SANDHILL CITIES

MAKING THE MODERN SOUTH

DAVID GOLDFIELD, SERIES EDITOR

SANDHILL CITIES

METROPOLITAN
AMBITIONS
IN **AUGUSTA,**
COLUMBUS, AND
MACON, GEORGIA

J. MARK SOUTHER

LOUISIANA STATE UNIVERSITY PRESS
BATON ROUGE

Published by Louisiana State University Press
lsupress.org

Designer: Kaelin Chappell Broaddus
Typefaces: Miller Text, text; S&S Baldwins Basic and Pro,
Copperplate Gothic 29 BC and 30 BC, display

Maps created by Mary Lee Eggart.

Cover image courtesy of Reese Library Special Collections,
Augusta University, Augusta, GA.

Cataloging-in-Publication Data are available from the Library of Congress.

ISBN 978-0-8071-8489-9 (cloth: alk. paper) —
ISBN 978-0-8071-8516-2 (pdf) — ISBN 978-0-8071-8515-5 (epub)

for my parents

CONTENTS

List of Illustrations   ix

Acknowledgments   xi

⌐⌐≈⌐

Introduction   1

ONE ✌ The Heart of Georgia   17

TWO ✌ The Winter Capital of America   45

THREE ✌ Metropolis of the Chattahoochee Valley   69

FOUR ✌ Planning "The South's Most Progressive City"   94

FIVE ✌ What Augusta Builds, Builds Augusta   120

SIX ✌ Building the Future from Our Past   147

Epilogue: Where Soul Lives   173

≈⌐≈

Notes   191

Bibliography   243

Index   261

ILLUSTRATIONS

MAPS

Georgia's fall-line cities and their imagined trade territories   8

Macon and the Heart of Georgia   18

Augusta and the Central Savannah River Area   47

Columbus and the Chattahoochee Valley   71

FIGURES

Broad Street in Augusta, ca. 1925   10

Macon in 1912   24

Crop-dusting demonstration, 1925   29

Proposed routes for the Dixie Highway, 1915   33

Baconsfield Park, 1933   38

Macon tourist guidebook, 1941   43

The Tafts at the Bon Air, 1908   46

Boston auto tourists in downtown Augusta, ca. 1920   57

Augusta tourism brochure, 1927   61

Augusta National Golf Club, 1935   63

Columbus promotional booklet, 1906   74

Southwest Georgia electric power advertisement, 1928   76

Auburn–Georgia game at Memorial Stadium, 1942   83

Howard Bus Line advertisement, 1929   89

Columbus promotional brochure, 1955   96
Fort Benning soldiers on Broadway, 1942   98
Military police patrolling Fourteenth Street Bridge, 1954   107
Old and new courthouses, 1972   117
Clarks Hill Dam construction, 1948   126
Savannah River Plant workers at rooming house, 1952   130
Robbins City Trailer Park in Augusta, 1952   131
Workers at the new Columbia Nitrogen plant, 1964   140
Greater Macon Chamber of Commerce advertisement, 1968   150
Macon Coliseum under construction, 1967   155
Downtown Macon architectural tour brochure, 1987   163
Douglass Theatre, 1959   167
Historic Macon tourism brochure, ca. 1984   171
Macon music promotion advertisement, 2023   174

ACKNOWLEDGMENTS

I grew up in Gainesville, Georgia, in the 1970s and 1980s in a family with deep roots in the red clay of the upper Piedmont and Blue Ridge Mountains of northeastern Georgia. When I traveled to a larger Georgia city, it was usually to Atlanta to visit my aunt or shop at Lenox Square, or to Athens for University of Georgia football games. Even though the state's fall-line cities were only about a two-and-a-half-hour drive away, they were to me little more than yellow shapes on the state road maps I enjoyed collecting or the occasional pictorial articles that appeared in my mother's *Southern Living* magazines. Like so many vacationers, we bypassed them on our way to Atlantic coast beaches. I first set foot in a Georgia fall-line city when my high school band performed at the Fountain City Marching Festival in Columbus's Memorial Stadium.

Sandhill Cities, then, probably owes its first debt to my father, William Parks Souther, whose aversion to driving through cities planted the seeds of my curiosity about Augusta, Macon, and Columbus. More directly and much more recently, the book concept sprang from my sense that too few urban historians pay attention to small and midsized cities. When I was a graduate student at Tulane in the late 1990s, Clarence Mohr introduced me to the first wave of 1970s and 1980s historical treatments of southern cities, including Blaine Brownell's *The Urban Ethos in the South* and *Cotton Fields and Skyscrapers* by Making the Modern South series editor David Goldfield. Don Doyle's *New Men, New Cities, New South* left me wondering how those cities that were neither New South dynamos like Atlanta nor tradition-bound seaports like Charleston might fit if he had expanded his analysis. Unfortunately (or perhaps fortunately for me), no one had published a comparative study that foregrounded those cities that stood on or beyond the fringes of the leading southern metropolitan areas. Thus, *Sandhill Cities* owes a debt to pioneer scholars of the urban New South and Sunbelt South, but my choice to research the Georgia fall-line cities gave me a reason to make up for lost time in acquainting myself with the urban history of my home state. Indeed, this choice spurred me to visit Augusta and Macon for the first time and to return to Columbus after many years.

As with all books, this one has accumulated many professional and personal debts, and I hope I have remembered all who played roles in bringing *Sandhill Cities* to fruition. Library and archive staff were essential in guiding me to many of the primary sources for this project. Working with them was among the most enjoyable parts of this project. Augusta Museum of History executive director Nancy Glaser personally arranged my access to archival materials that formed the cornerstone of my understanding of Augusta's history, and she also went out of her way to track down the perfect photo of William Howard Taft at the Bon Air Hotel. At the Georgia Heritage Room at the Augusta–Richmond County Public Library, Tina Monaco proved to be one of this project's staunchest supporters, offering encouragement and continued help long after I had completed my research trips. Her colleague Tina Rae Floyd also ensured that I had productive research visits. At the Reese Library Special Collections at Augusta University, I thank Maranda Christy, Kara Flynn, and Tammy Westafer. At Historic Augusta, Inc., executive director Erick Montgomery and Robyn A. Anderson trusted me to use their collections without oversight in a quiet, comfortable space. In Macon, archivist Muriel Jackson gave generously of her time to ensure that I missed nothing of pertinence in the extensive holdings of the Middle Georgia Archives at Washington Memorial Library. Her colleagues in the archives—Olivia Bushey, James R. O'Neal, Alicia Owens, Lee Ann Shoemaker, and Felicity Watts—all deserve my gratitude for assisting me during my multiple research visits. At the Columbus State University Archives in Schwob Library, director David Owings and his associates Tom Converse and Jessie Merrell supplied me with a steady stream of materials and showed much interest in my project. Additionally, I thank Mazie Brown for assisting with my research at the Hargrett Rare Book and Manuscript Library at the University of Georgia and Connie Finnerty and Julia Gardner at the Cornell University Library Division of Rare and Manuscript Collections.

I also appreciate Aimee Brooks at the Columbus Museum, Tommy Brown and Jennifer Wiggins at Auburn University Archives & Special Collections, Margaret Dunlap at Richland Library, Marie K. Force at Delta Flight Museum, Melissa Hanson of the Savannah River Site Cold War Historic Preservation Program, Mary Linnemann at the University of Georgia Hargrett Rare Book and Manuscript Library, and Jessica Walden at Visit Macon for helping me obtain some of the illustrations in this book. I am deeply grateful for the talent and dedication of Mary Lee Eggart, who crafted the maps in *Sandhill Cities*, and Timothy Pearson, who prepared the index.

Two generous Faculty Scholarship Initiative grants from the Cleveland State University Office of Research funded multiple research trips to libraries and archives in the three cities and at the University of Georgia. A John Nolen Research Fund Award supported my research in the Cornell University Library Division of Rare and Manuscript Collections.

Friends and colleagues deserve heartfelt thanks for supporting this undertaking. Virginia Causey, Kari Frederickson, Alan Lessoff, Tom Okie, and Mark Rose read one or more chapters and offered astute comments and suggestions that helped me sharpen my analysis and, at times, saved me from overlooking important scholarship or insights. Thanks, too, go to audience members who commented as I tested my ideas at the 2019 and 2022 Society of American City and Regional Planning History conferences and the 2018 and 2023 Urban History Association conferences. I also greatly appreciate the anonymous peer reviewers, whose expertise has made this a better book. Others who have been a supportive presence along the way include Matías Martinez Abeijón, Francesca Russo Ammon, Ella Howard, Eric Light, Glenn McNair, Todd Michney, Jack Mitchener, Meshack Owino, Sarah Jo Peterson, Meredith Drake Reitan, and David Stanek.

At LSU Press, I am immensely grateful, again, to Rand Dotson, who was the acquisitions editor for my first book, *New Orleans on Parade*, two decades ago. I also thank others at LSU Press: Neal Novak, Catherine L. Kadair, Min Marcus, and James Wilson, who guided *Sandhill Cities* through production; copy editor Dabian Witherspoon; and designer Kaelin Chappell Broaddus. Deep admiration and gratitude go to Making the Modern South series editor David Goldfield, who believed in my first book project and reassured me when he affirmed that a comparative history of three midsized Georgia cities would be a welcome addition to this series. Just as he was for *New Orleans on Parade,* David was an amazing mentor to me as I worked on this, my third book.

Family members were some of the biggest cheerleaders for my work. My parents, William and Sandra Souther, have decades of experience being patient and supportive of a succession of academic projects like this one. In this case, the COVID-19 pandemic added measurably to their wait. My aunt, Lynn Godshall, a career journalist with a deep love of books and the life of the mind, was a kindred spirit on the journey. My mother- and father-in-law, Connie and Tom Salyers, listened with care to the ups and downs of the research and writing process. My deepest gratitude goes to my wife, Stacey, who made many sacrifices in balancing her career (and mine) with raising our daughter across the lifespan of this book's production. Keely was not yet two years old when I started researching my previous book, *Believing in Cleveland,* and was in the fourth grade when I published it and started working on *Sandhill Cities.* She will be a senior in high school as this volume arrives on bookstore shelves.

SANDHILL CITIES

INTRODUCTION

America is still moving southward. Over the decade ending in 2020, two-thirds of the twenty-five fastest-growing United States metropolitan areas were in the South.[1] Places like Orlando, Raleigh, and Austin bespeak an economic transformation more than a half-century in the making, one that saw the nation's workforce tilt from production to service and knowledge. Often lost in this narrative of rapid southern growth and change is its unevenness. More than a tale of a Sun Belt rising at the expense of a Rust Belt, the history of the South is one of uneven development. When this unevenness is acknowledged, it skews toward the starkest examples of impoverished rural communities and burgeoning metros. *Sandhill Cities* trains its lens instead on an area of the South that developed between the extremes.

Sandhill Cities is a history of twentieth-century Columbus, Augusta, and Macon, which rank today as Georgia's second-, third-, and fourth-largest cities. All are consolidated city-counties, with populations of just over 200,000 in the first two and over 150,000 in the third. The Augusta metropolitan area comprises more than 600,000 residents, roughly twice that of metropolitan Columbus or Macon but only one-tenth that of Atlanta. Columbus is best known for Fort Moore (formerly Fort Benning), but it also spawned Royal Crown Cola and Aflac. Augusta enjoys international recognition as the home of the Masters Golf Tournament while its Medical College of Georgia lends regional stature in healthcare. Macon may be less widely known despite its Ocmulgee Mounds National Historical Park and International Cherry Blossom Festival. After long marginalizing Black cultural contributions, boosters have since embraced their cities' musical legends—James Brown, Ma Rainey, Otis Redding, and Little Richard—an embrace evoked in Macon's modern slogan "Where Soul Lives." Large African American populations have also made these cities politically important to Democrats' hopes in recent years as the fall line has become a blue belt in a mostly red state.

Rather than a trio of urban biographies, *Sandhill Cities* centers on how growth coalitions, which southern urban historian Blaine A. Brownell dubbed the "commercial-civic elite," framed the state of their cities and pursued what this book characterizes as "metropolitan ambitions."[2] Traditionally, the term "metropolitan" has tended to describe large cities, but the Bureau of the Census offers a more precise, functional definition. Census-designated Metropolitan Statistical Areas (MSAs) typically include one or more counties around a city of 50,000 or more people. The selection of counties to designate rests upon "meeting certain requirements of metropolitan character," which include thresholds of commuting and population density.[3] *Sandhill Cities* recognizes that these are problematic criteria to apply to earlier periods. Moreover, this book is less interested in defining metropolitanism in absolute terms than in relative ones. It explores metropolitan ambition as a state of mind that fixates on cities' growth, impelling pro-growth leaders to pursue growth or at least cultivate a physical appearance and a promotable image as metropolitan. It also reveals the challenges these leaders faced and the social, economic, and environmental costs of their actions.

Sandhill Cities takes its name from the sandhills, a band of rolling, sandy slopes that run from southwest to northeast between Georgia and North Carolina. The sandhills lie along the fall line, a roughly twenty-mile-wide geological boundary where rivers descend from the Piedmont Plateau through a series of rapids to the Coastal Plain. Rapids furnished waterpower and marked the head of navigation for rivers flowing into the Gulf of Mexico or the Atlantic Ocean. As a result, several cities, including those in this study, were founded at the base of the fall line between the mid-eighteenth and early nineteenth centuries. The fall line also became a boundary of social demarcation. Most white residential development after the late nineteenth century spread to the higher, rolling ground of the Piedmont to the north, while Black expansion was largely limited to the flatter land to the south with its gnats, mosquitoes, heat, and increased exposure to flooding and industrial pollution.

From Virginia to Louisiana, earlier cities had emerged along tidal rivers and bays near the ocean. Charleston was the largest southern city in the British North American colonies and remained one of the U.S.'s ten largest cities as late as 1840. Savannah ranked as Georgia's principal city before yielding to fast-growing Atlanta after Reconstruction. As historians David Goldfield and Don Doyle have argued, most southern coastal cities, built from wealth generated by antebellum plantation agriculture and oceangoing trade, lost ground after the Civil War to newer, dynamic inland cities that embraced railroad-age industrial and commercial investment. Goldfield identified the most prosperous New South cities as those "serving other masters besides or excluding King Cotton." Doyle wrote similarly of a divergence between cities that clung to tradition and those that embraced change.[4]

While focusing on the emergence of the New South, Doyle's approach meshed with other scholars' interest in a broader Sunbelt region as a counterpoint to Rustbelt urban decline after World War II.[5] In recent decades, most southern urban historians have researched the largest cities, especially Atlanta and New Orleans, although Houston and Charlotte have yet to receive their due.[6] Some historians have published more-or-less comprehensive urban biographies of midsized southern cities.[7] Others have studied individual, midsized cities in a tighter timeframe or through a thematic lens.[8] Few have spanned the decades before and after World War II while also connecting to both urban and southern historiographies.[9] Scholars have pointed to a "second line" of city-building activity from Montgomery to Richmond that trailed the original string of coastal cities, but they have seldom examined how these fall-line cities fared in the twentieth century—and never in a comparative manner.[10]

Seeking to avert urban historians' gaze on larger, mostly northeastern and midwestern cities, *Sandhill Cities* revisits formative scholarship on the urban South, which emerged in the pioneering work of Blaine Brownell, David Goldfield, and Howard Rabinowitz. These historians explored the tension between change and continuity and the relationship between southern cities and their historically agrarian region. While they agreed that southern cities shared much in common with cities in other regions, Goldfield's *Cotton*

Fields and Skyscrapers posited that southern urbanism possessed distinctive, persistent features, including a close relationship between cities and their rural hinterlands.[11] *Sandhill Cities* embraces this tension. Borrowing from historian Alan Lessoff, it also argues that smaller cities' boosters, especially those outside so-called megaregions, had to accept that their cities were satellites of larger metropolitan cities and therefore constrained by decisions made elsewhere.[12] Their situation reflects their slowness to pivot from embracing traditional southern agriculture but also the challenge of overcoming the inertia forged by previous leaders' decisions. Georgia's fall-line cities are products of an old economy that discouraged urban development but are also, like similar cities outside megaregions, unlikely candidates for developing the impetus to leap from a groove etched by geography and human actions.[13]

Sandhill Cities explores Georgia's fall-line cities and their trade territories in relation to each other, Atlanta, and their trade territories. Fall-line cities engaged in urban rivalries, but these tended to consume only modest local energy because the cities were widely spaced. Each city's relationship with Atlanta grew increasingly complex over time. The sandhill cities, especially Macon (only eighty-five miles southeast of Atlanta), were torn between emphasizing their proximity to the capital city and their distance from it. Their relationships with their trade territories were more constant and visible.

In the antebellum period, trade area boundaries had been fluid, depending on thousands of individual decisions that hinged on business relationships, knowledge of commodity markets, supply costs, road conditions, and disease outbreaks, among other factors.[14] Post–Civil War railroad expansion produced greater efforts to define and promote trade territories, although these remained unfixed. Railroads demarked regions based on their service areas. For example, in 1895, the Georgia Railroad, with its trunk extending from Augusta westward to Atlanta and branches serving Macon, Athens, Gainesville, Washington, and Jefferson, promoted "Eastern Middle Georgia," a 144-mile-wide circle whose edges touched its headquarters city of Augusta and the state's largest city. Along its trunk, at least three towns were named for company officials. With characteristic exaggeration, the railroad proclaimed that this area suffered no weather extremes and enjoyed a nearly perpetual growing season. Its emphasis on diversified agriculture not only reflected a key New South preoccupation but also made clear that many southern cities, including Augusta, still existed largely to serve agrarian pursuits.[15]

Local boosters more often placed their own cities at the center of their regional conceptions. This mentality was inseparable from the importance that Georgians attached to access to county seats and rural representation in the General Assembly. Put simply, more counties meant shorter travel to town and greater legislative clout, and it also served town boosters. As one historian observed, "the county seat, the little urban center, took possession of the countryside," and indeed the fall-line cities' leaders did likewise.[16] Hinterlands provided customers for merchants' wares as well as the crops and livestock to sell, export, or process. Cotton reigned well into the twentieth century, but boosters also urged their cities' development as service hubs for emerging agricultural pursuits. Augusta and Macon supported peach growers, while Columbus served pecan and peanut producers. All three encouraged investment in livestock, dairy, grasses, fruits, vegetables, and forest products. Boosters also connected their trade territories to industrialization efforts built around existing manufacturers that either processed rural products such as cotton, clay, and timber or supplied rural people with fertilizers and farm equipment.

Through World War II, trade territories loomed large in boosters' metropolitan ambitions. Beyond molding their cities into markets and marts, ringing rural counties exaggerated the stature of what were in fact relatively small cities. The sheer number of counties claimed by the fall-line cities further exaggerated their stature thanks to the presence of so many relatively small counties, a result of Georgia's proliferation of county charters in the several decades after the Civil War.[17] In 1910, Augusta and Macon each had about forty thousand residents, a population New Orleans had reached nearly a century before. Columbus had only a little more than twenty thousand, a mark Atlanta had surpassed soon after the Civil War. Emphasis on a large trade area might also allay outside investors' concerns that large Black populations suppressed these cities' purchasing power.[18] With twenty-odd counties shaded around a single ink spot on a map, a city seemed more consequential. By the Second World War, the Macon Chamber of Commerce branded a twenty-six-county Middle Georgia area as the "Heart of Georgia" and, even more boldly, the "State of Macon."[19] Similarly, Columbus promoters assembled eastern Alabama and western Georgia counties into a Chattahoochee Valley centering on their city, and Augustans eventually adopted a regional name—Central Savannah River Area—to bond with rural neighbors on both sides of the river. While *Sandhill Cities* frames the fall-line cities as boosters did, in the context of their trade territories, it acknowledges what they seldom articulated—that their cities were satellites of Atlanta. In addition, by the 1960s, surrounding rural counties began suburbanizing, forcing city leaders to reckon with how to mitigate negative impacts on their urban cores.

Why Augusta, Macon, and Columbus? First, there is value in choosing cities in the same state. Of course, Augusta and Columbus developed close relationships with communities across state lines and are closer to Columbia and Montgomery, respectively, than to Macon. Nevertheless, their leaders often framed their cities' problems and opportunities in the context of Georgia's economy and politics and shared concerns about their relationship to Atlanta. Georgia history also shaped how they packaged cities for outsiders. Boosters took pride in the fact that all three had begun as garrison towns that helped wrest Georgia's frontier from Native Americans and later dodged Sherman's fury on his March to the Sea.[20]

Second, although most of the South's fall-line cities depended to varying degrees on agriculture and agriculturally related industry, military installations secured and safeguarded by influential southern Democrats in Congress, and tourism based on romanticizing antebellum and Civil War history, the Georgia cities differed in important ways. Apart from Augusta's brief stint as a state capital, they stood apart from most major southern fall-line cities, which were state capitals. Capital cities developed durable administrative functions that provided not only an economic base but also visibility and clout that could attract outside investment. Moreover, unlike Richmond, Raleigh, and Columbia, none had a large university, although Augusta's Medical College of Georgia became an important unit of the University System of Georgia. Therefore, the Georgia fall-line cities may be more easily compared to each other than to their counterparts in neighboring states.

Third, these cities lay in rural sections that did not measure up to megaregions such as the Texas Triangle, Piedmont Atlantic, and Florida. They pursued similar growth agendas and planning strategies as larger cities, but their lingering reliance on agricultural and extractive activities cast long shadows over their economies. The South's larger metropolitan areas like Atlanta, Houston, Dallas, Austin, Nashville, Raleigh-Durham, and Charlotte avoided this outcome by building new economic clusters that included finance, insurance, government, education, healthcare, and high technology.

Conversely, New Orleans, Savannah, Charleston, and Florida's cities embraced leisure and tourism as an economic pillar. Georgia's fall-line cities took a less clear path that highlights the tension between inertia and momentum in southern metropolitan ambitions. They also demonstrate that some challenges of midsized cities cut across region and may also be found in Peoria, Grand Rapids, and Erie. Matching the exemplars of neither Sunbelt boom nor Rustbelt decline, Georgia's sandhill cities arguably reveal as much about modern urban America as major cities like Phoenix and Detroit.[21]

As the reader will discover, a large proportion of the fall-line cities' civic boosters hailed from old-line families in their respective cities or their hinterlands. Men with agriculturally derived wealth and influence dominated the ranks of each city's commercial and industrial firms, financial and real estate sectors, newspapers, utilities, railroads, municipal offices, and chambers of commerce. Sometimes their influence retarded economic change as they continued to focus on traditional pursuits, but other times, they proved as agile as newcomers in diversifying their activities for both personal gain and civic boosterism. For example, *Macon Telegraph* co-owner and editor W. T. Anderson, grandson of one of Middle Georgia's largest cotton planters, became a staunch advocate of using his city's central position in the state to court highway development and tourism. Likewise, Columbus's George W. Woodruff, who built his nineteenth-century fortune in Empire Mills (once the South's largest flour mill), contributed generational wealth that helped propel his sons into twentieth-century leadership in the Coca-Cola Company, banking, streetcars, and electric power in Atlanta, as well as in Columbus-based real estate and insurance concerns. One of Woodruff's grandsons, James W. Woodruff Sr., not only invested in dairy and beef cattle, cotton, and peanuts but also went on to serve as Columbus's most fervent lobbyist for a modern inland port and later for historic preservation and heritage tourism.[22]

As the reader will quickly discover, *Sandhill Cities* draws heavily upon information available in the three cities' daily newspapers and publications produced by chambers of commerce. Unlike many larger cities, midsized cities tended not to preserve as rich a variety of archival materials for the urban historian to explore, and the failure to value Black perspectives has a greater skewing effect than usual because roughly four in ten people in these cities were African American. Fewer personal papers, letters, and other such doc-

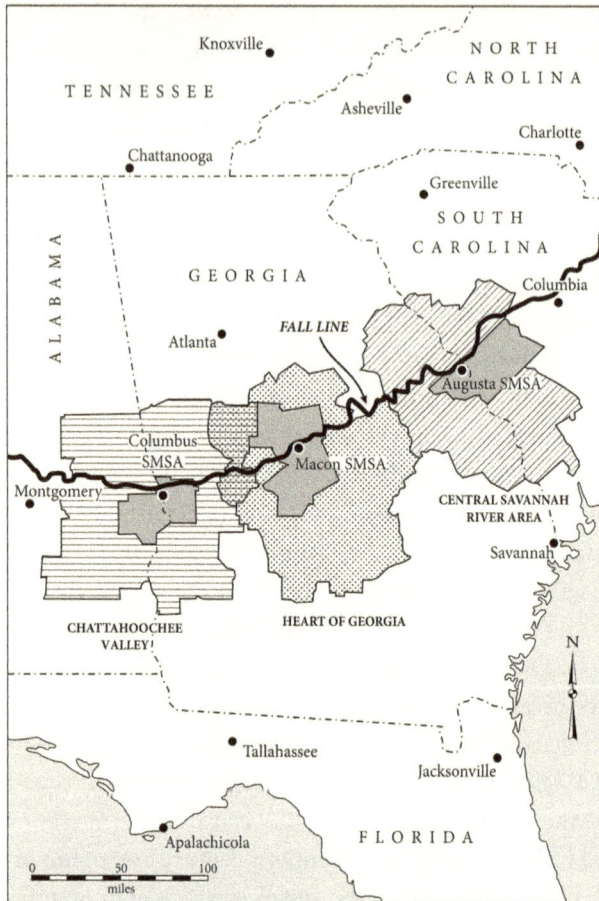

GEORGIA'S FALL-LINE CITIES AND THEIR IMAGINED TRADE TERRITORIES. This map shows the 1970 boundaries of the three cities' census-defined standard metropolitan statistical areas. The trade territory boundaries correspond to those defined locally in Columbus in 1935, in Macon in 1943, and in Augusta in 1950.

uments expound or counter the journalistic record. However, the book also finds newspapers and other booster publications invaluable because they reveal so much about the big plans and the priorities of those who hatched them. As the sociologist Harvey Molotch rightly observed, newspapers tied their own fortunes to metropolitan growth, which increased their circulation and ad sales. They were the mouthpieces for the "community elite," or "growth machine," to promote a vision for the one thing that unified them: the idea that place-based growth was desirable and even essential. Moreover, as Julia Guarneri has argued, newspapers worked hard to pull small-town and rural residents into their cities' orbits by getting them to see "both real and imaginary ties." While exploring this booster enterprise, *Sandhill Cities* also mines the relatively few alternative sources, reads newspaper accounts against the grain, plumbs the meaning of their veiled commentaries, and asks what their silences and omissions reveal.[23]

To set the stage for this book's focal period, roughly the 1910s to the 1980s, it will be helpful to introduce each of the three cities, including their founding, early development as trade centers, cotton-economy connections, Civil War impacts, New South agendas, and the contours of their twentieth-century development. As will become clear, the sandhill cities shared a number of commonalities in their development.

Georgia's second-oldest city dates to 1736 when James Oglethorpe authorized laying out a city at the head of navigation on the Savannah River. Augusta's gridiron street plan paralleled the river and centered on a military drill ground. Augusta was in its early decades a colonial garrison town designed to soothe contentious trade relations between Carolinians and Creek Indians. After an Indian cession in 1763 opened lands between the Savannah and Ogeechee Rivers to white settlers, it evolved into a market town that supplied farmers and handled their produce.[24]

After British troops captured Savannah in 1778, Augusta was one of the convening places for a state legislature that was perpetually on the move during the remainder of the Revolutionary War. In 1780 the city's grid, anchored by two extremely wide streets, was extended east and west along the river to accommodate a growing population (see Fig. 1). Augusta's rising importance as an inland trading center led to a rotation of legislative sessions with Savannah starting in 1782, but the prevailing interest in developing the backcountry pointed to a future of state governance away from the Lowcountry. Legislators authorized a new capital named Louisville along the fall line on the Ogeechee River and planned to model it after Philadelphia. In the meantime, Augusta served as capital from 1786 until 1796 and became a staging ground for westward migration. That migration into the backcountry cost not only Augusta the capital but then also Louisville, which held capital status for less than a decade before legislators moved the seat

FIG. 1. BROAD STREET IN AUGUSTA, CA. 1925. Originally designed as a 300-foot-wide drill ground, Broad Street was replatted in 1780 as a 165-foot-wide street. Over the next century, it emerged as the nation's second-widest principal commercial street, after New Orleans's Canal Street. Note the intrusive placement of the city's outsize Confederate monument, which required Broad Street's parallel streetcar tracks to bow around its marble base. Courtesy of Reese Library Special Collections, Augusta University, Augusta, GA.

of government to Milledgeville, thirty miles northeast of Macon, where it would remain until 1868.[25]

Until the late eighteenth century, Augusta served a bustling tobacco trade, but it pivoted to cotton after Eli Whitney's 1793 invention of the cotton gin. After the first steamboat arrived in 1816, the city handled much of the upland cotton export. The cotton boom created a mercantile elite in Augusta and an extensive network of plantations worked by enslaved people of African descent that enriched a small but powerful white planter class. A railroad network began to form in the 1830s and, with the 1845 completion of the Augusta Canal to harness the Savannah's waterpower, brought an industrial boom centering on textiles.[26] The city's population grew fivefold in the half-century after 1810, topping twelve thousand by 1860.

The Civil War brought continued prosperity. The city's canal and railroads helped it attract the Confederate Powder Works, and several factories turned to the manufacture of uniforms, shoes, and pistols. General William T. Sherman avoided Augusta on his March to the Sea in 1864, sparing it the destruction suffered by Atlanta. At the end of the war, thousands of freedmen fled plantations in surrounding rural counties and resettled on the low-lying plain just outside the city's southern boundary on land known as Verdery's Territory, forming a Black neighborhood that local whites variously called the Negro Territory, the Territory, or simply the Terry.[27]

Augusta's economic growth accelerated after the war. A canal expansion in 1875 brought more intensive textile development, including the enormous King and Sibley mills, which led Augusta to cast itself as the "Lowell of the South," a moniker that Columbus also used. The two cities' promotional hooks reflected the broader "cotton mill campaign" centered in the Carolinas, in which civic boosters' "town spirit" was inseparable from their efforts to replicate the textile empire that had long enriched New England. An expanding rail network also helped the city nearly quadruple the number of cotton bales it handled in the half-century after Reconstruction, leading boosters to dub it the "Second Largest Inland Cotton Market in the World."[28] Augusta, whose population tripled to almost forty thousand from 1860 to 1900, remained an important center of cotton, textiles, cottonseed oil, fertilizers, bricks, and clay products, but it also enjoyed a national reputation for its sandhills winter resorts.

As the century progressed, Augusta leaders secured major federal support for dams on the Savannah for hydropower, flood control, and navigation. The city also added a permanent military sector, paper mills, and chemical plants to offset the decline of cotton and relied on an emerging international reputation for golf to negate its loss of winter resort status. Like other fall-line cities, Augusta saw substantial Black in-migration, especially as plantation work shrank with mechanization. Despite successes in realizing some metropolitan ambitions, Augusta failed to annex suburban areas, causing it to suffer the effects of white flight starting in the 1950s.

Macon was founded in 1823 below the fall line on the Ocmulgee River near Fort Hawkins, a former frontier garrison and trading post authorized by President Thomas Jefferson in 1806 to facilitate trade with the Creek Nation. According to local lore, ancient Babylon inspired the city's grid of 180-foot-wide avenues intersected by 120-foot streets.[29] Like Augusta, the city established itself as the center of a thriving rural trade, with farmers trekking there from more than sixty miles away in all directions. Middle Georgia cotton production enriched antebellum Macon but at the cost of so much erosion that the Ocmulgee became unnavigable without persistent dredging.[30]

Like Augusta, Macon welcomed the industrial boost brought by the Civil War. Three major factories produced cannons, shells, rifles, pistols, and other military equipment, and more soldiers trained at its Camp Oglethorpe than at any other facility in the South. Macon's rail network also supplied Confederate forces during the Atlanta Campaign. Union bombardment of Macon accomplished little besides lending romance to the Cannonball House, a future United Daughters of the Confederacy shrine and tourist attraction. Sherman's troops bypassed Macon as they did Augusta.[31] As in other southern cities, Macon saw an influx of freedmen. In the year after the Confederate surrender at Appomattox, its Black population doubled. In addition to preexisting African American pockets on back alleys scattered about the city, emancipation led to the appearance of shantytowns in Pleasant Hill and Unionville, Black settlements located just outside the Macon city limits.[32]

After the war, Macon resumed its growth. Its population tripled between the Civil War and 1900, but cotton dependency and the impoverishment of a large segment of the region's population through sharecropping and tenancy kept Macon, like Augusta, from enjoying more impressive growth.[33] As an illustration, Atlanta's population exploded in the last four decades of the nineteenth century, adding more than 80,000 new residents to the 9,552 it had on the eve of the Civil War, compared to 27,000 newcomers to Augusta, 15,000 to Macon, and only 8,000 to Columbus.

Macon's heavy investment in railroads made it Georgia's principal hub with six lines in the 1880s, but Atlanta's railroads emerged from the economic turmoil of the 1890s on a stronger footing, reducing Macon's share of traffic. Nonetheless, Macon's rail and steamship connections and location in one of the South's most productive cotton-growing areas made it an important regional transportation and industrial center. In the 1880s, Macon added more factories than any Georgia city except Augusta, although its growth was also inseparable from agriculture, notably textiles, brick and tile, cotton choppers and compresses, cottonseed oil, fertilizer, meatpacking, and fruit canning.[34]

Several decades into the twentieth century, Macon remained an important agricultural market city. While it never matched Augusta's resort reputation and river development, the city attracted an army air base that, with other military investments, new industries, cotton mechanization, and a turn toward peanuts, poultry, and soybeans, delivered modest economic diversification.[35] Macon leveraged its central location in Georgia to become a convention center and highway hub and eventually exemplified the state's fall-line cities' use of the Charleston and Savannah models of historic preservation and tourism to drive central-city and downtown revitalization.

Macon proved more successful than Augusta in capturing suburban growth through annexation, including more than tripling its area and nearly doubling its population overnight in 1961. However, despite their early checkerboard racial patterns, all three cities became more segregated through discriminatory real estate practices like those practiced nationwide. By the eve of World War II, these cities exhibited some of the nation's highest proportions of D-rated (red-shaded) residential areas in the infamous federal real estate maps. Macon ranked third, Augusta ranked eighth, and Columbus ranked ninth.[36] Even its dramatic annexation, an echo of Atlanta's 1952 Plan of Improvement, yielded to continued white flight beyond its new borders, concentrating poverty in the city and plunging Macon into a long population decline starting in the 1970s.[37]

Laid out in a grid of wide streets along the Chattahoochee River on Georgia's western border in 1828, Columbus was the state's last major planned city. Substantial growth awaited the expulsion of most of the Muscogee (Creek) Nation to Oklahoma in the following decade. Columbus's economy, like that of Augusta and Macon, relied heavily on its river. In 1828, the city dammed the Chattahoochee to operate a gristmill, and the first textile mill soon opened along the riverfront. However, unlike Augusta, which invested public funds in a canal to serve multiple industries, Columbus permitted John Howard to build a new dam just large enough to supply his own mill's needs. Columbus officials also failed to invest robustly in railroads that might have helped diversify the city's economy. Although Columbus had some factories that produced iron, steam engines, machinery, leather products, shoes, ink, whiskey, and some other goods, cotton was by far the dominant local industry.[38]

As in Augusta and Macon, historian Virginia E. Causey writes, the Civil War brought the Chattahoochee River city "growth and prosperity unimaginable to the most enthusiastic antebellum boosters." Columbus turned out more war materiel for the Confederate army than any other city except Richmond. It almost survived the war as unscathed as its counterparts, but the Battle of Columbus in 1865—which boosters later pressed to have designated as the war's last major battle—wrought severe damage to the city's industry. Nevertheless, Columbus experienced rapid industrial recovery by the decade's end.[39]

After the war, the East Commons on the city's fringe rapidly filled with African Americans. Few found employment in the dominant, profoundly white textile industry, whose textile barons controlled much more than mills and mill villages. William H. Young's Eagle & Phenix mill was Columbus's principal employer, but its hydropower monopoly discouraged other industries or even additional investment in textiles. The city's postbellum efforts to finance railroads also fell far short of matching the rail hub that Macon enjoyed.[40]

In the twentieth century, Columbus's trajectory paralleled that of Augusta and Macon. As in those cities, cotton continued to dominate. Before Augusta's big push to develop its river's hydropower potential, Columbus staked its future on becoming the "Electric City." Local boosters also were the first among those in the sandhill cities to secure a major, permanent military base as an engine for economic growth. Camp Benning (later Fort Benning) profoundly shaped Columbus's economy and culture after World War II, compensating for the eventual decline of textiles.[41]

More than Augusta and Macon, postwar Columbus became a mill-and-military metropolis with little opportunity to add economic pillars. Just as it had lacked sufficient railroad connections, Columbus also remained isolated in the highway age. Off the beaten path of the Dixie Highway in the 1920s, it was, until 1979, the largest American city without an interstate highway. But, unlike Augusta and Macon, which faced limits in public support for further annexations or city-county consolidation, Columbus and Muscogee County managed to consolidate in 1971. Columbus's breakthroughs in attracting more outside investment and effecting tourism-led downtown revitalization, combined with the enduring boon of Fort Benning, enabled it to match the moderate growth of Augusta and Macon, but all three cities fell far short of Atlanta's continuing boom.

Sandhill Cities, the first book to connect the twentieth-century histories of the three major Georgia fall-line cities, takes a selective, thematic approach. Each of the first three chapters examines a theme in one city from about 1910 to 1940. Chapter 1 opens with Macon leaders' attempts to lure the state capital from Atlanta. It also explores how boosters attempted to use Macon's central location to elevate its stature through initiatives to serve as the Middle Georgia hub for diversified agriculture and as a tourist destination on the Dixie Highway. Chapter 2 centers on Augusta's bid to use its sandhills climate and topography to preserve its reputation as a leading winter resort as Florida's development threatened to eclipse it. The chapter traces attempts to leverage President William Howard Taft's visits to brand Augusta as the nation's "winter capital," to make the city a regional clearinghouse for highway information, and finally to start the new Masters Golf Tournament to try to reanimate the Garden City's sagging reputation. Chapter 3 probes how Columbus looked to its fall-line position on the Chattahoochee River to bolster industrialization, dispense electricity to rural southwestern Georgia, tap into Gulf of Mexico trade, and develop a military base. The chapter also explores how a riverside location that doubled as a state border made Columbus a neutral ground for major interstate football rivalries but also frustrated efforts to regulate Fort Benning soldiers' access to vice-ridden Phenix City, Alabama.

The last three chapters turn to the period between the 1940s and 1980s, although each focuses more tightly on one of three overlapping twenty-year periods: the 1940s–60s in Columbus, 1950s–70s in Augusta, and 1960s–80s in Macon. Chapter 4 returns to Columbus, exploring efforts to capitalize on the Fort Benning military buildup and then to sustain the wartime boom through metropolitan planning, as well as how disagreements across city, county, and state borders and the figurative color line compounded limitations posed by forces beyond the Columbus area. Despite these difficulties, the city managed to become the first consolidated city-county in Georgia. Chapter 5 turns to Augusta's renewed push for regional cooperation to secure Savannah River improvements and attract new industry. It also examines the economic, social, and environmental effects of Augusta boosters' enticement of paper mills and chemical plants to the swampy fringes of the city. Chapter 6 highlights Macon's shift from foregrounding industrialization to using historic preservation to combat the effects of suburban sprawl on downtown, entice white-collar employers and tourists, and recapture Macon's longtime aspiration to be "The Heart of Georgia." The chapter traces the role of a new mall in unifying preservationists, city officials, and merchants around the idea of crafting a historic downtown cityscape, and the effects of white leaders' choices in a city that was close to half Black.

Sandhill Cities tells a story that echoes in midsized cities nationwide that have stood outside or on the edges of megaregions. It illuminates how traditional southern economic, cultural, and social preoccupations, including long-standing racial segregation, bred a conservative mindset that hampered the work of reinvention that might have fulfilled the most hopeful of boosters' metropolitan ambitions. The Georgia fall-line cities sustained neither spectacular growth nor decline. Relying, in turn, on agriculture, agriculturally based manufacturing, river development, military training, and tourism, they failed to break their dependency on both the assets and liabilities of their physical geography and the decisions of outside capitalists, governmental leaders, and the traveling public on where to invest or spend their money. If *Sandhill Cities* shows why there was little hope that the fall-line cities might become another Atlanta, more importantly, it provides insights into how these midsized cities' biggest cheerleaders imagined charting their own evocations of the "Atlanta Spirit." What follows is the story of the myriad ways they pursued their metropolitan ambitions and a sense of why metropolitanism, for all but the largest cities, excited perennial striving toward an illusory finish line.

ONE

THE HEART OF GEORGIA

On a steamy August day in 1911, nearly three hundred members of the Georgia General Assembly converged in an unlikely place. Although Atlanta had been the state's capital since 1868, these lawmakers assembled for a barbecue under the shade trees around the Log Cabin Club just outside Macon, a city of forty thousand near the geographic center of the state. The "avowed prohibitionists" consumed more than five thousand bottles of locally brewed American Queen beer and a hundred gallons of Burgundy punch with their barbecued pork and lamb, Brunswick stew, and deviled eggs. However, more than beer and barbecue enticed these men to Macon. For nine months, Macon leaders had been agitating to relocate the state capital from Atlanta to their city. Now the Central Capital Association was hosting an inspection of two sites it was proposing for a new capitol building on the sandhills overlooking Macon should the visiting legislators vote to approve the move.[1]

Macon leaders' bid to poach the capital reflected a last-ditch effort to shrink the growing gap between their city and Atlanta. Part of a larger regional shift from coastal to inland development, Atlanta's growth outpaced that of Savannah.[2] Atlanta also siphoned investment that might have flowed into Augusta, Macon, and Columbus. But even as Atlanta was styling itself the "Gate City of the South," the sandhill cities busied themselves trying to develop into metropolitan centers while serving as regional hubs of agricultural diversification, transportation, and tourism. In Macon, metropolitan development became intertwined with rivalries with Atlanta over the seat

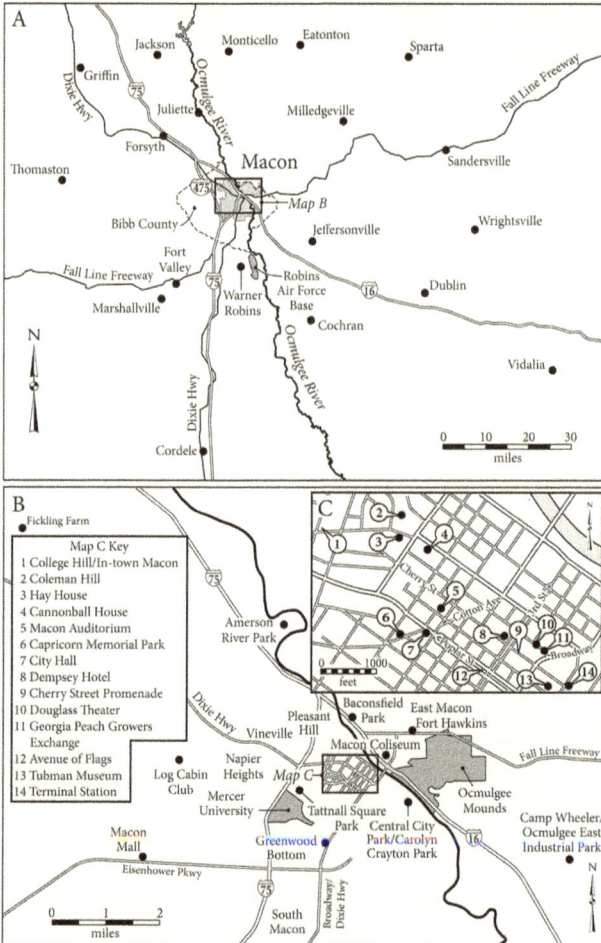

MACON AND THE HEART OF GEORGIA.

of state government and with Augusta to be Georgia's "third city" behind Atlanta and Savannah. While its decade-long effort to get the capital proved unsuccessful, Macon surpassed Augusta's state rank in 1920 and played an expansive, ongoing role as the hub of Middle Georgia.

In addition to the capital removal effort, Macon boosters spearheaded initiatives to become the hub of the state's peach belt and a destination for conventions, tourism, and retail trade. Leveraging fertile soil, cheap labor, and especially its central location, Macon boosters imagined their small metropolitan area as the hub of a vast agrarian region encompassing one-third of Georgia's population. In rhetorical flourishes that grew bolder as Macon's fortunes diverged from those of Atlanta, they styled their city as the "Heart of the Georgia Peach Belt" and "The Heart of Georgia."[3]

MOVE THE CAPITAL INTO GEORGIA

Macon leaders skirmished with Augusta over "third city" status while banking on their "Central City" reputation to attract the state capital. The capital removal effort arose in the autumn of 1910.[4] Atlanta leaders had expressed interest in luring Mercer University away from Macon to their city following intimations that the Georgia Baptist Convention was considering moving the college. The capital city's opposition to Macon leaders' efforts to secure a more advantageous Central of Georgia Railway passenger train schedule prompted further irritation. Macon boosters were also in the thick of a "Greater Macon" annexation campaign and an effort to use their central location in the state to make Macon similarly central in its economic and political influence.[5]

Boosters were desperate to stem Macon's relative decline in relation to Atlanta's boom. Though amplified by state politics, their concerns were hardly uncommon. Indeed, their counterparts in Nashville, Memphis, and Birmingham were variously resentful and envious of Atlanta's phenomenal expansion.[6] Macon boosters hoped to benefit from broad discontent, especially in South Georgia, toward what many saw as Atlanta's ruthless gambit for regional dominance. To some degree, this distrust of urban industrial society was a politicized residue of old planter arguments for the superiority of agrarianism. It would soon produce Georgia's county-unit system, which supported what political scientist V. O. Key Jr. later dubbed the "Rule of the Rustics" by minimizing rural counties' political disadvantage.[7] One *Macon Daily Telegraph* editorial portrayed Atlanta almost as a foreign foe: "There is no city, town or hamlet in Central and South Georgia but [that] has felt the sting of Atlanta's grab. . . . She has built Atlanta at the expense of Georgia." The editorial was careful to characterize capital removal as "a Georgia movement, and not a Macon scheme." Countering the boosterish notion of an "Atlanta spirit," it argued, "Georgia needs a Capital in keeping with the

Georgia spirit. She needs a Capital among Georgians." To accentuate Macon's centrality and Atlanta's peripheral location, the *Telegraph* titled the editorial, "Move the Capital into Georgia."[8]

While Atlanta and its immediate suburbs were growing rapidly in the opening decade of the new century, the *Telegraph* was correct in observing on the day of the General Assembly delegation's visit that Georgia's southern counties had grown much faster than those to Macon's north over the previous ten years. The census would soon confirm that between 1900 and 1910, twenty-five of thirty-one counties whose populations grew more than 25 percent were below the fall line, and about twice as many southern counties as northern ones had posted growth rates of at least 15 percent.[9]

Macon's rivalry with Atlanta for the seat of government was inseparable from its ambition to rise above its fourth rank in population in Georgia. Doing so required diverting its fixation from its rural hinterland to its nearby suburban periphery. Its immediate objective was to overtake Augusta. In 1909, Macon had moved with urgency to annex its growing suburbs. This effort to realize a "Greater Macon" crystallized at a mass meeting of the Citizens' Annexation Association. Leading Macon wholesale grocer and Bibb County Commissioner Augustine J. Long had called the meeting to stir support for annexing East Macon, Napier Heights, and South Macon.[10] Macon succeeded in March 1910, just weeks before census takers arrived.[11] Municipal and business leaders hoped these annexations might help Macon eclipse Augusta. Convinced that annexations would boost Macon to at least 50,000 people, Greater Macon backers anticipated overtaking Augusta, which had numbered just under 40,000 in 1900 and had not annexed land in nearly thirty years. Perhaps it might even close the gap with Atlanta, which had counted just under 90,000 residents in that year. If nothing else, a newspaper in the Wiregrass town of Waycross noted, "Macon seems to have imbibed some of the Atlanta spirit."[12]

When the census was released that fall, Macon tallied 40,665, beating Augusta's 37,826. While Augusta leaders fumed that their city could not possibly have lost 4 percent of its population since 1900, the *Telegraph* was exultant. Macon's growth rate of more than 74 percent had slightly surpassed that of Atlanta and was the highest among Georgia's larger cities. The *Telegraph* had pointed a decade earlier to the need for suburban annexation to produce apparent growth after posting minimal growth in the 1890s. But now it failed to acknowledge the boost derived from the recent annexations spurred by the impending census.[13] Unwilling to accept the disappointing results, the Augusta Chamber of Commerce plotted to send two hundred volunteer enumerators fanning across the city for a dawn-to-dusk census recount on a Sunday, when it assumed more workers would be at home. The citizen census found a net increase of 3,479 over the federal census, with nearly half in the city's mill villages and African American neighborhoods.[14] The *Augusta Chronicle* and *Macon Daily Telegraph* traded barbs over the recount. Macon, the *Telegraph* averred, "is growing like prime alfalfa," but the paper, showing signs of resignation, added that the city "doesn't need the official figures to assure her prestige."[15]

After reviewing the recount, the Census Bureau announced a revised population of 41,040, lifting Augusta above Macon by just 375. Macon boosters were indignant. Chamber president Emory Winship sent the *Chronicle* a telegram insinuating that Augusta, President William Howard Taft's winter home, "boasts in her confines men high in influence at Washington."[16] As Macon leaders seethed, Augustans staged a celebratory downtown night parade. With their hands clutching red signal torches furnished by the Georgia Railroad and their pockets filled with "cannon crackers and giant torpedoes," thousands of marchers joined with colorful floats and banners inscribed with messages such as, "Macon, 40,665—15 square miles; Augusta, 41,040—5 square miles."[17]

In the meantime, a day after the Augusta recount was reported, the Macon Chamber of Commerce held a meeting to discuss removing the state capital from Atlanta. Macon boosters repeatedly urged lawmakers to abide by their constituents' wishes. To shape public opinion, the *Telegraph* dutifully reprinted articles and editorials from dozens of newspapers in other cities and towns, especially those in portions of the state south and east of Atlanta. While these deliver no verdict on popular opinion, they provide insight into why Georgians supported, opposed, or were indifferent toward capital removal.

Those newspapers that favored moving the capital to Macon tended to be located in Middle or South Georgia. They cited various reasons for supporting a move. Although Griffin was located closer to Atlanta than Macon, the *Griffin News* argued that cheaper accommodations made the latter more attractive. Some newspapers pointed to the faster population growth in South Georgia, suggesting the need for a more centralized location. For example, the *Tifton Gazette* in the Wiregrass town of Tifton observed that "the counties that were once pine barrens are becoming the Egypt of the South," implying recent growth in cotton cultivation. The *Dawson News* in southwest Georgia decried the unfairness of making South Georgians travel 200–300 miles by train to reach Atlanta.[18] Others applauded the removal plan because they believed that Atlantans were arrogant. Echoing the *Telegraph*'s call to "Move the Capital into Georgia," the *Cochran Journal* in its namesake Middle Georgia town wrote acerbically, "Atlanta is beginning to realize that Georgia is not confined within her city limits." The *Meriwether Vindicator* in Greenville, a small town south of Atlanta and west of Macon, complained that Atlanta "has taken up the idea that it is really the only luminary in stellar space and the other cities shine only from the reflected light of its great heavenly body." For Milledgeville, more was at stake than a preference for the capital's return to Middle Georgia. The *Milledgeville Union-Recorder* wrote that "our people remember how the Capital was taken from this city by a carpetbag and Republican administration, without the consent of the people of the State." Its conjuring of southern white hostility toward Reconstruction underlined the idea that Atlanta, with its notable northern investment, "was never entitled to the Capital."[19]

More than a matter of public opinion, the Central City needed legislators' support, which depended on furnishing funds to defray the expense of building a new capitol. The tin-domed Georgia State Capitol, completed in 1889, was among Atlanta's largest buildings, but it had reached its capacity by 1910. Some felt the time was ripe for building a larger capitol elsewhere rather than seeing state employees parsed into additional downtown Atlanta office buildings.[20] To that end, Macon's Central Capital Association undertook a fundraising campaign that garnered $200,000 in initial pledges. Eager to portray a campaign enjoying broad support, the *Telegraph* noted the willingness of the city's Black community to subscribe funds, highlighting a $100 pledge from the city's oldest African American congregation, Steward Chapel A.M.E. Church on Cotton Avenue, and $10 matching pledges from its pastor and presiding elder. The paper also pointed to the $600 subscribed by the Middle Georgia hamlet of Juliette in neighboring Monroe County.[21]

While Macon leaders assembled funding, they also reinforced their message that Macon was ideally situated to be the capital. Their effort was built on the "Greater Macon" movement. Even before the capital removal campaign started, the *Telegraph* had sponsored a slogan contest in 1910 to select a tagline to appear on a large electric sign for which boosters were also scouting possible sites, ultimately choosing "Macon—The Magnetic Center."[22] After the capital removal campaign started, the Central Capital Association sent thousands of buttons with the message, "Macon is the Place for the Capital. The Magnetic Center," to other cities and towns. The *Columbus Ledger* editor remarked that while its readers generally favored Macon over Atlanta, they probably would not wear the buttons.[23] Nor could Macon's backers make headway where it counted most—among state legislators. In 1911, Bibb County Representative Joe Hill Hall introduced a capital removal bill in the Georgia House, but it died in a narrow committee vote.[24]

Although Macon's campaign sputtered, the city made an important advance in building its capacity to serve as the state's capital. Hall had told those assembled at the inaugural capital removal meeting that Macon needed "a Kimball House," a reference to Atlanta's principal hotel.[25] Though some boosters wanted to build a resort hotel to compete with Augusta for northern winter tourists, the capital removal effort and local leaders' desire to expand Macon's capacity as a convention city led instead to building the Dempsey in 1913. The nine-story, 225-room downtown hotel, located at Cherry and Third Streets, gave the city one more asset to tout to lawmakers. Chamber leaders proposed that the Dempsey's rooftop was ideal for the large electric sign they had been discussing. By this time, the boosters had replaced their short-lived "Magnetic Center" slogan with another, "The Heart of Georgia," a name first suggested in the 1910 slogan contest by Anna Jordan of Monticello, a small town and the county seat of Jasper County thirty-five miles north of Macon. Jordan's slogan eventually saw wide use, though it never appeared in the electric "blaze of truculent glory" that the *Telegraph* had envisioned.[26]

As in 1911, renewed efforts to pass a capital removal bill failed again in 1916 and 1919, suggesting the challenges of stepping out of Atlanta's long shadow. In the latter year, a group of Macon business leaders led by *Telegraph* co-owner and editor W. T. Anderson worked with Bibb County commissioners to offer Tattnall Square Park for a new capitol and to authorize a $1 million construction bond issue. The group also negotiated an option to purchase B. P. O'Neal's eighteen-columned antebellum home atop Coleman

FIG. 2. MACON IN 1912. This view from the roof of a downtown building faces northwest with the sandhills rising in the distance. In 1919, Macon capital removal advocates initiated the purchase of B. P. O'Neal's columned antebellum mansion on Coleman Hill (in the distance immediately left of the church steeple in the center in this photo) to offer as a governor's mansion. The effort never proceeded beyond an option to purchase the house because state legislators declined to abandon Atlanta. Courtesy of Middle Georgia Archives, Washington Memorial Library, Macon, GA.

Hill as a governor's mansion (see Fig. 2). The *Telegraph*'s Atlanta news bureau manager also secured a pledge from House Speaker John N. Holder to do all he could to give Georgians an opportunity to vote on capital removal. Holder promised to do so while adding that, as a citizen of Jackson County in Northeast Georgia, he would cast his vote to keep the capital in Atlanta.[27] As the summer legislative session commenced, Macon capital removers faced a new group called the Atlanta Committee. Headed by New South prophet Henry W. Grady's son-in-law Eugene R. Black and backed by Coca-Cola executives, the Atlanta Committee dissuaded legislators from bringing capital removal to a vote. Some Middle and South Georgia lawmakers were so incensed that they even tried, unsuccessfully, to introduce a bill to ban the sale of the Atlanta-made soft drink in Georgia.[28]

With that, the capital removal effort subsided, although concerns over the Ku Klux Klan's emergence as an "invisible" government in Atlanta led Anderson to threaten removal once more in 1924.[29] However, just as the Greater Macon movement spaded the ground for future efforts to absorb suburban growth through annexation or city-county consolidation, capital removal prefigured subsequent initiatives to reinforce Macon's leadership in Middle Georgia. If Macon could not become the political seat of Georgia, it would cast itself instead as the hub of a Middle Georgia agricultural empire.

THE HEART OF THE GEORGIA PEACH BELT

In a 1924 issue of *Macon Magazine*, a chamber of commerce publication, Craddock Goins of Milwaukee wrote that, "regardless of whether Macon . . . will be the Capital City in politics, it stands an excellent chance of becoming the South's Dairy Capital." Goins compared the boll weevil's impact on Georgia cotton in the previous decade to the chinch bug's devastation of Wisconsin's wheat crops in the 1870s. He believed Middle Georgia might emulate Wisconsin, which had built its famed dairy industry around insect-resistant forage crops like alfalfa.[30] Indeed, the Macon chamber's agriculture department was thinking along the same lines as it prepared to promote poultry, dairy, and livestock farming as part of the Middle Georgia Development Campaign (MGDC). But rather than a dairy capital, Macon would be a fruit capital.[31] The idea of southern cities as supporters of surrounding farming areas was hardly unique to Macon, and the agricultural depression that gripped the South only reinforced this inclination. Although even Atlanta boosters believed that "farms are the city-builders," the sentiment was particularly compelling in the fall-line cities, whose less robust positions in the national economy made them more dependent on their hinterlands.[32]

Efforts to diversify Middle Georgia agriculture to ease cotton dependence had germinated in the nineteenth century but were slow to take root. Among potential replacements for cotton, pecans and peaches attracted considerable investment. In the 1870s, Macon banker I. C. Plant had planted one thousand paper-shell pecan trees on his Ocmulgee River farm, and Samuel and Lewis Rumph of Marshallville in Macon County (twenty miles southwest of Macon) had pioneered propagation of Elberta and Georgia Belle peaches and enticed northern investment in southern horticultural pursuits.[33] Despite no shortage of promotion, including staging the Georgia Peach Carnival in 1895, Macon had been slow to reap rewards as a market, mart, and center for agricultural extension, processing, and distribution because of the lingering centrality of cotton. However, agricultural diversification elicited growing interest in the 1910s. Under the leadership of J. F. Jackson, a Midwestern transplant, the Macon-based Central of Georgia Railway initiated the Central of Georgia Test Farms program in 1911, which persuaded farmers to allocate a portion of their acreage to cultivation under the railroad's supervision in return for the company's guarantee against loss. By 1914, twenty-nine test farms totaling 1,135 acres operated in the area.[34] The looming threat of the boll weevil, which was gnawing its way through Middle Georgia's cotton crop by 1916, only furthered the crop diversification agenda championed by agricultural scientists, extension agents, and boosters.[35]

In addition, with many African Americans abandoning rural Middle Georgia counties to pursue jobs in Macon, Atlanta, or northern cities, the prospect of losing Black farm labor arose. In October 1916, a purported labor agent conned nearly three hundred Black Maconites into purchasing railway tickets to Michigan with false promises of high-paying work, only to leave them to be arrested or dispersed at the train station. Although the departures failed, the specter of a Black exodus concerned white leaders. W. T. Anderson used his editorial voice frequently to present the region as "almost indigenous to the negro," a place where "white and black understand each other."[36] While concerned about the loss of Black farm labor, some leaders also saw opportunity in the upheaval. They hoped to attract "white settlers" from outside the South to hasten Middle Georgia's transition from sprawling cotton plantations, many lying fallow, into smaller farms producing peaches, pecans, watermelons, cantaloupes, truck crops, meat, poultry, and dairy products.

Macon boosters' embrace of agricultural diversification was inseparable from their effort to strengthen trade ties throughout Middle Georgia. They channeled some of their energies into encouraging pasture development to support a livestock industry and replenish soils depleted by decades of continuous cotton production. As with its earlier test farms, Central of Georgia provided important leadership by paying half the cost of seeding grasses and clovers on forty-four test pastures totaling 1,068 acres in the winter of 1921 to demonstrate the profitability of pasturing in Middle Georgia. By decade's end, the program had grown to 64,000 acres.[37] Concurrently, the Macon chamber launched a series of its own initiatives. The chamber hoped to foster crop diversification, encourage in-migration of white farmers to increase buying power in Macon's trade territory, and develop services to shepherd the city's transition to a broader agricultural market. In addition, the chamber focused on enticing more manufacturers of cotton and clay products, but, in contrast to Augusta and Columbus, limited waterpower hampered Macon's industrial capacity into the 1920s.[38]

In 1921, the chamber set up its farm markets bureau to help farmers dispose of crop surpluses. Its functions soon expanded to the promotion, standardization, and distribution of a widening range of farm products. Additionally, the chamber offered farm demonstrations and hired county agents to support Middle Georgia farmers and increase their ties to Macon.[39] The chamber followed two years later by supporting the MGDC and the new Georgia Peach Growers' Exchange (GPGE), and in 1925, it contracted with an upstate New York aircraft manufacturer to make Macon the crop-dusting hub of the South. These efforts, as William Thomas Okie argues, reflected a recommitment to a longstanding dream that united New South visionaries and horticulturists in "whitening the black belt," although in the case of peaches, Black pickers were merely "hidden in the foliage." Replacing cotton with crops whose cultivation might attract white farmers, then, did more to shape the image than the reality of Macon's rural periphery. Throughout the 1920s and 1930s, almost half of the population of Bibb and surrounding counties was African American.[40]

The Middle Georgia Development Campaign was a response to the abandonment of cotton growing over the preceding decade. Between 1910 and 1923, in eight counties surrounding Macon, the area devoted to cotton plummeted from 333,905 acres to 98,800 acres. The Chattahoochee Valley, for its part, suffered almost as precipitous a decline in cotton acreage, while the Augusta area saw a more modest loss of about three-eighths of its area under cotton cultivation. Middle Georgia landowners absorbed some of this decline by turning to peaches, whose 1923 value was 70 percent more than that of cotton, but the broader picture revealed some three million acres of idle land in Middle Georgia. The survey also found that nearly nine-tenths of farm inquiries received by the Macon chamber originated in eight midwestern and Great Lakes states where commercial and industrial encroachment was driving up land values. As a result, the chamber formed a land settlement committee in 1923 that cooperated with J. F. Jackson and other railroad companies' agricultural development agents to encourage the profitable cultivation of idle land in Middle Georgia.[41]

Though unable to win the state capital, Macon staked a symbolic claim as the "Heart of the Georgia Peach Belt," a seat for supporting the cultivation, marketing, packing, and shipping of peaches. The immediate eight-county Macon trade territory had quintupled the number of trees to more than five million since 1910 and accounted for half of the state's annual peach crop. By comparison, the Columbus area's peach trees increased in number by about one-third to about 380,000, while the Augusta area's peach sector slumped by about one-fifth to fewer than 200,000 trees.[42] After fifteen years of working through the Atlanta-based Georgia Fruit Exchange, growers met in Macon in 1923 and agreed to dissolve that entity and form a true cooperative, the Georgia Peach Growers' Exchange, to be based in Macon. The GPGE sought in part to address the problem of excess production. Peaches deemed too soft to ship tended to be used to feed livestock but also to be dumped in creeks or ravines. With its main office on Broadway in downtown Macon and a branch office in Marshallville, the GPGE standardized packaging, coordinated government inspections, contracted with an Atlanta marketing firm, and enlisted experts from the U.S. Department of Agriculture (USDA) and American Can Company to introduce peach farmers to other options such as canning, preserving, or pickling peaches to boost profits. Although it lasted for more than four decades, the GPGE failed to unify much more than one-third of the state's peach growers, diminishing its ability to fulfill boosters' hopes.[43]

In 1924, the Georgia State College of Agriculture and USDA co-hosted the nation's first public crop-dusting demonstration in Athens. Army pilots flew three Huff Daland biplanes retrofitted for aerial dusting to showcase the perfection of calcium arsenate dusting experiments against the boll weevil, which were first undertaken the previous year at the USDA Delta Laboratory in Tallulah, Louisiana. In February 1925, the Macon chamber contracted with Huff Daland to organize a dusting subsidiary headquartered in Macon. Within a week, Huff Daland Dusters had set up an office downtown, while the City of Macon started construction on a hangar at Camp Wheeler. In March, eighteen Huff Daland airplanes arrived in Macon, giving the Middle

FIG. 3. CROP-DUSTING DEMONSTRATION, 1925. Macon boosters, USDA officials, and company leaders attend a crop-dusting demonstration by Macon-based Huff Daland Dusters, the precursor of Delta Air Lines. Macon leaders hoped the company would play a role in making their city the service hub of the Middle Georgia "Peach Belt." Courtesy of Delta Flight Museum, Atlanta, GA.

Georgia city the nation's largest private aircraft fleet (see Fig. 3). The company boasted that it would "wage war upon enemies of cotton and other crops" such as pecans and peaches. Its planes also briefly became symbols of Macon as an agrarian metropolis, appearing in local demonstrations. The first plane made its ceremonial debut at the Fort Valley Peach Blossom Festival by "dusting" attendees with a "trail of peach petals." Another dusting demonstration accompanied a Georgia Association tour and barbecue at the Macon Packing Plant, a new chamber venture to help farmers with "the storage and orderly distribution of their perishable products" such as peaches.[44]

As with the Georgia Peach Growers' Exchange, the impact of Huff Daland Dusters proved disappointing. When local demand for its services underperformed expectations after only a few months, the company relocated to Monroe, Louisiana, to serve Mississippi Delta cotton growers before pivoting to passenger service in 1928 and eventually returning to Atlanta as Delta Air Lines in the 1940s.[45] Although neither venture fulfilled the Macon chamber's high hopes, each reflected an expansive metropolitan vision that connected city and countryside. Peaches continued to be a focus. By 1930, they accounted for between one quarter and three-eighths of the farm acreage in Crawford, Jones, and Peach counties and nearly one-fifth of Houston County's farmland. The latter also invested significantly in peanut cultivation, and while Macon never became a "dairy capital" as Goins predicted, dairy farms accounted for about one-sixth of the farming areas of Bibb and Monroe counties.[46]

A similar agriculturally oriented metropolitan vision was present in Augusta and Columbus. Neither city proclaimed itself the hub for a particular commodity like peaches, but both of their respective trade territories substantially increased their production of cowpeas, peanuts, and other legumes, which were both profitable and beneficial for replenishing soils exhausted by intensive cotton production. Still, cotton retained a firm grip, especially around Augusta, where the reduction in cotton growing was much more modest than around the other two cities.[47] In sharp contrast, Macon leaders believed their city was positioned ideally to usher in a new agricultural economy centered around the peach. Though their schemes to capitalize on agricultural diversification were never fully realized, Macon boosters' embrace of Middle Georgia's Peach Belt made their city a bellwether for a future in which the fall-line cities would have to recalibrate the focus of their efforts to market themselves as regional hubs.

MACON AND THE DIXIE HIGHWAY

Two years after the first Huff Daland airplane spread peach petals over Fort Valley's Peach Blossom Festival visitors, a U.S. government plane scattered poppies over the Dixie Highway where it crossed Echeconnee Creek, an Ocmulgee River tributary that formed the southern border of Bibb County. The flyover was part of the Memorial Day 1927 dedication of the "model mile" of the Dixie Highway Road of Remembrance lined by one hundred pecan trees and bronze markers. Conceived by the Bibb County Dixie Highway Auxiliary in 1922 to honor World War veterans from Bibb County, the project also promoted highway beautification to call tourists' attention to Macon. The Road of Remembrance showcased Maconites' outsize influence in the campaign to build the Dixie Highway, the South's most impactful transportation advance of the interwar period.[48]

The Dixie Highway was among the so-called marked trails that emerged from the Good Roads Movement of the early twentieth century. This movement transformed a patchwork of locally maintained farm-to-depot roads into a national highway. The Dixie Highway and other improved southern highways had a transformative effect on the region, supporting the industrialization of agriculture, encouraging automobile-centered tourism, and contributing to the integration of the South into the national economy.[49] Macon leaders played key roles in planning and promoting the Dixie Highway from the inception of the Chattanooga, Tennessee–based Dixie Highway Association (DHA) in 1915. W. T. Anderson, along with *Atlanta Constitution* editor Clark Howell, was among the fourteen original directors of the DHA and was instrumental in shaping the designation of routes through Georgia.[50] In addition, Macon clubwomen became active in the Dixie Highway movement. Less than three months after the DHA was organized, the women formed the Bibb County Dixie Highway Auxiliary to foster highway beautification. One of its founders was Alma Anderson Massey, the wife of a cotton gin manufacturer and sister of the newspaper editor. In 1916, the Bibb auxiliary became the prototype for other auxiliaries in the ten-state area covered by the Dixie Highway. In 1924, under Massey's leadership, the Bibb auxiliary spearheaded the formation of the National Dixie Highway Auxiliary (NDHA) with headquarters in Macon.[51]

Between the inception of Dixie Highway planning and the outbreak of World War II, boosters sought to use highways to expand Middle Georgia trade and build up Macon's convention and tourist business. Their efforts mirrored those across the South, where boosters were particularly keen to use highway improvement as a lever for economic development. North Carolina, for example, went so far as to market itself as "The Good Roads State."[52] Like their efforts to make Macon the state capital and the hub of peach culture, this endeavor deepened their ties with other Middle Georgia communities and reinforced Macon's identity as "The Heart of Georgia." But as they learned, maintaining Macon's position as the trade mart of Middle Georgia in the auto age would require more than a central location. Once Dixie Highway paving approached completion, Macon boosters pivoted toward highway advocacy for the surrounding farming region in the mid-

1920s. They also discovered that it would take more than the highway to make Macon a destination rather than a mere stop between Michigan and Florida. In the depths of the Great Depression, they would try to develop an attraction to draw tourists to Macon.

It was never in doubt that the Dixie Highway would run through Macon. While the well-established winter resort of Augusta lay along a straight line between Sault Ste. Marie and the fast-emerging resort city of Miami, Macon's location to the south of Atlanta made it the surer bet as highway planners considered how best to open Miami to motorists from the Great Lakes. Here was an example of how Macon sometimes benefited from its location in relation to the capital city. In contrast, Augusta boosters would have to scrap for a branch route. Their effort ultimately benefited less from Augusta's reputation as a winter resort than W. T. Anderson's support for a multi-route system instead of a single long-distance highway. For its part, Columbus lay too far west to merit serious consideration.[53]

Anderson was adept at blurring the line between magnanimity and self-interest. In 1914, a national advertiser had asked him Macon's population. When the man told him that despite a population of 50,000, Macon essentially had 30,000 because 40 percent were Black, Anderson formed the "Negro edition" of the *Macon Daily Telegraph*, averring that African Americans were "entitled to be included." Likewise, rather than insist on a single Dixie Highway, he announced his support for alternate routes (see Fig. 4).[54] Because the Dixie Highway would rely on counties to pave their own stretches of roadway, dual routes might spur competition to hasten improvements, boosting the entire region. While Macon might have benefited more by being along the sole route of the South's greatest marked trail, Anderson understood that supporting competing routes from Atlanta to Macon and from Macon to Florida would double the number of improved highways converging on his city. However, he and two other DHA directors broke with Howell and the majority of directors who favored a third branch, dubbed the Old Capital Route because it would connect the former capitals of Milledgeville and Louisville and pass within thirty miles of another, Augusta, on its way to Savannah and Jacksonville, Florida.[55]

Despite the triumphalism that greeted each DHA announcement, route designations preceded most road improvements. Well into the 1920s, large segments of its various routes remained unpaved and susceptible to damage

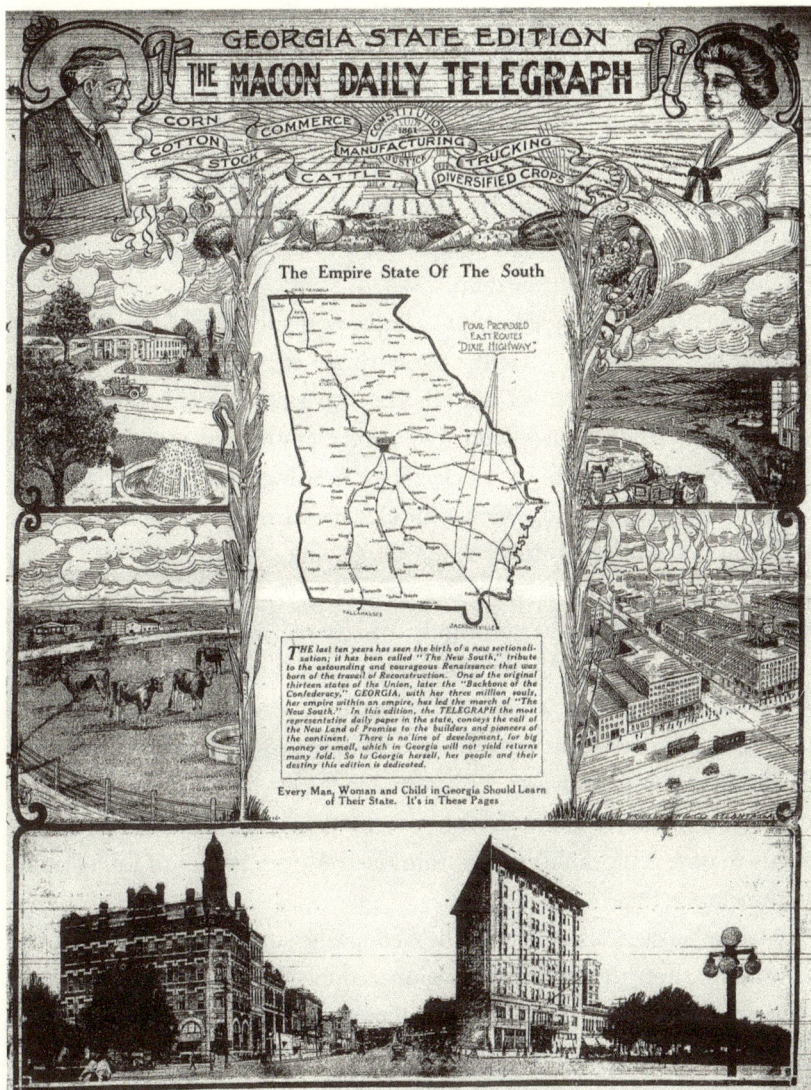

FIG. 4. PROPOSED ROUTES FOR THE DIXIE HIGHWAY, 1915. The Dixie Highway network is the focal point of this newspaper section cover. The surrounding art suggests the centrality of the highway in Macon boosters' hopes of further developing the agricultural backbone of their city's economy. Macon was a nerve center for Dixie Highway planning but continued to lag further behind Atlanta. *Macon Daily Telegraph*, August 19, 1915. Courtesy of Middle Georgia Archives, Washington Memorial Library, Macon, GA.

from downpours. Although the Dixie Highway was their primary concern, Macon leaders, like their counterparts in other southern cities, wanted to promote better roads more generally at a time of surging automobile ownership. Their efforts far surpassed ensuring the upkeep of Bibb County's highway spokes around the Macon hub. They also extended to assisting with highway improvements throughout Middle Georgia to support economic development and, with women's leadership, making Bibb County the regional model for highway beautification.

Macon boosters fostered highway improvements to build "good will" beyond Bibb's borders, especially on the fringes of their trade territory that overlapped with other cities' hinterlands. The Macon chamber met in 1925 with officials from Johnson and Wilkinson counties east of the city to discuss lobbying state highway officials for a new highway from Wrightsville to Macon. Lacking a bridge across the Oconee River, Wrightsvillians had to travel far out of their way to reach Macon. Calling these counties' soil "as fine as that of the Mississippi valley," the *Macon News* noted that a new highway would shorten the route from eighty to sixty miles and foster agricultural development, making it closer to Macon than to Augusta. The paper added, "Much of the trade which logically belongs to Macon now goes to Savannah or Augusta, so we would consult our selfish interests by encouraging their proposed highway." Similarly, the Macon Lions Club facilitated the formation of a highway association in Cordele, seventy-five miles to the south, to raise funds to pave a 160-mile stretch from the southern border of Bibb County to the Florida line.[56]

Macon boosters also used Middle Georgia's gradually improving highway network to strengthen their city's regional connections. In 1925, the chamber sponsored a series of "good will" tours that visited dozens of towns to present a band concert, give a speech, and meet local officials. Chamber manager Malcolm Ainsworth insisted that "[w]e are not going out to advertise Macon." Rather, chamber president and *Telegraph* co-owner Peyton T. Anderson claimed, they sought "to gather the heads of various business houses together and take them through Macon's legitimate trade territory so that they may become personally acquainted with the people who visit their stores when in Macon."[57] Despite these statements, the loop tours clearly sought to enlarge "The Heart of Georgia." They extended outward from Macon, sometimes using stretches of the Dixie Highway system, and progressed along the edges of Middle Georgia before returning. One such tour went as far east as Vidalia and Sparta, whose merchants and farmers were just as likely to trade in Savannah or Augusta. Two others surpassed the midpoint between Macon and Columbus. The *Columbus Ledger* regarded the goodwill tours with alarm, asking what Columbus leaders were doing to counter these tours that were "bound to make inroads on the local trade territory." The tours appear to have achieved their goal. As the newspaper in the Wiregrass town of Ashburn effused, the Macon tours showed that "there was something doing in Georgia and that Macon was near the vortex of activities."[58]

Women in the Bibb County Dixie Highway Auxiliary shared boosters' ambitions to use the Dixie Highway to promote tourism. Building on the Macon chamber's increasing use of the slogan "The Heart of Georgia" and sponsorship of a free tourist camp in Central City Park, the Bibb auxiliary worked to expand upon the earlier "parking" of the centers of downtown Macon's extraordinarily wide streets with verdant lawns, flowering shrubs, and rows of oaks between the 1880s and 1910s.[59] In 1921, the women began marking and beautifying the Dixie Highway in Bibb County, starting with a "model mile" of pecan trees, crepe myrtles, and spirea along Forsyth Road in Vineville, Macon's fashionable suburb in the fall-line hills. Horticulturist and landscape designer Robert C. Berckmans, Macon's parks superintendent and a descendent of the founders of Augusta's famed Fruitland Nurseries, assisted the auxiliary.[60]

As roadside beautification proceeded, the women mobilized to make the entire Dixie Highway a "Road of Remembrance" despite the disbanding of the Dixie Highway Association and the federal government's rollout of a national numbered highway system in 1927. In the following year, the NDHA helped organize ten new chapters in Middle Georgia and Wiregrass counties, perpetuating the Dixie Highway's unifying potential even as its segments became subsumed into several numbered routes. After Massey showed them Bibb County's model mile, the NDHA chapters in Monroe and Lamar counties to the northwest of Macon planted several hundred trees along U.S. 41. The NDHA also benefited when Berckmans persuaded the National Pecan Growers Association to donate 1,350 trees in 1928.[61] Although the Road of Remembrance was never completed on the entire 5,800-mile Dixie Highway system, the Macon-based NDHA, with the Bibb auxiliary at its core, kept Macon on the minds of people throughout the system's ten-state region and continued to unify "The Heart of Georgia" in common purpose.

Despite its promise, the Dixie Highway failed to bring substantial development to Bibb County, whose population increase from 56,646 to 83,783 in the three decades after 1910 appears less impressive when viewed in the context of six surrounding rural counties that lost a total of more than 26 percent of their people. Most tourists passed through Macon on their way elsewhere, just as they had done on passenger trains. Nor did the city break the hold of agriculture and agriculturally based industry. As a result, Bibb County experienced lackluster growth. In contrast to 1920s population growth of 37 percent in Fulton County (Atlanta) and 30 percent in Muscogee County (Columbus), where Fort Benning offered a boost, Bibb County expanded by only 8 percent. While annexations magnified Atlanta's and Columbus's appearances of growth, Macon's failure to annex its suburban edges matched a similar failure in Augusta. Augusta managed, nonetheless, to increase by almost 8,000 people (ten times Macon's increase) and to retake the rank of Georgia's third most populous city, a cause for melancholy among Macon's boosters.

ONE CONTINUOUS GARDEN SPOT

As the Great Depression deepened, Macon leaders continued their well-rehearsed reliance on serving as the hub of Middle Georgia. The city's WMAZ radio station, operated by the Macon Junior Chamber of Commerce (Jaycees), amplified the idea that Macon served a vast farming territory. Reminiscent of earlier capital removal claims that Macon served the "real" Georgia, the station pitched the "State of WMAZ," fifty-four counties (appropriately peach-shaded in one ad) with more than 800,000 people. Although the one-thousand-watt station ignored the fact that Atlanta's WSB, only ninety miles away, had fifty thousand watts of broadcasting power, it beckoned prospective advertisers with an agricultural nod, "Cut yourself a big slice of Georgia."[62]

WMAZ was hardly exceptional in conflating metropolitan stature with the trade territory. Less than three weeks into President Franklin D. Roosevelt's first term, a Macon chamber ad trumpeted, "A New Deal for Macon's Cash Registers!" Appropriating the Roosevelt agenda's name, the ad promised "millions of additional dollars from the farms and towns in this section." Underscoring the persisting intent to develop millions of arable acres in the two-dozen counties for which Macon provided a market and distribution point, it pointed to the half-million people within seventy-five miles "who look to Macon as the logical market for their produce." It reaffirmed a long-standing tendency among Georgia sandhill cities' boosters to define the scope of their metropolitan ambitions not as a city and its suburbs but as a city surrounded by an agricultural empire.[63]

The "New Deal" ad also signaled the chamber's commitment to "maintain an active interest in all problems affecting our neighbors and to co-operate with them in every way possible. We know that as our neighbors prosper and grow—so shall Macon prosper and grow." Its pledge to use Macon's central location to attract more conventions continued a longtime pursuit. It also echoed earlier pitches that cast metropolitan ambitions to become the state capital in the altruistic terms of serving the two-thirds of Georgians who lived closer to Macon than Atlanta. Its promise to push for paving all highways in Middle Georgia, likewise, continued the city's earlier leadership in securing the Dixie Highway. But in another sense, the chamber's "New Deal" signaled a stronger embrace of tourism in its pledge to continue marking Middle Georgia highways "to divert tourist travel through Macon," as it had done in Griffin and Milledgeville the previous autumn.[64] Moreover, Macon leaders' embrace of regionalizing beautification efforts built upon earlier work by the Bibb auxiliary but made tourism an overt aim. Elaborating upon an old notion that Macon's natural advantages in climate and soil supported lushly planted parks and parkways in town and scenic farms and orchards in the countryside, the boosters' regional movement envisioned a more embellished, automobile-oriented landscape that would steer tourists toward local attractions. Though hatched by boosters, Macon's initiative required federal and state government support, expertise from professional horticulturists, and participation by garden clubs and the public.

In 1935, after three hundred Works Progress Administration (WPA) workers improved Macon's parks and county roads, former mayor G. Glen Toole, who by that time headed a roadway beautification committee, planned to line Forsyth Road (U.S. 41) with clusters of mimosa, crabapple, dogwood,

FIG. 5. BACONSFIELD PARK, 1933. Mayor G. Glen Toole promoted city and regional beautification efforts in the 1930s, taking advantage of New Deal funds to implement many of his ideas. Toole directed the planting of thousands of camellias, azaleas, and other flowering shrubs and the creation of a lagoon and winding paths in Baconsfield Park, which he and other Macon boosters hoped might rival famed gardens elsewhere in the South. Courtesy of Middle Georgia Archives, Washington Memorial Library, Macon, GA.

and palms. Although Toole was dissatisfied with the "rigid line of trees on highway banks" that were the NDHA's legacy, his choice of Forsyth Road reprised the women's earlier decision to plant their "model mile" close to Macon's wealthier northern suburban section. Toole hoped it would be one of many beautified highways leading to Macon from all directions and making it a greater tourist destination. He also sought to tap the federal spigot to nourish his vision of additional highway beautification, levees along the northeast bank of the Ocmulgee River, and a sunken garden with winding roadways in Baconsfield Park, where the city parks department had recently planted thousands of azaleas and camellias (see Fig. 5).[65]

Sharing Toole's interest in regional beautification, W. T. Anderson promoted a vision that encompassed surrounding counties. At a Kiwanis luncheon at the Dempsey Hotel in 1936, he remarked on how tourists made annual pilgrimages to Charleston, Savannah, and Mobile to see beautiful gardens, adding that "there isn't any reason why we can't make this the flower city of the South." Anderson urged enlisting "every man, woman and child, white and Negro," showing his penchant for imagining a shared sense of community, even though many Black Maconites lived on unpaved back alleys hardly conducive to beautification. Anderson suggested giving citizens a camellia cutting in a can to take home, plant, and cultivate, following it with a contest for the best results after one or two years. The Kiwanians responded by forming a beautification committee. Echoing the mayor, one Kiwanis officer commented, "We must do something to make Macon seem to those who pass through it, better and more attractive than the hundreds of other towns of the same size."[66] Anderson also carried his beautification vision to surrounding counties. He told the Kiwanis Club in Jackson, the seat of Butts County, that beautifying highways would foster "friendship and interest among middle Georgia residents" and "make central Georgia one continuous garden spot which would attract thousands of visitors here each year." Like the vision of diversified agriculture, it might also remake landscapes built to support cotton. In Milledgeville, Anderson told garden club women of the need to demolish the "tumbled-down, abandoned shacks" that marred the scenery along highways into cities and towns, a reflection of the ambivalence with which whites looked upon the vestiges of the cotton South.[67]

The Macon chamber promised to meet any other county's highway beautification effort at the county line. The first to pledge cooperation was Bleckley County, located immediately southeast of Bibb County on the Cochran Short Route that passed through the county seat of Cochran and offered the shortest drive from Macon to the coast. The Cochran Short Route's inclusion in the regional project owed to its generous rights-of-way, which pointed to a hurdle—persuading property owners to grant quit claims to meet federal highway right-of-way minima for beautification. All other highways radiating from Macon had even narrower rights-of-way. Within several months, the chamber had secured deeds from all property owners between the Bibb-Bleckley line and Jeffersonville, enabling beautification to proceed.[68]

In his speeches, Anderson pivoted effortlessly between grandiosity and simplicity. At Georgia State Women's College in Milledgeville, he called for a statewide "Georgia Gardens" program with Macon "acting as the hub." Referencing Thomasville's rose gardens and Savannah and Charleston, Anderson remarked, "We visit these cities and come back enthusiastic about the beauties and delights of fairylands built by human hands." Conversely, in neighboring Jones County, he told Kiwanians that beautification need not be expensive. "Everyone," he averred, "can root japonicas or oleanders, or go into the woods and get dogwood and crabapple."[69] Indeed, his pragmatism and idealism were inseparable. In his speech in Jackson, Anderson cast beautification as environmental remediation. As elsewhere in the Lower South, deforestation and cotton monoculture had scarred the land across Middle Georgia, subjecting it to erosion. "If you want to see a tragedy written in flowing blood, look at our Georgia streams running to the sea," Anderson observed. "They are bright red, colored with the fine top soil [*sic*] of our good land, washed away by rain. . . . What has this to do with beautification? Plenty. As we plant to beautify we plant to prevent erosion." Another Anderson editorial even characterized highway beautification as a lifesaving action. He suggested planting Cherokee roses, the Georgia state flower, "just beyond the shoulder of the roads with the double purpose of beautification and of safe-guarding [*sic*] travelers from the ambling cows and pigs which at any unguarded moment may cause a wreck."[70] These practical justifications underscored that Macon boosters saw their metropolitan ambitions— whether capital removal, agricultural extension, highway development, or beautification—as catalysts for regional reinvention.

Anderson's Georgia Gardens idea never took root statewide, but this did not stop the *Telegraph* from crediting Macon for beautification efforts elsewhere, which likely owed more to homegrown interest, WPA funds, Savannah's influence, and the involvement of professional consultants in other Georgia cities. In late 1936, the town of Waynesboro (south of Augusta) launched a beautification plan assisted by Savannah Tree and Park Commission superintendent W. H. Robertson. Augusta, a city that already had a long tradition of embracing landscape planning, also consulted with Robertson and commissioned University of Georgia landscaping professor and state highway engineer Hubert B. Owens to devise a city beautification plan.[71] While Macon boosters' latest bid to showcase their regional leadership accomplished no more than previous ones, it unfolded alongside another effort to give Macon a distinctive destination. During the Depression, Macon leaders became keenly interested in developing a "river garden" along the Ocmulgee River that might compete with famed attractions like Magnolia Gardens and Middleton Gardens near Charleston and the recently opened

Bellingrath Gardens outside Mobile.[72] In addition to Toole's improvements in Baconsfield Park, other similar attractions opened to the public in the 1930s, including Bibb Manufacturing executive James H. Porter's Porterfield estate in southern Bibb County, with its ten thousand rose bushes, and future American Camellia Society founder William G. Lee's azalea and camellia gardens just upriver from Baconsfield Park.[73]

Ocmulgee Fields emerged as the most promising place for Macon to develop an attraction of national renown. Realizing this tourist potential would test boosters' ability to embrace preserving what many viewed as a wasteland. Native Americans in the tenth to twelfth centuries had farmed the rich bottoms along the Ocmulgee and built a complex of earthen mounds. When Hernando de Soto traversed the area in 1540, some descendants of this society remained, and later the Lower Creeks used the site until they ceded the mounds to the United States in 1826, three years after Macon was chartered. In the next century, the mound complex suffered degradation as a result of the construction of a railroad, Confederate earthworks, fertilizer factory, brickyard, clay mine, and dairy farm, as well as due to hill climbing by motorcyclists in the 1920s.[74]

Macon attorney and amateur historian Gen. Walter A. Harris became fascinated by the remnants of mounds at Ocmulgee Fields and tried to interest the Smithsonian Institution's Bureau of American Ethnology in preserving the site in 1922. After seven years, he finally succeeded in getting bureau chief Dr. M. W. Stirling to visit the mounds. Four years later, Harris and associates convinced the Jaycees to sponsor a civic effort to purchase the mounds and give them to the city government. Georgia congressman Carl Vinson, a Milledgeville native, helped them obtain Civil Works Administration (CWA) support for the Smithsonian to undertake excavations. He also introduced a bill in 1934 that led to the establishment of Ocmulgee National Monument on the condition that locals assemble two thousand acres around the mounds.[75]

Local apathy proved a daunting obstacle. Harvard researcher Dr. Arthur R. Kelly attested that, although the archaeological and tourist potential of Ocmulgee Fields rivaled that of Puebloan sites in the American Southwest, "never before in doing site explorations . . . have I seen so little general interest or concern evidenced as in Macon." Nevertheless, Harris continued to appeal to merchants, gas and oil stations, hotels, and other businesses that would benefit if the mounds became a tourist destination.[76] One local business leader averred that it would be "suicidal" if Macon forfeited the national monument and likened its importance to building the Dempsey Hotel in 1913 and the Macon Auditorium in 1925.[77] The Jaycees agreed to form an Indian mounds committee to raise acquisition funds. Support ranged from business leaders to New Deal workers to schoolchildren who sold postcards of the mounds and donated lunch money. Still, the remaining acquisitions were hard-fought. Bibb Manufacturing refused to sell a tract it was reserving for a future textile mill expansion and fought federal condemnation before eventually agreeing to transfer a portion of its property. Although the assembled area of 678 acres was far short of the goal, the NPS agreed to accept the mounds.[78]

If many Maconites were indifferent toward the mounds, the *Macon Telegraph* wanted to bend the national monument toward Anderson's vision of tourist attractions. Although the purpose of saving the site was to preserve its archaeological value and reconstruct the mound complex to depict the cultures of Mississippian peoples who grew maize, the *Telegraph* imagined flower gardens, again referencing Magnolia Gardens and Middleton Gardens as models. An editorial insisted that more attention to the landscape was important because "many visitors are not specialists and they will be attracted most by a beautiful environment."[79] With this in mind, the Macon chamber formed its own Indian mounds committee and hoped to attract thousands of tourists to an "Indian festival, to compare with Mardi Gras," and the Jaycees sought to highlight the park by cooperating with the WPA to publish *The Macon Guide and Ocmulgee National Monument* in 1939 (see Fig. 6).[80]

Macon's newfound fascination with the mounds became enmeshed in boosters' fusing of traditional and modern pursuits. As the WPA guide observed, "Macon cannot be defined as belonging either to the Old or the New South but as a city blending elements of both in its entity." While calling attention to modern downtown buildings and industrial plants, the guidebook explained that "Macon retains many aspects of the farmers' market town that it was before the War Between the States. This is particularly noticeable on Saturdays, when farm wagons and mud-caked Fords creak and sputter down the main thoroughfares."[81] Indeed, Macon leaders had spent the Depression

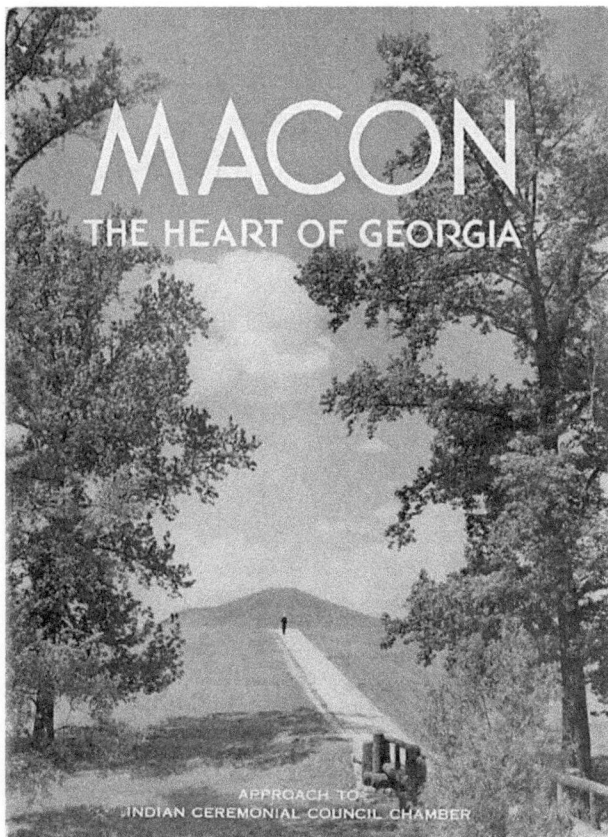

FIG. 6. MACON TOURIST GUIDEBOOK, 1941. This guide employs Macon's long-standing slogan "The Heart of Georgia" and showcases the Ocmulgee Mounds, an attraction that local boosters hoped might make their city more than a stopping point for tourists passing through the state on their way to or from Florida. Courtesy of Middle Georgia Archives, Washington Memorial Library, Macon, GA.

years much the same as the previous decades: touting the mostly agricultural Middle Georgia trade area and attempting to make "The Heart of Georgia" a tourist destination.

Macon's seemingly ambiguous position in the New South was partly a result of its marginalization amid Atlanta's meteoric growth. But it also reflected Maconites' ambivalence toward modernization that made them see their city's future in embracing familiar forms of development.[82] Maconites had staked much of the appeal of capital removal on the idea that Macon was the heart of an authentic version of Georgia unmarred by the "carpetbagger" mindset many still attributed to Atlanta. They had embraced the idea that Macon was the natural hub for an ideal state economy based on cotton, diversified crops, and industries that sprouted from Middle Georgia's natural resources made possible by its warm climate and rich soil.[83] They had also embraced modern highways while crafting a tourist image drawing on the same romantic southern imagery that the Dixie Highway's name evoked. Their attempt to incorporate Ocmulgee Fields into a seamless story that anchored Macon's present in a pageant of progress from Creeks to Confederates—replete with plenty of camellias and the promise of a local answer to Mardi Gras—revealed much about how Macon boosters imagined the New South in "The Heart of Georgia."

TWO

THE WINTER CAPITAL OF AMERICA

On the morning of December 18, 1908, a Southern Railway passenger train rolled into Union Station, an imposing Spanish Renaissance–style depot that announced Augusta's metropolitan ambitions. A special train car carried president-elect William Howard Taft, his wife Nellie, their sons Robert and Charles, and Taft's private secretary and valet. An estimated four thousand Augustans greeted the train, giving the Republican a cordial reception in this Democratic bastion of the Solid South. Augusta Chamber of Commerce president, bank executive, and Waynesboro native Lynwood C. Hayne addressed Taft in the cavernous station, concluding with "the confident hope and belief, that you will fully realize in this garden spot of the Sunny South, all of your pleasurable anticipations of rest and recreation." The entourage then motored three miles west from Union Station to "the Hill," as the winter colony of Summerville was called. There the Tafts would spend two nights as guests of Landon A. Thomas, the president of the John P. King Manufacturing Company, one of several large cotton mills that had lent Augusta the sobriquet "Lowell of the South." Thereafter, the Tafts planned to settle at Terrett Cottage, an antebellum home whose side yard opened onto the magnolia-studded grounds of the Bon Air Hotel, where the family would take their meals (see Fig. 7). By afternoon, the president-elect was acquainting himself with the sand greens at the Augusta Country Club.[1]

Taft had chosen Augusta for his winter sojourn on the advice of his family physician in Cincinnati. When Dr. Frederick Forchheimer recommended Au-

FIG. 7. THE TAFTS AT THE BON AIR, 1908. The Taft family made numerous visits to Augusta, where President Taft liked to play golf. Here they are pictured in front of the Bon Air Hotel, the social center of the city's winter resort colony of Summerville atop the sandhills. Local boosters hoped that Taft's preference for Augusta might lend the city a reputation as "The Winter Capital of America." Courtesy of Augusta Museum of History, Augusta, GA.

gusta, he was, in fact, thinking about the village of Summerville that perched on the sandhills overlooking the city from three miles to the west. The escarpment that lent the Hill its nickname stood some 350 to 500 feet above sea level and about 200 to 350 feet above the elevation of Augusta's business district along the Savannah River.[2] Just as Macon's fall-line location in "The Heart of Georgia" shaped that city's efforts to serve as governmental seat, agricultural mart, highway hub, and convention and tourist destination for the state, Augusta's sandhills embodied its boosters' hopes to make the city the "Winter Capital of the United States."

In all three of Georgia's major fall-line cities, suburbs on the sandhills— Vineville in Macon, Wynnton in Columbus, and Summerville in Augusta— became the most desirable residential sections by the early twentieth century. While Augusta boosters invested in sandhills resort promotion and

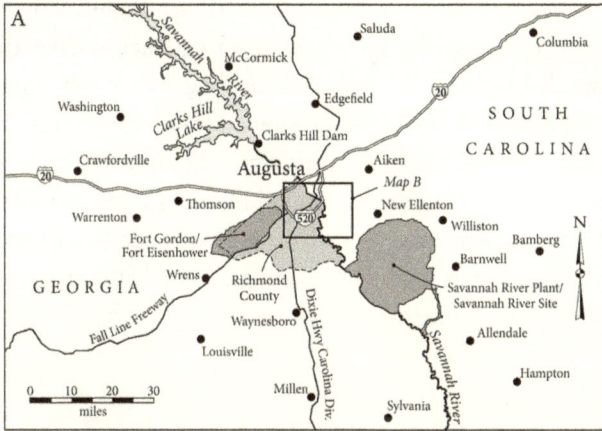

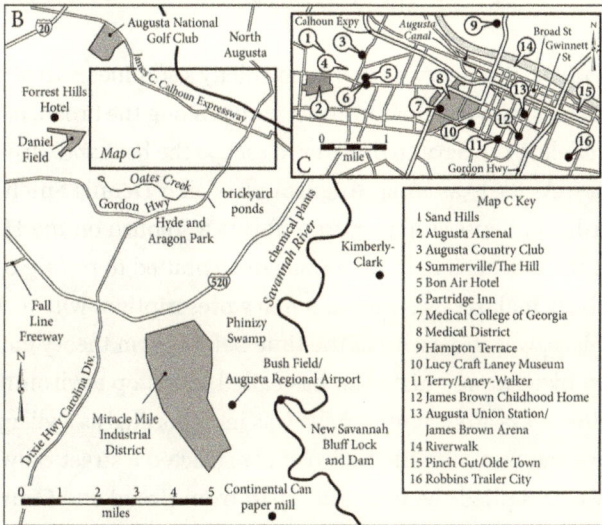

AUGUSTA AND THE CENTRAL SAVANNAH RIVER AREA.

suburban residential development on the Hill, recurring river floods, a disastrous fire, and disinvestment consigned much of the city, especially its largest Black neighborhood, the "Negro Territory" or "Terry" (now known as Laney–Walker), to deteriorate even as its leaders dubbed Augusta the "Garden City of the South."[3] By embracing winter tourism while continuing to rely on cotton and cotton-dominated industry, Augusta leaders lavished hospitality on a narrow range of potential visitors.

With the emergence of Florida's semitropical resorts, Augusta would struggle to maintain its tourist appeal. Southern highway development opened new routes, making it even harder to attract tourists than when doing so entailed lobbying for favorable passenger train schedules. During the Great Depression, Augusta boosters reprised earlier attempts to leverage President Taft's choice of Augusta as his winter home, this time seizing upon the fame of Atlanta golfing champion Bobby Jones to try to make Augusta the "Golf Capital of America." Despite Augusta's reputation, it proved little more capable than Macon of commanding tourists' attention to spur economic development in the interwar years.

THE WINTER CAPITAL

Before the 1880s, Summerville had been chiefly a summer retreat for prominent Augustans who left their in-town homes along the broad, oak-shaded streets paralleling the Savannah River to escape the heat and threat of tropical diseases. As early as 1804, Augusta physician Dennis Smelt had prescribed for his patients suffering from fevers a sojourn on the Hill, which was free of the miasmas that the physician attributed to rotting cottonseed but were likely malaria or typhoid. Smelt's prescription, which connected health to place, was indicative of the time before germ theory emerged, an era marked by what one historian has called "nonstop environmental appraisal."[4] Five years after Summerville was incorporated as a village in 1861, the Augusta and Summerville Railroad constructed a street railway whose mule-drawn cars plied the four-mile span from Broad and Centre (Fifth) Streets (two blocks from the river) to the U.S. Arsenal in Summerville. Just as streetcars encouraged suburban development in other cities in the latter half of the nineteenth century, the forty-minute run enabled wealthy Augustans to take up healthful suburban living on the sandhills. Summerville's population more than quadrupled over the next fifteen years, and the village evolved from a local summer retreat to a national winter colony where a growing number of northerners rented cottages or built winter homes.[5]

Although local leaders sought to make the sandhills and Augusta synonymous in the national mind, the city's challenging environment made clear that Summerville, although nearby, was a realm apart. Augusta's location several miles below the fall line, where the Savannah River's course widened from a narrow gorge onto a broad plain, subjected the central city to recurrent flooding. In the most severe floods in Augusta, the water rose high enough to spread like a sheet across the relatively flat street grid. On September 11, 1888, the worst flood in a half-century struck Augusta, making "every street a canal." The muddy waters "swirled along the counters of Broad street [sic] and licked the show windows." The *Augusta Chronicle* declared that the flood "was an impartial, and entirely democratic freshet" and shared anecdotal evidence to argue that the disaster had reduced all Augustans— Black or white, rich or poor—to similar helplessness.[6] The evolution of the Hill from winter colony to annexed suburb would make it increasingly disingenuous to claim that all Augustans shared the same environmental hazards.

As in Asheville, North Carolina, where George Washington Vanderbilt's completion of his castle-like Biltmore House augmented the elite reputation of a mountain city known for its temperate climate, Augusta boosters sought to add similar cachet to Summerville.[7] After years of pronouncements about the healthfulness of the sandhills and the need for a winter hotel, Augusta's repute as a resort became firmly established with the construction of the Bon Air Hotel.[8] After a stint selling patent medicines in New York City, Augusta native Dr. William Henry Tutt took advantage of the excitement that swirled around the 1888 Augusta Exposition to raise capital for a Summerville hostelry through the Sand Hills Hotel Company. Framed and finished in Georgia longleaf pine wood, the rambling, Queen Anne–style, 140-room Bon Air opened in December 1889. As historian Edward J. Cashin observed, "Augusta, the Lowell of the South, was about to become the Saratoga of the South."[9]

The Bon Air had a slow start. Augusta boosters remained more attuned to the cotton trade, textile manufacturing, and civic events that showcased these enterprises. In the resort's inaugural season, a recently formed Augusta Carnival and Trades Display Association staged a New Orleans–style carnival that drew tens of thousands of Augustans and visitors to Broad Street, a downtown thoroughfare second nationally in width only to the Crescent City's Canal Street. The Augusta Cotton Exchange and dozens of mercantile and industrial firms entered colorful, horse-drawn floats in a night parade that rolled through downtown. The *Augusta Chronicle* averred that Broad Street was "one glittering bower of light. Fairyland could not exceed it in beauty." In the following January, so many visitors thronged the city for the second Augusta Carnival that every downtown hotel and boardinghouse was filled beyond capacity, forcing many people to leave town while "others slept in offices, hall-ways, in hotel lobbys [*sic*], on steps and many even on naked floors." Perhaps the city's inability to accommodate a surge of visitors convinced city leaders that a third edition of the winter carnival was unwise, but, in any case, Augusta held no subsequent carnivals.[10]

Downtown Augusta's capacity for conventions and tourism shrank in the depression that followed the Panic of 1893. The *Chronicle* lamented the "hotel problem" in 1900, noting that the city now had only one remaining commercial hotel. On the Hill, it was a different matter. In 1901, the newspaper observed that the Bon Air was flush with 219 guests.[11] After 1890, when former Indian Territory agent and Kansas City real estate broker Daniel B. Dyer assembled Kansas City financial backers to purchase and electrify the Augusta Street Railway, the Bon Air and Broad Street were a mere fifteen-minute ride apart, with cars departing each end every seven and a half minutes.[12] While the electric car line made Summerville a popular attraction for downtown hotel guests and the city an allure for Bon Air patrons, the interchange between them withered by 1900. The *Chronicle* commented on Bon Air guests: "It is quite an unusual sight to see of them [*sic*] in the city, unless in the morning, when out for a little shopping. From morning until night the time is whiled away on the golf links."[13] Golf had arrived in Augusta in 1897 when the Bon Air leased ninety acres of nearby property to lay out a nine-hole course. When the Augusta Country Club formed four years later, it replaced the Bon Air links with an eighteen-hole course open to hotel guests. A later addition of another eighteen holes in 1909, several months after Taft's first visit, elevated the resort's golf reputation when a growing number of southern resorts were adding courses.[14]

When not golfing, Bon Air guests enjoyed the natural environment of the sandhills. They traversed miles of bridal paths on horseback beneath the "fragrant pine forests" and hunted quail, woodcock, and snipe. Guests seemed unable to resist bringing nature back with them. So many of them picked yellow jessamine on their strolls that the flowering vines nearly disappeared by the early 1900s. Tourists' fascination with mockingbirds also "created a market, and the negroes of the community made a business of catching the nesting birds and shipping them north," leaving Summerville yards eerily silent until tourists learned that the birds would not sing in captivity.[15] Visitors' desire to possess the natural landscape of the Hill remade much of it into golf courses and manicured suburban estates and threatened its native flora and fauna, but the desire of a growing number of affluent Hill residents to preserve the naturalistic allure of their surroundings and a degree of separation from the more intensive commercial and industrial development on the river bottoms probably discouraged them from investing in additional hotels that might replicate the Bon Air's success.

Augusta's winter resort attracted its share of northern capitalists and their families, but as the *Chronicle* regularly pointed out, building upon this foundation was a perennial challenge. Its mid-January to mid-April season was inherently limiting. Despite assurances that Augusta's climate was mild and equable, the season was subject to weather-induced interruptions and abrupt changes. When Arctic air descended over northern states, Augusta found itself inundated with more tourists than it could accommodate. But mild weather in the North sometimes delayed the southward movement. Additionally, the cold spells that periodically struck Augusta could send the Bon Air's guests packing for Florida earlier than planned. Likewise, Florida's building heat inevitably gave the city a return flow of guests late in the season, but an early onset of warm weather in Augusta or moderate temperatures in tourists' hometowns often threatened to cut the season short.[16]

Though subject to the vagaries of weather, the hotel's popularity increased, particularly after the introduction of golf. By 1903, this demand led Augusta railroad and marble-mining tycoon James U. Jackson to open the three-hundred-room Hampton Terrace Hotel on a high bluff in North Augusta, a suburb on the sandhills across the Savannah River in South Carolina.[17] Over the previous two years, Jackson had built an electric interurban railway that connected the Park in the Pines Hotel in the resort town of Aiken to North Augusta and, with his purchase of Dyer's street railway, from there to the Bon Air. Jackson's Aiken–Augusta Electric Railway enabled tourists to travel by train to Union Station and then reach their choice of sandhill resorts on the interurban.[18] Jackson's hotel, whose guests enjoyed the adjacent golf links and hunting on a fifteen-thousand-acre game preserve, more than doubled Augusta's capacity to host winter visitors, but demand continued to outstrip the availability of rooms, stimulating a series of expansions of the Bon Air and Hampton Terrace.[19]

Summerville's reputation—and therefore also Augusta's—as a winter haven solidified when the nation's richest man joined the president-elect in regular visits there. Standard Oil baron John D. Rockefeller had discovered the pleasure of golfing at the Bon Air almost two years before Taft's first visit.[20] Rockefeller's arrival in January 1909 for his third Augusta sojourn trailed Taft's by a month. As they rode west, up the Hill from Union Station, both men probably saw little evidence that their host city had suffered another devastating flood after thirteen inches of rain fell in a day's time a few months before. The Savannah had swollen to nearly thirty-nine feet at Augusta, unleashing a "red and raging flood" that rose as high as the windows of streetcars and formed "dangerous whirlpools at the street corners." One *Chronicle* writer had seized upon the disaster to claim that the "entente cordiale between the races—the white man and his black brother— was something typical of the South. No distinction was made in the efforts to save life and property." But in contrast to one "poor old negro preacher" whose cottage "the flood carried . . . literally into and down the river" and the loss of sixty drowning victims in the central city, Augusta's sandhills resort colony remained fully intact for Rockefeller and Taft to enjoy. As the writer had commented, "Fortunately, the two immense winter tourists' hotels, the Bon Air and Hampton Terrace, . . . were well above the freshet level."[21] The Hill was becoming part of Augusta in the local mind.

Nevertheless, the resort colony on the Hill remained unable to accommodate all who hoped to visit, a situation the *Augusta Chronicle* continued to bemoan. In 1909, the Bon Air's former chief clerk Morris W. Partridge bought the Meigs House across Walton Way and opened the greatly expanded structure as the Partridge Inn. Still, tourist demand continued to exceed the space.[22] The *Chronicle* began to liken the sandhills climate to a "mine," excoriating local businessmen for their indifference toward further hotel development. Referring to Los Angeles, which it called "one of the toughest cow towns in the Southwest" as recently as thirty years before, an editorial argued that unlike "desultory" Augustans who "staked out only a few surface veins," Angelenos "did not pursue the 'pick and pan' method of working Los Angeles' climate mine; they staked out everything in sight." The editorial insisted that if Augusta's climate was "good enough for the President of the United States" and "the richest man in the world," it was certainly "good enough for tens, and even hundreds, of thousands of people who are looking for a climate 'claim.'"[23]

Though the *Chronicle* lauded Partridge's entrepreneurship, publisher and editor Thomas W. Loyless wondered whether the continued underdevelopment of the "climate mine" of Augusta's fall-line hills was the product of a lack of enterprise, foresight, or capital.[24] A native of Dawson in rural southwestern Georgia, Loyless had moved to Augusta in 1902 and had watched Augusta's struggle to accommodate winter tourist demand for nearly a decade. Perhaps more importantly, the *Chronicle* had more than the typical interest of a newspaper because one of its major stockholders was (until 1911) Daniel B. Dyer, who owned large swaths of real estate on the Hill. Dyer had tried to make his properties more attractive by planning a circumferential automobile boulevard, but it had failed to attract local investors.[25] Dyer and Loyless served on a chamber committee tasked with finding investors to finance a new resort hotel. By December 1911, they were among the directors of a syndicate that planned to build Aumond, a residential, golf, and hotel development about one mile west of the new city limits that now encompassed the recently annexed Summerville.[26] Although the undertaking owed in part to Dyer's and Loyless's actions, the *Chronicle* portrayed it as "the direct outcome of a series of articles and editorials . . . in which we put squarely up to the people of Augusta the importance . . . of developing Augusta's 'climate mine.'" But the Aumond campaign fell far short of its goal, crushing plans for the new hotel, a failure blamed on yet another river flood that depressed the capitalization effort.[27]

The next few years underscored the fragility of Augusta's winter resort as a focus for realizing its boosters' metropolitan ambitions. When Taft's 1912 reelection bid failed, Augusta's image as the winter capital faded. The Hill, whose climate and topography had encouraged the illusion, benefited from Augusta's misfortune again three years after Taft's departure. Although repeated floods finally galvanized support for a levee along the Savannah River in 1916, that same year brought a devastating fire that displaced some three thousand Augustans. The fire began at Broad and Eighth Streets on March 22. Fanned by strong winds, the flames turned the night sky orange as they swept through more than two dozen blocks of downtown and the adjacent Pinch Gut neighborhood to its east. The inferno gutted the sixteen-story Empire Life Building, then under construction, and destroyed nearly seven hundred fifty buildings. Along Greene Street, once Augusta's showplace boulevard, the fire reduced stately mansions and ornamental gardens to rows of chimneys looming over scorched stumps.[28] The 1908 and 1912 floods and the 1916 fire hastened the flight of affluent whites to the Hill, which transformed Pinch Gut from a wealthy intown neighborhood into a rooming-house district.[29]

Elevation safeguarded the winter resorts from floods, but the choice to build the hotels from the abundant yellow pine harvested from the forests of eastern Georgia and western South Carolina subjected these buildings to a different threat that imperiled booster hopes. A New Year's Day fire in 1917 rendered the Hampton Terrace a smoldering ruin, while another conflagration consumed the seasoned pinewood of the Bon Air four years later.[30] Although the fires miraculously claimed no casualties, they left only the much smaller Partridge Inn to carry on the city's resort business. The diminished capacity came at a time when Augusta was struggling with the volatility posed by new, competing highways that upended decades of reliance on fixed railroad routes. Two years later, the city lost its biggest cheerleader for resort development when *Chronicle* editor Loyless sold the paper and moved to Columbus to invest in its morning newspaper, the *Enquirer-Sun.* Loyless also leased an old inn in the fading spa town of Bullochville north of Columbus and, with the help of a testimonial from a boy "cured" of polio after swimming in its spring-fed pool, helped Columbus-born New York banker George Foster Peabody entice Franklin D. Roosevelt and rebrand the village as Warm Springs.[31]

At a time when southern resort hotels were at their apogee, boosters hoped to reconstruct the Bon Air Hotel as soon as possible, especially because attempts to rebuild the Hampton Terrace had proven fruitless and Macon and Columbus boosters were pressing for tourist hotels in their respective cities.[32] Through the efforts of Sandford H. Cohen, known for his tourism promotion efforts in Asheville, a new Bon Air Hotel Corporation formed. Thomas Barrett Jr., son of a two-time Augusta mayor, became its president and, with assistance from the Committee of Fifty in the chamber of commerce, helped raise funds to rebuild Augusta's famed winter hotel. Called the Bon Air–Vanderbilt to reflect its management by the Vanderbilt

Hotels of New York, the eight-story, 308-room stucco hotel opened in January 1923.[33]

Although the Bon Air–Vanderbilt restored some of the resort's capacity, boosters discovered that the shift from passenger trains to private automobiles meant that the reputation of the sandhills alone could not keep Augusta on the tourist map. Like their tourism-minded counterparts in Asheville who championed the Blue Ridge Parkway, Augusta boosters were eager to secure their city's place in the emerging network of modern highways. Shortly after the turn of the century, Augusta had seemed well-positioned to attract auto tourists. Although the earliest automobiles were a novelty on Augusta streets, by 1908, garages and repair shops were becoming almost as common as livery stables.[34] Well-groomed sand-clay roads and vitrified brick streets were also not hard to find. Judge William F. Eve, who had overseen Richmond County's roadbuilding and road maintenance since 1879, gained the nickname "father of good roads in Georgia" by devising a model plan for improving county roads. After a lease on county convicts expired that year, Eve set them to work on chain gangs, working outward five miles from the central city on each highway until all were smooth, sloped, and oiled, then proceeding farther on each road until reaching the county line, and finally improving intersecting roads. Eve's convicts, like those in other Georgia Black Belt counties that took advantage of harsh policing of African Americans, literally smoothed the way for the Bon Air to claim that with roads "constantly being extended and improved[,] . . . many guests find it desirable to bring their machines." When he wasn't on the country club links, Rockefeller could sometimes be found motoring around the sandhills in his "big red Peerless."[35]

At a time when interest in "marked trails" was rising, Richmond County's reputation for good roads languished following Eve's retirement in 1909, which led to a precipitous reduction in the county's convict road force.[36] By 1915, with tourists complaining about the worsening condition of the county roads and early planning underway for a Dixie Highway to connect the

Midwest and South, the county recommitted its full convict force to its roads.[37] Augusta promoters understood the Dixie Highway's potential for their city. The city's Merchants and Manufacturers Association pointed to the expected windfall that Augusta would enjoy when midwesterners found their way over from the Dixie Highway in Atlanta.[38] Augustans were elated when Georgia Chamber of Commerce president Charles J. Haden suggested that the Dixie Highway's logical southern terminus was Augusta rather than Miami. Haden said the latter terminus would necessitate passing "through the very hardest part of the country." Augusta and Savannah boosters shared his interest in seeing the highway reach the Savannah Valley rather than bisecting southern Georgia. Of course, the claim belied the fact that the Wiregrass counties comprised the fastest-growing part of the state. The *Chronicle* characterized a more easterly route as being "skirted with massive trees" and affording "ever-changing scenery, a continuous panorama."[39]

After Dixie Highway Association (DHA) directors Clark Howell of Atlanta and W. T. Anderson of Macon agreed in 1916 to channel the highway from Chattanooga through Atlanta to Macon and divide it into three forks from there, Augusta would be only thirty miles from the highway's Old Capital Route at Waynesboro in neighboring Burke County, but Augusta boosters still hoped to steer more tourists through their city. Lying thirty miles north of just one of the three spurs of the Dixie Highway offered little to Augusta. Accordingly, the Augusta chamber formed a good roads committee in 1918 and succeeded in lobbying the DHA to establish the Carolina Division, which branched off at Knoxville and proceeded southward through Asheville, Greenville, and Augusta before linking with the Old Capital Route at Waynesboro.[40]

Just as the Bon Air had established Augusta as a railroad-age winter resort, city boosters hoped to preserve Augusta's advantages as an auto-age destination by promoting good roads and setting up a tourist information bureau. In 1919, former piano and phonograph merchant Charles F. Rossignol patented a visible gasoline dispenser for filling-station pumps and soon turned his Broad Street shop into an auto accessory store. Frustrated that tourism promoters along competing routes to Florida were distributing maps that omitted Augusta, Rossignol began driving the roads in Augusta's hinterland and noting their condition. Literally drawing from firsthand knowledge, he started placing his meticulous map of regional highway distances and condi-

FIG. 8. BOSTON AUTO TOURISTS IN DOWNTOWN AUGUSTA, CA. 1920. Augusta boosters made concerted efforts to court auto tourists in the 1920s. This photo on Broad Street shows motorists who participated in a Boston-to-Augusta auto excursion sponsored by the Automobile Legal Association. The hand-drawn regional highway conditions map, an innovation of automotive merchant and Augusta Motor Club secretary Charles F. Rossignol, appears at left. Courtesy of Augusta–Richmond County Public Library System/ Georgia Heritage Room, Augusta, GA.

tions, rendered in white chalk, on a large blackboard on the sidewalk in front of his store (see Fig. 8).[41] By 1920, Rossignol, whose display grew to four maps based on information gleaned from regional correspondents, had emerged as a guiding force in courting auto tourism for the city and a seeming antidote to being bypassed by the main trunk of the Dixie Highway.[42]

After the 1921 Bon Air fire, Rossignol worked tirelessly as secretary of the Augusta Motor Club to route as many tourists through the city as possible and, with the city's hotel accommodations much reduced, to encourage establishing an auto camp that might help capture tourist spending in Augusta.[43] He approached the city's leading hotel and garage operators with what he called "the biggest stunt in the way of advertising that was ever pulled off." With a raft of pledges in hand, Rossignol partnered with the *Augusta Chronicle* to produce forty thousand copies of his Official Highways Guide, in which he included detailed, hand-drawn maps with up-to-date guidance on regional road conditions.[44] The *Chronicle* continued to print Rossignol's biannual guides and provided an office adjoining its building lobby for him to dispense information to visitors. The chamber's good roads committee also worked with Rossignol to place Augusta mileage signs along every highway leading to Augusta from as far north as Virginia.[45] Rossignol's task was not without challenges. The Dixie Highway Carolina Division became progressively poorer to the south of Greenville. One stretch was so bad in rainy weather that McCormick County farmers drove forty miles north to trade in Greenwood rather than brave an unpredictable twenty miles to reach Augusta. These conditions led some Greenville filling stations to divert motorists from Augusta and steer them through Anderson, Hartwell, Athens, and Macon.[46] To counter the problem, Rossignol organized western South Carolina business leaders to help distribute Augusta's highway guidebooks. In Edgefield, Rossignol told local officials that advertising to the north would open the region to agricultural diversification, making cotton a "fancy crop" produced so sparingly that farmers would again be able to regulate its price.[47]

Rossignol's expertise made Augusta an indispensable hub for highway information during a period when southern highways presented unpredictable conditions. So did his unrelenting campaign to get the city to provide a first-rate auto camp.[48] After an abortive effort to create a tourist camp along the Savannah River on the edge of downtown, Rossignol secured a commitment from filling station operator Charles P. Boardman to provide the use of space behind his business at Wrightsville Road and Fifteenth Street.[49] Rossignol had high hopes for the camp, which attracted some five thousand visitors over its first five months, but became increasingly dissatisfied with the city's failure to support improvements. By spring 1922, after an extended period of rain, the low-lying camp turned into a bog, forcing tourists to resort to laying bricks from a pile at an adjacent abandoned construction site to avoid slogging through ankle-deep mud. The *Chronicle* quipped that the camp "might do very well on the back of a plantation," betraying its insensitivity to the fact that most Black Augustans living nearby in the Terry suffered similar hardships on their unpaved streets and alleys throughout the year, conditions that were familiar to African Americans in other southern cities. More concerning for the newspaper was the idea that rival Macon had a first-rate municipal camp in its Central City Park.[50] In September, the Committee of Fifty petitioned the city council to improve or relocate the tourist camp. After another month of inaction, the *Chronicle* expressed disbelief that it seemed easier to raise $1 million to build the new Bon Air–Vanderbilt than to get the city to spend three thousand dollars for a decent camp.[51] The city then considered using a corner of the municipally owned Allen Park on Walton Way, but this proposal raised the hackles of the Augusta Woman's Club, which pointed out that it might be "unsightly to tourists who wintered at Augusta hotels." Ignoring the opposition, the city finally provided a better facility.[52]

Even as he styled Augusta the "Highway Center of the Southeast" and pressed for a high-quality auto camp, Rossignol understood that lingering stretches of unimproved highways were not all that might undercut Augusta's transportation advantages. As paving progressed on the Central Route of the Dixie Highway through Macon and the new Coastal Highway, which promised a shorter path from Virginia to Florida via Charleston and Savannah, Augusta faced the challenge of being in a tax-averse state whose legislators refused to pass a statewide bond issue to ease the local burden of improving roads in small, rural counties. In contrast to Chatham County (Savannah), which used a one-to-one state-to-local match to pave its roads and those in neighboring rural counties, Richmond County failed to do so until it finally approved a countywide bond issue in 1925.[53] Augusta leaders did what they could to prepare for competition from the coming Coastal Highway. Their hopes rested on efforts to improve the remaining problematic stretches of highways in surrounding counties as well as on the completion of paving on U.S. 1. In April 1926, they paused to celebrate a milestone in this endeavor. Officials gathered near the Fifth Street Bridge that crossed the Savannah River to unveil the first marker on the eighteen-hundred-mile route between Fort Kent, Maine, and Miami.[54] Five months after the Coastal Highway opened in July 1928, the No. 1 Association formed under the leadership of Waycross and Augusta boosters to promote U.S. 1.[55]

In the early 1920s, while Macon was styling itself "The Heart of the Peach Belt," Augusta's self-proclaimed role as "Highway Center of the Southeast" had telegraphed the city's metropolitan ambitions throughout the region. By the time Rossignol died in 1928, the completion of long stretches of paved highways in the Southeast had already made road-condition mapping less critical.[56] The Coastal and Central Dixie Highways, by then renamed U.S. 17 and 41, had siphoned tourist traffic away from Augusta, leaving U.S. 25, the former Dixie Highway Carolina Division, as the only well-used corridor through the city. The decline had reduced local officials to worrying about the fact that U.S. 1 signage directed motorists to use Twiggs and Seventh Streets, which carried them through the Terry, directly past the brothel at 944 Twiggs Street where future "Godfather of Soul" James Brown would move several years later from Barnwell, South Carolina, to live with his aunt. One city councilman complained in 1929 that this route was extremely unattractive and gave no inkling of the beauty to be found elsewhere in the Garden City, primarily on the Hill, whereupon the Augusta chamber mulled requesting a redesignation of the route but took no action.[57]

This concern reflected a problem that Augusta never solved. The growing popularity of Florida's many resort communities along the Atlantic and Gulf coasts relegated Georgia's fall-line cities to the status of stopovers. Improved mosquito control, a clear public preference for more reliable winter warmth, and frenetic development and advertising diminished the attractiveness of the sandhills, leaving Augusta promoters hard-pressed to tap the flow of motorists on their way to or from Florida.[58] They did what all promoters do—assess their product and advertise it. Though long a noted asset, golf was poised to remake Augusta's identity.

THE GOLF CAPITAL OF AMERICA

Before going on to become the first golfer to win the "Grand Slam" by sweeping all four major championships of the time over the next several months, Atlanta's Robert Tyre (Bobby) Jones Jr. played in the Southeastern Open Golf Tournament in Augusta on March 30 and April 1, 1930. Although he refused to become a professional golfer, Jones had built an international reputation over the past several years by regularly beating the best pros in open tournaments. After playing the first two rounds of the Southeastern Open at the Augusta Country Club, the tournament players finished on the course at the Forrest Hills–Ricker Hotel, which had opened just outside the city limits on the sandhills in 1927, giving Augusta a second large resort hotel for the first time since the Hampton Terrace fire.[59]

On the strength of the Forrest Hills–Ricker and the Bon Air–Vanderbilt, boosters ramped up promotion of Augusta as a winter resort. Inspired by the Forward Atlanta program, the chamber launched its Greater Augusta Ad-

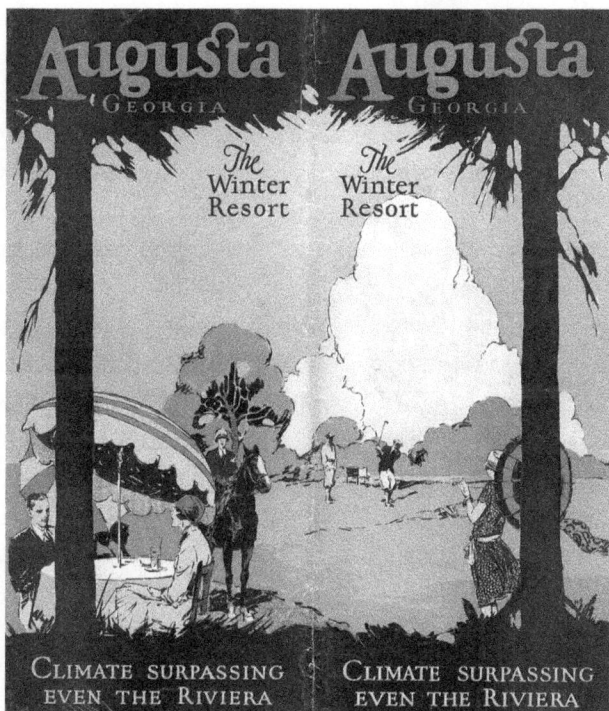

FIG. 9. AUGUSTA TOURISM BROCHURE, 1927. The opening of the Forrest Hills Hotel in 1927 rekindled determination to reclaim tourism business lost to Florida. This brochure extolled the city's excellent golf courses and a climate purported to be better than the Riviera. Courtesy of Reese Library Special Collections, Augusta University, Augusta, GA.

vertising Campaign in 1927 and spent more than $17,000 (nearly $300,000 in today's money) over the ensuing year to market the city nationally.[60] The campaign's "Augusta, Georgia, the Winter Resort" booklet cover featured a colorful golf course scene framed by silhouetted palmettos and the subtitle "Climate Surpassing Even the Riviera" (see Fig. 9). Ignoring Florida's undeniable popularity, the booklet touted weather statistics that showed that Augusta enjoyed more sunny days than Nice, France, and Naples, Italy. It also emphasized golf and other outdoor sports and recreation offerings and printed testimonials from prominent New York, Chicago, and Pittsburgh businessmen. In 1928, the campaign requested a chamber appropriation of $50,000 annually to promote Augusta even more widely.[61]

After the onset of the Great Depression, however, the chamber found that it was unable to support this commitment. The spectacle of Georgia's golfing star winning the Southeastern Open offered welcome, free publicity, but the event's mark on the city soon faded. Nevertheless, a June 1930 *Chronicle* editorial pointed out, "We have a friend in Bobby Jones, who will always be glad to come to Augusta, and where Bobby Jones is in the next ten years, there will be the golfing capital of the universe." But Jones's announcement that he would retire from competitive golf after winning the Grand Slam dampened the promise of the Southeastern Open as an annual event. Although Augusta would hold the tournament once more in 1931, hopes of realizing the *Chronicle*'s stated ambition of "making this city the golfing capital of the world each spring" seemed no more durable than an earlier claim as the "Winter Capital of America" had been after President Taft left the White House in 1913.[62]

Atlanta Journal sportswriter O. B. Keeler had made periodic visits to Augusta in the 1920s to cover horse shows and tennis tournaments, and on some of these trips, Jones accompanied him and played on the city's golf courses. One of Jones's dreams for his retirement was to build the ideal golf course by borrowing features from the world's greatest courses. Jones befriended cottonseed oil executive and Augusta Country Club president Fielding H. Wallace, Bon Air–Vanderbilt Vice President Thomas Barrett Jr., and prominent local amateur golfer Alfred S. Bourne, all of whom understood what Jones's vision might mean for Augusta, but it was Jones's friend Clifford Roberts who convinced him to look around Augusta for his dream course. When Barrett showed him the former Fruitland Nurseries tract, Jones was convinced he had found the ideal site.[63] Located on Rae's Creek just west of the country club, the one-time indigo plantation had belonged to Dennis Redmond since 1853. An early promoter of crop diversification, Redmond started a nursery business and experimented with growing fruit crops. He named his property Fruitlands and built a large concrete home in the style of a West Indies plantation manor. Three years later, Dr. Louis E. Berckmans and his son Prosper J. A. Berckmans, both horticulturists from Belgium, bought Redmond's property and gradually expanded Fruitland Nurseries into the South's largest such operation. It became known for the dissemination of azaleas, camellias, Amur privet hedges, arborvitae, and wisteria across the Lower South, as well as for early innovations in peach cultivation. After the Berckmans family sold the Fruitland trade name to another nurs-

FIG. 10. AUGUSTA NATIONAL GOLF CLUB, 1935. In the depths of the Great Depression, Augusta leaders took heart when champion golfer Bobby Jones made the development of the Augusta National Golf Club his retirement project. The club, which occupied a one-time indigo plantation turned plant nursery and fruit orchard, became home to the Masters Tournament and compensated for the fading of Augusta's reputation as a winter resort amid Florida's growth. The Fruitlands Nursery office still stood (at right) at the time of this photo. Joseph M. Lee III Collection, Courtesy of Augusta Museum of History, Augusta, GA.

eryman in 1918 and the land itself seven years later for what became another failed effort to build a new tourist hotel, the property languished until Jones selected it for his golf course.[64]

Jones, Roberts, and other associates acquired the old Berckmans tract in 1931. They retained the famed Scottish golf course designer Alister Mackenzie to work with Jones to develop the course. In a reflection of their high hopes for what the project might mean for Augusta, Jones's friends christened it the Augusta National Golf Club. Jones and Mackenzie modeled each hole on some of Jones's favorite holes at other courses. They selected a different flowering plant as the namesake for each hole and included prominent plantings of these in their landscaping, with Prosper J. A. Berckmans Jr. and Louis Berckmans advising on which shrubs merited salvaging from the property's days as a nursery.[65] At a time when capital was scarce for launching major ventures such as golf courses, the club proved unable to build a new clubhouse. Thus, Fruitlands became the permanent clubhouse, and the view of its white columns framed by an alley of magnolias became one of the most iconic images associated with both the sport and Augusta (see Fig. 10).[66]

Several months after Augusta National opened in 1933, its officers determined that it should host a major tournament to revive the unrealized vision behind the Southeastern Open. In a shrewd marketing ploy that demonstrated their awareness of the challenges they faced, they coaxed Jones to postpone his retirement to compete in the tournament. Club secretary Fielding Wallace then appeared before the city council to ask it to appropriate $10,000 to underwrite the Augusta National Invitation Tournament, promising that it would bring twenty thousand visitors who would spend at least $1 million in the city to see thirty of the world's greatest golfers. One councilman saw the idea as an unfair subsidy to the wealthy and unwarranted because the golf course was located outside the city limits while another called it "foolish" given the state of the city's finances. Nevertheless, the city council approved the appropriation. The *Chronicle* applauded the decision as a powerful response to the fortunes lavished on golf at Pinehurst, North Carolina, and Miami and Palm Beach, Florida, and called the winter resort and the Savannah River "the two greatest opportunities for this city to progress and develop into the metropolis of the Southeast."[67]

Staging the Augusta National Invitation Tournament, colloquially known as "the Masters" from its inception in 1934 and officially renamed five years later, prompted more than merely advertising the event and wiring the course to support the planned national radio broadcasting by CBS. The expected twenty thousand visitors far outstripped the limited number of hotel rooms in Augusta. In addition to about 850 rooms in three tourist hotels on the Hill, the city had one 300-room commercial hotel, five small hotels, and six boardinghouses. The shortfall led to the formation of a housing bureau headed by Augusta real-estate broker Camilla von Camp to identify rooms in private homes. The Sand Hills Garden Club also aligned its annual garden tour with the Masters, with proceeds supporting the club's effort to renovate the old Medical College of Georgia building as its Garden Center.[68]

While no precise statistics supported its organizers' predictions, the inaugural Masters filled Augusta's hotels and boardinghouses, gave many Augustans a taste of what would be called the "gig economy" much later, and led hotelier Morris Partridge to remark on the "large number of fine new automobiles we see on the streets." The void that followed it underscored the enduring problem associated with Augusta's tourism sector: It did not sustain year-round profits and employment.[69] *Chronicle* sports columnist Tom Wall reflected on this problem. He wrote that "the town by the yellow Savannah took on the aspect of a winter resort equal to any in the south," but he wondered what attractions Augusta offered during the rest of the winter season. "Augusta has climate and Augusta has golf," Wall concluded, but these were no longer sufficient to support the local tourist trade.[70]

Augusta's "golf capital" hopes persisted, but the future of Jones's great experiment remained uncertain. New club memberships lagged, depriving the event of much-needed income. The city's appropriation for the Masters declined sharply after 1934, and an inexplicable objection by the Forrest Hills Hotel manager to the continued municipal subsidy provoked a standoff in 1937 in which the chamber refused to accept any appropriation that did not provide for the Masters. And, in the tournament's first six years, Augusta's heralded climate seemed illusive as rainy weather forced delays and even cancellations of whole days. By 1939, a newly formed Business Men's Masters Tournament Association undertook a campaign to try to bring more local spectators to the struggling tournament.[71]

Worse, despite predictions that the outbreak of war in Europe would stimulate domestic tourism, the U.S.'s entry into the conflict did the opposite.[72] The management at the Forrest Hills Hotel worried that the droning of military planes at nearby Daniel Field might drive away its golfers.[73] The Bon Air, which the Vanderbilt hotel interest sold in 1941 to a Spartanburg, South Carolina–based life insurance company, converted from a winter resort to a year-round "popular-priced" hotel marketed as a place for military families to stay. As wartime restrictions reduced tourism, this owner unloaded the Bon Air two years later to the Auto Finance Company of Augusta, and after two more years, it sold out to the Sheraton Corporation.[74] In October 1942, Clifford Roberts announced that the Masters would be paused for the duration of the war, citing transportation challenges, the enlistment of many members and players in the armed forces, and the anticipation that the military might take over the city's resort hotels. Soon afterward, the U.S. Army acquired the Forrest Hills Hotel and converted it for military use as Oliver General Hospital. Augusta National decided to turn the fairways over to pasture a herd of feeder calves once it was assured that the cattle would not disturb the horticultural splendor along the links.[75] As with Macon's Ocmulgee Mounds, Augusta's Masters Tournament might promise civic transformation, but this would have to wait.

The Augusta National and the Masters Tournament fit seamlessly into the profile that Augusta boosters had crafted for their city for decades. The relatively mild, dry winter climate of the sandhills had supported booster ambitions to make Augusta a "winter capital" for the nation's most influential and illustrious people to escape the harsh weather of the North, and the well-drained soil of the sandhills lent ideal conditions for a "golf capital." Likewise, both features of the sandhills had encouraged affluent white Augustans to cultivate the "Garden City of the South" on the Hill. Beyond the reasonably well-maintained downtown, the rest of the city on the river plain became careworn in the two decades after the great fire of 1916. In contrast to the enveloping parklike setting of the Hill, the city maintained only fifty acres of bona-fide parks, one-fifth of what the National Playground and Recreational Association prescribed for a city of Augusta's population. And, as a 1924 civic study commented, these parks were ostensibly open to the public yet excluded the approximately 45 percent of citizens who were African American. For Black Augustans, apart from those who worked as caddies for white golfers at the country club, there was only Brownstone Park, a privately owned plot outside the city limits.[76]

As in Macon, the sudden availability of WPA funds brought long-overdue attention to the city's once exemplary intown parkways whose lack of cultivation now contrasted starkly with the manicured grounds of Augusta National, Augusta Country Club, Forrest Hills, and estate gardens on the Hill. Using federal subsidies, the city formed an Augusta Beautification Commission in 1936 and engaged Hubert B. Owens of Athens to develop a Savannah-inspired beautification plan. Unsurprisingly, the plan failed to extend southward into the Terry, where most Black Augustans resided. Only after Black real estate broker S. L. McCoy questioned the Terry's omission in 1938 did the city agree to include Gwinnett Street, but even then it merely appointed a chairman, R. A. Dent (a Burke County native and co-owner with his brother of furniture and flooring stores in the Terry), to organize Black property owners and tenants. WPA support finally brought the paving of Gwinnett Street. Long after most primary streets in the white sections of Augusta were paved, however, some 85 percent of the Terry's streets remained unpaved and thus alternatively dusty and muddy, a condition that would have been all too familiar to African Americans in most other southern cities.[77]

When WPA writers prepared the Augusta volume in the *American Guide Series* that same year, they described the Terry's unpaved streets and alleys, lined with alternating rows of "shabby wooden houses" without electricity and "bungalows of more solid construction." The Augusta guide provides impressionistic glimpses of the mostly unseen lives of the Black Augustans who toiled in the Terry's brickyards, fertilizer plants, and lumber mills or cooked dinners, washed laundry, or sang spirituals for patrons in tourist hotels on the Hill. Below the sandhills, away from the golf courses and estate gardens that inspired Augusta's official nickname, Black Augustans cultivated nature to the extent their crowded dwellings permitted. As the Augusta guide observed, even the meanest shacks "have tiny porches filled with verbena, ferns, and geraniums. Lard cans painted in bright colors hold green plants and palms. Morning glories, white clouds of clematis, and all kinds of green climbing things cover the unpainted clapboards, while roses and gardenias bloom luxuriantly though untended."[78]

Augusta boosters, in their effort to fashion the "Golf Capital of America," perpetuated the city's uneven development and reinforced the social and cultural chasm marked by its fall-line hills. They also proved incapable of using even the golfing equivalent of the Kentucky Derby to provide more than a veneer of the metropolitan stature they wanted. Away from the Hill's posh hotels and golf courses, the city saw few tangible benefits. Boosters had hoped to induce industrial firms to build new plants in and around the city during the interwar years, but most of their efforts had relied on attracting influential executives to visit in the winter months with the idea that they might find Augusta an attractive place to invest. In 1931, citing a claim that Los Angeles had become an industrial city by promoting tourism, the chamber ran a full-page *Chronicle* ad that requested support for a $25,000 annual campaign to advertise Augusta to tourists.[79] It made no mention that its allocation of four times as much advertising to tourism as to industry just four years earlier had coincided with a clear decline in industry. Indeed, as boosters promoted golf and a resort lifestyle, Augusta stagnated. In contrast to the 1880s, when Augusta had enjoyed a 274-percent rise in manufacturing employment, the 1919–29 period saw a 1-percent decline, and the next decade brought a further drop of 13 percent.[80]

Just as Macon boosters expected more from their central location in Georgia than it could deliver, Augustans' metropolitan ambitions relied too much on the supposed natural advantage of the sandhills climate. With Augusta's greater distance from Atlanta and proximity to a much larger river than Macon's Ocmulgee, the city's leaders dreamed that one day a Savannah River lined with factories and plied by oceangoing cargo ships might make Augusta a major inland port and metropolitan area. At the same time and much like Macon, Augusta had shepherded an economy based on serving as a market and supplier to King Cotton. Both cities fostered economic diversification, but their efforts were constrained by their histories of reliance on agriculture and industries that simply processed agricultural products.

Both cities shared a similar climate and topography thanks to their fall-line location, but Augusta, with its location midway between New York and Florida along the Southern and Atlantic Coast Line railroads, had been better positioned for resort development. Lacking such a connection, Macon leaders had tried to use their location to become a seat of state government and a clearinghouse for diversified agriculture. Once the Dixie Highway's main trunk was paved and could funnel traffic from the Midwest through Atlanta to Florida, Macon began a belated bid to become a regional tourist destination while Augusta clung to its entrenched reputation as a winter capital and attempted to update that to center on golf. For Augusta, the influence of tourism accentuated the division between favored suburbs in the sandhills and increasingly impoverished urban areas on the plain below. The hardship of the Depression years (and in Augusta's case, the misfortune of environmental challenges) left both cities' metropolitan ambitions and many of their people with an uncertain future.

THREE

⌐∞⌐

METROPOLIS OF THE
CHATTAHOOCHEE VALLEY

⌐∞⌐

In 1950, Boston newspaperman Amory Coolidge was riding a southbound train to Columbus, Georgia, to cover the city's impressive growth when he struck up a conversation with Edward Hamilton, a Columbus manufacturing tycoon. The next day, Hamilton took Coolidge on a tour of the city. He explained that Columbus was the South's greatest textile center and that dams north of the city furnished hydroelectric power to run its mills and regulate water levels downriver to Apalachicola, Florida, "which is our port on the Gulf of Mexico." He turned next to the central city, pointing out the "great Football Bowl at Golden Park" as one of a spate of civic endeavors, along with being Georgia's first city to adopt the commission-manager form of government and city-county consolidation. Upon concluding his tour, Hamilton told Coolidge to be sure to visit Fort Benning, home of "the greatest outdoor war school in the world," which had made Columbus "not only metropolitan but cosmopolitan." To underscore the giant military post's influence, Hamilton concluded, "Columbus is Fort Benning and Fort Benning is Columbus."[1]

Hamilton and Coolidge were characters in a fictional story narrated by Columbus clubwoman Rosa C. Gordon at a meeting of the Woman's Reading Club in 1922 and published by the *Columbus Enquirer-Sun* under the title "Utopia in Columbus, or, Looking Forward 30 Years." Yet, Gordon's vision, loosely modeled on Edward Bellamy's *Looking Backward, 2000–1887*, revealed much about the city of her own time despite her attempt to imagine its future. She was the wife of Frederick B. Gordon, who may have been her inspiration for Hamilton. He had organized the Columbus Manufacturing Company in 1899 to operate a cotton mill that was the city's first to use surplus hydroelectric power from the first dam on the Chattahoochee.[2] The Gordons knew well the metropolitan ambitions of Columbus boosters in their day—maintaining the city's hold as a major textile center while promoting efforts to realize the river's hydroelectric and navigation potential, develop Columbus into a regional sports capital, and exploit Fort Benning to bring economic growth.

Just as boosters attempted to build a metropolitan future around Macon's central location in Georgia and Augusta's sandhills topography and subtropical climate, their counterparts to the southwest sought to harness fall-line assets to transform Columbus from a river-hugging cotton-mill town into an expansive metropolitan area that could overcome the division and marginalization that the state border posed for it, the surrounding western Georgia area, and eastern Alabama communities. Although the textile industry would remain a pillar of the city's economy and identity, boosters tried to recast Columbus as the metropolitan hub of the Chattahoochee Valley. Through their efforts, it emerged as a center for promoting river development. While the electrification aspect of their vision faced mostly into Georgia, the dream of becoming an inland port cemented bonds across the Georgia–Alabama border and even southward to the Florida Panhandle. Furthering these efforts to forge stronger bonds with Columbus's trade territory, civic leaders also tried to use a neutral position on the river border of two states to make Columbus a host city for regional sports events. Additionally, they worked to secure, preserve, and support Fort Benning, one of the nation's foremost military reservations, and they and Benning officials worked cooperatively to forge a multicentered Chattahoochee Valley metropolis that might blur the lines between Alabama and Georgia and between city and post.

Columbus's 1928 centennial celebration marked a pivotal time in the city's metropolitan development. In the preceding years, Columbus had annexed new suburban residential allotments with fanciful names like Dinglewood, Peacock Woods, and Wildwood Park in the fall-line hills to its east, and Columbus had built a viaduct and two underpasses across the longtime barrier posed by the sprawling railyard on downtown's eastern flank. The city had

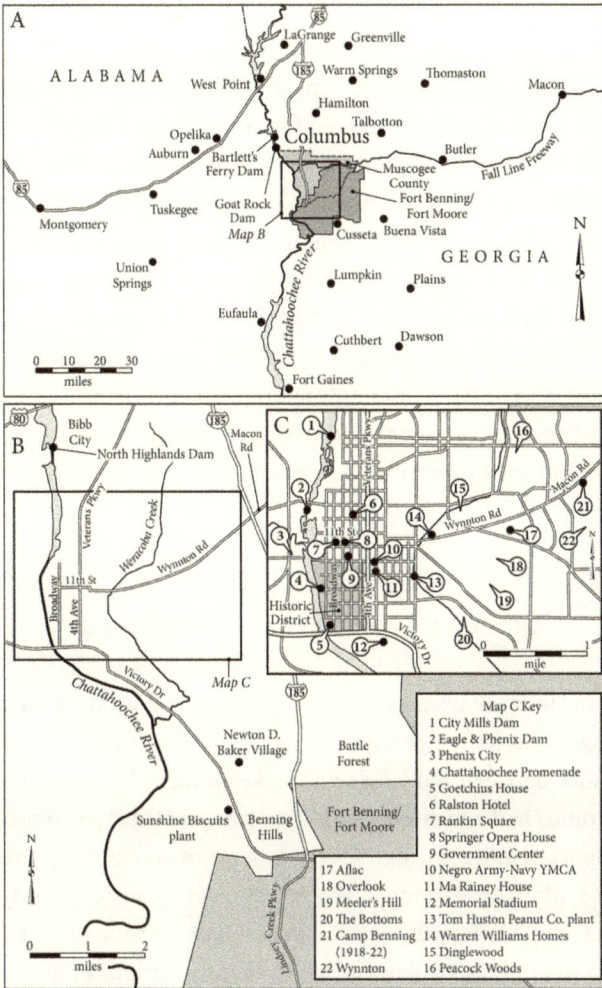

COLUMBUS AND THE CHATTAHOOCHEE VALLEY.

also hired eminent Cambridge, Massachusetts planner John Nolen to draw a blueprint for future development whose national stature aligned with Columbus boosters' lofty metropolitan ambitions and perhaps the desire to see the city rise to parity with the much larger Montgomery, Macon, and Augusta. In addition, the centennial capped a decade of breathless promotion of the seemingly limitless potential of Chattahoochee River hydropower and navigation, the state line as an asset to Columbus's ambition to become a regional sports center, and the U.S. War Department's investment at Fort Benning.

As in Augusta and Macon, the onset of the Great Depression less than two years later proved a trying period for Columbus, testing the resilience of its dominant textile industry. Columbus leaders also faced challenges having less to do with the national economy than with a problem that all three fall-line cities would increasingly endure in the future: the diminishing ability of local leaders to guide their city's paths due to decisions made in other places. These challenges constrained boosters' efforts to use Columbus's location on a river and state border to benefit from electric distribution, port development, and hosting interstate sporting events. However, much more than agricultural extension and tourism in Macon and Augusta, military development offered Columbus a stronger pillar for a metropolitan Chattahoochee Valley.

THE PLACE WITH THE POWER AND THE PUSH

In thirty-four miles between West Point and Columbus, the Chattahoochee River plunges 362 feet, a greater fall than the Niagara River makes in the same distance between Lake Erie and Lake Ontario.[3] Since its founding in 1828, Columbus had a history of yielding control of the river to private interests to support manufacturing.[4] By the late 1880s, as electric power became essential for urban development, the excess power generated by dynamos in three of the city's textile mills proved inadequate because of seasonal variations in the river's flow. Seeking relief, G. Gunby Jordan, a native of Sparta, Georgia, who had married into a prominent Columbus family and risen into the ranks of the city's textile-dominated business establishment, worked with the Macon-based textile firm Bibb Manufacturing Company to form the Columbus Power Company. The new firm purchased water rights along both sides of the Chattahoochee River at Lover's Leap, two miles upriver from the city, where it completed North Highlands Dam in 1901. This was the dam that powered Gordon's cotton mill.[5]

Unfortunately, however, the river's relentless fluctuations impeded the dam's usefulness to the city. Over the next two years, the Boston engineering firm of Stone and Webster, working through Savannah-based representative

George Johnson Baldwin, worked clandestinely with Columbus real estate tycoon John F. Flournoy to acquire water rights along a fifteen-mile stretch of the river above North Highlands Dam. They consolidated Stone and Webster's holdings in local railroads and electric, gaslight, and streetcar service into the Columbus Electric Company, which in turn absorbed Columbus Power and assumed its name in 1906. Baldwin also thwarted Mayor Lucius H. Chappell's effort to form a municipal power company. As a result, Columbus was beholden to local textile operators and Boston capitalists who monopolized the river but failed to unlock its full hydroelectric potential.[6]

Among the Columbus business leaders who chafed at Stone and Webster's control was engineer B. H. Hardaway, whose construction company had a long history of building bridges, dams, and other infrastructure in the city. Hardaway maneuvered quietly to assemble local investors to buy riverfront property sixteen miles upriver in Harris County at a point known as Goat Rock, where granite outcrops studded the Chattahoochee as it coursed through a narrow, pine-forested gorge. Using their holdings as leverage, Hardaway and his syndicate cut a deal for Columbus Power and Stone and Webster to cooperate in building a dam large enough to serve a growing city and provide a current to power regional development (see Fig. 11).[7]

On December 19, 1912, about 1,200 officials and business leaders from throughout the Chattahoochee Valley gathered to dedicate the new Goat Rock Dam that spanned the river, "joining the two states in concrete." At the ceremony, Mayor Chappell "baptized" a goat with a flask of muddy river water before flipping the switch that activated the powerplant. Goat Rock was the Columbus area's sixth dam, but it was the first to serve a wider vision of using electric transmission to expand the Electric City's influence over its trade territory. Though the mayors of Hamilton in Harris County, Georgia, and Opelika in Lee County, Alabama, ceremonially shook hands across the state line while standing atop the dam, the promise of Goat Rock strongly favored the Georgia side of Columbus's trade territory. In Alabama, the plant served mainly the neighboring river towns of Girard and Phenix City.[8]

In contrast, through its construction of high-voltage transmission lines, Columbus Power directed the current generated by falling waters at Goat Rock not only toward Columbus but also northward to support cotton-mill development in Georgia Piedmont towns along a line from West Point to Newnan, the latter of which was nearly twice as far from Columbus as it was

FIG. 11. COLUMBUS PROMOTIONAL BOOKLET, 1906. This illustration touts Columbus as "The Electric City of the South," reflecting boosters' ambitions to use the Chattahoochee River's precipitous drop at the fall line to make Columbus a regional force in hydroelectric power generation and distribution. The angelic figure in this design shines a spotlight on Columbus as an industrial city. At the time, the city ranked second in Georgia behind Atlanta as a manufacturing center. Courtesy of Columbus State University Archives, Columbus, GA.

from Atlanta.[9] Emboldened by the completion of Goat Rock Dam, in 1913, the Columbus Board of Trade coined a new slogan for the city: "The Place with the Power and the Push." Under the direction of cane syrup manufacturer J. Ralston Cargill, one of the city's staunchest boosters, the organization published a promotional booklet the following year that used the new slogan in its title. In addition to emphasizing that Columbus was the southernmost point of hydroelectric production and northernmost inland port with the shortest water route to the Panama Canal, the booklet touted Goat Rock as one more step toward an eventual "staircase of dams" whose power would drive the city's growth.[10] After the consolidation of the Columbus Power, Columbus Railroad, and Columbus Gas Light Companies in 1922, the resulting Columbus Electric & Power Company (CE&P) set out to build the next step up the "staircase." Four years later, its completion of an even larger power-plant at Bartlett's Ferry Dam, located twenty miles north of Columbus and four miles beyond Goat Rock Dam, augmented the latter's ability to supply power to industry in western Georgia. The dam also laid the groundwork for expanding Columbus's influence south and east into the Wiregrass region.[11]

A few months later, CE&P organized a subsidiary, South Georgia Power Company, to acquire hydroelectric and steam plants previously operated independently in several cities and towns in southwestern Georgia. Using a sixty-mile, 110,000-volt transmission line from Columbus to Americus and a network of smaller lines from there, CE&P and its subsidiary planned to redirect excess power from Bartlett's Ferry to augment existing production. CE&P triumphantly proclaimed that it had acquired "some 10,000 square miles of territory," and while electric power was only one tie binding this vast area to Columbus, it was an economically and symbolically important one.[12] After two years of building new power lines to stitch together its electrical network, CE&P used the occasion of the Columbus centennial in April 1928 to publicize its 608-mile web of lines across nearly forty counties in the context of Columbus's metropolitan ambitions. Blurring the line between news and advertising, a combined *Columbus Ledger* and *Enquirer-Sun* centennial section featured several pages on CE&P's endeavors in what the company named "Southwest Georgia." Though Columbus lay on the western fringe of Southwest Georgia, a map depicting power lines strongly suggested the Electric City's central importance to a region shaped roughly like a right triangle with points at Newnan to the north, Blakely to the south, and Douglas to the southeast (see Fig. 12). Importantly, Southwest Georgia overlapped the southern part of Atlanta's trade territory and cut deeply into the areas that otherwise looked to Macon and Albany. Through electrical service, the boosterish feature claimed, "[t]he smallest place in this territory has been taken out of the country town class . . . and has been put on a metropolitan footing."[13]

FIG. 12. SOUTHWEST GEORGIA ELECTRIC POWER ADVERTISEMENT, 1928. Columbus Electric & Power Company formed a subsidiary called the South Georgia Power Company in 1928, hoping to bring additional growth to Columbus by combining Chattahoochee River and Flint River hydropower with steam plant–generated electricity to support regional industrial and agricultural development. Courtesy of Hargrett Rare Book & Manuscript Library, University of Georgia, Athens, GA.

CE&P and its subsidiary announced a publicity campaign in August 1928 to encourage agricultural development in Southwest Georgia as a precondition for industrialization, promising, "Factories FOLLOW the Plow." Working with specialists from the Georgia State College of Agriculture in Athens and rural county extension agents, the power company pursued much the same goal as the Macon Chamber of Commerce had earlier in the decade. Citing the region's progress over the preceding two decades in moving away from cotton dependency through the cultivation of pecans, peaches, peanuts, and truck vegetables; raising of livestock; and processing of cane syrup and dairy products; CE&P pledged to turn Southwest Georgia into "an independent industrial section" through what it called an agricultural "college course." This "course" was really a plan for at least forty weekly installments of expert advice on farming methods published as ads in the *Columbus Ledger*. The campaign got underway in January 1929 but ended abruptly in May, only halfway through its intended run.[14]

The bid to promote agricultural development to industrialize Southwest Georgia failed to anticipate what happened just months later. In the summer of 1929, the New York–based Commonwealth & Southern Corporation, a utility holding company that had recently consolidated control over an Atlanta-based holding company that had acquired Georgia Power in 1926, took over the Columbus Electric & Power Company while allowing its name to persist. Although Columbus leaders delighted in the fact that Gunby Jordan was named chairman of the Columbus subsidiary's board and expressed hope that the city would retain a degree of autonomy to use electricity to bind Southwest Georgia to the Electric City, Columbus was, once more, swept into the orbit of outside capital. Georgia Power president Preston S. Arkwright was named president of the Columbus subsidiary, and Columbus leaders now comprised only one-third of officers, sharing control with Atlanta and New York men.[15]

By 1930, just two years after the bullish visions that accompanied the centennial, the idea that a staircase of dams would enable Columbus to steer its economic destiny was on the rocks. Under Commonwealth & Southern control, Georgia Power continued to promote agricultural and industrial development around Columbus but only insofar as Columbus was part of Georgia. In contrast to the Southwest Georgia agricultural education campaign, Georgia Power initiated a contest with prizes for the best farm demonstrations. In place of Columbus's focus on all counties in southwestern Georgia, it limited eligibility to a handful of selected counties scattered statewide. Ads for the Georgia Power Company Profitable Farming Award carried the company's telling new slogan (coined by Arkwright), "A Citizen Wherever We Serve." Like Augusta and Macon, Columbus was one of several division offices for an Atlanta utility that itself answered to New York.[16] Columbus might benefit, but no more or less than other Georgia cities. City leaders would need another way to assert a competitive advantage.

The loss of control over using electricity to serve Columbus's metropolitan ambitions was only part of the problem for local boosters. Implicit in the city's claim to be "The Place with the Power and the Push" was that damming the Chattahoochee River not only generated power but also, through controlled releases from these dams, literally pushed water downriver to maintain the depths necessary for navigation between Columbus and the Gulf of Mexico. Georgia Power had shared CE&P's philosophy of favoring hydroelectric over other forms of electric generation until a severe drought struck Georgia in 1925. By the next year, river levels had fallen so low that navigation ceased on the Chattahoochee and power plants' ability to produce electricity was limited. Arkwright vowed to lessen Georgia Power's dependence on rainfall by investing in more coal-fired steam plants.[17]

Between the mid-1920s drought and their loss of local control over the "staircase" upriver, business leaders formed another organization that would attempt to place Columbus at the center of a Chattahoochee Valley where river navigation stimulated metropolitan development. But this hope required appealing to the federal government, which alone had the capacity to reengineer the river down to the Gulf. The navigation campaign grew out of the passage of a congressional bill introduced by Senator William J. Harris from Cedartown in western Georgia on behalf of the Columbus Chamber of Commerce in 1924 to authorize a survey to determine the feasibility of extending the Intracoastal Waterway east from New Orleans to Apalachicola and developing a system of locks and dams to provide a year-round barge channel upriver to Columbus. In August 1928, just two weeks before CE&P's announcement of its Southwest Georgia agricultural campaign, J. Ralston Cargill, by then the secretary of the Columbus chamber, assembled businessmen at the Ralston Hotel (named for Cargill in recognition of his leading role in expanding Columbus's hotel accommodations), where they agreed to form the Chattahoochee Valley & Gulf Association (CVGA) to unify the existing lobbying efforts by individual chambers of commerce.[18]

With Cargill at the helm, the CVGA continued to press the federal government to authorize the waterways project. Although the Intracoastal Waterway extension won approval, Chattahoochee River improvements remained elusive into the 1930s. To exercise a stronger collective voice, representatives from thirty counties on both sides of the Chattahoochee convened in March 1935 at James W. (Jim) Woodruff Sr.'s country estate on Lake Cora in Harris County, where they agreed to form the Chattahoochee Valley Chamber of Commerce (CVCC), which would be based in Columbus. As constituted, the CVCC ultimately represented seventeen counties in western Georgia and eight in eastern Alabama. Upon its creation, Woodruff assumed the mantle of river development from Cargill while also fostering industrial and tourism development and securing greater state support for highway improvements to reduce the isolation of the Chattahoochee Valley.[19]

With Woodruff personally bankrolling new river surveys and lobbying trips to make its case, the CVCC secured congressional support for canalization of the Chattahoochee and Flint Rivers in 1939, but World War II intervened, stalling progress. Only in 1946 would Congress finally authorize the development of downriver locks and dams to support barge navigation up to Columbus, and the project would not reach fruition until eighteen years thereafter. The endeavor took so long that Jim Woodruff Jr. was shepherding the work by its completion, but Jim Woodruff Sr.'s unflagging effort led him to be called "The Father of the Chattahoochee" and to be the namesake for the lock and dam that created Lake Seminole on the Apalachicola River, the gateway to a system of locks and dams on the Chattahoochee and the linchpin of Columbus's port dreams.[20]

THE ATHLETIC CENTER OF THE SOUTHLAND

Reliable navigation remained perennially beyond Columbus leaders' reach in the interwar period. Yet, in forging relationships throughout the watershed, Cargill and Woodruff had reinforced Columbus as the metropolis of the Chattahoochee Valley, a conception that mirrored Macon leaders' efforts in Middle Georgia. Both men also championed other metropolitan ambitions for this trade territory. One of these sprang from the notion that Columbus's location along the Georgia–Alabama border provided a neutral ground for interstate football rivalries. This idea meshed well with Cargill's active encouragement of Columbus's tourist trade. With effort, Columbus might turn the disadvantage of a peripheral location in Georgia into an economic asset. The idea was hardly unique; other southern cities also hosted collegiate games because they provided more attendance and hence more revenue than college towns could muster in a time before campuses had large sports stadiums.[21]

The same river that had been called a southern Niagara now promised another economic boon. Rather than mills along its downtown riverfront or dams upriver, however, this new pillar of Columbus's metropolitan ambition relied on lands where the Chattahoochee's banks curved around the southern end of the city. In 1910, the Georgia General Assembly authorized the sale of the South Commons, a roughly triangular parcel five blocks south of downtown along the river, by the common commissioners to the city government. Like Savannah, Augusta, and Macon, Columbus had been planned with commons surrounding city lots. The East Commons had been sold decades earlier to build a large railyard. The South Commons, which had been the site of the Driving Park horse track for three-quarters of a century, might have been sold to manufacturing interests if commons commissioner T. E. Golden had not conveyed the land to the city with the stipulation that it be reserved for recreational use.[22] The following year, *Columbus Ledger* linotype operator and sportswriter J. Cam White spearheaded a guarantee-fund drive that persuaded Mercer University to move its home game against Clemson Agricultural College from Macon to Driving Park. Downtown merchants festooned Broad Street storefronts in the schools' colors to excite community interest in the game.[23]

Although the Electric City was an unlikely location for a football game between Georgia and South Carolina teams, the Mercer–Clemson game inspired subsequent efforts to use the city's state-line location to lure games between Georgia and Alabama teams. In the fall of 1912, local leaders secured the Georgia–Alabama game and the matchup between Mercer and Alabama Polytechnic Institute (Auburn), leading the *Enquirer-Sun* to predict that "the landing of a game in this city will be a plum that most of the colleges will want." Jim Woodruff's younger brother, twenty-four-year-old former Georgia Bulldogs quarterback George C. "Kid" Woodruff, echoed the newspaper's assertion. He argued that Columbus had enough Georgia alumni to make the game against the Crimson Tide an annual event in Columbus and persuaded downtown merchants to decorate again in the colors of the competing teams.[24]

Although Columbus hosted no collegiate games from 1913 to 1915, the city's experience in the two preceding seasons provided a template. In 1916, the Columbus chamber and the Rotary Club invited Georgia and Auburn to play annually in Columbus. Montgomery and Macon also courted the game, which had been played mostly in Atlanta since the 1890s. However, Auburn was closer to Columbus than to Montgomery or Macon, and Columbus had considerable Auburn and Georgia alumni bases. Columbus was also the hometown of the Woodruff brothers, each an alumnus of one of the schools, who played host to athletic officials to promote Driving Park.[25] With the Central of Georgia and Southern Railways running special trains to Columbus and advertising the game in stations within a 100-mile radius, the chamber envisioned the border rivalry being the most-attended football game in the South's history.[26] Muscogee County lent convict laborers to erect additional bleachers and clear stems and stalks to turn a rented cottonfield into an "auto park" for the game. The Woodruffs' efforts on local alumni committees and in concert with the Ralston and Waverly Hotels (the respective headquarters of Auburn and Georgia fans) resulted in staging a parade and filling Driving Park with more than two thousand fans.[27]

After two consecutive wartime years when games were suspended, Columbus leaders resumed their efforts in 1919. Agreeing with the *Ledger* that the city's border location was a distinct asset, Georgia and Auburn athletic officials committed to playing their next three matchups in Columbus.[28] When Oglethorpe University in Atlanta and the University of Florida agreed to play each other in Columbus in 1920, the *Enquirer-Sun* exclaimed that the Electric City was now on "the Southern football map."[29] While the Oglethorpe–Florida game offered more in the form of publicity than large numbers of visitors to Columbus, the Georgia–Auburn game's overflow crowd led to the addition of enough temporary bleachers to boost Driving Park's capacity for the 1921 game. Even that was not enough to seat the estimated 15,000 who turned out, and the success, along with the promise of bearing all hosting costs besides the teams' travel expenses, enabled Kid Woodruff to secure commitments from both universities to play in Columbus at least through 1927.[30]

With the Georgia–Auburn game secured for another five seasons, George Woodruff and the city's Georgia–Auburn committee presented a proposal to the Rotary Club in 1922 for a 25,000-seat concrete stadium in Golden Park, as the South Commons had been renamed.[31] Just two months after calling Columbus "the athletic center of the Southland," the *Ledger* warned of the precarity of this status following the opening of Montgomery's Cramton Bowl.[32] After two more years of discussion, the city commission appropriated $50,000 in bond revenues, much less than needed to make the stadium as large as its backers hoped. The resulting Memorial Stadium was a 15,000-seat, horseshoe-shaped structure with the capacity to support later expansion. Woodruff obtained municipal support for selling reserved seats to augment fundraising for an arcaded stadium entrance as a war memorial. Memorial Stadium opened, fittingly, in 1925 when Auburn played a Georgia team now coached by Woodruff.[33]

The mid-to-late 1920s marked a time of effervescent boosterism in Columbus, as was true in many cities. Boosters hoped to diversify Columbus's textile-heavy economy in part through developing tourism. Like the fast-approaching centennial celebration, Memorial Stadium reinforced their hope of attracting more visitors to the city. The *Ledger* pointed in 1926 to Atlanta's successes in attracting college football "classics" and argued that, with its new stadium, Columbus might now fill the fall calendar with additional college games.[34] However, local boosters found it hard to answer the *Ledger*'s call. After a meeting of the Georgia–Auburn Football Association, the Kiwanis Club resolved to try to lure the Georgia–Alabama game away from Birmingham, which was building Legion Field, and even spoke audaciously of trying to poach the Alabama–Auburn game, also played in the "Magic City."[35] After two more years with no headway, Columbus suddenly faced the unthinkable. With the new Sanford Stadium just months from completion on its campus, the University of Georgia announced it would play the 1929 game against Auburn in Athens instead of Columbus. At a Columbus Junior Chamber of Commerce meeting, Woodruff said if the Jaycees would sponsor it, Columbus could have the 1929 Georgia–Tulane game and squelch the grumbling about losing the city's great football classic. With Woodruff's aid through the Georgia–Auburn Football Association and his connections as a former Georgia coach, the Jaycees secured a Friday night Georgia–Tulane game, followed by the Georgia–Auburn freshman game the next day. Despite this face-saving action, the *Ledger* had grown impatient. In an editorial, the paper complained that Memorial Stadium had been built at considerable cost with the idea that it would be used more than once a year, adding that the venue was "'rusting' from lack of use" (see Fig. 13).[36]

African American civic leaders played a major role in responding to the *Ledger*'s call by attracting gridiron clashes between Georgia and Alabama Black colleges. In a 40-percent Black city surrounded by rural counties with majority-Black populations, they knew they could generate interest. Although Columbus's white boosters, like their Macon and Augusta counterparts, preferred to sequester the African American community away from the city's prized civic spaces, their failure to attract big-time games on a

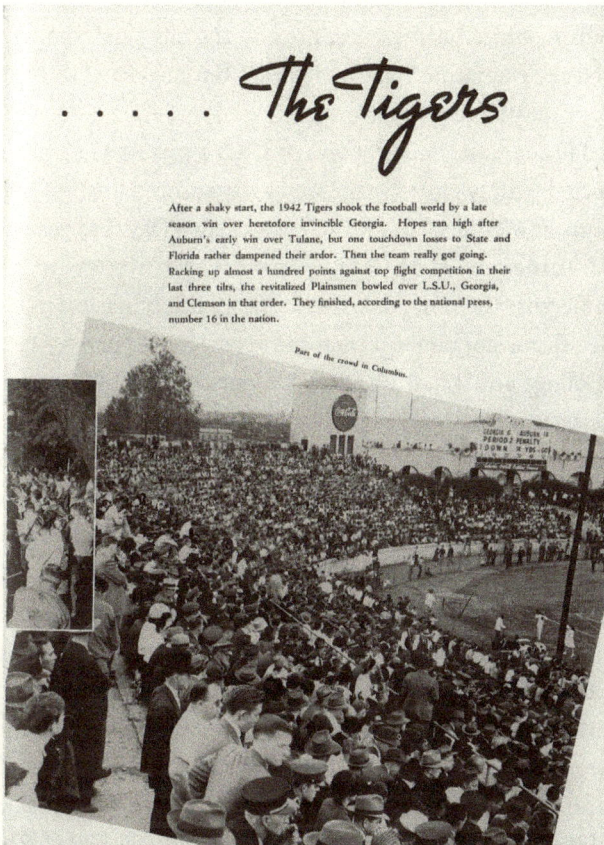

The Tigers

After a shaky start, the 1942 Tigers shook the football world by a late season win over heretofore invincible Georgia. Hopes ran high after Auburn's early win over Tulane, but one touchdown losses to State and Florida rather dampened their ardor. Then the team really got going. Racking up almost a hundred points against top flight competition in their last three tilts, the revitalized Plainsmen bowled over L.S.U., Georgia, and Clemson in that order. They finished, according to the national press, number 16 in the nation.

Part of the crowd in Columbus.

FIG. 13. AUBURN–GEORGIA GAME AT MEMORIAL STADIUM, 1942.
Opened in 1925, Memorial Stadium reflected an assumption that Columbus's border location could be an asset in attracting major intercollegiate football rivalry games to the city, which already hosted the annual matchup between nearby Auburn and Georgia. When this dream failed to materialize, the city's Black leaders began organizing HBCU "classics" at the stadium in the 1930s, drawing mixed responses from white leaders. *Glomerata*, vol. 46 (1943). Courtesy of Auburn University Archives & Special Collections, Auburn, AL.

consistent basis opened the door for African American use of Memorial Stadium, which in turn presented the opportunity to substantiate Columbus's athletic center claim. However, Black football promoters would draw mixed responses from white business leaders and the city's newspapers, who acknowledged the economic benefit of games but neglected to connect them to broader promotional efforts.

Founded in 1929, the Social and Civic Club 25, or So-C-25 (so named because it started with twenty-five members), sponsored the first Black college football game at Memorial Stadium on Armistice Day that year. Black physicians E. J. Turner and K. H. Terry, who were also investors in Washington Heights, billed as "the only high class, Colored Subdivision in Columbus," spearheaded the promotion of a game between Montgomery's Alabama State Teachers College and Atlanta's Clark University.[37] Columbus newspapers applauded the game but cast its African American promoters as junior partners seeking to emulate "the program" of white booster organizations and as needing charitable support from whites. The *Enquirer-Sun* was careful to point to the places where Blacks could buy tickets on the fringes of downtown and those for whites on the former Broad Street, renamed Broadway preceding the centennial to emulate New York's famed thoroughfare. While boosters urged merchants in "the colored section downtown" to decorate in the red of Clark and black and gold of Alabama State, they did not suggest the same on Broadway, although the Jaycees and Columbus Electric & Power raised a large advertising banner there and one five-and-dime offered special prices on decoration materials in the schools' colors. A pregame parade observed the color line on its way from Sixth Avenue at Eighth Street to the stadium. An estimated five hundred white spectators attended the game in a whites-only section cordoned off from thousands of Black fans.[38]

White promoters continued to cling to the hope of attracting more white college football games to Memorial Stadium. Although the Georgia–Auburn game resumed in Columbus in 1930 and occurred annually until the Second World War halted intercollegiate sports, they found little success in enticing additional games.[39] Besides Georgia–Auburn, African Americans proved to be the only consistent source of college football action in Memorial Stadium. Alabama State returned annually for the Armistice Day Classic, playing Clark again in 1930 and Florida A&M in 1931 before taking up a standing meeting with Atlanta's Morris Brown College in 1932 and for several subsequent years.[40] Then, in 1936, Black real estate broker E. E. Farley worked with other local African American leaders to bring the football game between the Tuskegee Institute and Morehouse College to Columbus in 1936.[41] As with Georgia–Auburn and Alabama State's several preceding games, Columbus proved a viable neutral venue with many alumni of both schools living in the area. The Tuskegee–Morehouse game would eventually become Columbus's longest-running annual gridiron battle, surviving long after Memorial Stadium lost the Georgia–Auburn game in 1959 amid the shift of Southeastern Conference and other major-conference games to campus-based stadiums on "home-and-home" schedules.[42]

Through the war years, the annual "classics" between what later became known as historically Black colleges and universities (HBCUs) would play only a limited role in advancing the metropolitan ambitions of white Columbus boosters. In part, this was a result of a lack of overnight accommodations for Black visitors. Prior to World War II, the city's only Black hostelry was Lowe's Hotel, a small Fifth Avenue apartment hotel. Although railroads ran special trains for some of these games, many visitors needed to arrange to stay overnight with friends or relatives.[43] The limits on Blacks' ability to support the Electric City's ambition to be the "Athletic Center of the Southland" extended to the combined fascination and condescension that whites expressed toward HBCU teams and fans. A *Ledger-Enquirer* sportswriter's coverage of the 1942 Tuskegee–Morehouse game laid bare these racist attitudes. He depicted Black fans as unruly and the quality of football as mediocre, writing that the fans "went native" when their marching band played and that "[t]he longest pass in the game was a whiskey bottle that came sailing out of the Morehouse stands onto the grass." While acknowledging that some regarded the annual classic as the city's best game, he remarked that this was true only of its "entertainment and novelty," and he concluded that even Tuskegee, "which will rate high in the nation among colored teams, could never defeat an average white college eleven."[44]

At bottom, Black participation in boosters' vision and white press encouragement of token white patronage were props used to portray race relations as amiable. For many more years, Columbus whites, unwilling to embrace Black sports and unable to muster the resources to continually expand Memorial Stadium or control white athletic programs' decisions for how best to build their fan bases, would struggle in vain to build a football destination status comparable to that achieved by Birmingham's Legion Field, let alone match Augusta's golfing fame.

Columbus had entered the twentieth century in similar circumstances as Macon and Augusta. All three cities relied heavily on cotton-dominated agriculture and industry, and all three sought economic diversification. However, only Columbus developed an entirely different economic pillar that produced significant growth prior to the 1940s. Despite attempts to use its river to achieve greater stature through electric distribution, river shipping, and sports spectacles, that pillar turned out to be federal military investment. While Macon and Augusta saw only brief surges of investment in military bases during World War I that largely abated until the onset of World War II, Columbus leaders managed to lobby for a permanent military presence between the wars that enabled their city to rise to comparable metropolitan stature with Macon and Augusta. The maintenance of a military presence required ongoing civic efforts but also positioned Columbus to outperform the other two fall-line cities in the interwar years. Only half as large as its fall-line counterparts in 1910, Columbus had risen to 90 percent of Macon's size and 80 percent of Augusta's by 1940.

In 1917, Columbus boosters hoped to attract an Army training camp but were disappointed when their city was not selected, especially after other fall-line cities—Fayetteville, Columbia, Augusta, Macon, and Montgomery—were named as sites. The chamber of commerce's newly formed encampment committee persuaded federal officials to inspect the city, but the resulting visit produced only a suggestion that Columbus would be chosen in any future round of selections. In December the committee traveled to Washington, DC, to lobby for a camp. Though they were unsuccessful, the War Department announced plans in the following spring to move the Infantry School of Arms from Fort Sill in Oklahoma and named Col. Henry E. Eames to guide site selection. The chamber dispatched John A. Betjeman, a civil engineer on loan from the Jordan Company (Gunby Jordan's real estate business), to advocate for Columbus alongside Senator Harris. Columbus realtor M. Reynolds Flournoy scouted sites, settling on a Macon Road farm three miles east of Columbus. When the government finally named Columbus as its site, he arranged a six-month lease and helped relocate the farmer. Col. Eames secured commitments from Columbus businesses to build the camp on the promise of being reimbursed. Workers transformed the Macon Road cottonfield into a camp in under two weeks while the first troops from Fort Sill were en route to Columbus.[45]

Camp Benning served its wartime purpose but soon revealed limitations, chiefly its lack of satisfactory rifle ranges, which prompted Col. Eames to search for a larger site. A tip from Columbus lawyer B. S. Miller led Eames to Arthur Bussey's Riverside plantation nine miles south in Chattahoochee County. There, he found a 1,800-acre, oak-shaded tract, much of it "almost as level as a floor."[46] Bussey, who owned fertilizer and brick companies, had bought the property in 1909 and, in the spirit of agricultural diversification that was sweeping the South, transformed it into a "model" plantation producing cotton, sugarcane, corn, dairy, and other farm products.[47] As impressive as the land's large, level tract was, the highly varied sandhill topography surrounded it, enabling training exercises to simulate the world's battlefields. These considerations shaped the War Department's intent to purchase 115,000 acres in Chattahoochee and Muscogee counties.[48] The choice of lands reflected an understanding that the loss of such a vast area, when coupled with the barrier posed by the river, required minimizing disruption to the city's future expansion. Accordingly, the post's northern boundary traced "an irregular line east of the city to avoid valuable grounds and existing factories on the eastern outskirts."[49] Although the War Department condemned Bussey's farm, the signing of the Armistice led the government to order a construction hiatus less than two months later.[50]

The war's end also stirred local dissension over the idea of a permanent military presence. Boosters embraced Camp Benning's role in their metropolitan ambitions, a position echoed in articles and editorials in the city's two daily newspapers. The Columbus chamber was composed mostly of bankers, realtors, and insurance men who stood to benefit from the economic boost generated by the base. Their ardent support for creating a much larger, permanent Camp Benning set them at odds with textile operators, who worried that their workers might leave the mills for higher-paying government jobs, and with planters and farmers, who feared losing their land to eminent domain.[51] While textile interests did not organize against land acquisition, farmers did. In December 1918, Dr. Charles Howard Jr. of Cusseta in Chattahoochee County called a mass meeting to "save the city and both counties." A *Ledger* editorial expressed "real astonishment" that anyone could oppose what it viewed as the best development ever to come to "this district," adding that farmers could find "thousands of acres of idle lands" a short distance from Columbus and Cusseta. Rhodes Browne, a banking and insurance executive and former Columbus mayor, insisted that nine-tenths of Columbusites favored Camp Benning and warned that they "will remember where that agitation originated."[52]

Proponents showed up to counter opponents at the mass meeting. After Howard warned that Chattahoochee County would lose its agricultural identity, realtor Gunby Jordan called for a "spirit of harmony" and sense of common purpose in "the upbuilding of the entire district." Going further, Judge B. S. Miller told the crowd that the post was good for Columbus, by which, he explained, he meant everywhere within a 100-mile radius. After another local judge promised to form a twelve-member Chattahoochee County advisory board to mediate the land acquisition process, boosters defeated Howard's resolution opposing Fort Benning, instead endorsing the post and the metropolitan vision it advanced.[53] Their success smoothed the way for land purchases, although the federal government decided to acquire 98,000 acres, less than originally intended.[54]

The establishment in 1919 of a permanent Camp Benning (colloquially called Fort Benning well before its official renaming in 1922) indeed changed Columbus's relationship to its rural hinterland. As Fort Benning grew, some boosters argued it might hasten agricultural diversification in the Chattahoochee Valley, especially livestock and dairying.[55] Although the military post unquestionably opened a new market for farm produce, the vastness of the installation pushed those benefits farther outward from the city. By 1935, Chattahoochee County had the fewest farms and lowest farm-product value of any county in the bistate trade territory. With few farms to require farm labor, it also had only a 30 percent African American population in a trade area that averaged 53 percent Black.[56] When the city hired the Jacksonville-based planner George W. Simons Jr. to study Columbus in 1948, Simons pointed out that the removal of so much land from farm production three decades earlier had more than negated any benefit of selling truck crops to the city and Fort Benning, adding that the military had eclipsed agriculture as a pillar of Columbus's economy.[57]

MACK
BUSES

———

Commenced Business
August 13, 1921

———

Millions of Passengers

Millions of Miles

No Serious Accidents

PACKARD
CARS

———

We employ only ex-
perienced drivers —
usually men with fam-
ilies. They are closely
supervised—trained in
the elements of safety
and courtesy; eyes ex-
amined periodically.
You will find us accom-
modating and desirous
of serving you.

Scene on Fort Benning Boulevard, showing one of our Parlor Car Buses on its way to
Fort Benning.

HOWARD BUS LINE, Incorporated

Phone—City
410

TRANSPORTATION
Columbus————Fort Benning
"Sincerity is our service"

Phone—Post
224

FIG. 14. HOWARD BUS LINE ADVERTISEMENT, 1929. The establishment of regular bus
service between downtown Columbus and Camp Benning in 1921 reinforced social and
economic connections between city and post, helping unify them as a military metropolis.
The Howard Bus Line eventually formed the first route in the city's metropolitan transit
system. *Industrial Index*, May 29, 1929. Courtesy of Columbus State University Archives,
Columbus, GA.

Although Fort Benning removed most of the farmland ringing Columbus on the south and east, it did not immediately transform the nine-mile
span between city and reservation. In Fort Benning's early years, it was
paradoxically dependent on and isolated from Columbus. The unimproved
red-dirt road between the city and post was almost impassable after heavy
rains.[58] When the federal government lifted its construction moratorium
in 1919, workers strung electric and telephone lines and built a railroad between the city and the post.[59] In August 1921, on the recommendation of the
chamber's camp activities committee, Benning officials granted a concession
to the Atlanta-based Howard Taxi and Bus Company to offer regular bus
service between downtown Columbus and the post.[60] The bus line was a
crucial factor in knitting a seamless metropolitan social fabric across civilian
and military lines (see Fig. 14).

Boosters were quick to identify Fort Benning's role in training officers as a ticket to wider recognition for this emerging military metropolis. One chamber of commerce ad even called Columbus "The West Point of the South," and the post lent a cosmopolitan air to the city by bringing in men from all over the nation and even overseas. As one local observer noted, "the presence of so many distinguished military men adds further to the zest of a warm-hearted Southern city." One local historian later remarked on "the sight of the Army uniforms and the long lines of khaki on Broadway."[61] Civic leaders sought to connect with the officers at the post, hosting social and recreational events for them such as golf matches at the Columbus Country Club, which through the chamber's brokering offered half-rate officer memberships.[62] Unsurprisingly, the influx of young, single men yielded so many local marriages that one booster christened Columbus "The Mother-in-Law of the Army."[63]

Another "marriage" of sorts came with the paving of the main road between the city and post in 1925. Even before the completion of Benning Boulevard, Mayor Homer Dimon proclaimed that "Columbus and Benning have been hyphenated" and "will be one family," adding that "greater Columbus is coming through a greater Benning."[64] Indeed, thanks to the new highway, Columbus was no longer merely "The Mother-in-Law of the Army"; now the city was effectively married to the military base. In a June 2, 1925, ceremony held in Springer Opera House, Columbus and Benning officials staged a mock wedding with a bride, groom, bridesmaids, and groomsmen representing the city and post, complete with the 29th Infantry Band's rendition of Wagner's "Wedding March." The new road encouraged officers and soldiers to partake of city offerings, such as the Muscogee Club's oyster pan roasts and the Ralston Hotel's "fresh Chicago meat" and nightly entertainment, and Columbus citizens to attend military demonstrations on the reservation.[65]

Beginning in the 1920s and continuing through the following decade, Fort Benning underwent improvements that transformed it from what some had derisively dubbed a "peacetime Valley Forge" into "a city within itself."[66] Concurrently, civic efforts to provide better transportation, services, and social opportunities ensured that the thousands of Fort Benning officers, enlisted men, and military families would be a part of Columbus and support its leaders' metropolitan ambitions. Local commentators variously described Fort Benning as a suburb, an industry, or a metropolitan center. In effect, it was all three. The growing base developed ample services and amenities, which met military personnel needs and even made it a destination for civilians and tourists. By the late 1930s, Fort Benning was the largest employer in Columbus, producing a $2 million monthly payroll (about one-fourth of the total in the city's textile mills) that soldiers eagerly spent in the city.[67] Even before the surge that followed the nation's ramping up of military preparedness, ongoing federal investment at Benning in the interwar period helped Columbus begin its transformation from a compact mill town along the river into a sprawling suburban landscape anchored by downtown and the post to its southeast.

Fort Benning's allure grew as the post advertised itself as a metropolitan amenity. Benning's new image as a model military base reflected a spectacular construction boom. By 1933, the post had more than three hundred buildings and fifty miles of paved streets, handsome brick barracks, pastel-shaded stucco officers' houses, and a long list of amenities that included two theaters, a stadium, and a golf course.[68] The post's new Spanish Colonial Revival-style Officers' Club, which opened in 1934, further cemented social ties with the city, becoming a who's who of Columbus with names like Jordan, Woodruff, Kirven, Swift, and Hardaway.[69] The post's expansion continued through the 1930s, setting Columbus apart from Augusta and Macon. While the populations of Richmond and Bibb counties grew by about 12 percent and 9 percent respectively in the Depression decade, Muscogee County expanded by more than 31 percent.

Although Mayor H. C. Smith called Fort Benning "our most important suburb," he seemed to recognize the reservation as more than an appendage of the city when he quipped that if the post continued growing, it would "not be long before . . . we consider our city a suburb of Benning."[70] Indeed, the post, through its massive military and civilian payrolls and ceaseless support of the building trades, played an important role in facilitating the suburbanization of the city's south side. In a promotional booklet published around 1934, Columbus real estate interests hoped to entice Benning officers to buy suburban homes by emphasizing the presence of the base as a continuing amenity. They juxtaposed photos of modern suburban homes and antebellum mansions, pairing them with assurances that Columbus was "a pleasant community of people with charm and culture."[71] As much as Fort Benning brought a "cosmopolitan" flair to Columbus, boosters continued to deploy traditional white southern culture in their appeals to outsiders, just as their counterparts did in other southern cities.

Civic leaders generally welcomed Fort Benning as an integral part of an emerging metropolitan Columbus, but the river and the color line each posed limits to the metropolitan unity the post otherwise fostered. Numerous vice operators in Phenix City exploited the availability of thousands of young men unmoored from the restraints of their families and communities. On weekends, soldiers ventured across the Dillingham Bridge to partake in the Alabama town's tawdry nightlife, so much so that in March 1924, the Infantry School's commandant, Brig. Gen. Briant H. Wells, issued a ban on crossing the river that stood for five years. Even after it was lifted, Phenix City remained a problematic presence, underscoring that the state border sometimes undercut the ideal of a unified Chattahoochee Valley metropolis.[72] Military and civic leaders were even more intent on limiting the presence of African American soldiers in the city. Fort Benning, like Columbus, was separate and unequal with rigidly segregated facilities. Post officers forbade Black enlisted men from visiting white sections of Columbus, and the Howard bus line refused service into the city, meaning that Black soldiers had to walk or hail a jitney outside the post gates, a hassle that led many to resign themselves to remaining on the reservation.[73] Whether by drawing boundaries at the river or between the races, Columbus boosters showed the limits of their visions of metropolitan unity.

Much more than other booster pursuits in the interwar years, the cultivation of military investment paid dividends for Columbus's metropolitan ambitions. Unlike the limitations that hindered river development and interstate sporting events, Fort Benning firmly established itself as an integral part of the city. Columbus leaders had come to see Fort Benning not only as the chief contributor to metropolitan expansion but also as inseparable from it. In the interwar years, Columbus had blazed a path toward what would become far more common in the fall-line cities' future: the concurrent, interlinking ascent of the Cold War military-industrial complex and the Sunbelt metropolitan boom. American entry into World War II would produce local and federal commitments to expand Fort Benning to an extent never imagined when the reservation moved from the city's eastern edge to the piney woods to its southeast after the First World War.

Though military leaders had chosen Columbus as a major training center because of its varied landscape at the nexus of the river and sandhills, Fort Benning enabled Columbus to transcend the determinism of its Chattahoochee Valley site. In the coming decades, as global competition squeezed an increasingly vulnerable textile industry, Fort Benning would become the city's key shaper. As the next chapter demonstrates, it would steer civic priorities during the war as leaders grappled with how to serve the needs of a suddenly swollen military population. The military base would also fuel a postwar suburban boom, filling nearly every free parcel of land in Muscogee County and making Columbus both the fastest-growing of Georgia's fall-line cities and one that, despite significant planning challenges, eventually pioneered the forging of a more unified metropolitan area.

FOUR

⌁

PLANNING "THE SOUTH'S MOST PROGRESSIVE CITY"

⌁

In a 1943 issue of the Columbus-based regional trade publication *Industrial Index*, Pearl Smith Truman, the president of a local business college, opined that the military buildup in recent years had transformed her city. "Less than five years ago," she wrote, "Columbus was still in the town class, but now since the 'Brown River' from Mighty Fort Benning flows steadily through the streets, the town has become a city." While World War II deferred the dream of engineering the muddy Chattahoochee into a canal to the Gulf, Columbusites tapped the figurative stream of khaki-uniformed soldiers only recently pressed into service. Columbus's metropolitan ambitions took a new direction during the war, when the public, private, and military sectors had to coordinate their activities to accommodate hundreds of thousands of mostly young men from around the nation. Doing so not only demonstrated patriotism but also promised to burnish the city's image.[1]

Truman also lamented, "If only these splendid men did not have to go to war after all their training . . . what a grand city could be developed right here!"[2] As in other cities, however, the war catalyzed a mindset that metropolitan planning could preserve the wartime progress and provide the basis for a brighter metropolitan future. Indeed, from 1940 to 1970, Columbus saw its greatest growth since the antebellum period, nearly tripling in population. This expansion did not merely advance boosters' metropolitan ambitions. It also taxed government and business leaders' ability to upgrade roads and water and sewer lines, find suitable land to attract industry, and revitalize and provide services to an aging central city, concerns that Augusta and Macon leaders also shared.

While Columbus leaders supported balanced postwar metropolitan growth, they faced vexing problems. In contrast to Atlanta under the long tenure of Mayor William B. Hartsfield, they proceeded tentatively in metropolitan planning, possibly reflecting a complacency encouraged by continuing reliance on Fort Benning and the city's textile industry. Additionally, the growing scourge of organized crime in neighboring Phenix City tarnished the entire area's reputation and compounded the challenges of cooperative planning among municipalities and county governments. Even on the Georgia side of the border, efforts at regional planning repeatedly devolved into squabbles between city and county commissioners. The resulting turmoil delayed downtown revitalization and slum redevelopment and jeopardized eligibility for some federal funding.

Along with division and delay, Columbus, unlike Macon and Augusta, suffered liabilities peculiar to its location. Fort Benning and an unprotected river floodplain limited suburban expansion to the south and east, channeling most postwar development to the north and northeast. In 1956, Columbus was the nation's largest city left off the interstate highway system and became one of the last major American cities to enact a comprehensive zoning code. Industries that might have considered Columbus found little suitable land, boosters unable to assemble attractive incentives, and better options closer to the emerging freeway system. By 1962, when metropolitan unity stood at its lowest ebb despite strong area growth, few could imagine that in less than a decade Columbus would be Georgia's first consolidated city. Although the *Columbus Ledger* christened Columbus "The South's Most Progressive City" in 1922 and used the tagline on its masthead until 1966, the western Georgia city spent most of the postwar half of that period struggling to give meaning to the claim (see Fig. 15). During World War II, however, Columbus's metropolitan destiny seemed close at hand.

DUTY AND OPPORTUNITY IN THE CITY OF THE FORT

Georgia's fall-line cities had attracted large Army training camps during World War I, but soon after the war, Augusta had lost Camp Hancock, and

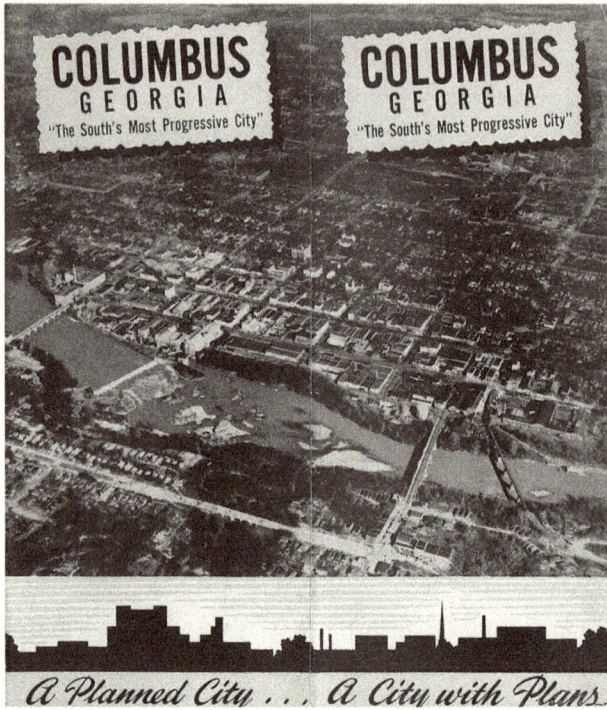

FIG. 15. COLUMBUS PROMOTIONAL BROCHURE, 1955. This brochure's use of the slogan "The South's Most Progressive City" and the tagline "A Planned City . . . A City with Plans" reflected a renewed attention to metropolitan planning catalyzed by World War II. Despite its origin as a well-planned city, Columbus had done little to implement a plan by John Nolen in 1926 and was now struggling to act on a 1948 plan by George W. Simons Jr. Courtesy of Columbus State University Archives, Columbus, GA.

Macon had forfeited Camp Wheeler. In 1941, these cities enjoyed a renewed military commitment. Augusta's airport became the Daniel Army Airfield, the sleepy old Augusta Arsenal on "the Hill" morphed into a bustling bombsight factory, and Camp Gordon opened several miles west of town. Middle Georgia became the beneficiary of a new air base through a combination of factors. When Army Air Corps officials expressed interest in building an airbase near Columbus in 1940, Eagle & Phenix Mills chief W. C. Bradley opposed it out of fear that it might exert upward pressure on the textile industry's low wages. Taking advantage of Columbus's forfeiture and with help from their congressional district representative Carl Vinson, Macon leaders invited military officials to tour potential sites in Middle Georgia, acting on a new chamber of commerce policy of assembling free land for military installations. They ultimately purchased a large dairy farm sixteen miles south of Macon near the whistle-stop town of Wellston. Although the military reportedly favored Atlanta, Wellston's flat topography and the gift of more than three thousand acres tipped the scale, netting the Warner Robins Army Air Depot, which later became Robins Air Force Base. Vinson's skill in leveraging federal dollars, which also netted Macon a naval ordnance plant employing 8,000 workers, brought tens of thousands more jobs to Warner Robins over the course of World War II. Among them was Otis Redding Sr., a Black former sharecropper who had left Monroe County for Terrell County before moving to a new federal housing project on the south side of Macon. Redding's son, then a toddler, would go on to fame as a rhythm and blues artist.[3] Bradley had foreclosed the possibility of the airbase and thereby unwittingly aided Macon, but the Columbus textile industry could not thwart the expansion of Fort Benning. Like Macon and Augusta, Columbus would see thousands of other new arrivals like the Reddings fleeing the dead end of Black Belt tenancy and sharecropping to take advantage of newfound opportunities.

When President Franklin D. Roosevelt issued Proclamation 2352 in September 1939 in response to Germany's invasion of Poland, he catalyzed a military buildup that sent the First Infantry Division to Fort Benning and brought a new wave of growth to Columbus. From a population of around 6,000, Fort Benning ballooned to about 45,000 by the following spring, leading boosters to claim a metropolitan population of 100,000 for the first time.[4] The influx produced a critical housing shortage that prompted a return to building wooden cantonments on the base like those in its early days and a six-hundred-unit defense housing project called Newton D. Baker Village for white officers and their families.[5] The mobilization's impact on Columbus was similarly sudden and unmistakable (see Fig. 16). "Brown army vehicles of almost every size and description" filled downtown streets. A massive new Howard bus station included the longest lunch counter in Georgia, which of course was racially segregated. The influx heralded unprecedented business opportunities. Soldiers streamed in and out of Broadway restaurants; barber shops; pharmacies; and music, photographic, jewelry, and dime stores. One observer noted that "a lot of khaki goes into the suds

FIG. 16. FORT BENNING SOLDIERS ON BROADWAY, 1942. As the nation girded for war, Fort Benning became one of the nation's largest infantry training centers. The influx of GIs gave downtown Columbus an unmistakably martial atmosphere as khaki-clad soldiers spent their leisure time patronizing local businesses. Photo by Lloyd E. Kelly. Courtesy of The Columbus Museum, Columbus, GA.

of the downtown washeries."[6] Remarking in 1940 on the economic boon of militarization, a cynical Philadelphia newsman wrote, "Columbus is a very greedy little pig, hoisting the American flag, because its tradespeople behold a dollar sign amid its stars and stripes."[7] In addition to filling cash registers, the influx promised a bonanza for landlords. Many thousands of newcomers fled the impoverishment of tenancy and sharecropping to become civilian war workers. They filled rooming houses in town and poured into trailer parks off the road between the city and Fort Benning. The Jones Trailer Camp charged $2.50 a week for each trailer space, which one occupant complained was "nothing but a mud hole," adding that his family had no alternative because the rooming houses in the city forbade children.[8]

The problems that accompanied the wartime transformation brought civic leaders back to a similar sense of urgency that animated the original fight to secure and then preserve the training camp more than twenty years earlier. To maintain its momentum, Columbus, like other cities with military bases, would have to do its part to meet GIs' housing and social needs. Columbus leaders understood that "duty and opportunity" were inseparable. Echoing the sentiments of boosters who had feared the potential loss of Columbus's training camp after World War I, a newspaper editorial in late 1940 contended that the city might lose the benefit of growing military preparedness without a concerted effort to build new houses. "Never before, and perhaps never again," it concluded, "will we have so tremendous an opportunity to grow rapidly into a greater metropolis."[9] The imposition of rent control in Muscogee and Russell counties in 1942 curbed exploitation by landlords, but it proved harder to satisfy the need for more housing. Developers managed to build a handful of new subdivisions for military families south of town under the National Defense Housing Program, notably the aptly named Benning Hills, but as elsewhere the demand would remain undersupplied until after the end of the war.[10]

Perhaps no one grasped the imperative of serving GIs' social needs better than Walter A. Richards, a civil engineer and industrial executive who served as president of the Columbus Chamber of Commerce in 1941–42. Writing in the *Columbus Enquirer* in the latter year, Richards observed, "We, as a community, have a rare opportunity to render a real war time [sic] service by helping to make these boys happy while they are our guest and at the same time spread good will [sic] for our city by having them say a good word for our city when they leave us."[11] A native of Washington, DC, Richards had moved to Columbus after serving in World War I. During his 1922–25 tenure as city manager, he hired John Nolen to draft the city's first master plan. After returning in 1928 following a stint as the city manager of Daytona Beach, Florida, Richards became vice president of Columbus's Tom Huston Peanut Company and was named president four years later when banks assumed control of the firm after its ill-fated foray into frozen peaches.[12]

In December 1940, on the eve of Richards's second term as chamber president, Mayor Edward Murrah asked him to serve as chairman of the Columbus Defense Service Committee (CDSC), a new nongovernmental organization intended to coordinate the various social programs offered for Fort Benning personnel by the city's department of recreation, churches, civic and fraternal organizations, and national organizations such as United Service Organizations (USO) and Young Men's Christian Association (YMCA). Planning activities for the GIs was as important for keeping them out of trouble as it was for showing them warm hospitality. After an inspection tour by Secretary of War Henry L. Stimson highlighted grave "moral conditions" in the Columbus–Phenix City area, the city worked with Phenix City and Fort Benning officials to curb vice while turning to the CDSC and its community partners to recast the city's image in a rosier hue by rallying Columbusites to steer soldiers away from vice dens.[13]

Richards was versed in the problems of "social disease," having been appointed a few months earlier to head the city's Hygiene Council in concert with Benning officials, local health authorities, and a U.S. Public Health Service liaison.[14] Understanding the danger that a lapse in public health might pose for the city's image, he labored to convey the importance of a communitywide effort to welcome GIs into wholesome social settings. Just as Richards had found it necessary as city manager to counter public apathy toward urban planning and complaints from municipal leaders about the cost of hiring Nolen, he had to warn that a redoubled effort was needed to support a sixfold increase in military personnel at Fort Benning, especially providing "a substitute for their home life." Speaking to a women's club in late 1941, Richards sought to lift what he sensed was flagging interest in hospitality, urging his audience to devote a quarter of their leisure time to "boosting soldier morale and entertaining soldiers in our homes."[15]

In his bid to instill a habit of civic hospitality, Richards courted many Columbus organizations. Churches were a natural ally. Trinity Episcopal Church provided space for the CDSC's headquarters and was among the dozen churches that went on to operate complimentary leisure spaces for military officers and personnel each weekend.[16] In addition, the CDSC kept a registry of young women volunteers, dubbed "Military Maids," for dances and other social events in concert with the city recreation department, churches, USOs, Howard Bus Line, and Fort Benning. In an article promoting a meeting of the Military Maids at one local church, *Columbus Enquirer* society-page editor Mrs. George (Effie Mae) Burrus Jr. took implicit aim at the temptations of the city's nightlife by writing, "LIPSTICK. Used properly by our American girls, it will go a long way in winning the present war."[17]

The provision of wholesome venues assumed heightened importance when Black soldiers were involved. White Columbus leaders, who had viewed the influx of African American fans for HBCU football games warily in the 1930s, were blunt in warning that the enlarged contingent of Black troops might overwhelm Fort Benning's capacity to provide separate recreational activities for them on the base. Doing so required careful planning to protect the city's reputation. Richards singled out the lack of a Black recreation center as a "problem" requiring "immediate attention."[18] The CDSC's answer was to advocate a new "colored" Army and Navy YMCA in town, which of course meant separating it as much as possible from the existing Army–Navy YMCA on Eleventh Street in the heart of downtown at some point. *Ledger-Enquirer* publisher Maynard R. Ashworth, who served as chairman of CDSC's "committee on colored men's program," worked with a so-called advisory colored committee to plan the new YMCA. At the suggestion of E. E. Farley, Black real estate broker and grocery store operator Lizzie Lunsford offered to fund the construction of a building on property she owned at 841 Fifth Avenue and rent it for the facility. Lunsford and her children Lula and Walter had inherited this and other property, including a drugstore, seven years earlier from her late brother, a prominent merchant.[19] The city and county commissions, flush with federal support for recreation programs, agreed to fund an Army–Navy YMCA for whites but left fundraising responsibility for the Jim Crow "Y" to the CSDC and its African American partners. The Negro Army–Navy YMCA, the world's first, opened in July 1941 and doubled as a USO club.[20]

Despite the CDSC's efforts to steer soldiers away from trouble, within a year, Columbus posted the highest rate of sexually transmitted disease in the eight-state area overseen by the Army's Fourth Corps. In February 1942, the city counted 122 cases, with an additional 32 in Phenix City. The figures were far more than those in most other southern cities and amounted to more than Atlanta, Macon, and Augusta combined. Only New Orleans came close, with 111 cases. A group of ministers urged Columbus and Muscogee commissioners to undertake tighter vice control. Brigadier General Walter S. Fulton, the commanding officer at Fort Benning, coordinated anti-vice efforts with Columbus and Phenix City officials starting that spring.[21]

Local boosters were more effective in strengthening social connections between Columbus and Fort Benning, burnishing the image of a military metropolis that had emerged in the interwar years. City and military leaders cooperated in staging Army Day festivities in April 1942. "The pavement trembled" on Broadway as tanks and other armored vehicles highlighted a downtown parade, and military equipment displays appeared in storefront windows. Fort Benning also drew large audiences to its "open house" to view tactical demonstrations.[22] In 1943, after the city's USO Travelers' Aid Station counted a record 3,696 requests for rooms in a single month, the chamber of commerce operated a billeting office on Broadway to assist in finding accommodations in private homes for thousands of out-of-towners who visited loved ones stationed at the post. Under the management of Oscar Betts, a Georgia Tech–educated engineer turned hotel manager and an ardent supporter of close civic-military cooperation, the Ralston Hotel hosted officers' dances in its swanky Mirror Room and served holiday dinners to large numbers of troops.[23] Although Fort Benning, which now sprawled over 182,000 acres spanning two states, had "assumed the proportions (if not the aspect) of a metropolitan center," boosters' efforts cemented both the image and reality of Columbus as "The City of the Fort" in which city and base were "almost synonymous."[24]

By 1943, having grown into its larger role as a hostess city, the so-called Mother-in-Law of the Army now demanded a new planning effort. Richards reprised a role he had come to know well: warning against complacency. Although he headed a peanut-processing company whose business reflected Columbus's historic connections to its agricultural hinterland, he was at heart a metropolitan booster with a technocrat's mind. Echoing similar commitments to postwar planning seen in other American cities, Richards described his vision for reviving Columbus's long-dormant planning to encourage orderly growth and redevelopment, urging his peers not to lose "the artificial stimulus of the war" but instead to "capitalize on the gains we have made."[25]

Despite forming a municipal planning board in 1922 and accepting Nolen's 1926 plan that pointed to a future Columbus with diversified industry, a strong downtown, and beautiful parks, boulevards, and civic spaces, the city government had failed to realize many of Nolen's suggestions.[26] The textile industry, with its low wage structure, continued to dominate Columbus's economy, and it seemed likely that Fort Benning's influence would shrink after the war.[27] Unplanned residential and commercial development on the city's fringes and the constraints posed by the river and Fort Benning limited the prospects for attracting new industries. Older sections of town, including the Bottoms, where freedmen had settled on flood-prone former Commons land along Weracoba Creek, suffered deplorable housing conditions. As in Augusta's Terry, Atlanta's Buttermilk Bottom and Vine City, and countless other impoverished Black communities across the urban South, many African Americans in the Bottoms lived on dirt streets in shacks without plumbing facilities. Suburban growth stoked by the military base taxed the city's "crazy patchwork" of narrow, often mismatched streets and roads.[28]

Richards reconstituted the Greater Columbus Committee in March 1944, taking the name of a short-lived organization that had championed annexation after World War I. This eighteen-member temporary committee set out to create a formal planning body to serve not only the city but also the metropolitan area. The resulting Columbus Planning Association (CPA) formed in August with Richards serving as general chairman.[29] The CPA planned to study metropolitan needs and make recommendations, but it had no formal budget or jurisdiction. As important as it was that Columbus had a body that understood the need for sound planning to guide its future, the creation of this new group without more than an advisory role portended significant limits to metropolitan planning in the years ahead.

The CPA's members looked to the postwar period with an optimism buoyed by the sense that Columbus was well-positioned to avoid an economic slump. In the summer of 1944, the *Industrial Index* reported that the area's manufacturing employment was likely to remain stable because "[n]ot a single strictly wartime industry has come into the Columbus area" and the city's preexisting manufacturers, having met war production demands, were already converting back to meeting their normal production demands. Their optimism seemed warranted when a Census Bureau official included Columbus among the nation's fourteen "Class A-1 markets" with "superior prospects" for postwar growth.[30] Adding to their confidence was the CPA's success in securing voter approval in 1945 for the annexation three years later of five square miles of suburban areas, especially to the southeast toward Fort Benning. The annexation would almost double the city's area and add about 20,000 citizens, raising Columbus's population to nearly 80,000, enough to lift it from fifth to third in the state.[31]

Columbus needed to overcome serious deficiencies to fulfill its leaders' metropolitan ambitions. Some challenges resembled those in other cities, especially an aging downtown and blighted central-city neighborhoods. The *Columbus Ledger* pointed to the city's "down-at-heel look" as an impediment to their ambitions as early as 1944.[32] Weeks before V-E Day, the *Ledger* referenced a Georgia Power ad that warned of the deleterious effects of urban obsolescence. Questioning if Columbus was in any condition to welcome "returnjng soldiers, sailors, Marines and WACs," the editorial intoned that the city needed to address its "junk heaps, tumbled-down shacks, [and] unpaved sidewalks." The next day, the *Columbus Enquirer* asked readers if they had taken a close look at the buildings along Broadway. "If you have," the editorial noted, "we'll bet you were assailed by a feeling of shame. . . . Why is it that Columbus—the metropolitan city that it is—has such flimsy, ugly structures along its main business thoroughfare?" It warned that such conditions would repel industrial prospects.[33]

While local leaders did little to address their downtown's unprogressive appearance, they made a promising start to replacing substandard housing. The Georgia fall-line cities were particularly afflicted with blighted housing that entrapped most African Americans and white cotton mill workers. In the Home Owners' Loan Corporation appraisals, Macon, Augusta, and Columbus ranked in the top ten among U.S. cities for the highest percentage of their residential areas shaded red on the map and given a D or "Hazardous" rating.[34] By 1944, the federal government was prepared to fund a housing project for Black war workers in Columbus as a Jim Crow counterpart to Baker Village. The U.S. Housing Authority identified a sloping, D-rated site for the project in Meeler's Hill. However, white residents of the adjacent A- and B-rated Overlook neighborhood on the crest above balked. Civic boosters hoped to placate Overlook residents and use the project to wipe away "the huddle of Negro shacks at the foot of Wynnton Hill" on the Weracoba Creek floodplain, on the eastern approach to downtown and buffered by a C-rated neighborhood. When the alternative site's cost exceeded the government's allotment by $100,000, the city and county commissions appropriated nearly half the cost of the Warren Williams Homes, while the Columbus Planning Association raised the remainder.[35] In what the federal housing authority called the nation's only example of businessmen donating cash gifts for public housing, Columbus's white establishment demonstrated a greater resolve to "protect" their own property values from the perceived taint of Black residency than they would be able to summon for planning in the years ahead.[36]

Despite early signs of a planning revival, the next decade brought a haphazard, intermittent effort. Two months after the war ended, Richards joined the Columbus City Commission. He pressed the city and county to hire a planning consultant to prepare Columbus's first master plan since Nolen's in 1926. After a yearlong delay, the local governments finally hired Jacksonville-based planner George W. Simons Jr., who completed his plan in 1948. Simons called for enacting zoning, redesigning the city's inefficient street system, eliminating blighted areas, and improving the city's appearance and image. He also pointed out that Fort Benning had occupied so much land in unincorporated Muscogee County that city-county consolidation was the only way to ensure orderly metropolitan expansion. In the coming two decades, a number of cities reached the same conclusion, viewing consolidation as a useful mechanism for addressing the economic inefficiencies and social concerns created by rapid metropolitan expansion.[37] The CPA quietly disappeared after the delivery of the Simons plan. Unfortunately, Richards's resignation as mayor in 1949 left a planning void that others did not fill. Only in 1953 did the city and county pursue developing comprehensive zoning codes, hiring Simons to implement his recommendations of five years before. Zoning lagged for another three years, by which time it was viewed as critical for guiding an even larger impending annexation that would more than double Columbus's area to 26.6 square miles in 1958.[38]

In the year after the CPA's inception, the chamber of commerce formed its New Industries Committee. Chaired by Maynard Ashworth, who had led the CDSC's effort to build a Black servicemen's YMCA, the committee fell far short of its promise. It set a goal of raising only $10,000 in stock, a paltry sum compared to the $100,000 raised for site acquisitions and national promotion by the Macon Area Development Committee, an entity formed by the Macon chamber in 1944. The modest goal reflected the weakness of Columbus's chamber, whose 1944 overall budget was about half that of Macon's and Augusta's and was reportedly the lowest among thirty-two U.S. cities of similar size.[39]

The lack of resolve to raise more funds left Columbus woefully short on industrial land. Constrained by Fort Benning's sprawling footprint and running out of options elsewhere that did not conflict with the patchwork of suburban residential areas developed in the absence of zoning, the new industries committee's meager budget and the high cost of scarce land discouraged action. With no reserved land or incentive packages to compare with those provided by more aggressive southern communities, the chamber nonetheless rolled out a flashy industrial marketing campaign in 1949 with 10,000 copies of a brochure cleverly titled "America Discovers Columbus, Ga."[40] Unsurprisingly, the effort attracted few new industries. In 1952, Sunshine Biscuits built what would turn out to be the only new plant employing more than five hundred workers in the entire quarter century after World War II. Columbus's experience stood in stark contrast to the Atlanta metropolitan area, whose three largest counties accounted for one-third of all new manufacturing jobs in Georgia between 1947 and 1958.[41]

The city's state-border location also continued to sow division, hampering metropolitan cooperation. This division pointed to the limits of Rosa Gordon's ability to surmise the future in her short story in the early 1920s. Her fictional industrialist Hamilton, looking backward from the vantage point of 1950, told fictional newspaperman Coolidge that, a decade before, the citizens of Phenix City and Girard had persuaded the Alabama legislature to cede their territory to Georgia, enabling Columbus to extend its city limits to a "perfect circle ten miles in diameter." This enabled Hamilton to describe the fictitious Hotel Utopia on the western bank of the Chattahoochee River as a Columbus landmark. The reality was that, while Phenix City depended economically on Columbus, many of its business operators benefited from lying beyond the regulatory reach of their Georgia neighbor.[42]

Phenix City had long been a source of consternation for Columbus and Fort Benning officials. The Russell County town had battled its entrenched vice operators in spasmodic bursts, often under pressure from state and military officials, only to lapse into indifference. Despite accolades for stamping out liquor violations in 1946 and gambling operations in 1951, progress was ephemeral, leading to fears that the wide-open town would impede industrial recruitment.[43] In 1953, one of Phenix City's most outspoken anti-vice activists, attorney Albert L. Patterson of the Russell Betterment Association, warned that a textile firm reportedly interested in the area might not overlook the "terrible conditions" that persisted along the Chattahoochee between the Dillingham and Fourteenth Street bridges. Ten months later, after winning the Democratic primary for Alabama Attorney General on the

FIG. 17. MILITARY POLICE PATROLLING FOURTEENTH STREET BRIDGE, 1954. After the murder of Albert Patterson in Phenix City, the Alabama governor declared martial law. In this photo, Fort Benning military police patrol the Fourteenth Street Bridge over the Chattahoochee River alongside the Muscogee Manufacturing mill on the Columbus side of the bridge. Vice operations in Phenix City had periodically prompted Fort Benning officials to forbid soldiers from crossing the river and posed a continuing challenge to boosters' efforts to unify a bistate Chattahoochee Valley metropolitan region. Photo by Tim Chitwood. Courtesy of Columbus State University Archives, Columbus, GA.

strength of his vow to root out organized crime, Patterson was murdered in an alley near his office.[44] The brazen killing cast a pall over the entire Columbus area. The murder prompted Alabama Governor Gordon Persons to declare martial law and dispatch National Guardsmen to the border city, and it led to a resumption of military policing of the bridges over the Chattahoochee (see Fig. 17). But the crisis also produced enough outrage to catalyze a permanent cleanup.

Four months after Patterson's murder, the changes were sufficient for the *Columbus Ledger* to proclaim that Columbus's Alabama partner, once a "divorcee," was ready to reunite with the "South's Most Progressive City." The paper urged industries to take a fresh look at Phenix City, which had more land available for industrial development than on the Georgia side of the river. Fort Benning officials rescinded the latest of their proscriptions against soldiers visiting Phenix City just a month later in another sign of healing metropolitan fractures.[45] With the vice problem in Phenix City finally resolved and another significant annexation poised to lift Columbus's population well over 100,000, boosters renewed their push for a metropolitan planning effort that might span the river, but they met stiff resistance from Muscogee County commissioners who clung to their dwindling influence in the face of an expansionist city. Their opposition, which recalled concerns about the loss of rural lands for Fort Benning four decades earlier, brought turmoil at a time when unified planning might have advanced Columbus's fortunes.

In 1957, the Columbus chamber held a screening of an Atlanta booster film titled *Now for Tomorrow* at the Ralston Hotel. The film had been produced two years after Atlanta tripled in area through an annexation that Mayor Hartsfield had urged as part of a "Plan of Improvement" to retain white political power over an increasingly Black city. It recounted how Atlanta leaders had formed the Atlanta Metropolitan Planning Commission, the nation's first multicounty planning agency, in 1947 and pointed enthusiastically to the city's metropolitan strides.[46] Inspired by Atlanta's example, in 1957, the Columbus chamber persuaded city and county commissioners to ask the Georgia General Assembly to pass enabling legislation needed to charter a ten-member, multicounty Metropolitan Planning Commission (MPC), which formed in Columbus the following year.[47]

Soon after persuading the city and county to form the MPC, the chamber hired the Industrial Development Branch of the Georgia Tech Engineering Experiment Station to study Columbus's economic potential and problems.[48] The report, released in 1959, confirmed the city's dilemmas. For one, the area was too reliant on military and mill jobs. Fort Benning produced more than one-sixth of the trade area's payrolls, and eight large textile mills with low profit margins and low wages accounted for nearly three-fifths of all manufacturing employment in the city. At a time when Columbus remained a regional destination for many farmworkers displaced by mechanization, the city was suffering a sustained decline in manufacturing employment, and the risk of military cuts at Fort Benning was ever-present. The Georgia Tech report urged developing industrial employment in the surrounding rural counties to reduce the pressure on Columbus. The report also pointed to the city's decidedly un-metropolitan appearance. It characterized downtown storefronts as "countrified" with many stores displaying merchandise on the sidewalks and argued that downtown "completely fails to give the impression of a modern progressive metropolitan center." Indeed, the city had made no progress in improving its downtown storefronts to match the new landscaping and fountains in the Broadway parkway championed by women of the United Garden Clubs in 1955.[49]

The chamber expected the MPC to act on the Georgia Tech report since the planning body ostensibly represented the city and surrounding counties. Unfortunately, however, the MPC, like the earlier Columbus Planning Association, started with no budget and considerable confusion as to its purview.[50] Its formation under these circumstances reflected Atlanta-inspired metropolitan ambitions by boosters who lost sight of unifying governmental stakeholders around a common vision. From its inception, the MPC also faced strong opponents in the Muscogee County Commission, including cattle rancher and county commissioner Roy M. Waller. When the MPC was forming, Waller chastised a Columbus chamber official for suggesting qualified candidates for membership and predicted that the MPC would be "stacked" with city residents to the exclusion of rural Muscogee citizens. Indeed, the MPC's members turned out to reflect the city's growth coalition, especially its real estate industry.[51]

In 1959, Roy A. Flynt Jr., a traffic engineering planner whose father was the Georgia Highway Department planning engineer, became the MPC's full-time director.[52] Among his recommendations was to turn several blocks of Broadway into a pedestrian mall supported by peripheral parking garages, as Simons had suggested in a downtown study the previous year.[53] Despite hiring an expert planner, the MPC became mired in political intrigue when its chairman, a local realtor, began closing the commission's meetings to the public and the press. As secret meetings continued, both the city and county commissions threatened to withhold funds. When the MPC lobbied state highway officials for a freeway connector between Columbus and I-85 at LaGrange, Waller and fellow county commissioners excoriated it for overstepping its authority. Two months later, Flynt resigned.[54]

The MPC's woes brought handwringing among Columbus boosters who saw their metropolitan ambitions imperiled. A chamber official observed with only modest exaggeration that Sunshine Biscuits had been the only outside industry to locate in Columbus since 1828 and warned that if Columbus did not straighten out its planning turmoil, "not one new industry will come to Columbus when the river is completed."[55] Various observers had suggested periodically that the city's influential textile operators wanted to keep out new industries for fear of introducing unionized labor and higher wage scales that might siphon away their own workers. Textile magnates had shunned an Army air base for this reason in 1940. In 1947, the chamber's new-industries chairman, Georgia Power sales manager Muse E. Mann, hinted at the problem: "Our labor situation is such that some of the new industries we can't justify in bringing to Columbus." Ten years later, local leaders launched the Columbus Industrial Development Committee (CIDC) with the express purpose of acquiring industrial land. In its promotional booklet, local cotton-gin manufacturer Harold G. Lummus was quoted as saying, "[W]e can't rely on one industry and one source of income." But after four years the CIDC had yet to acquire a single option on land, which one officer tried to explain away with the insistence that its biggest advantage was "the symbol it represents."[56]

Regardless of whether the failure to assemble industrial land reflected an unadmitted desire among textile operators to discourage new factories, the result was the same, and it was no secret that Columbus's leaders were in disarray. Although a new director (James Wright) was secured, the MPC's troubled state led the county commission to withhold funds and to try, unsuccessfully, to persuade the city commission to join in forming a consolidated planning commission, as had been done in 1952 in both Augusta and Macon.[57] By October 1961, with no resolution in sight, an exasperated *Ledger* editorial office lamented, "Round and round we go and where we stop nobody knows. That's the status of community planning here today."[58] Soon afterward, Wright also departed, sending the MPC into a tailspin from which it would not recover. Amid increasingly bitter interactions between the city and county, the MPC was allowed to collapse in February 1962.[59]

That same year also saw the calm desegregation of downtown department stores and lunch counters and the defeat of a bid to consolidate city and county governments. The consolidation effort reflected the work of a city-appointed citizens committee headed by James W. Woodruff Jr., by then the manager of Columbus Broadcasting, *Ledger-Enquirer* publisher Maynard R.

Ashworth, and John B. Amos, president of the Columbus-based American Family Life Assurance Company (later Aflac), formed in 1955. It came as a number of cities, including Nashville, Indianapolis, and Jacksonville, were weighing consolidation as a useful mechanism for addressing the economic inefficiencies and white flight that accompanied rapid metropolitan expansion. Tellingly, despite the pragmatic decision to support downtown integration, white civic leaders saw no need to include a single Black representative on the twenty-one-member committee.[60] Intended to foster governmental efficiency, take a logical next step in a city that had already annexed most of the county's population outside Fort Benning, and project the air of a progressive metropolis, the consolidation campaign floundered because of negative publicity incited by Waller and two like-minded county commissioners. In 1955, Waller had expressed hyperbolic disdain toward annexation, calling it "cannibalistic" and quipping that he would appreciate "30 days' notice before they move the city limits to the county line so I can move my cows into Harris County." Conjuring images of socialist Cuba seven years later, Waller dubbed consolidation a "metro-Castro type government," an epithet he delighted in repeating at every opportunity.[61]

Agreeing with Waller, Cusseta Road furniture store owner W. S. Persons headed an anti-consolidation group called the Committee of the Plain People that placed numerous fearmongering ads in the *Ledger* in the weeks preceding the consolidation referendum. Its ads were a reminder that many in the outlying areas distrusted the Columbus growth coalition's metropolitan ambitions. One ad charged that the *Ledger-Enquirer* "monopoly press" was bent on "REPRISAL . . . to *get the jobs* of the three commissioners who opposed them on MPC." Another ad more ominously showed a cartoon of a man wearing a "Plain People" shirt punching consolidation backers and urged readers to "drop in on them at their plush offices 'downtown' to talk things over!"[62] The negative publicity helped defeat consolidation, with 58 percent of voters rejecting it. Although the tony Wynnton neighborhood, an "island suburb" like Atlanta's Buckhead and Charlotte's Myers Park, supported the merger by a two-to-one margin, the city in aggregate disapproved by a narrow majority, and county voters rejected it by a four-to-one margin.[63] Soon afterward, Persons became the campaign manager for segregationist and future Georgia Governor Lester Maddox, who shared his suspicion of strong government, in his unsuccessful bid for Lieutenant Governor.[64]

Two months prior to the consolidation defeat and at precisely the time when the MPC was terminated, an inspection team from the National Association of Real Estate Boards (NAREB) visited Columbus as part of its "Build America Better" campaign, an anti-blight initiative started a decade earlier by an anti-public housing Los Angeles developer. The resulting report, titled *Toward a New Columbus*, appeared in May 1962.[65] It echoed the economic outlook in the Georgia Tech report from three years earlier, pointing to the uncertain future of Fort Benning and the influx of rural workers when mills were shedding jobs through automation. Calling Columbus "a city in transition" from "a mill town and agricultural center to a diversified modern city," the report noted the need to recruit new industries more aggressively and improve the city's physical appearance. Despite Columbus's foray into federally funded urban renewal in the Bottoms in 1957, the report decried the "creaking remains of neglected ante-bellum [*sic*] mansions" and "discouraging squalor of shotgun shacks" that lined the approaches to downtown as "a poor invitation indeed to a supposedly modern community," adding that "downtown Columbus is just plain dowdy." As inertia gripped downtown revitalization planning, the NAREB report pointed to the potential of a historic preservation movement that would soon take root in all three Georgia fall-line cities. While noting the "shabby, forbidding" residential blocks to the south of downtown, the report pointed approvingly to the "magnificent, old trees," "colorful mansions of the gingerbread era and earlier," and proximity of the river. It suggested that "conservation-centered urban renewal" of this area could "create a new market for retail stores" downtown, an idea that would soon also animate local preservationists and their counterparts in Augusta's Pinch Gut and Macon's College Hill neighborhoods.[66]

Of course, Columbus's poorest citizens lived away from that enclave judged as having conservation potential. Neither helped by conservation nor displaced by demolition, they held their own in a city that had beckoned thousands to leave their rural homes for an elusive better life. A *Ledger* reporter introduced Johnnie Mae Sampson and her four children, who lived in a house that resembled "a sharecropper's cabin in the Mississippi Delta." The Sampsons, who were Black, had worked on a farm shelling peanuts and chopping cotton before moving to Columbus in 1960. While the city's leaders were scrambling to resuscitate metropolitan planning, Mrs. Sampson's husband died from drinking paint thinner when he was unable to afford whiskey. It is not recorded whether he had tried to find industrial work, but Columbus's dominant textile operators, like their counterparts throughout the South, remained notoriously hostile to African American millhands in the 1960s. The widowed Sampson's fifty-hour-a-week job as a maid and her daughter's beauty parlor job barely paid the rent for their shack with an outdoor privy and no bathtub. The lack of progress in "The South's Most Progressive City," which had long ranked second in the state behind Atlanta in manufacturing employment, crushed more than the metropolitan ambitions of growth-minded Columbus leaders.[67]

STUMBLING TOWARD A GREATER COLUMBUS

Jarred by the collapse of metropolitan planning, rejection of consolidation, and unflattering portrayal of the city in the Build America Better report, the county commission made a conciliatory overture to the city commission in 1963, asking for a fresh start at joint planning. The city agreed, and in October the newly constituted Columbus–Muscogee County Planning Commission (CMPC) met for the first time.[68] The CMPC faced the fallout of two years' worth of virtually nonexistent planning at a time when the rules for obtaining federal grants were changing in ways that required more substantive area planning. To qualify for urban renewal funds, Columbus planners could no longer simply draft a site plan as they had done for the Bottoms in the 1950s. They also had to provide a comprehensive city plan. For some federal aid, even a city-county planning unit was no longer sufficient. If the CMPC had any hope of reversing Columbus's omission from the Interstate Highway System seven years earlier, it would need to comply with the Federal Aid Highway Act of 1962, which required planners in urban areas with populations over 50,000 to devise a "contiguous, comprehensive, cooperative transportation planning process" by July 1, 1965, for highway funds sought after that date. The task of developing a single transportation plan for an entire metropolitan area was more complicated for those that straddled state borders because the Georgia state government, which had to approve metropolitan transportation plans, did not recognize bistate planning commissions. Augusta and North Augusta, South Carolina, cooperated without formal agreement to skirt this regulation, and now Columbus and Phenix

City would need to do likewise.[69] The absence of an interstate highway and a continuing failure to assemble industrial land—despite the formation of the CIDC for exactly this purpose—probably cost Columbus and Phenix City the opportunity to land a $20 million U.S. Rubber tire plant, which instead went to a 640-acre tract provided by the Opelika Industrial Development Board along the projected route of I-85 some thirty miles northwest of Columbus. A *Ledger-Enquirer* columnist quipped that Columbus was on its way to being "a suburb of Opelika," adding that "the time to get ready . . . slipped past us years ago."[70]

Columbus leaders would have to bide their time to obtain either urban renewal or federal highway funds. In the process of making up for lost time, the Columbus–Phenix City area would lag Macon and Augusta for the remainder of the decade. Unfortunately, like the Metropolitan Planning Commission before it, the CMPC faced its own hardships. Amid a nationwide shortage of qualified city and regional planners, the CMPC's first chief planner resigned after only eight months, leaving Columbus's participation in preparing the transportation study in limbo and jeopardizing eligibility for urban renewal while the city and county failed to find a replacement until ten months later.[71]

By 1968—twenty years after George Simons's recommendation to fight blight through rehabilitation, redevelopment, and zoning—most of Columbus's substandard housing remained. With work on the comprehensive plan progressing slowly, the prospect of urban renewal remained distant. The CMPC looked to Mills B. Lane Jr., president of the Atlanta-based Citizens and Southern (C&S) National Bank. Lane, whose father had founded C&S in Savannah in 1906 before moving its headquarters to Atlanta, had become the bank's president in 1946 and built C&S into a powerful component of Atlanta's rising stature as the progressive hub of the New South even as he poured his personal fortune into historic restorations in Savannah. Lane's bank-financed "Savannah Plan" for slum rehabilitation inspired the commission to urge similar action in Columbus.[72]

But one month after CMPC director Ed Baker appealed to twenty local industrial executives to help finance slum eradication, not one had replied. Undeterred, the CMPC declared a "war against slums" with its homegrown Operation Reclaim initiative, whereupon the Columbus-based Royal Crown Cola and W. C. Bradley companies finally responded to Baker. Ignoring areas that had been identified as the city's bleakest for decades, Baker then announced that the city's rehabilitation priority would be the 390-acre historic area south of downtown along the river, which NAREB had found promising six years earlier. The decision pleased the Historic Columbus Foundation (HCF), a preservation group formed in 1966 and modeled after the Historic Savannah Foundation.[73]

Meanwhile, to facilitate transportation planning, the CMPC shepherded a new organization to review applications for federal aid from area communities in both Georgia and Alabama. The resulting Chattahoochee Valley Council of Local Governments, unlike the Chattahoochee Valley Chamber of Commerce three decades before, failed to achieve a unified vision. Rather, Baker admitted, it was a tool born of necessity to meet federal requirements for cooperation in planning. Metropolitan fractures over transportation appeared despite efforts to find common ground. To meet the requirements of the jet age, Columbus would need federal funds to upgrade or relocate its airport, but the Georgia prohibition of planning across state lines reinforced the inclinations of officials in Muscogee and Russell counties to press for what was best for their own jurisdictions. A similar problem emerged over the need for more bridges to connect Phenix City and Columbus, with officials on each side unable to agree on a proper location for a new bridge.[74]

Amid these squabbles, Baker resigned in July 1969. It soon came to light that Baker had accused CMPC members and Columbus and Muscogee officials of "foot-dragging" and that the CMPC had demanded his resignation. Baker was incensed by conflicts of interest among CMPC members—as more than half were in the real estate industry—and charged that they were dismissive toward established planning practices whenever these stood in the way of rezoning parcels in which they had a stake. He added that one member had told him, "Ed, you need to meet the one hundred people that really run this town," leading him to tell the *Ledger* that he did not know who they were "because I was working for 190,000 people."[75] Baker's departure led the CMPC to hire an Atlanta-based firm to complete the Columbus–Muscogee portions of the transportation study. It also led to civic discussions about the need for a planning commission more reflective of the broad community.[76]

After the city-appointed Citizens Advisory Committee for Community Improvement called for shrinking the planning commission to five to seven members representative of the whole community, the city commission appointed a five-member Planning Advisory Commission in 1970.[77] That same year, consolidation was up for another vote. The *Columbus Enquirer* noted that in Nashville and Jacksonville, the first cities in the Southeast to consolidate with their counties, citizens had enjoyed tax cuts. It also pointed to other advantages: Columbus would become Georgia's second-largest city and "first in progressive spirit"; a "blue chip government" could help Columbus attract "blue chip industry"; and, as in Jacksonville, consolidation would provide free publicity to "put Columbus on the map."[78]

City and county voters responded by approving consolidation by more than a four-to-one margin.[79] Although a majority of county voters opposed consolidation, as they had in 1962, this time the measure found stronger support inside the city. Importantly, in 1969, voters had already heeded Mayor J. R. Allen's call to approve annexing the 42.5-square-mile balance of the county (except for Fort Benning and the riverside mill village of Bibb City) so that Columbus might avoid the mistake Macon had made in 1961, when it had nearly doubled its population by more than tripling its area to 49 square miles but had to settle for federal allocations based on its 1960 population for the remainder of the decade.[80] Having annexed virtually all of Muscogee County, there was now little room to argue against ending the duplication of government services. In addition, by that time Columbus accounted for more than 90 percent of Muscogee County's population, up from under three-quarters several years earlier. Also helpful was the compromise proposal that the resulting Columbus Commission would have six at-large and four district commissioners. Coupled with the impact of the Voting Rights Act of 1965, this arrangement favored some African American representation. In contrast to Richmond, Virginia, whose business establishment's refusal to accommodate Black desire for district representation led to the failure to consolidate with Henrico County, Columbus's compromise produced a commission that initially had two Black members.[81]

As the 1970s dawned, Columbus boosters sensed that their city was turning a corner. In 1970, two months after the consolidation victory, Mayor Allen pointed to the 234-foot-tall Government Center rising on Ninth Street. It replaced the old domed, neoclassical Muscogee County Courthouse whose long neglect mirrored that of the city (see Fig. 18). Allen exclaimed that

FIG. 18. OLD AND NEW COURTHOUSES, 1972. Columbus and Muscogee County finally consolidated their governments after decades of discussion and failed attempts, creating Georgia's first and the Southeast's third consolidated city and supporting boosters' long-standing effort to effect greater metropolitan unity. Locals applauded the new thirteen-story Government Center for lending a more metropolitan image to what had long been likened to an overgrown mill town. Photo by Herb Cawthorne. Courtesy of Columbus State University Archives, Columbus, GA.

Columbusites would marvel at this "new and ultra-modern building and say, 'Look what we have got in Columbus,'" adding that the tower would "cement this progressive-type attitude sweeping through the city."[82] Hailed as Columbus's first skyscraper, Government Center was a monument to the long struggle for metropolitan stature and a symbol of the city's success in overcoming the lingering power of entrenched rural interests to create Georgia's first consolidated city-county.[83]

Along with a consolidated government widely cited as an aid to luring new industry, in 1970 Columbus received state approval of the Columbus–Phenix City Transportation Study, the last such study in Georgia to be completed.[84] The approval paved the way for seeking federal support for road improvements, which promised to relieve the traffic snarls produced by Benning Hills, Battle Forest, and scores of other postwar suburban subdivisions that had grown in tandem with Fort Benning. By the end of the decade, Interstate 185 would link the city's Lindsey Creek Parkway (finally built over four decades after John Nolen had envisioned it) to I-85, shortening the driving time to Atlanta. Columbus leaders, quipped a *Ledger* reporter, celebrated "as if the city had just become a part of the United States."[85]

Although consolidation also overcame the power of an establishment top-heavy with descendants of old-line textile families by replacing its boards with new departments filled with more diverse appointees, the result was not always a more equitable metropolitan area. The city finally had a unified Department of Community Development with a planning division, but it maintained chasms formed and reinforced by the empowered few. The new department guided Columbus's first urban renewal undertaking since the Bottoms project in the late 1950s. The Southwest Columbus–Weracoba Creek Urban Renewal Project combined support for the demolition of the dilapidated neighborhoods on the Weracoba Creek floodplain with preservation in the new Columbus Historic District along the Chattahoochee River south of downtown. Sensing the city's new direction, longtime navigation advocate Jim Woodruff Jr. purchased and moved the endangered 130-year-old, New Orleans–style Goetchius House several blocks to a riverside lot at the south end of Broadway that his father had bought with the idea that it would be a good dock site. After the U.S. Army Corps of Engineers's inability to maintain a sufficient river channel had made Columbus's inland port a failure, Woodruff opened a restaurant in the Goetchius House in 1971 with an eye to attracting heritage-minded tourists.[86]

Across the railyard to the east, the persistence of heavy policing, unpaved streets, dilapidated housing, broken streetlights, and flooding hazards in Black neighborhoods remained sore spots a decade after the moderate, pragmatic, prosperity-minded downtown establishment had quietly desegregated stores and lunch counters. Following the dismissal of seven African American policemen for protesting police department discrimination, violence erupted in downtown Columbus in June 1971. Demonstrators firebombed downtown stores, setting the stage for two tense months that saw attacks on patrol cars and more than 150 cases of arson. The unrest mirrored similar assaults on downtown businesses in Augusta and Macon the previous summer and again in 1971 in Macon at the same time as the Columbus rebellion.[87] These outbreaks, which also occurred in many other U.S. cities from the mid-1960s to early 1970s, were a painful reminder of how little the need for social equity occupied the minds of white boosters fixated on their metropolitan ambitions.

Metropolitan ambitions in Columbus had animated planning in the 1940s–60s as they did in Macon, Augusta, and other cities in and beyond the South. Columbus's forays into metropolitan planning faced a myriad of challenges, some of which reflected unique local circumstances and others of which were regionally or nationally common. The expansion of Fort Benning rapidly swelled Columbus's population and stimulated commerce but also taxed infrastructure from roads to schools to utilities, much as it did in Huntsville, Mobile, Norfolk, and other southern cities. The military influx channeled wartime planning toward providing services and hospitality both to manage and cultivate the city's newcomers in the interest of making Columbus an orderly and attractive community that might reap peacetime rewards from its display of patriotic duty. After the war, planners grappled with the same problems faced by other cities: race and class division, rural-to-urban migration, central-city decay, suburban flight, and economic transition. Columbus's challenges were compounded by its proximity to a state border, distance from the developing interstate highway network, entrenchment of the textile industry with its depressive effect on wages and skills, and Fort Benning's removal of so much downriver land that might have supported industrial diversification. Although Columbus planners were pioneers among the Georgia fall-line cities in achieving city-county consolidation, the area's relentless decentralization blunted the potential of consolidation to unify a metropolitan region.

FIVE

WHAT AUGUSTA BUILDS, BUILDS AUGUSTA

"Is this a 49th state? It's not Augusta—It's not Georgia—It's not South Carolina—Let's give it a name!" This call to action appeared in the *Augusta Chronicle* in 1950. It followed a meeting of mayors and other representatives from eastern Georgia and western South Carolina towns in downtown Augusta to discuss coordinating the development of the city's trade territory. At the time, the U.S. Army Corps of Engineers had nearly completed a mile-wide dam and spillway on the Savannah River twenty-two miles upstream, forming the third-largest reservoir east of the Mississippi. The delegates agreed to endorse a contest to name this region, which consisted of twelve Georgia counties and eight in South Carolina with a combined area larger than New Jersey. In addition to sponsorship by the city's daily newspapers and radio stations, Augusta Mayor W. D. Jennings and Walter Harrison of Millen, Georgia, contributed to the $250 purse for the contest.[1]

After reviewing more than twenty-five hundred entries, a panel selected "Central Savannah River Area," the entry submitted by C. C. McCollum, a retired school superintendent from the sandhills town of Wrens in Jefferson County, thirty-three miles southwest of Augusta. Soon the nickname typically appeared as "CSRA." Naming Augusta's trade area was the latest example of the strong inclination toward regional development as a tool for advancing metropolitan ambitions in the Georgia fall-line cities. Unlike in Macon with its central location fully within Georgia, Columbus and

Augusta were border cities whose trade areas spilled into adjacent states. Columbus boosters had styled their city as the metropolis of a region they called the Chattahoochee Valley, and now Augusta sought to do likewise. The word "Central" did more than provide a mental image of the CSRA's location along a river boundary between two states. It also emphasized that Augusta was central rather than peripheral, an important distinction at a time when Atlanta had long since come to dominate outsiders' imagination of Georgia. "Names carry great weight," Augusta Chamber of Commerce secretary Lester S. Moody exclaimed. "In fact," he added, "there is magic in names."[2]

Yet something other than magic underlay the CSRA's promise. Effervescent boosterism accompanied the anticipation of the new Clarks Hill Dam and the deepening of the river channel to support navigation between Augusta and Savannah. Moody had championed improvements to the nation's eighth-largest river by volume since his arrival in Augusta in 1926. The Florida native believed that the dam's flood-control, hydroelectric, and navigation benefits would enhance agricultural and industrial development and help Augusta become a major metropolitan area, a goal shared by his Columbus counterpart, James W. Woodruff Sr. When the chamber launched its monthly newsletter, *Building Augusta and the Central Savannah River Area*, in 1951, its tagline, "What Augusta Builds, Builds Augusta," suggested that it behooved Augusta boosters to continue to shepherd the development of outlying rural counties. Up to that time, boosters had assumed the future would bring more of the same to the Savannah Valley: agriculture and agriculturally based industry.[3]

Moody and other Augusta leaders never imagined that, five months after the naming contest, the U.S. Atomic Energy Commission (AEC) would select a 315-square-mile area of the CSRA along the South Carolina side of the river for a massive plant to produce materials for hydrogen bombs.[4] Constructed in less time than it took to fill Clarks Hill Lake, the Savannah River Plant (SRP) drew national attention and inspired Augusta boosters to seek new industries.[5] In the 1950s and 1960s, the Augusta Chamber of Commerce and two new organizations, the Committee of 100 and the Central Savannah River Area Planning and Development Commission, spearheaded industrialization throughout the city's trade area, but apart from the SRP, the lion's share of growth came in Richmond County. The resulting development of a major chemical and pulpwood products concentration, especially in the low-lying areas immediately south and east of Augusta, included some of the nation's biggest corporations: Du Pont, Kimberly-Clark, Monsanto, and Procter & Gamble. Their presence overcame an otherwise stagnant, agriculturally based manufacturing sector and, along with a robust military presence, helped propel Augusta's Sunbelt growth. But modern, automated processes diminished their employment potential, posing a conundrum for primarily Black farm workers impelled by mechanization to seek urban futures. The plants also further degraded nearby Phinizy Swamp and the mostly African American neighborhoods to its west. As for the river that encouraged industrialization, the dream of making Augusta the preeminent inland port of the Southeast, like the similar vision in Columbus, never materialized. By the early 1970s, it would be unclear whether shipping and manufacturing were reliable pillars of further economic development.

HIGHWAY TO THE SEA

Despite the interruption of the Civil War and growing competition from railroads, Georgia's navigable rivers continued to facilitate cotton culture and the distribution of timber logged from the state's swamps and forests through the end of the nineteenth century. However, by the end of the first decade of the new century, poor soil conservation in farming and the indiscriminate cutting of timber eroded the Piedmont's red clay, which washed downstream during heavy rains and silted up already-shallow rivers in the upper coastal plain to the point that navigation became unprofitable in the fall-line cities.[6] The Savannah River could run as shallow as three feet in some places during dry spells; a man walked across it at Fifth Street in 1927. Yet it was also capable, as seen in chapter two, of swelling into a torrent that could inundate Augusta and outlying Savannah Valley farms during periods of heavy rain in the mountains and foothills to the northwest. Such floods had posed a perennial hazard until the city completed a fourteen-mile levee along the river's west bank in 1915, which displaced the flooding risk from Augusta to "the African American market gardeners and brick makers" in the unprotected town of Hamburg across the river "who contributed to feeding and building Augusta."[7]

The twin problems of flooding and unnavigability led Augusta leaders to take a wide view of the proper sphere for efforts on their city's behalf. Although Macon leaders made sporadic attempts to restore their city's lost stature as an inland port, Columbus and Augusta boosters made more persistent advances toward that end in the middle decades of the century. The Augusta campaign, like Macon's bid to become a regional clearinghouse for services to agricultural diversification in "The Heart of Georgia" in the 1920s, reflected boosters' interest in bending regional planning of their watershed to Augusta's advantage. Unlike Macon's agricultural campaign, however, Augusta and Columbus boosters' river ambitions required massive federal investment.

Soon after Moody moved to Augusta, he met with *Augusta Chronicle* editor and navigation advocate Thomas J. (Tom) Hamilton to discuss the Savannah River's potential. A native of Grovetown in neighboring Columbia County, Hamilton left Mercer University after his junior year to take a job as a reporter for the *Augusta Herald* before rising through the ranks of both papers in the 1910s. After World War I, he inaugurated a long-running list of "Ambitions for Augusta" on the *Chronicle's* editorial page and made river channel development his passion. Using the bully pulpit of the editorial page, Hamilton "spread the gospel of a Deeper Savannah River" and made the *Chronicle* "a potent and dependable weapon" for his cause. As a result of the congressional lobbying that Hamilton and Moody agreed to undertake, within a few months they obtained a Corps of Engineers survey. The Corps recommended a series of dams to supplement the levee's flood protection and provide more reliable channel depth. The first of these, the New Savannah Bluff Lock and Dam, opened thirteen miles downstream from Augusta in 1937. Their additional work to secure soil conservation laws in Georgia and South Carolina persuaded President Franklin D. Roosevelt to authorize a major dam near the hamlet of Clarks Hill in McCormick County, South Carolina. Land acquisition for the reservoir began in 1938, but the project still faced headwinds in the Senate. In addition to persistent Augusta lobbying, Senator Burnet R. Maybank of South Carolina and Senators Walter F. George and Richard B. (Dick) Russell Jr. of Georgia mounted "vigorous opposition" to the removal of Clarks Hill from the flood-control bill, ultimately securing the project. After congressional approval of the bill in 1944, the Army Engineers initiated planning.[8]

After World War II, Augustans' efforts to obtain federal support for river development opened a rift with Atlanta interests. Between 1910 and 1927, Georgia Power Company built six hydroelectric plants in the extreme northeastern corner of the state on the Tallulah River, which joined the Tugaloo River to form the Chattooga, a tributary of the Savannah. With extensive landholdings along the Georgia side of the Savannah River in Lincoln County, the company had feared federal condemnation of its property. At its request, Moody had felt compelled to travel to Washington, DC, where he obtained an assurance that federal officials would negotiate with Georgia Power when assembling land for the Clarks Hill project. Then, in August 1946, Moody received a mysterious invitation to a luncheon at the Sheraton Bon Air from Georgia Power's Augusta agent.[9]

When Moody arrived, Georgia Power president Preston S. Arkwright was there to propose that his company seek a license from the Federal Power Commission (FPC) to build Clarks Hill Dam. Nineteen years earlier, Moody, Hamilton, and other Augusta proponents of a dam at Clarks Hill had consulted Arkwright before seeking a federal commitment to Savannah River development. Motivated by the impact of a severe drought in the mid-1920s, Arkwright had disclaimed interest in dam development and indicated that Georgia Power was willing to purchase electricity "at the switch-board" from the U.S. government at Clarks Hill. Although Georgia Power had gone on to obtain an FPC license in 1928, the company surrendered it in 1932 and later assured Moody that it had no intention of building another dam in the Savannah Valley. Later, in 1946, thanks to the high price of coal, Arkwright was once again interested in hydropower. He claimed to be concerned about waiting for the federal government to fulfill its promise, but Moody made clear that, in courting federal support, he and others in Augusta had made binding commitments.[10]

After being assured that Georgia Power would relent, Moody was stunned when he picked up the morning paper and found the front-page headline, "Georgia Power Co. Willing to Take Over Clarks Hill."[11] Two weeks later, Georgia Power Vice President Charles A. Collier returned to ask for Augusta chamber directors' support for the utility's subsidiary, Savannah River Electric Company (SREC), to build and operate the dam with a powerhouse on the Georgia side rather than in South Carolina, as the federal government planned to do. Collier asserted Georgia Power's interest as a landowner and holder of an extensive existing market for selling electricity. Going further, he asked, "Is Augusta going to say 'no' to a private enterprise that is willing to spend $45,000,000 and say to the world that Augusta stands for state socialism?"[12]

Later that week, Moody blasted Collier's position. He argued that Georgia Power and other private companies might own the riverbanks, but "the people" owned the river itself and the latent power "locked in the mighty waters of that stream." He added that if the FPC believed the federal government was better positioned to develop the river, it was bound under law to reject private licensing. Moody rejected Georgia Power's interest in claiming the power plant for Georgia. After all, he reasoned, "Many of our leading business men [sic] and outstanding citizens came to this city as country boys from the red hills of Edgefield, McCormick, Saluda, Aiken, Barnwell and other neighboring counties in that state." Underscoring his sense of shared destiny between the city and its hinterland in both states, he argued that Augustans were just as interested in the advancement of South Carolinians. Moody dismissed Collier's charge of socialism, concluding, "If working to improve the condition of the people living in the Savannah River Basin area is socialist, then I am a socialist."[13]

When Georgia Power persisted in making its case to the FPC, Moody turned to South Carolina Governor Strom Thurmond for help. Though remembered as a staunch segregationist who headed the States' Rights (Dixiecrat) Party's presidential ticket in defiance of Harry S. Truman in 1948, the governor did not oppose all forms of government intervention. An Edgefield native, Thurmond understood the benefits of federal development of the Savannah River basin and wanted to get his state's share of its advantages. Accordingly, Thurmond argued against Georgia Power and helped secure the FPC's endorsement of Army Engineers construction. A last-ditch SREC appeal failed in October 1947, leading to the resumption of Clarks Hill construction (see Fig. 19).[14]

The opening of the dam in 1954 rendered the Augusta levee obsolete by enabling a controlled release of water to prevent the river from rising above flood stage during heavy rains. Clarks Hill also would prove a tremendous asset in Augusta leaders' efforts to entice new industries, but initially, it produced disappointing results for navigation. The dam's opening coincided with another extreme drought that delayed raising Clarks Hill Lake to full-

FIG. 19. CLARKS HILL DAM CONSTRUCTION, 1948. Through the congressional lobbying efforts of Augusta Chamber of Commerce Secretary Lester Moody and other civic leaders in Georgia and South Carolina, the Central Savannah River Area secured federal appropriations that created the 70,000-acre Clarks Hill Reservoir. Clarks Hill played a pivotal role in attracting the Savannah River Plant and numerous chemical plants and paper mills to the CSRA in the 1950s and 1960s. Photo by Russell Maxey. Courtesy of Richland Library, Columbia, SC.

pool elevation, leaving the channel south of Augusta as shallow as three feet. This was under half of the anticipated seven-foot minimum and a far cry from earlier dreams of a thirty-foot channel to rival that of the Houston Ship Channel in Texas. Augusta's largest brick manufacturer, Merry Brothers Brick and Tile Company, had increased production in anticipation of shipping more of its product down the river, but its sister company, Merry Brothers Shipping, found itself unable to load barges to the minimum draft needed to break even financially.[15]

Like Camp Gordon, whose future appeared tenuous amid President Dwight D. Eisenhower's economizing until Lester Moody successfully lobbied Georgia's Senate Armed Services Committee Chairman Dick Russell to retain it, the river's potential remained uncertain in the mid-1950s. The drought only increased Augusta boosters' resolve to push for continued federal involvement in improving navigation. Their efforts resulted in a new municipal dock and Governor Marvin Griffin's designation of Augusta as an inland port in 1956, along with Moody's success in winning a federal appropriation for a nine-foot channel south of Augusta the following year to make the Savannah River what he called a "Highway to the Sea."[16] Though the river's potential remained unfulfilled, its promise alone had helped the CSRA win another federal investment to bolster Augusta's metropolitan ambitions.

TIN-HATS AND TRAILER CAMPS

In 1951, as the Savannah River's waters gradually submerged the stump-dotted red hills to form fingerlike coves above Clarks Hill Dam, another landscape transformation was about to start about twenty miles southeast of the city. Lester Moody waxed philosophical when interviewed for an article in *The New Yorker* describing the upheaval wrought by the Savannah River Plant (SRP), a project being developed by the Wilmington, Delaware–based chemical company E. I. du Pont de Nemours under a contract from the AEC on a mammoth tract spilling across portions of three South Carolina counties. "It's going to mean empire-building to us," Moody declared. "Augusta is going to grow and grow and be prosperous. Of course, the folks around Ellenton are being inconvenienced, but you can't have progress with sentiment. . . . The hand that shuns the thorn can't have the rose."[17]

Moody's comments were another reminder of the connection between Augusta's metropolitan ambitions and the fortunes of the expansive CSRA, but the impending boom would create winners and losers, as historian Kari Frederickson has observed. For low-wage textile mill workers in Aiken County's Horse Creek Valley, the SRP promised better-paying employment, a fact that forced one mill to undertake a public-relations campaign to dissuade workers from leaving. Additionally, the sudden availability of thousands of construction jobs forced wage hikes to stanch the departure of cotton pickers. The SRP might have produced a larger exodus of Black farmworkers had Du Pont not bowed to local discriminatory customs.[18] It came as agricultural diversification was finally taking root, with cotton yielding to what David Goldfield has called "the green wave of pasture, soybeans, and corn." Indeed, as agrarian employment dipped during the 1950s, African Americans found their job opportunities constrained by their lack of skills and racial discrimination. Rather than flocking to the SRP, many gravitated to Augusta. The city's Black population increased from about 41 to 45 percent, while Aiken County experienced a net out-migration of 1,573 African Americans.[19] Some six thousand people, including the mostly Black townspeople of Ellenton and a handful of smaller hamlets, and many more who occupied rural farmhouses and sharecropper shacks, would face a forced evacuation. Hardly unique, the evacuation was part of a long history of Black loss of land and communities.[20]

The SRP sprang from a confluence of geopolitical and local geographical factors. The alarming discovery that the Soviet Union had closed the nuclear gap in just four years by exploding its first atomic bomb in 1949 led President Truman to authorize the development of a far more powerful weapon. On August 1, 1950, the AEC commissioned Du Pont to build and operate a new plant to produce plutonium, tritium, and other bombmaking materials. Du Pont obtained the contract because of its experience building and operating the world's first plutonium reactors at Hanford, Washington, during World War II. The AEC selected the South Carolina site after evaluating 114 locations in eighteen states. The site checked all the boxes: a large expanse of cheap land with a relatively low population and gently sloping and well-drained topography, a relatively isolated location at a reasonable distance from areas capable of absorbing population growth, and an area with low labor costs. Ironically, the area's liabilities—worn-out former cotton lands that the Augusta chamber had been attempting to recast by promoting model farms raising livestock or growing fruit, nut, and truck crops, as well as a low-wage labor market that was also a legacy of King Cotton—were now assets. An earlier, unsuccessful effort by Lester Moody, South Carolina State Senator Edgar Brown of Barnwell, and South Carolina's Research, Planning, and Development Board to land Du Pont's Orlon factory put the CSRA on their radar. Especially important was the Savannah River, whose Clarks Hill Dam could ensure the availability of millions of gallons of water to diminish the heat produced during manufacturing.[21]

When the AEC evacuation order came, residents had a choice: sell their houses and move or hire professionals to move their houses. Ralph South, a forty-five-year-old professional house mover from a small eastern Colorado town, heard the news of the plant on the radio and decided to journey across the country to Ellenton with his eighteen-year-old son Gerald to make some money moving houses. In fact, South had the distinction of moving the first house, that of a Black farming family. In January 1951, a Columbia newspaper photographed South leaning out of his truck cab to direct Gerald and another man, who were securing Hampton Irvin's tin-roofed, weathered-clapboard house, which was perched on the flatbed with members of Irvin's family standing on its front porch to watch the feat.[22]

In addition to relocating thousands of residents displaced from the project site, the CSRA needed to accommodate tens of thousands of construction workers. At first, it seemed that Augusta might bear the brunt. The Federal Security Administration's initial report on population change in 1951 predicted that, in the next two years, the Georgia side of the river would receive close to half of the influx. The Augusta metropolitan area, comprised of Richmond and Aiken counties, would add 100,000 to its existing 162,000. While it suggested that Bamberg and Barnwell counties in South Carolina would see the largest percentage increases, the sheer number expected in and near Augusta startled local leaders.[23] Actual growth fell considerably short of expectations, but the Augusta metropolitan area still grew by an estimated 59,293 between 1951 and 1953.[24]

Unlike at Manhattan Project facilities at Hanford, Los Alamos, and Oak Ridge, the AEC opted not to build government housing for the Savannah River Plant, leaving the provision of housing to the private sector. One AEC representative, evincing a typical Cold War mindset, insisted that "Americans just don't like to live in government towns," but as Frederickson argues, the government also did not want to provide them.[25] Especially in South Carolina but also in and around Augusta, the resulting housing crunch was a bonanza for builders, landlords, motor-court owners, and trailer-camp operators. Some "tin-hats," as the construction workers were called, paid $1.25 a night to sleep on cots in the Augusta YMCA, while others slept in shifts in $8–10-per-week rooming houses on the fringes of downtown (see Fig. 20). One such property, a Greene Street mansion that had sat empty in 1951, had eighty-two roomers in 1952.[26] Some workers and families resorted to living in barns, sheds, tents, and, in at least one case, even a dog kennel.[27]

Trailers were the answer for many workers with families, just as they

FIG. 20. SAVANNAH RIVER PLANT WORKERS AT ROOMING HOUSE, 1952. During the construction of the Savannah River Plant near Aiken, South Carolina, the Augusta area's housing shortage became acute. Federal officials counted mostly on the private sector to furnish housing. In this photo, two SRP workers wearing their "tin hats" sit on the porch of a Seventh Street rooming house, one of many on the fringes of downtown Augusta. Courtesy of U.S. Department of Energy.

had been for military families in Columbus during World War II. Trailer camps sprouted in pastures, cotton patches, and pecan groves along highways and in backyards in area towns.[28] The *Wall Street Journal* reported that farmland worth as little as $75 an acre in 1950 fetched ten times as much for trailer campsites in 1952. Farmers lucky enough to have frontage along the highways leading to the SRP found trailer rentals more lucrative than cotton, corn, or peanuts. At least one winter resident did the same with his Aiken farm. At the height of construction, an estimated eighteen thousand people occupied trailers in 130 parks in South Carolina and thirteen in Georgia.[29] In addition to contracting with a Columbia-based construction firm for temporary barracks for up to 4,500 single men in Allendale, Barnwell, and Williston, Du Pont arranged with the Philadelphia-based John A. Rob-

FIG. 21. ROBBINS CITY TRAILER PARK IN AUGUSTA, 1952. Wives of Savannah River Plant workers visit outside one of the one thousand mobile homes in this trailer park off East Boundary and Gwinnett Streets on the eastern fringe of Augusta. The John A. Robbins Company of Philadelphia also built three similar camps in South Carolina. Although the SRP construction boom subsided after a couple of years, the Augusta area's industrial development remained strong through the 1960s. Courtesy of U.S. Department of Energy.

bins Company to build four Robbins Trailer City camps for married workers in Augusta and Aiken, Barnwell, and Williston, South Carolina, with a combined four thousand units.[30] By July 1952, in Augusta, one thousand "round silver trailers" dotted forty blocks in a new gridded tract at Gwinnett Street (now Laney–Walker Boulevard) and East Boundary Street (see Fig. 21). To make the camps more livable, Robbins provided postal service, laundries, and other basic amenities, as well as grass seed and gardening tools to encourage residents to make the grounds attractive. Flanked by the city's Black Cedar Grove Cemetery, Charleston and Western Carolina Railroad yards, and Merry Brothers brickyard ponds, Augusta's trailer city, like its first municipal tourist camp thirty years before, was on marginal land. Lacking trees, its twenty-six-foot-long metal tubes broiled in the summer sun. The mercury soared as high as 106 degrees, the hottest the city had ever recorded, during a month-long heat wave that claimed twenty-six lives.[31]

Along with military families who were moving into the Augusta area during the Korean conflict, other SRP workers chose modest homes in new subdivisions. Builders took advantage of the demand to offer mass-produced suburban homes. The Defense Housing and Community Facilities and Services Act of 1951 designated a "critical defense area" that encompassed eight counties on both sides of the river, relaxed credit controls, and provided special FHA mortgage-insurance terms. Developers built 3,225 rental and 625 owner-occupied houses, about one-third of them in Richmond County, under this program. They also separately built more than five thousand houses in dozens of area subdivisions in 1951–52, including the 575-home Crosland Park in Aiken, which emulated an onsite "assembly-line" system pioneered by William Levitt and Sons on a former Long Island potato farm after World War II.[32] Another company, Knox Brothers, manufactured prefabricated housing in its Thomson, Georgia, factory and assembled them on site. Headed by Peter S. Knox Jr., Knox Brothers grew out of a lumber business started by his father in 1932. It had pioneered prefabrication methods at Camp Gordon under an army contract in 1938 before developing Augusta's growing suburban fringes after World War II. Knox advertised its "Tree-to-Key Know-How," a reflection of the elder Knox's insistence on controlling everything from growing pine forests to building homes.[33] Like the trailers whose owners sometimes "just drive into an empty lot or a backyard and set up housekeeping, without benefit of proper water, power or sewage connections," the growth of subdivisions outstripped the area's capacity to provide utilities. Into the 1960s, the cities of Augusta and North Augusta continued to dump raw sewage directly into the river, while unincorporated Richmond County befouled Phinizy Swamp with its sewage.[34]

The Korean War years crushed any hope that Augusta might return to its old, familiar rhythms after World War II. The stimulus of Clarks Hill Dam, Camp Gordon, and the Savannah River Plant brought Augusta more fully into a new era. Less than fifteen years earlier, the city's WPA guide had described a languid city in which "[n]othing must take up too much energy."[35] In 1952, the chamber of commerce boldly predicted that within two years Augusta would become "the largest metropolitan area between Richmond and Atlanta." As had long been the case in Georgia's fall-line cities, the chamber cited an expansive trade area to puff up its apparent population. In a 1952 industrial promotional book, the chamber asserted that Augusta was "naturally and economically integrated" with nineteen Georgia and twelve South Carolina counties where 672,742 people lived. "This area," it averred in a momentary abandonment of the CSRA moniker, "is known as the Greater Augusta Area."[36]

When Dorothy Kilgallen visited in 1953 on assignment for a *Good House-keeping* article, she observed that Augusta "is a town named for a princess, but early in 1951, in a swift, almost transvestite, metamorphosis, it became a virile, booming young giant. . . . It is as if Scarlett O'Hara had come home from the ball, wiggled out of her satin gown, and put on a space suit." Kilgallen described a mélange of "white mansions and magnolias, honky-tonks and the H-bomb . . . casual G.I.s from Camp Gordon, and . . . proud D.A.R.s from the best families." Her account of a night on the town, complete with jazz and striptease, also demonstrated why many SRP workers opted to live in Augusta or at least to spend leisure time there. Despite a law that ostensibly restricted liquor purchases to package stores, she reported that forty to fifty places in the city served mixed drinks.[37]

Kilgallen's depiction of Augusta as a boomtown worried boosters who were uneasy about the cultural and social implications of Sunbelt development. They were already well aware that the city's camellia-scented, green-shadowed veneer, polished in the prewar years, had faded amid an unsettling modernization.[38] An *Augusta Chronicle* editorial lamented that "a rash of magazine and newspaper articles" depicted the city as a "Southern version of Reno or Las Vegas." The influx of SRP tin-hats and the dubious national publicity they drew to Augusta and its environs conjured the same indignation that prominent Augustans had exhibited toward tin-can tourists in the 1920s and Erskine Caldwell's *Tobacco Road* in the Depression. It may have also called to mind how the vice-ridden nightspots of Phenix City sullied Columbus's reputation. Mayor Hugh L. Hamilton demanded that Kilgallen apologize for her portrayal of Augusta but also invited her to return so he could have "the privilege of escorting you to some of the beautiful homes, gardens, golf courses, historic sites, and to personally introduce you to some of the finest people in the world who make Augusta their home."[39]

While Augusta leaders fretted about the Savannah River Plant's impact on the city's image, they worried more about what would happen to its labor market and economy when the construction ended. In January 1951, prior to SRP construction, the two-county metropolitan area had 47,000 workers, under 6 percent of whom labored in the construction trades. Two years later, the workforce had soared to 87,480, with about 39 percent employed in construction. When only nonconstruction jobs are tallied, the expansion was much more modest, rising from 44,360 to 53,070.[40] If most of these "tinhats" departed, the area's economy would surely recalibrate to something closer to what it had been before unless permanent jobs could be created. Manufacturing seemed the best bet, but except for the six-hundred-worker Lily-Tulip Cup plant that opened in 1946, no major industries had located in the area since before the Great Depression. Expansions of existing manufacturers merely offset contractions of others' workforces.[41] The losses included Georgia-Pacific, originally founded in 1927 as Georgia Hardwood Lumber Company, which departed for the Pacific Northwest in the late 1940s. Just as Columbus druggist John Pemberton had moved to Atlanta before inventing Coca-Cola and Macon had lost the company that ultimately became Atlanta-based Delta Air Lines, Augusta eventually would see Georgia-Pacific headquartered in the Georgia capital.[42]

Before the SRP, textile mills had dominated the Augusta economy, just as in Columbus and, to a somewhat lesser extent, in Macon. Textile production concentrated in two belts—one in the Horse Creek Valley, and another along the Augusta Canal just west of downtown. The largest, the King and Sibley mills, each employed well over one thousand operatives. As late as 1953, textiles accounted for more workers in Richmond and Aiken counties than the combined total of the next three largest sectors: stone, clay, and glass; food and kindred products; and lumber and wood products. Among the latter, clay products were most noteworthy.[43] Thanks to rich deposits of clay minerals, notably kaolin, that ran in a belt underneath the Georgia and Carolina sandhills, the manufacture of bricks, tile, and other ceramic products became another key industry in the three sandhill cities. By the 1920s, Augusta ranked first in the Southeast as a brickmaking center. Located on the edge of Phinizy Swamp, the city's brickyards, along with ditches dug by the WPA in the 1930s to mitigate malarial conditions, transformed hundreds of acres of former gum and cypress swamp through the extraction of clay, leaving pits that became ponds. Merry Brothers, a brickyard dating to 1899, was among Richmond County's largest industrial employers. Another was Ohio-based Babcock and Wilcox, which had built a kaolin kiln to make firebricks in Augusta in 1928 and later expanded into ceramic insulation products for high-heat industrial uses and rocket boosters. To the extent that the area had a chemicals sector before the SRP, it was confined to processing cottonseed oil and making fertilizers needed by the surrounding region's farms and plantations.[44]

Augusta's major manufacturing sectors were essentially stagnant in terms of employment by the early 1950s. Excluding chemicals, the area's manufacturing employment dropped from 16,620 to 15,800 between 1952 and 1955. In contrast, the chemicals sector, which had never employed more than a few hundred people, suddenly jumped from 510 to 8,300 in that same period, largely a result of Savannah River Plant jobs. Cotton mills employed nineteen times as many workers as chemical plants in 1952. Just three years later, chemicals employed 87 percent as many as textiles, causing Augusta to diverge from Columbus, where textiles continued their unbroken dominance.[45] Once the SRP's 36,000-worker construction-phase payroll plummeted and the facility settled at its expected operational workforce of several thousand employees, would Augusta and the CSRA have anything to offer to turn some of these transient workers into permanent residents? This question led the chamber of commerce to appoint a special committee to explore ways to ensure that the answer would be "yes."

In the 1950s, southern boosters made a renewed effort to diversify urban economies that depended too heavily on entrenched traditional industries. Southern cities such as Knoxville, Tennessee, and Spartanburg, South Carolina, formed industrial recruitment committees and offered subsidy packages to court plant relocation. A few tried instead to "hatch our new industries rather than steal them." In Huntsville, Alabama, for example, boosters created the Huntsville Industrial Center to try to attract space-age industrial research laboratories to overcome the 1949 closure of the city's Redstone Arsenal, while promoters in the Raleigh–Durham area leveraged the presence of nearby universities to start Research Triangle Park.[46] Likewise, Birmingham, Alabama, chamber of commerce officials had formed a Committee of 100 in 1949 to seek industrial diversification to break dependence on a steel industry recently wracked by steel and coal strikes. Within two years, the so-called Pittsburgh of the South had attracted $153 million in industrial investments. In 1952, three members of Augusta's chamber committee visited Birmingham to learn about its Committee of 100. Impressed by the initiative, the delegation soon formed an Augusta counterpart with the same name, one of a number of such organizations in southern cities.[47] Augusta's Committee of 100 had a slow start. Chaired by Josef C. Patchen, an Augusta engineering firm partner who also raised beef cattle and hogs on his thousand-acre experimental farm in Burke County, the group worked first to recruit members and raise funds.[48] In 1956, after amassing $50,000 in subscriptions, the Committee of 100 became a separate organization and hired Allen H. Douglas as its managing director. The thirty-three-year-old Savannah native planned to concentrate on attracting chemical, electronics, and metallurgy manufacturers, a marked departure from the focus on livestock, food processing, and ceramics that a Georgia Tech study commissioned by the chamber's postwar planning committee had suggested twelve years earlier.[49]

Like Columbus and Macon boosters, the Committee of 100 discovered that recruiting industries was extremely slow and time-consuming. After a year with no results, an *Augusta Chronicle* editorial in April 1957 pointed to growing frustrations in the business community that led to the formation of a new business-promotion organization. The editorial warned that an allied effort was critical "for the development of Augusta into a metropolitan city."[50] Hurrying to squelch these discordant tones, the Committee of 100 hosted an open house four days later at the Richmond Hotel with chart displays showing more than 2,300 individualized contacts it had made with manufacturers nationwide. A newspaper article a month later quoted Douglas's plea for Augustans to be optimistic because optimism was essential for wooing industrial decision-makers.[51]

The city's fortunes appeared to be shifting by year's end. On Christmas Eve, the *Chronicle* reported that the B. F. Goodrich Company of Akron, Ohio, had bought 274 acres seven miles south of downtown for a possible rubber plant, news that Patchen said might "help everyone in the area to have a happy holiday season." Two months later, in a hopeful but cryptic sign, the Committee of 100 reported the acquisition of some nine hundred acres to the city's south by an unspecified industry. Perhaps they took some comfort in simply being able to announce some progress.[52] Patchen and Douglas remained tight-lipped about the transaction as they tried to manage public expectations. In June 1958, the Committee of 100 revealed that General Electric would convert a former wholesale grocery warehouse on the edge of downtown into a television picture-tube plant that would employ about seventy workers.[53] After six years of talk, the Committee of 100 finally had something to show, leading Augusta chamber president Murphy Holloway to exclaim triumphally, "Ten years ago, Augusta was more or less content to be the 'Garden City of the South.' Today, this isn't so. The atmosphere has changed completely."[54]

In December, the Committee of 100 finally revealed the plan for the nine hundred acres it had teased ten months earlier, but at this point, most readers probably missed the connection because the *Chronicle* opaquely described a 2,600-acre site on the Central of Georgia Railway near the Savannah River eleven miles south of the city. It reported that Stamford, Connecticut-based Continental Can Company would build a "mammoth" paper mill on this land that would have an initial payroll of four hundred and be a boon to the region's foresters and woodmen. The casual observer might have been forgiven for assuming that Augusta boosters' success was merely one more sign of the phenomenal rise of the pulp and paper industry that had rapidly reforested much of the region's gullied farmland, but those boosters had to do more than stand by and watch the "'big parade' of paper companies into the South."[55] Several weeks later, the circumstances surrounding Continental Can's selection of Augusta came into sharper focus when the Committee of 100 announced that to win over company executives, it had pledged to cover the $250,000 cost of 1,750 acres, a prime example of the aggressive inducements that southern cities and towns used in the postwar years. Now it did not have sufficient funds to fulfill its promise and was launching a campaign to try to collect that sum in a week's time.[56] Judging from the defensive tone of articles on the subject over the ensuing two weeks, Patchen and Douglas probably lost more than a little sleep. The Committee of 100 claimed it had kept quiet about the deal and its lack of funds because it was in a fierce competition with other cities' subsidies to try to win the plant. One day later, the *Chronicle* reported $25,000 in public subscriptions, and Douglas appeared on local television to explain that the Committee of 100 had promised the land over a year before but "couldn't show our hand" until the company announced its decision. He said that the Committee of 100 had "exhausted every other avenue" and "had no recourse but to turn to the people for help."[57]

The *Chronicle* dutifully printed daily updates on how much money had been raised to bail out Augusta's industrial scouts. A week later, more than half of the sum was in hand, but after a second week, the headline "Factory Fund at $194,000; More Likely" suggested the awkward position in which the local boosters found themselves.[58] Those old enough to remember the abortive drives to finance winter resort hotels in the 1920s must have felt a familiar hollowness. But on the fifteenth day since the revelation of the Committee of 100's predicament, the *Chronicle* declared, "The CSRA Has Spoken." Augusta's three largest banks (Georgia Railroad, C&S, and First National) had agreed, "of their own volition," to advance the remaining $50,000, a sign of "their conviction" that the business community would finish the job. The newspaper failed to report whether they did so, but the bailout nonetheless enabled a ceremonial deed transfer to Continental Can, and it finally became clear that the 2,600-acre plant site included acreage reported a year earlier, which the company had bought, and the larger tract secured by Augusta boosters and the banks that prevented a fiasco.[59]

Had the banks not intervened, the Continental Can effort might have left the Committee of 100 badly battered. As it turned out, securing the paper mill supported a future narrative about the Committee of 100 that effectively erased its first four years inside the Augusta chamber by dating it only to 1956, which enabled a more triumphal story to match that of its Birmingham counterpart.[60] Augusta's spin on the Continental Can story clearly succeeded, for five years later, when Columbus's industry-seeking efforts were just emerging from nearly two decades of inertia, an envious *Columbus Ledger* would claim that the Committee of 100 had secured the plant largely through small citizen donations.[61] Regardless, the Continental Can success proved a turning point, for the Committee of 100 had bigger news: Central of Georgia Railway had purchased a 400-acre hog farm seven miles south of Augusta and adjacent to the 274 acres that B. F. Goodrich had yet to develop. There, the railroad planned to develop Richmond County's first industrial park, which it dubbed the Miracle Mile Industrial District.[62]

By 1960, following a string of new or expanded plants, the Committee of

100 was ready to tout its successes. Tourism had long been an instrument for seeking further economic investment in Augusta. In the postwar era, the Masters Tournament enjoyed new heights of popularity. President Dwight D. Eisenhower joined Augusta National Golf Club in 1948 and made forty-five visits during his two-term presidency. CBS began nationally televising the Masters in 1956, bringing Augusta imagery into millions of Americans' homes. By 1960, the Committee of 100 had a compelling message to put before visitors in town for the annual tourney. In a large ad, it told "Mr. Spectator" that "Augusta not only has excellent GOLFING . . . it has INDUSTRY as well!" Beneath drawings of a golfer and a scientist framed by a rocket, test tubes, and a train passing factories, it trumpeted $105 million of industrial investments over the previous two years. With a map of its twenty-county area, now conflated with Augusta itself, the ad emphasized that the Committee of 100 stood ready to serve those "looking for a large town . . . or a small town near a metropolitan center."[63]

Twenty-five years earlier, an Augusta promotional book predicted that by 1975 "that section east of East Boundary and between the Savannah road [*sic*] and the river will have been drained and industrialized, with huge industries all the way to New Savannah Bluff."[64] In the mid-1960s, this prediction seemed well on its way to fulfillment. Rapid development in and around the Miracle Mile turned a vast expanse of second-growth pine forest and remnant swamplands south and east of the city into a green and gray patchwork of woods and industrial complexes, mostly paper mills and chemical plants. Between 1961 and 1965, the Miracle Mile added a Procter & Gamble detergent plant on the parcel previously held by B. F. Goodrich as well as Du Pont and Monsanto chemical plants. The Miracle Mile's success led Central of Georgia to purchase additional acreage in 1963. More plants opened around Continental Can to the south of Bush Field (now Augusta Regional Airport), including Olin Mathieson and Philadelphia Quartz chemical plants and Southern Glassine and Cox Enterprises paper mills. Another concentration emerged along Sand Bar Ferry Road to the city's east on both sides of the Savannah River, including Columbia Nitrogen's fertilizer plant and a Columbia Nipro chemical plant, both jointly owned by Pittsburgh Plate Glass (PPG) and Dutch State Mines Netherlands, and a Kimberly-Clark paper mill at Beech Island, South Carolina (see Fig. 22).[65]

FIG. 22. WORKERS AT THE NEW COLUMBIA NITROGEN PLANT, 1964. In the 1960s, Augusta boosters used generous incentives to lure many chemical plants to new industrial districts carved from the swampy expanses to the south and east of town. Columbia Nitrogen was among those that opened off Sand Bar Ferry Road near the Savannah River. The workers in this photo were riding in a golf cart made by another Augusta-based manufacturer, Club Car Inc., established in 1961. Photo by Fitz-Symms Distinctive Photography Studio. Courtesy of Augusta Museum of History, Augusta, GA.

The Committee of 100 had formed to recruit industry throughout the CSRA, but about six-tenths of the area's industrial development since the late 1950s had occurred in Richmond County.[66] Only three CSRA counties in Georgia—Richmond, Columbia, and McDuffie—had seen employment growth in the 1950s. Conditions were ripe for another organization to serve the region's rural counties. Such an organization emerged in Thomson, the seat of the Knox Brothers lumber and prefabricated-home empire, springing from an idea hatched in 1958 by boosters in McDuffie, Warren, Columbia, Wilkes, and Lincoln counties. Inspired by a regional commission in Rome, Georgia, the group decided to form the Central Savannah River Area Planning and Development Commission (CSRAPDC) in 1961 to serve all twelve CSRA counties on the Georgia side of the river.[67]

Over the next several years, the CSRAPDC functioned more as a regional complement to the Augusta–Richmond County Planning Commission and similar entities in area towns than an industrial development organization. In addition to working on regional recreation, water, and sewer plans, the CSRAPDC also supported the Committee of 100 and local industrial development bodies. It created an overall economic development program and sought grants to support it from the Economic Development Administration (EDA), one of President Lyndon B. Johnson's War on Poverty initiatives to foster development in economically distressed areas. An early success was its role in forming the Forward Four Counties Development Company in McDuffie, Taliaferro, Warren, and Wilkes counties, which obtained an EDA grant for a new industrial park in Warren County. This pilot project provided a template for several other subregional industrial parks.[68]

The CSRAPDC also attempted to catalyze further development south of Augusta. In 1968, the planning commission worked with the Committee of 100 and the newly formed Augusta–Richmond County Industrial Development Authority to finalize plans for a five-thousand-acre Riverview Industrial Park in Phinizy Swamp. With its EDA application, Augusta leaders hoped to establish a railyard there to eliminate the long-standing problem of railroad tracks crisscrossing downtown at street level. This plan meshed with Augusta planners' concurrent interest in downtown revitalization. Had boosters not failed to secure land, their twin downtown revitalization and industrial efforts might have erased what remained of an already-stressed swamp environment.[69]

The mid-1960s marked another inflection point for CSRA industrialization. A deemphasis on industrial development was underway nationally, and Augusta was no exception. A 1966 study by the Georgia Department of Public Health surveyed attitudes held by "a representative cross-section" of Augusta leaders about the most important recent and current community initiatives. While the most-cited recent initiative was "development of industry," ranking just ahead of "efficiency in government" and "efforts toward peaceful desegregation," the most-listed current need was "downtown traffic and parking improvement." In contrast, "continuing development of industry" was among the least-cited current needs. The survey found much interest in focusing on health, government, transportation, social relations, and social services, while economic development ranked lowest.[70] Augustans did not suddenly disdain economic development; rather, they started to see that traditional development, despite its successes, left many unmet community needs. Accordingly, civic leaders began to seek more broad-based community development, encompassing environment, healthcare, recreation, education, and welfare. But as the survey also showed, the condition of downtown and the central city was emerging as a key preoccupation, as was true in Macon and Columbus.[71]

By 1969, boosters felt less inclined to push for new industry, leading them to fold the Committee of 100 into the renamed Chamber of Commerce of Greater Augusta. The organization's name, unlike the "Greater Augusta" that boosters had applied to the whole trade territory in the early twentieth century, now described the narrower geography of what the U.S. Census Bureau called the Augusta Standard Metropolitan Statistical Area (SMSA). Between 1930 and 1960, metropolitan Augusta's population had risen 67 percent, while the non-metropolitan remainder of the CSRA had declined by nearly 20 percent. As the city's SMSA grew from two to seven counties in the years that followed, the metro-rural divergence persisted, exposing the limits of the CSRA conception.[72] Rural counties' industrial capacity was limited by their low and mostly unskilled workforces, while their continuing agricultural decline offered little prospect for enriching the metropolitan area at the center of the CSRA. Consequently, fall-line city boosters, who had once been as interested in rural agriculture as in urban manufacturing, refocused their efforts on serving their metropolitan areas and, with widely varying results, seeking to capture growth through annexation or consolidation. Of the three, Augusta fared by far the worst, failing to extend its city limits beyond a meager 16.5 square miles until its eventual consolidation with Richmond County a quarter century later.[73] In the meantime, Augusta's tightly drawn city limits would remain a civic fixation that made leaders focus more on the suburbs than outlying rural counties. The problem was hardly unique to Georgia's fall-line cities or even to other southern cities. As just one example, the decline of steel and coal production in the "Pittsburgh district" of western Pennsylvania and northern West Virginia led Pittsburgh boosters to reframe their ambitions for metropolitan growth around the city and its suburbs.[74]

As the regional vision faltered, so did the core pursuits of CSRA boosters: industrial development and river navigation. Augusta boosters announced fewer and fewer new industries and expansions as the 1970s and 1980s wore on. Columbus and Macon, which had lagged Augusta in new industrialization in the late 1950s and early 1960s, hoped to break the grip of textile dependency with their first industrial parks, which opened in 1964, although Macon's interstate highway connections and proximity to Atlanta's Hartsfield International Airport positioned it better than the more isolated Columbus.[75] Navigation proved a conundrum for all three of Georgia's sandhill cities. It required capital outlays that only the federal government could afford. Federal officials were loath to fund channel improvements or maintenance in the absence of clear signs of growing commercial use of rivers, but it was hard to produce such growth given the plateauing of industrial development and the continued lack of a reliable channel depth that made shipping unprofitable for companies. By 1971, Columbus's modern port, created less than a decade earlier, was pronounced a failure after silting up to the point that two companies—Dow Chemical and PPG—that had been attracted by the promise of the port had departed the city. By the end of the decade, Augusta's inland port had met the same fate.[76]

The failure to sustain industrial and river development into the 1970s led to greater reliance on military payrolls and, eventually, the low-wage service jobs that would come with the rise of heritage tourism by the 1980s. But boosters' previous successes in the 1960s, which were precipitated by the stimulus of Clarks Hill Dam and the Savannah River Plant, also carried social and environmental consequences. The industries to the immediate south and east of Augusta strained both people and the natural environment. Despite hundreds of millions of dollars of investment, Augusta's industrial boom produced relatively few jobs because of their use of labor-saving automated equipment, a variation on the theme of industrial automation that gutted many cities' manufacturing employment in and after the 1960s. Very few paper and chemical plants on the edge of Augusta employed more than two hundred workers. Some, including the Du Pont and Philadelphia Quartz

plants, employed only about a dozen people each. And, as in Savannah earlier, these jobs were located on the periphery of the city, away from where
the greatest employment needs were.[77]

Thanks to its conservation of a vast 315-square-mile forested tract, a "verdant island" that was even visible from space, the Savannah River Plant
itself had only modest health implications for the surrounding region, but
inside its facilities was a different matter. The SRP's production of radioac-
tive materials exposed its operators to carcinogens, and ultimately tens of
thousands sought compensatory action.[78] Lacking the same forest buffer
as the SRP, the city's southside neighborhoods bore the brunt of Augusta's
"new" industries in and around the Miracle Mile. As in cities elsewhere,
working-class—and especially Black—Augustans had always borne the brunt
of manmade environmental hazards. Jim Crow customs and policies had
channeled most Black Augustans into the city's south side, and as mechanization forced thousands of African Americans off farmland, discrimination
and industrial encroachment constrained their suburban housing options
mostly to a narrow band east of U.S. 1 and west of Georgia Highway 56 (New
Savannah Road).[79]

After World War II, a number of rural migrants to Augusta built houses
in Aragon Park and Hyde Park, adjacent outlying developments earmarked
for Black buyers on the floodplain to the south of the city limits. In the first
half of the 1960s, Augusta echoed the civil rights advances made elsewhere
in the South by desegregating its public accommodations and beginning
to integrate public schools. An expanding Black electorate had also helped
two Black candidates win election to the city council. Still, racial inequities
persisted in the provision of basic utilities and services, leading citizens to
form the Hyde and Aragon Park Improvement Committee (HAPIC) in 1968.
Industrial downsizing would open the way for HAPIC to begin to press for
environmental remediation, but by the time residents were better informed
about nearby sources of pollution, it was too late to prevent the many rare
cancers and other diseases that long-term exposure had inflicted.[80] As was
true nationwide, Augusta boosters' singular pursuit of industry while preserving Jim Crow revealed the limits of the civil rights revolution to overcome persistent urban racial inequality and its public health consequences.

Just as these and other surrounding Black neighborhoods saw CSRA
boosterism further degrade public health conditions, they also endured its

magnification of the long-standing liabilities of occupying a floodplain. For well over a century, more affluent Augustans on the Hill had lived without fear of environmental hazards. Out of sight and out of mind, Phinizy Swamp had long been the receptacle for Augusta's untreated sewage, and by the 1960s, it was also befouled by chemical pollutants in an echo of what had happened on the lower river after Savannah's push for chemical industry development in the 1930s.[81] The postwar reengineering of the Savannah River to fulfill Augusta boosters' vision may have saved the city from flooding and stimulated the area's attractiveness to industry, but it did so at the expense of Black Richmond Countians. Every time Clarks Hill Dam released higher volumes of water, it forced the closing of the Butler Creek gate downriver at New Savannah Bluff, which in turn prevented Oates Creek from draining into the Savannah River. As a result, southside residents endured the recurring problem of Oates Creek spilling out of its banks and causing raw sewage and liquid toxins to back up into their yards and homes. Only in 1988, after more than two decades of federal and county inaction, did a firm plan begin to redress the oversight of earlier Augusta leaders preoccupied with flood control for the central city.[82]

Generations of fall-line city boosters had looked to their rivers and their trade territories as economic assets. They had long exploited rivers' capacities as conduits of commerce and generators of the power needed to operate mills. While Macon had carved out a particularly expansive Middle Georgia region that some boosters went so far as to dub the "State of Macon," Columbus and Augusta had labored to overcome the added challenge of unifying trade areas that spanned state borders. The Chattahoochee River had produced division, notably in Columbus's direction of river-generated electricity toward Georgia and Phenix City's challenges to Fort Benning officers and Columbus industrial recruiters alike. In contrast, Augustans proved especially adept at forging ties across the Georgia–South Carolina line. The CSRA conception epitomized postwar Augusta's cultivation of a regional approach to economic development. In addition, with cooperation from their congressional representatives in both states, Augusta boosters secured stronger federal commitments, delivering the region its largest reservoir, "permanent" status for its major military installation, and a mammoth atomic plant that singlehandedly recast the CSRA's economic structure. Despite the massive infusion of federal largesse, however, Augusta struggled to escape a new form of economic dependency that was every bit as profound as the dead hand of Columbus's entrenched textile industry. Moreover, the dream of becoming a sustainable inland port proved elusive despite Augustans' best efforts, and the long-awaited growth of "new" industries produced disappointingly few jobs while degrading the environment and accenting the social disparities that traced the fall line there as in other sandhill cities.

SIX

𝔅UILDING THE 𝔉UTURE FROM 𝔒UR 𝔓AST

On July 30, 1975, hatchbacks and station wagons buzzed past the peach trees, sourwoods, crepe myrtles, dogwoods, live oaks, and pines that lined the sea of asphalt surrounding Macon Mall. The carefully selected trees, its Montgomery-based developer claimed, evoked "Historic Macon." If so, these nods to the shopping center's namesake city were forgotten the moment shoppers left the steamy heat and entered the two-level, air-conditioned mall on this opening day. They strolled on patterned brown-and-tan carpet concourses, rode the escalators and glass-bubble elevator, and beheld the luxuriance of tropical trees and plants. Some lunched at Chick-fil-A, others at Morrison's Cafeteria. Perhaps some left clutching bags filled with suede bell-bottoms, a digital watch, a Polaroid camera, aquarium fish, or a Linda Ronstadt eight-track.[1]

Designed to be the new retail hub of Middle Georgia, the 1.2-million-square-foot mall transformed the prospects for downtown Macon.[2] Downtown's share of Bibb County retail sales had declined gradually over the preceding decade after the opening of the much smaller Westgate Mall in 1961, but few downtown stores had closed. In contrast, Macon Mall slashed downtown's share by about half in one year.[3] Davison's, an Atlanta subsidiary of Macy's that had acquired department stores on Augusta's Broad Street and Macon's Cherry Street in 1944, closed its Macon store upon opening at Macon Mall. So did Sears and Belk-Matthews.[4] Although Macon was 35 percent African American, one downtown promoter's comment after the mall's opening made clear that most merchants cared mainly about white shoppers: "Today's shopper is older, blacker, less educated and less affluent than the downtown shopper of two years ago."[5] In choosing to locate in the mall, the local merchants that left downtown and national retailers that entered the Macon market for the first time trailed the white flight to the suburbs. Those merchants that stayed, including the Macon-based Burden-Smith and Jos. N. Neel department stores, tried to ignore the local wag who quipped that "the mall will do for downtown Macon what Sherman did for Atlanta."[6]

Macon Mall's developer may have wanted its landscaping to suggest "Historic Macon," but the mall's announcement in 1973 galvanized a campaign to use Macon's actual historic cityscape to revitalize its downtown. Over the previous two decades, Macon leaders, like those in Augusta, Columbus, and countless other midsized cities, had refocused their boosterism on their metropolitan area rather than on the larger surrounding trade territory, but they also began to worry about suburbia's impact on the central city in the early 1970s. Although they continued to promote modern downtown office buildings and suburban industrial parks alongside a selective portrayal of Macon's heritage, their fixation on competing with Atlanta for investment yielded to a growing interest in learning from Savannah's use of its historic architecture to create a tourism-based economy. Macon boosters' recast metropolitan ambitions signaled an acquiescence to becoming a satellite of Atlanta.[7]

The mall accomplished what a decade of gradual decline had not; it produced a sense of urgency to revitalize downtown. The relatively late arrival of Macon's first major mall—sixteen years after Atlanta's Lenox Square and ten years after Columbus Square in Columbus—shaped the response to downtown decline in Macon, just as it did in Augusta, where two suburban malls opened within a week of each other in 1978.[8] The tardy appearance of major malls in two of Georgia's three fall-line cities helped their downtowns dominate their trade areas long enough for planners to observe how other cities had responded to similar problems. It also shortened the period when planners remained in thrall to massive clearance and modernist towers and plazas and, especially in Macon, nurtured a shared vision among a rising cadre of historic preservationists and downtown revitalization planners and backers. The Greater Macon Chamber of Commerce had long portrayed Macon as a mélange of romantic past and dynamic present, a blend that local boosters increasingly emphasized in the 1960s. As late as the early 1970s, boosters used historic sites mainly as hooks for luring industry, business, and conventions, but the mounting impact of suburbanization, particularly after Macon Mall opened, encouraged a deeper commitment to reviving a historic cityscape as a tool for urban revitalization. By the early 1980s, Macon's mostly white civic leaders had reached a consensus that located the city's future in its past.

MACON ON THE MOVE

As boosters reimagined the future of surrounding counties as suburban rather than rural after World War II, they began to emphasize diversified industrial, commercial, and service development to accompany agriculturally oriented industries and military bases. The Macon Area Development Committee (MADC) attracted many new industries in the immediate postwar years, especially in ceramics, paper, and building materials, before losing momentum. Then Macon leaders found new inspiration in Augusta's industrial boosterism of the late 1950s.[9] In 1962, after Bibb County representatives secured enabling legislation in the Georgia General Assembly, the city and county joined in support of forming the Macon–Bibb County Industrial Authority. William A. Fickling Sr., a native of the sandhills town of Butler who had started Macon's leading real estate firm in 1937 and served as chairman of the MADC, became the industrial authority's chairman. While Columbus boosters were grasping at straws to try to have a new interstate highway route designated for their city, Fickling had been instrumental in the late 1950s in getting state and federal officials to route Interstate 75 parallel to the old Dixie Highway through Macon rather than bypassing the city a few miles to the west. The decision would aid industrial development and downtown access but also slice through Pleasant Hill, Macon's largest Black neighborhood.[10] Voters approved the industrial authority to sell bonds, assemble land, and build and lease buildings to recruit industry. In 1963, the Greater Macon Chamber of Commerce introduced its new "Macon on the Move" slogan, which reflected boosters' anticipation that interstate highways would aid industrialization. In 1964, the city conveyed land adjacent to the Macon Municipal Airport in southern Bibb County to the industrial authority to develop Airport Industrial Park, Macon's first zoned industrial district.[11]

Ad Appears Today In Wall Street Journal

Another ad promoting Macon as a Southeastern office center appears in the *Wall
Street Journal* today. The ad is part of a
series of national advertising prepared by
the Economic Development Department of
the Greater Macon Chamber of Commerce
and financed by Bibb County through the
Macon-Bibb County Industrial Authority.

The current ad, which pictures the new
Georgia Power Building, names Macon's
growth rate, central location and new facilities as reasons that businesses should locate
here.

FIG. 23. GREATER MACON CHAMBER OF COMMERCE ADVERTISEMENT, 1968. In the postwar decades, boosters promoted Macon as a Sunbelt growth center. Through advertising campaigns in national publications such as *The Wall Street Journal*, they touted Macon's location astride two interstate highways and pointed to its sprouting downtown skyline to assure investors that Macon was "thoroughly modern." Courtesy of Visit Macon, Macon, GA.

Macon's pursuit of industry, the growth of Robins Air Force Base in neighboring Houston County, and the coming of freeways prompted rosy predictions of further metropolitan growth. With I-75 and I-16 set to meet in
Macon, the city fared far better than Columbus, whose boosters' hopes for an
interstate remained remote.[12] A 1967 report by the National Planning Association projected that in the next eight years, the Macon metropolitan area
would outperform Phoenix and Atlanta in population growth and would
rank second behind Tallahassee in the Southeast. Macon chamber officials
greeted the report with the expected enthusiasm. Executive secretary Charles
Bundy commented that the coming transportation improvements positioned
Macon to take advantage of industries' growing concerns that Atlanta was
becoming "so big, so expensive."[13] With industrial authority support, the
chamber launched a series of national advertising campaigns starting in
1967, in which interstates added a new dimension to Macon's promotion
of its centralized location. In some of these ads, the right stem of the "N" in
"MACON" formed an I-75/I-16 signpost (see Fig. 23).[14] A subsequent cam-

paign, titled "Macon, Ga., an important place to be," featured cartoon-like ads depicting different aspects of Macon on a Georgia map and a tagline that extolled the benefits of locating "right in the middle." With these ads, the chamber exaggerated Atlanta's distance from the center of the state, much as Macon's capital removal advocates had done six decades earlier. Each ad depicted the capital city in the far northwestern corner of Georgia near Chattanooga.[15]

The industrial authority and chamber efforts indeed extended the economic lift provided by military investment. They fostered a business expansion that continued well into the 1970s, driven by the opening of Ocmulgee East Industrial Park on the site of Camp Wheeler. The campus attracted Tokyo-based YKK to build a zipper plant, followed by a regional office of the Government Employees Insurance Company (GEICO) and a Brown and Williamson Tobacco cigarette factory. These three firms alone employed several thousand workers. The combination of military and industrial investments in southern Bibb and Houston counties delivered strong growth to the Macon area, like its fall-line counterparts. Although Bibb County's population growth slowed dramatically in the 1960s, the Macon metropolitan area roughly doubled in the three decades after World War II. Unlike the three decades preceding the war, most growth was occurring in suburban areas. But successes in attracting new commerce proved unsustainable because Macon struggled to provide new water and sewer connections by the late 1970s.[16]

Meanwhile, local leaders expressed a similar confidence in downtown in the 1960s. Comforted by the absence of large suburban shopping centers that made Macon sixth among all U.S. metropolitan areas for the proportion of its retail trade located downtown even in the late 1960s, they believed downtown needed only modest interventions such as storefront modernizations, shopper incentives, and special events to attract Middle Georgians.[17] In 1963, the chamber formed a Downtown Council that persuaded merchants to add aluminum fronts to their facades, expanded the "park and shop plan" that validated shoppers' parking, added sidewalk planters on Cherry Street, and gave Macon's Christmas parade a Middle Georgia format by inviting floats, bands, and other entries from outlying counties starting in 1964.[18] In an inversion of the chamber's earlier goodwill tours, the Downtown Council also sponsored shopping tours in 1965 for women from several Middle Georgia towns to entice them to choose Macon over Atlanta or Savannah. Participants arrived at the S&S Cafeteria on Cherry Street for morning coffee and doughnuts and enjoyed a city tour, a fashion-show luncheon sponsored by local merchants, and an afternoon of shopping in "Downtown Macon, Middle Georgia's Fashion Center."[19]

Although city leaders continued to emphasize conventional ways of safeguarding downtown, the Macon–Bibb County Planning and Zoning Commission retained the Atlanta firm of Adley Associates in 1968 to guide its downtown planning. In the same year, Augusta's planning commission commissioned another Atlanta firm to plan its downtown, suggesting how planning principles in the fall-line cities were filtered through firms in larger southern cities, especially Atlanta.[20] The resulting report envisioned both cosmetic enhancements and more sweeping redevelopment. Mirroring local white leaders' attitudes, its suggested enhancements—a pedestrian mall on Cotton Avenue and mall-like streetscape enhancements on Cherry Street—contrasted sharply with its recommendations to clear and redevelop the buildings along Broadway and Fifth Street and incorporate portions of these streets into a boulevard to connect to I-16. Unnoted in the report was that the latter area attracted mostly African Americans. Also unmentioned was that the envisioned "new shopping complex" at Cherry and Fifth Streets would require demolishing the grand but careworn fifty-year-old Terminal Station.[21]

The "new shopping complex" corresponded to a plan revealed earlier that year. Atlanta's C&S Bank president Mills B. Lane Jr. announced his bank's intent to demolish Terminal Station to build a $30 million complex called Commerce Square with two department stores, a shopping mall, and two office towers. C&S and First National Bank and Trust, a subsidiary of Atlanta-based Trust Company, had long tethered Macon financially to Georgia's capital city. In Atlanta, Lane had recently done the seemingly impossible, financing a massive downtown stadium that lured the Braves from Milwaukee. This apparent miracle worker now wanted to deliver a major boost to downtown Macon.[22] Just as Lane had enticed the Braves with the promise of a stadium, he persuaded the Atlanta-based Rich's department store to abandon its plan to build a branch on land it had purchased in the Macon suburbs. Rich's committed to Commerce Square with conditions that included construction of a complete cloverleaf on I-16 and widening of the Fifth Street Bridge over the Ocmulgee River to facilitate regional access to the development. In another reflection of how the fall-line cities sought to

validate their metropolitan statures by courting concepts and capital origi-
nating in Atlanta, an executive in C&S's Macon office exclaimed that having
a Rich's "puts Macon in the big league."[23]

While Macon waited for the hopeful news that Commerce Square might
strengthen downtown as the hub of Middle Georgia, Mayor Ronnie Thompson, a Cherry Street jewelry store owner who had grown up in an Augusta
mill village during the Great Depression, regularly injected himself into
downtown matters in dubious or even harmful ways. In 1969, he oversaw the
addition of more than fifty flagpoles on Poplar Street to fly flags of every U.S.
state and territory, but the so-called Avenue of Flags did little to boost downtown business.[24] In the following year, he ordered police to "shoot to kill"
after members of the Black Liberation Front picketed Cherry Street stores to
protest the city's refusal to hire African American firemen and policemen or
pave dirt streets in Black neighborhoods. The mayor's heavy-handed stance
on "law and order" earned him the nickname "Machine Gun Ronnie." In a region whose metropolitan growth coalitions embraced a combination of what
one historian characterized as "rapid economic development and enforced
racial harmony," boosters worried that outsiders might perceive Macon, in
contrast to Atlanta, as a city *not* "too busy to hate."[25]

WHERE OLD SOUTH CHARM MEETS NEW SOUTH PROGRESS

Even as the chamber was pursuing its "Macon on the Move" campaign to
attract downtown retailers and offices and suburban industries, it began to
support efforts to highlight the city's historical assets—at least the ones that
sugarcoated or deflected attention from the bitter legacy of white supremacy.
Since the early twentieth century, boosters had used Macon's antebellum
homes, a reconstructed frontier fort, and Indian mounds to help the city
stand out as a place to relocate a business or hold a convention. By the 1960s,
with the convention and tourist trade on the rise and interstates poised to
augment Macon's central location in Georgia, local leaders hoped to cash in.

When the Georgia Chamber of Commerce launched its "Stay and See
Georgia" campaign in 1962 to try to make the state more than a stop on
the way to Florida, the Macon chamber appointed retired textile executive
John J. McKay Jr. to chair "attractions and tourism" on its Stay and See Ma-

con committee. McKay, the son of an insurance agent and a member of the local Daughters of the American Revolution (DAR) and United Daughters of the Confederacy (UDC), had grown up on the red-brick Orange Street in the historic College Hill neighborhood (named for the onetime Wesleyan College campus) on the sloping sandhills immediately west of downtown. Having nurtured a lifelong love for Macon's past, in retirement, he poured himself into developing slide lectures, mapping tours, and crafting brochures.[26] McKay helped the chamber frame Macon as the "Heart of Historic Georgia" and a city "Where Old South Charm Meets New South Progress" in brochures. These taglines were evolutions from earlier booster rhetoric. By embellishing the half-century-old "Heart of Georgia" tagline and building a conceptual bridge between Old South "charm" and New South "progress," McKay unified endeavors long pursued separately by clubwomen and businessmen in most cities. Indeed, McKay's work was a programmatic extension of efforts by women's ancestral organizations such as the DAR and UDC to safeguard and celebrate specific historic landmarks of the antebellum period.[27]

The chamber's new brochures packaged a mythic Macon, tying prehistoric past to heritage-steeped present. They presented the Ocmulgee Mounds as revealing the "hidden secrets" of prehistoric people and as a "sacred ground" of friendly Creek Indians who stood with the English against the "Spanish and hostile Indians" and later "negotiated" with Thomas Jefferson to bequeath their land (with no mention of their forced removal). Fort Hawkins, partially reconstructed in concrete by the Works Progress Administration for the DAR in 1938, was cast as Jefferson's "gateway to the Louisiana Purchase." Macon's planners purportedly used "ancient Babylon" as the model for laying out the "nation's best designed" business district. According to one brochure, the columned mansions on the hills just west of downtown "were saved for your enjoyment by staunch Confederate defenders." That Macon's beauty spots were "saved" exclusively for whites' enjoyment was underscored by the fate of Baconsfield Park, whose donor Augustus Bacon had deeded the land on the condition that the city prohibit Black use in perpetuity. While McKay was packaging the white city, Black Maconites were driven from Baconsfield Park on March 31, 1963, by a "pistol-waving caretaker," setting off a decade-long legal battle that eventually reached the U.S. Supreme Court. Although the Court ruled against the constitutionality of Bacon's stricture, the city

FIG. 24. MACON COLISEUM UNDER CONSTRUCTION, 1967. Boosters made explicit reference to the nearby Ocmulgee Mounds as the design inspiration for the pyramidal Macon Coliseum, a major new convention, sports, concert, and event facility located along I-16 across the Ocmulgee River from downtown. Located on what was once part of Muscogee (Creek) ceremonial grounds, the Coliseum relied on a federal urban renewal project that displaced more than four hundred families from East Macon. It became a key part of Macon's ongoing effort to use its central location in Georgia to lure state conventions and meetings. Courtesy of Middle Georgia Archives, Washington Memorial Library, Macon, GA.

would return the land to Bacon's heirs, who in turn sacrificed the park to developers rather than abandoning Jim Crow. In a city still struggling for civil rights advances, McKay's work likewise erased the more than one-third Black population's part in that history, save one brochure's mention that the Louisville Slave Market was only eighty-four miles east.[28]

While Macon's cultivation of an image as a historic but modern city focused mostly on an elite white conception of the antebellum period, the area's prehistoric past and Native American presence into the early nineteenth century added another dimension to 1960s presentations of Macon's heritage. Ocmulgee National Monument's Great Temple Mound became almost an unofficial trademark for Macon starting in the late 1960s. The park's earthen mounds inspired the new pyramidal Macon Coliseum that opened along I-16 across the river from downtown in late 1968 (see Fig. 24). The Coliseum, which occupied land that was originally part of the Ocmulgee Old Fields, relied on an urban renewal project that demolished the homes of 420 families, two-thirds of them Black. The mounds also inspired a similarly styled tourist information center that opened three years later along I-75. Located sixteen miles northwest of town, the mound-shaped center exhorted travelers to stop in Macon rather than skirting it on the I-475 bypass on their way to Florida.[29]

Along with inspiring additions to Macon's tourism infrastructure, the Ocmulgee monument served Macon boosters who understood the extent to which their city's metropolitan ambitions entailed accepting that Macon was a satellite unable to escape Atlanta's orbit. In 1969, two dozen Macon leaders presented the Middle Georgia city to some of the state's leading industrial developers at a chamber-sponsored luncheon at Atlanta's Capital City Club. Each developer received copies of promotional materials, including a booklet titled "Macon: An Important Place to Be," that situated the city in a historical frame. In one striking pairing, a woodcut of a Native American man clasping a bow and arrow appeared next to a photo of spectators inside the new Macon Coliseum. Its caption observed that the coliseum was "modeled after the ceremonial mounds at nearby Ocmulgee, where thousands of Indians once gathered." "From the Coliseum," it continued, "you can travel a thousand years in a couple of miles." The booklet used the mound builders to connect the past and present while ignoring the Trail of Tears. Not only had Native Americans inspired the coliseum's design, but also "the people we call Master Farmers established a tradition that the Coliseum continues: Macon is a meeting place for the entire Southeast."[30]

The mounds also became the site of an experiment calculated to enhance Macon's image as a center of historical attractions. In 1972, on the chamber's invitation, nineteen Muscogee (Creek) people moved from Okmulgee, Oklahoma, to work at Ocmulgee National Monument and the I-75 information center. Some served as guides, while others performed ceremonial dances or staffed the new Creek Indian Trading Post at the monument. The "reintroduction" of Creeks to Macon was the brainchild of chamber president Charles H. Jones, a native of Thomaston in Upson County about forty-five miles to the west.[31] It was not the first attempt to exploit Native American culture to enliven a site whose last occupants, the Creeks, shared at most an obscure connection to the earlier mound builders and had been driven off the land. In 1951, about three dozen Oklahoma Creeks went to the dedication of the park's new museum, and the chamber invited Creeks to participate in a two-day festival the following year.[32] Two decades later, Jones pursued a much larger ambition that might give Macon a year-round spectacle. Like McKay's whitewashed presentation of antebellum Macon, Jones's vision romanticized a prehistoric culture by importing Native Americans at a time when many of the city's African Americans still endured substandard housing on dirt streets. Jones's idea disregarded the fact that modern Creeks had neither a well-understood connection to the mound builders nor many inherited stories about their ancestors' lives in Middle Georgia. Rather than the "return" or "homecoming" that Jones imagined, their migration owed more to Native American desires to seek opportunities they lacked on the reservation.[33]

Jones's persuasiveness helped him win support from the National Park Service and, despite misgivings among some Creek elders, from Muscogee Nation chief Claude A. Cox.[34] With the blessing of the Inter-Tribal Council of the Five Civilized Tribes in Oklahoma, the promise of jobs, scholarships, and housing support, and a desire to escape the Muscogee Nation's high unemployment, the first Creeks began arriving in Macon in May 1972.[35] Although chamber leaders initially treated them like celebrities, the Creeks found their integration into Middle Georgia society stilted and their treatment at times demeaning. Only after they objected did the chamber take down an I-75 billboard for the tourist information center that read "Real, Live Indians."[36] Gerald Harjo had been promised a job as a guide but was tasked with mowing lawns, leading him to protest, "I didn't have to come all the way to Macon, Ga. to cut grass."[37]

The apex of local interest in the newcomers was Creek Indian Week, a several-day event in October 1972 to mark the Bibb County sesquicentennial and the National Parks centennial (measured from the establishment of Yellowstone). The Macon chamber, observed one Atlanta journalist, "blithely dubbed the return of the Creeks, 'The Trail of Cheers,' and struck medals commemorating the event."[38] The festival utilized the Ocmulgee National Monument, Macon Coliseum, and the Mulberry and Third Street Parks downtown, and included pottery-making and archery demonstrations, ceremonial dances, a miniature "Indian Village," and a downtown parade.[39] But the highlight was its historical pageant written and directed by a Fostoria, Ohio-based firm. The pageant included about three hundred children and several adults, but only two Creeks who sat "virtually motionless" and "pantomimed occasionally to the narrators' voices." The play ended with only a "perfunctory reference to the leave-taking of the Creeks" followed by "a burst of patriotic pageantry."[40]

Though they had imagined adventure and fulfillment, the Creeks faced daily indignities in Macon. Some monument visitors insinuated that Ben Checotah was not "a real Indian" because he was not wearing feathers, and some casually addressed Harjo as "chief" or ordered him to perform a rain dance.[41] As their novelty faded, many Creeks sensed that they were little more than living relics to people whose image of Native Americans was informed by Hollywood and television Westerns. Having grown frustrated by the insensitive questions and taunting by locals and tourists, two-thirds of the Creeks had paid their own way to return to Oklahoma by the end of 1975.[42]

The experiment of recreating a Creek village ended with hard feelings because the Creeks grew resentful of boosters' attempts to cast them as modern primitives in a rose-colored fantasy while losing sight of promises to support their real-world aspirations. Yet, it had served its purpose of stimulating tourism to the national monument and supporting the chamber's portrayal of Macon as lying at the heart of a distinctive region where a romantic past and dynamic present converged. Even as the Creek presence dwindled, the opening of Macon Mall had galvanized civic leaders in more concerted action to use historic landmarks not only as tourist hooks but also as a means of reinvigorating the central city.

CAPITALIZING ON CHARM

After five years of vacillation and dimming prospects, C&S admitted in November 1973 that the Commerce Square project was dead, a casualty of Macon Mall.[43] Eager to minimize the setback, Mayor Thompson declared that he would prioritize downtown revitalization in the remainder of his term. First, he led a delegation to Walt Disney World to study its monorail despite admitting that the city had sought "no consultation with professional designers." Just days after returning, Thompson led another junket to Germany and

Sweden, also at public expense, to collect ideas for a possible Cherry Street pedestrian mall, even though many U.S. cities had adopted this concept. Then, he took a delegation to Japan and Taiwan, ostensibly to recruit industry. The *Macon News* lamented that the "globetrotting mayor" was "more interested in playing at being mayor than in doing the work of a mayor."[44]

By making Commerce Square infeasible, Macon Mall effectively saved Terminal Station. It also reinforced an upswell in local interest in historic preservation, which became closely connected to downtown revitalization in part because Mayor Thompson's successor, Buckner F. Melton, with an eye toward recasting the city's image and attracting tourists, proved adept at making it fit seamlessly with downtown renewal.[45] Melton, a native of Arlington in rural southwestern Georgia, had an even broader vision for placing the central city at the heart of Macon's metropolitan ambitions. His administration encouraged renewal of the old industrial district east of Terminal Station, but an elaborate plan to fuse historic preservation, downtown revitalization, and reindustrialization failed because of the insurmountable problems of assembling sufficiently large industrial parcels to compete with suburban industrial parks.[46]

The mayor also hoped to salvage a regional reputation sullied by Thompson's antics. Melton and his Community Development director Mary Costello were especially aware of the need to atone for his predecessor's adversarial relationship with African Americans. To that end, they displayed a greater commitment to matching central-city revitalization with some meaningful progress in physical improvements in Black neighborhoods such as Pleasant Hill. However, these commitments trailed downtown efforts and largely came to fruition after Melton left office in 1979.

City Hall's shifting downtown strategies signaled a desire to mend Macon's image and grapple with suburbanization, but they also reflected a growing preservation movement that inspired many other cities around the country beginning in the mid-1960s; Macon was a bit ahead of the curve. Inspired by the example of the Historic Savannah Foundation, which had since its 1955 inception used preservation to make tourism a leading Savannah industry, all three major Georgia fall-line cities saw the potential of preservation to renew interest in intown living and thereby invigorate their downtowns to respond to suburban competition.[47] Macon's Middle Georgia Historical Society (MGHS) led the way in 1964, followed by Historic Augusta Inc. in

1965 and the Historic Columbus Foundation in 1966. As the decade closed, civic leaders in Columbus and Augusta commissioned Carl Feiss, a Cleveland, Ohio–born architectural historian who shaped the National Historic Preservation Act of 1966, to evaluate architectural inventories taken by local chapters of the Junior League, a national service organization comprised mostly of young, well-connected white women. Feiss also undertook a similar survey in Macon. Using these surveys, each city's preservationists defined and obtained the designation of an intown National Register district—with Columbus being first, in 1969—and, in the mid-1970s, set up revolving funds like the ones pioneered in Charleston and Savannah to acquire, restore, and resell residential properties in these districts.[48]

Macon's revolving fund sprang from a new preservation organization, the Macon Heritage Foundation (MHF), the product of the 1975 merger of the MGHS with a property owners' group called In-Town Macon Neighborhood Association (IMNA), which had formed the previous year. In-Town included College Hill and the residential area to the south around Mercer University. The largest homes on College Hill were imposing white-columned antebellum mansions, some of which had been converted into rooming houses during World War II. As early as 1958, in his survey of Macon's housing conditions, the Jacksonville planner George W. Simons Jr. had suggested forming a property owners' association that might "take voluntary action" to forestall blight.[49] Seventeen years later, Atlanta transplants Peter and Maryel Battin and their neighbors heeded this call when they organized to try to exert more control over the neighborhood where they had chosen to invest in restoration.[50]

The work of preservation-minded residents like the Battins, many of whom were forsaking suburban living to stake their future in the city, provided an important foundation for the city to build on. In a 1976 study, the planning commission observed that In-Town, which had been "on its way to becoming a slum ghetto," now, thanks to the IMNA, had "the potential to recapture the flair of 19th century Macon."[51] Just as Savannah's historic district had attracted a return of middle-class and affluent residents and a growing number of tourists that injected new vigor into downtown, municipal and business leaders in Georgia's sandhill cities began to find similar promise in their own architectural fabric that might counterbalance the poorer, mostly Black neighborhoods that otherwise predominated in the central city. Like the similar downtown-adjacent neighborhoods of Southwest Columbus and Augusta's Pinch Gut (which lumberman and suburban developer Peter S. Knox Jr. rebranded "Olde Town" as he became the leading restorer of historic houses in the 1970s), In-Town might also provide new middle-class patrons for downtown businesses. Significantly, through the MHF's efforts, the Macon Historic District that formed in 1975 also encompassed downtown.[52]

The Macon Heritage Foundation took an active interest in downtown from its inception, partly reflecting the personal commitment of Phil Walden, a native of Greenville, South Carolina, who had grown up on Macon's west side and attended Mercer. Better known as the former booking agent and manager for the Macon rhythm-and-blues artist Otis Redding and the co-founder of Macon's Capricorn Records, which helped launch the Allman Brothers Band that made Macon "the cradle of southern rock," Walden also became one of Macon's staunchest proponents of historic preservation. In 1975, he was named MHF's board chairman and appointed to the planning commission. That year, Capricorn acquired a nineteenth-century storefront on Cotton Avenue. Walden's company restored the building to house the recording studio's offices and transformed the vacant lot next door into Capricorn Memorial Park to honor Redding and Duane Allman, both of whom had died in accidents. The *Macon Telegraph* applauded Capricorn's work in an editorial titled "Capitalizing on Charm."[53]

Walden believed that Macon Mall need not bring the demise of downtown and hoped to encourage other owners to restore their downtown facades, although he was disheartened by their "flat refusals" to entertain the idea. While Walden and the MHF pressed for a zoning ordinance to make demolitions more difficult in the historic district, they settled for a carrot rather than a stick by looking at ways to incentivize property owners to restore downtown buildings. Despite his efforts, the city's elites were loath to fully embrace him. They chafed at his use of the Grand Opera House for a rock concert to support historic preservation, and he was reportedly denied financing from old-line Macon banks and "blackballed from admission to the Idle Hour Country Club, the only one in town that counts." Walden resigned after only one year on the planning commission, but by the time he left, the commission had produced a design study that ensured that facade rehabilitation would be a key part of Macon's strategy for recapturing its "charm."[54]

While property owners may have been hesitant, the announcement of

Macon Mall catalyzed a sense of urgency among downtown revitalization backers. Less than two months after the Commerce Square plan dissolved, the Macon chamber urged creating a downtown revitalization agency with the power to issue bonds. Georgia legislators quickly approved the formation of the Macon–Bibb County Urban Development Authority (UDA).[55] The agency's first major action was to accept a new downtown study by a design team sponsored by the American Institute of Architects and headed by Macon planner Robert Olson, which resulted in plans to create a plaza on Cotton Avenue between City Hall and Macon Auditorium (then undergoing a federally funded restoration), convert Cherry Street into a mall-like "promenade" between Third Street and Broadway, and clear and redevelop the largely African American block on Broadway between Mulberry and Cherry Streets.[56] Black businesses had occupied downtown's edges since Reconstruction. Early pockets were located just west on Cotton Avenue near City Hall and around the open-air cotton market on Poplar Street, as well as at Bridge Row near the Fifth Street Bridge on downtown's eastern fringe. The latter area gradually expanded southwestward along Broadway across Walnut and Mulberry Streets to Cherry Street in the early twentieth century. Remaking Cotton Avenue and Broadway was inseparable from long-standing white efforts to control, if not curtail, the Black presence downtown.[57]

Of the design team's proposals, the city prioritized the one that required the least investment. Unlike Augusta, whose leaders had recently commissioned I. M. Pei to develop a $4-million, four-block modified pedestrian mall on Broad Street, or Columbus, where Arthur Cotton Moore's aspirational design for a combined pedestrian mall and canal on Broadway was deemed infeasible, the UDA opted for a modest redesign of three blocks of Cherry Street that might catalyze public interest and lead to a broader revitalization.[58] Dubbed Cherry Street Promenade, this plan entailed no excavation or repaving. Indeed, it required little more than hauling in dirt to spread in raised beds lined by railroad crossties on portions of the right-of-way to form a two-lane serpentine roadway to replace the existing four lanes; planting trees, shrubs, and flowers; and installing new benches and canopies to create a mall-like environment. Best of all, the overlay cost only $100,000, one-fortieth that of Augusta's Bicentennial Park project on Broad Street.[59]

Soon after the Cherry Street Promenade opened in July 1976, the planning commission released its downtown design study. While the study called

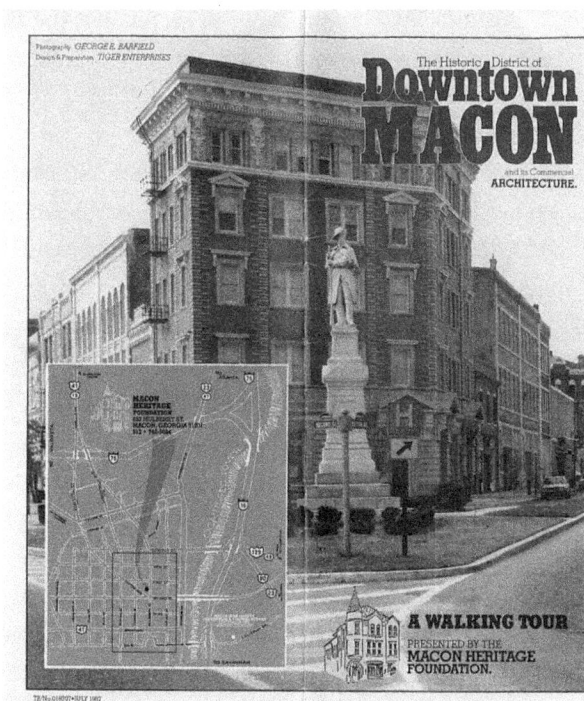

FIG. 25. DOWNTOWN MACON ARCHITECTURAL TOUR BROCHURE, 1987.
Following the 1970 designation of the Macon Historic District,
which encompassed all of downtown and the intown residential
areas to the west, a decade's worth of Community Development
Block Grant–funded facade restorations played a key role in making
downtown Macon a regional model for preservation-driven urban
revitalization. Courtesy of Middle Georgia Archives, Washington
Memorial Library, Macon, GA.

for eliminating downtown problem spots, it warned that the city "cannot
acquire and 'bulldoze' vast areas." Instead, it posited that the "beauty and
character of downtown Macon that is reflected in its existing architecture,
monuments, and parks" would be essential to the business district's future.
The plan proposed a "Facade Rehabilitation Incentive Program" centering
on Cotton Avenue to create a cohesive, historically evocative streetscape,
and it added that the improvements should eventually extend to additional
streets and alleys. This program would become the cornerstone of Macon's
approach to reviving its downtown's regional reputation (see Fig. 25).[60]

In 1977 the UDA and City Hall prepared to implement the facade program. This initiative to uncover downtown's "charm" represented a reversal of the Downtown Council's successes in getting many businesses to install false fronts in the 1960s and a departure from the UDA's suburb-inspired Cherry Street remake. The city would fund up to $15,000 toward restoring a facade if the owner agreed to spend at least the same amount, bring the building's interior up to code standards, and grant the city an easement to regulate exterior signage and undertake streetscape improvements such as repaving sidewalks, planting trees, and installing decorative lighting. While inspired by similar initiatives in Pittsburgh and Hudson, New York, this program was the first of its kind in Georgia and the first in the nation to be funded by a Community Development Block Grant (CDBG).[61] The facade program initially focused primarily on Cotton Avenue, inspiring a campaign to convert upper floors to apartments. The campaign's name, "Livin' on Cotton," suggested a complete disregard for descendants of enslaved people who had harvested the crop that was the street's namesake. The restored facades nevertheless drew praise in *Southern Living* magazine's "Future of the South" feature in 1980 and led Augusta's city government to implement its own program.[62]

In contrast to the facade program, many locals panned the Cherry Street Promenade. One woman complained that merchants had enabled officials "to destroy the charm of our city and make of it . . . a ragged forest of unattractive shrubs." Another resident wrote that the street was "not in keeping with our tradition," while another commented that despite the city's "columned houses," downtown parks, and wide streets, "Macon seems to have abandoned its own image."[63] As Olson suggested, however, the Promenade was not meant to be permanent, only to help locals take a fresh look at downtown's potential.[64] The lively debate that ensued over Cherry Street's future would, a few years later, lead to a more intensive revitalization that was rooted in the business district's historic "charm."

Twin commitments to central-city renewal and metropolitan expansion showed signs of rupturing as some leaders began to recognize these agendas as oppositional rather than complementary, part of a larger rupture in the Sunbelt growth agenda in the 1970s.[65] Although William Fickling, whose realty interests spanned the metropolitan area, insisted there remained a concert of interests, in 1977, the UDA tried unsuccessfully to persuade the Bibb County Commission to delay construction of a new sewer line to Bibb

County's northwestern border with Monroe County. Olson argued that it was nonsensical to entice investment to the suburban edge when downtown revitalization was just beginning to take root.[66]

Still, as leaders imagined Macon's future, they focused preponderantly on downtown or the metropolitan fringes. Their vision blurred as they peered into the city's deteriorating neighborhoods, where seventy-five miles of streets remained unpaved as late as 1976. One of those dirt streets, Orchard Avenue in Pleasant Hill, was near the Woodliff Street home of Macon's famed recording artist Little Richard, leading a *Telegraph* reporter to quip that when the musician penned his 1956 hit "Slippin' and Slidin'," he might well have been driving on this street after a rain.[67] Mayors Thompson and Melton had prioritized the increasingly white In-Town area before Melton began to support improvements in Pleasant Hill, where residents were still waiting for paved streets ten years after I-75 had shot through their neighborhood.[68]

These administrations similarly favored redeveloping downtown's historically Black fringe along Broadway and adjacent portions of Poplar Street, but the Melton administration made a genuine, if delayed, effort to assist in saving the Douglass Theatre, an iconic African American landmark on the west side of Broadway between Mulberry Street Lane (an alley) and Cherry Street. Born in 1870 in a one-room sharecropper house in Macon's outlying Black enclave of Unionville, Charles Henry Douglass left his floundering bicycle rental and repair business just after the turn of the century and began investing in real estate, soon accumulating sufficient wealth to open Macon's first Black hotel, the Colonial. In 1921, fed up with enduring Jim Crow in Macon's theaters, he opened the Douglass Theatre. Police and the Ku Klux Klan had periodically targeted Broadway, especially following incidents such as a 1922 poolroom shooting that precipitated a lynching followed by a mock funeral on the street and a narrowly averted attempt to burn the corpse in the Douglass Theatre's foyer. Despite the unrelenting risk of white violence, Douglass and other Black businessmen had persevered. In addition to offering vaudeville shows, the Douglass Theatre was a mainstay for Black movies and entertainers such as Bessie Smith, Ma Rainey, and Duke Ellington over the next two decades. After Douglass's death, the theater staged concerts by Little Richard, Otis Redding, Lena Horne, and James Brown.[69]

After the mid-twentieth century, white leaders' longtime habit of labeling the district in explicitly racist terms evolved as officials nationwide embraced the colorblind rhetoric of "blight."[70] Downtown revitalization supporters had urged the clearance and redevelopment of Broadway since C&S Bank's announcement of Commerce Square. They hoped that removing what they deemed blighted buildings would transform the blocks to either side of lower Cherry Street into an integral part of the white business district and create a solid corridor between the heart of downtown and the envisioned mall and office complex. They were hardly alone. Across the nation, cities were obliterating Black districts on the edges of their downtowns, including in other midsized southern cities such as Knoxville and Chattanooga.[71] By the mid-1970s, when Macon Mall upended downtown, the Broadway–Fifth Street corridor became central to planners' hopes that the city could encourage development downtown to counter the centrifugal effects of suburban competition. The transformation of Broadway into an I-16 connector promised to make this marginalized area the "front door" of a strengthened retail and office hub of Middle Georgia.[72]

The Cherry Street Promenade had reflected an effort to coax shoppers toward lower Cherry Street stores. Claims that its landscaping provided cover for criminals matched a similarly veiled white discomfort with the presence of African Americans and the documented crime rate in the surrounding blocks. The redevelopment area accounted for more than a quarter of Macon's prostitution arrests and liquor violations and 22 percent of its gambling arrests in 1974, and in the following year, it saw three homicides and twenty-one assaults.[73] Given white leaders' longtime disdain of Broadway, it might seem surprising that the planning commission's 1976 design study made an exception to its recommendation to bulldoze the Broadway–Fifth Street area, calling for carving out a small island of restoration in the 300 block of Broadway that included Douglass Theatre, which closed in 1973, and the long-shuttered Douglass Hotel (see Fig. 26).[74]

In 1978, however, the city purchased the Douglass block, planning to demolish it. Then a biracial citizen group managed to halt the demolition, convincing the city to allow time to find an entity able to buy, restore, and maintain it. Headed by James H. Wimberly, an African American social studies curriculum director in the Bibb County Schools and state director of the Association for the Study of Afro-American Life and Culture, the Broadway Arts Alliance (BAA) emerged from that citizens' committee and

FIG. 26. DOUGLASS THEATRE, 1959. Located on the eastern edge of downtown, Macon's most historic Black-owned theater closed in 1973 and faced possible demolition before the city government and a biracial coalition of civic leaders changed course and undertook a long, difficult path toward the eventual restoration of the Douglass as a hub of Macon's rejuvenated image as a cultural tourism destination. Courtesy of Middle Georgia Archives, Washington Memorial Library, Macon, GA.

hoped to make the old theater into a performing arts center.[75] In 1980, with federal and state funding, the city made repairs and engaged the architect and preservation specialist who had restored Columbus's Springer Opera House, which had catalyzed the preservation movement in the western Georgia city.[76] Although the BAA disagreed about how to proceed, Melton's successor George Israel's administration undertook further restoration work in 1981. While a feasible plan was not devised until a decade later with the nearby construction of the Georgia Music Hall of Fame, the city's efforts helped ensure that a key piece of Black history would be included in the larger downtown revitalization movement.[77]

Although the city pressed on in acquiring properties in the redevelopment area, concerns about blight spilled over to the 400 block of Poplar Street between Third Street and Broadway. A local reporter disapprovingly described a "grim" block of "soul food restaurants with adjacent package stores, low-light lounges, beauty and barber shops, a pool hall, a 'beer parlor,' a furniture store and vacant storefronts." The area's gradual slide concerned Black business owners who had watched for the past decade as the city privileged downtown's core and tried to open a "front door" off I-16. Former Great Lakes steamship cook Ed Leonard had operated the Carioca Dinette at 416 Poplar since 1948. At that time, the block was on the periphery of the main Black commercial strip on Broadway, but Leonard remembered how it had developed into a regional destination that attracted African Americans from across the city and rural Middle Georgia, and even tourists, to sample its nightlife and his restaurant's beef stew and short ribs. The city's demolition in the Mulberry–Broadway area and farther out Broadway in the Greenwood Bottom district in the second half of the 1970s finally left the 400 block as the only node of Black entertainment in the central city.[78]

In 1980, the city commissioned a reuse study of the block's eighteen buildings. The firms that consulted on the study urged renovation of what they called one of downtown's most architecturally intact blocks into offices, much as Columbus businessman Harry Kamensky had done after a visit to Denver's Larimer Square in 1976 inspired him to develop Rankin Square, a project that had fulfilled an earlier vision promoted by the Columbus–Muscogee County Planning Commission for "an old New Orleans-type" redevelopment of a downtown block. Rankin Square had forced out many Black-owned businesses, and Macon's Poplar Street plan appeared poised to do likewise. The study included a historical sketch that tellingly ended in the 1920s before turning to declining property values and rising crime since the 1960s, conveniently leapfrogging the block's postwar history as a Black business district. The proposed conversion would rescue the block from "blight and crime, giving a heightened image of vitality, history and security to the downtown area as a whole."[79]

When an Atlanta developer asked the city in 1982 to apply for an Urban Development Action Grant (UDAG) to support his plan to act on the Poplar study's recommendation, dozens of Black businesspeople voiced concerns about being displaced for "a white central business district." Four years earlier Dr. D. T. Walton Jr., a Black dentist on Cotton Avenue, had successfully pushed city officials to include Black participation in guiding the use of any UDAG funds obtained for downtown improvements, but now that promise seemed in question. Walton inquired why Poplar Street merchants were not accorded the same opportunities as Cherry Street merchants to participate in improvements. Mayor Israel pointed out that none of these merchants had applied for a facade grant but failed to acknowledge that it was harder for less-capitalized businesses to take advantage of such programs. Ironically, H. J. Russell, the developer behind the so-called 400 Poplar project, was African American. He owned Macon's ABC-affiliated television station, and his construction company was one of the nation's largest Black businesses. Like other out-of-town investors, Russell literally bought into the city's vision of using historic imagery for urban revitalization, telling the *New York Times*, "I'm high on Macon. It has some of the finest old buildings in the Southeast."[80] Russell's interest was arguably less significant on account of his race than as another indication of Macon's continuing role as a regional satellite of Atlanta.

A quarter century before Maconites committed themselves to reclaiming their historic cityscape, William Fickling was cultivating a landscape conducive to an event that would showcase the city's transformation far beyond Middle Georgia. In 1952, the real estate executive had been curious about a flowering tree in his garden. Suspecting it might be a Yoshino Cherry, Fickling took a cutting to Washington, DC, and found that it was identical to trees along the capital's Tidal Basin. In an echo of W. T. Anderson's earlier suggestion of encouraging Maconites to plant camellias, Fickling began propagating cuttings in a greenhouse on his North Macon farm and giving them away whenever the opportunity arose.[81]

Carolyn Crayton, who came to head the Macon–Bibb County Beautification Commission in 1974, had met Fickling after happening upon his blooming cherry trees four years earlier. She helped Fickling distribute and coordinate the planting of his trees, eventually numbering in the hundreds of thousands and turning the city pink each spring. In 1982, the city and county proclaimed his March 23 birthday Cherry Blossom Day.[82] Crayton began planning the inaugural Cherry Blossom Festival for the next year. Reminiscent of the Bibb County Dixie Highway Auxiliary sixty years earlier, her commission planted twelve thousand Yoshino Cherry trees on county highways and at every I-75 interchange between Atlanta and Macon, and

Georgia congressional representative J. Roy Rowland named Macon the "Cherry Tree Capital of the United States."[83]

The inaugural Cherry Blossom Festival featured a formal ball, the Cherry Blossom Queen coronation, the Cherry Cooking Contest, a fashion show, musical events, and tennis and golf tournaments. The Macon Historic District figured prominently. To open the nine-day festival, three Japanese-owned industries in Macon dedicated their gift of a large stone replica of a traditional lantern carved in Macon's sister city of Kurobe, Japan, which was installed amid the cherry trees in Third Street Park near Cherry Street. Along with a downtown parade and street dance, NBC's Willard Scott delivered his *Today Show* weather report from Third Street Park. The festival also included "Discover Historic Macon" tours of the Cannonball House (named for the cannonball that had struck it in the Civil War), Sidney Lanier Cottage (whose namesake poet penned "The Song of the Chattahoochee"), and the palatial, cupola-topped antebellum Hay House, where tourgoers enjoyed a Japanese tea ceremony.[84]

Cherry Street itself was undergoing a $5.5 million public-private rehabilitation to replace the Cherry Street Promenade with a more historically evocative streetscape flanked by restored facades and embellished with brick crosswalks, tree pits, and gas lamps. The project was dedicated in November 1983 during the Cherry Jubilee, a Downtown Council–sponsored street party likened to Mardi Gras.[85] The project's centerpiece was a restored Victorian-era fountain in the Third Street Park at Cherry Street. On the corner of Cherry and Third, the historic Dempsey Hotel reopened as senior-citizen apartments after closing in 1974 and undergoing a UDAG-funded renovation inspired by Columbus's example of refurbishing its Ralston Hotel for the same purpose. Two blocks east, Georgia Power Company was restoring the classic Terminal Station for a regional office and planned shops, a promising direction for a building threatened with demolition just a decade earlier.[86]

Although much of the central city did not receive such attention, the city had at least paved the streets and relieved the drainage problems. Suburban sprawl did not abate, but the central city proved resilient. The Cherry Street revival and cherry-themed events put the new heart of Macon on full display. Soon rivaling the cherry festival in the nation's capital with hundreds of thousands of attendees, the Cherry Blossom Festival garnered regional and

Macon is halfway between Nashville and Disney World. Stay with us NOW or on your way back.

WELCOME TO MACON! We're proud of Macon's claims to fame and we want to share them with you.

We want you to tour Macon's Historic District. Over 575 structures have been noted for their architectural significance and approximately 50 more are listed on the National Historic Register. Most of the original old Macon has been proclaimed a National Historic District.

Historic Downtown Macon beams with new energy and life after an extensive restoration project that brought back old fountain, carefully restored facades and eras that were once Regency.

QUOTES BY TRAVEL WRITERS

"Visit this Central Georgia city with a narrow maze of antebellum homes and hundred facades of 50 chairs and office buildings in 19th Century splendor."
Michael Hinsley, Chicago Tribune

"Macon is a tract that Sherman thankfully missed. But yes, visited."
Paula Crouch, Atlanta Journal-Constitution

"To be in Georgia and not visit Macon is like being in Spain and not going to Granada to see the Alhambra. For Macon is a magic city where Old South graciousness still persists and hundred excellent in taste and pretty pink Southern wisteria rig northwards."
Robert Turnbull, Toronto Star

"There's a lot to see in Macon! Two Days! Mini-shrine—Hay House and Georgian National Monument."
Jean Allen, Ft. Lauderdale News

"Le site de Georgia est par son grande age vie des, sites architecturaux (on plus importants de Amérique du Nord."
Marique Nowremian, French travel writer

Mid-March of every year Macon celebrates as the "Cherry Blossom Capital of the World." Macon has over 80,000 Yoshino Cherry Trees planted throughout the community. This week-long celebration, Macon's "Cherry Blossom Festival," features a parade, arts and crafts, music of every flavor—from symphony to dixieland, an international food festival, a street party, sporting events, special stage productions, celebrations and so much more you'll want to be there! This festival is listed as one of the top 100 festivals in the nation by the American Bus Association.

Ocmulgee National Monument, managed by the United States Department of the Interior National Park Service, is an archaeologically significant site. Thousands of years are portrayed and exhibited in the museum and many of the actual mound sites can be toured. Rose Hill Cemetery, also on the banks of the Ocmulgee, is one of the oldest surviving public cemetery parks in the United States. It is noted for its picturesque 19th century landscape design and the Confederate Square. The square encloses approximately 600 Confederate and Union soldiers' markers.

Within easy driving distance of Macon and Bibb County are other area attractions:
■ The Jarrell Plantation, Juliette
■ Clinton Historic District, Clinton
■ Old State Capital, Milledgeville
■ National Camellia Society, Marshallville
■ Georgia's Colonial Coast, which includes Savannah, St. Simons Island, Brunswick, Jekyll Island and Cumberland Island National Seashore, is 3½ to 4½ hours from Macon, traveling I-16.

Stay in one of Historic Macon's 2,500 hotel or motel accommodations. Dine in a wide range of restaurants

FIG. 27. HISTORIC MACON TOURISM BROCHURE, CA. 1984. In the 1980s, Macon tourism leaders continued to struggle to make their city more than a stopping point on the way to or from Florida. This brochure captures the city's embrace of its history as an attraction even as it seems to acquiesce to the fact that most visitors still paused for only a few hours or perhaps overnight. Courtesy of Visit Macon, Macon, GA.

national coverage that helped shine a spotlight on downtown Macon and its adjacent, historic residential district by the mid-1980s.[87]

The "charm" of the transformed central city paid more than cultural dividends. It also helped shore up a regional economic pillar and recenter the Middle Georgia economy downtown. Unfortunately, airline deregulation in 1978 limited the ability of smaller cities to take full advantage of growing national interest in heritage tourism by funneling more long-distance flights into a handful of large-city hub airports at the expense of midsized cities like Macon. Indeed, deregulation led Eastern Air Lines to exit the Macon market and Delta to pare down its service. Macon boosters urged the airlines to reconsider and mounted an energetic "Fly Macon" campaign to get Maconites to use the local airport instead of driving to Atlanta's Hartsfield International Airport but to no avail. The diminishment of Macon's commercial aviation potential added to growing concerns about Middle Georgia's ability to attract its share of development.[88]

In this climate, boosters found Atlanta a much-needed source of tourism, which promised to lift downtown out of its slump. Mayor William Lee Robinson was not exaggerating when he said in 1991 that Macon boasted "one of the most enviable downtown success stories in the Southeast."[89] Thanks to the Macon Auditorium restoration, the formation of a separate Convention and Visitors Bureau, and an enlivened downtown, Macon's annual convention attendance more than doubled to over 150,000 and downtown retail vacancies plunged from 35 to 10 percent in the decade after 1977. With downtown capturing 70 percent of Bibb County's office development in this same period, downtown employment rose from 7,750 to more than 10,500.[90] Many of these jobs filled newer buildings that had finally given Macon one more sign of metropolitan status: a downtown skyline. But others repopulated downtown's more diminutive historic buildings. Among Macon's biggest coups was attracting Aetna's regional insurance claims office from Atlanta to the former Davison's store on Cherry Street in 1981, a sharp contrast from when GEICO had selected an outlying industrial park.[91]

Earlier in the century, Macon boosters had looked jealously toward Atlanta and had hustled to try to bring the state capital to "The Heart of Georgia." Like Augusta and Columbus boosters, they had bet, in turns, on becoming a hub of diversified agriculture, river development, military activity, and industry. Even more than in those cities, they had also vacillated between basking in Atlanta's glow and laboring in its shadow. By the 1980s, they were determined to set Macon apart from Sunbelt sameness and understood the benefits of making it widely known that, as one tourism brochure highlighted, "halfway between Nashville and Disney World" one might find the "Antebellum Heart of the South" in the world's "Cherry Blossom Capital" (see Fig. 27).[92] Yet, these very formulations were hardly outside the national mainstream. They depended on accepting that midsized cities like Macon required more than charm for urban reinvention; they also demanded capital from large, networked cities like Atlanta to help underwrite their distinctive image.

EPILOGUE
WHERE SOUL LIVES

"Where Soul Lives." These words form a circular logo resembling a pink neon sign floating on a glowing purple brick wall (see Fig. 28). In 2016, Visit Macon began using this slogan to headline Macon's musical heritage. After spending the previous half-century burnishing their city's reputation as a place "Where Old South Charm Meets New South Progress," a dichotomy that reflected an ambivalence toward pursuing Sunbelt growth that might erode romance-steeped southern white traditionalism, boosters instead embraced a metropolitan ambition that celebrated rather than denied Macon's multiracial reality. As the hometown of Little Richard, Otis Redding, and the Capricorn Records label that made the city "The Cradle of Southern Rock," modern Macon packages its blues, soul, and rock 'n' roll roots through its museums, music venues, recording studios, and other landmarks. It even has its own Macon Music Trail app tour and Macon Music playlist on Spotify.[1]

Following decades of pitches seeking to capture the interest of white executives and white tourists, boosters now frame the sandhill cities as diverse and inclusive places. Macon's "Where Soul Lives" brand, according to Visit Macon, "aims at creating a sense of unity" around the notion of the city's "soul." While the brand debuted in 2016, it was more than a quarter century in the making. In 1991, under the leadership of executive director Janice Marshall, the Macon CVB worked with leaders in the city's African American community to develop the city's first Black heritage brochure, which guided tourists to twenty-one points of interest.[2] In 1998, the tourism bureau com-

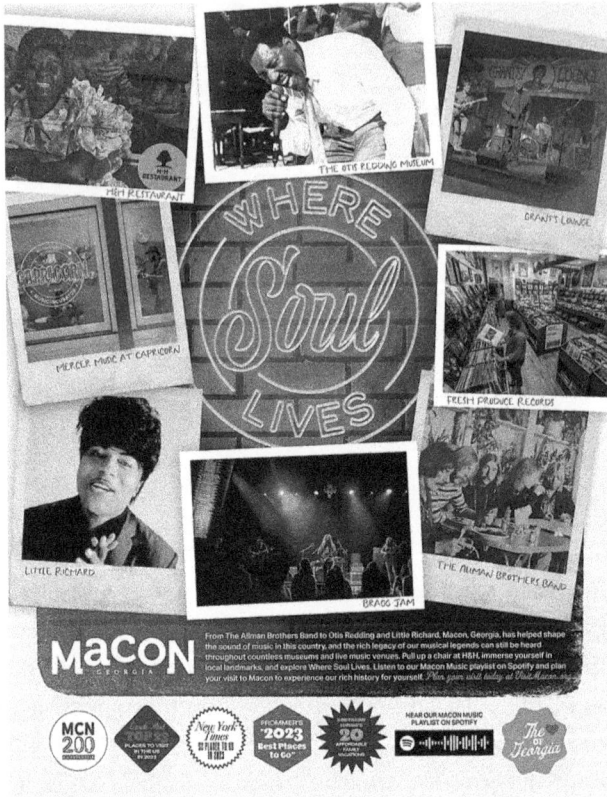

FIG. 28. MACON MUSIC PROMOTION ADVERTISEMENT, 2023. In the
past quarter century, Macon has exemplified the trend toward using
musical heritage as a focus for tourism promotion, a trend that is
also visible in Augusta and Columbus. Macon's seminal role in the
development of rhythm and blues and rock and roll led to the clever
branding slogan "Where Soul Lives" and the cultivation of tours
and other visitor experiences that tie this heritage to the cityscape.
Courtesy of Visit Macon, Macon, GA.

missioned a study that led it to adopt an earlier iteration of the tagline, "The
Song and Soul of the South." As part of the campaign, Marshall persuaded
Little Richard to serve as Macon's official goodwill ambassador and promote the city's musical legacy.[3] Phil Walden's daughter Jessica Walden and
her husband launched Rock Candy Tours in 2011, giving visitors a carefully
curated experience to match the image that attracted them. Like earlier images, however, the "Song and Soul" tagline also nodded to a romanticized

Old South in its not-so-subtle emulation of Disney's 1946 film *Song of the South*. A subsequent study in 2014 recommended a wider umbrella that cast "Soul" as both a marketable set of attractions and a mentality shared by all Maconites, leading to the "Where Soul Lives" brand.[4]

Even as Macon's promoters play a new tune, their appeal to music lovers is not unlike past appeals the fall-line cities made to peach farmers, winter golfers, military divisions, chemical manufacturers, and historic home restorers. The new messaging also exists alongside a decades-old claim about locational advantage. "With convenient access to multiple interstates and our central location in the heart of Georgia," a 2023 Visit Macon ad proclaims, "it's easy to see why they say that All Roads Lead to Macon." Bathed in orange, pink, and purple sunset hues, the ad features a bird's-eye view of downtown centering on the wide expanse of Poplar Street with cupolas and spires piercing through the trees on College Hill in the distance. Eleven decades after their predecessors adopted "The Heart of Georgia," Macon boosters continued to employ this slogan, which appears in the ad on a large red seal with a white heart at the center of the pink-shaded shape of the state.[5]

Macon may enjoy a central location in Georgia but, like Augusta and Columbus and the entire sandhills region, it has labored to fulfill its boosters' metropolitan ambitions ever since Atlanta's mythical, phoenix-like ascent from the ashes of Sherman's fire. In the 1890s, promoters had touted "Macon the Hub," referring to railroads that already enriched Atlanta more than the fall-line city. The coming of the Dixie Highway and, later, the interstate highway system reinforced Macon leaders' hopes of capturing a larger share of economic development. But as with railroads, highways were insufficient to close the gap between the fall-line cities and Atlanta. Georgia's capital won three interstate routes; Macon saw two, Augusta only one, and Columbus none until its spur opened in 1979. The sandhill cities' freeways brought mixed results, channeling interstate traffic around their periphery and propelling their suburbanization, even as they doubled as spokes for a new hub in Atlanta.

Boosters have long sought a freeway along the fall line. Since the early Cold War years, these efforts have stressed the defense benefits of connecting military installations, but they also reflect hopes of overcoming a perennial lack of traffic flow along the fall line. Plans to build what became known as the Fall Line Freeway gathered momentum in the 1980s, but the proposed route would have sliced through environmentally sensitive swamps and culturally significant grounds near the Ocmulgee National Monument outside Macon. Public opposition led officials to designate I-75 as Bibb County's portion of the route, and most of the 215-mile corridor ultimately consisted of widened existing state roads. The Fall Line Freeway fell short of interstate standards and did little to cut against the grain of freeways radiating from Atlanta. Boosters' hopes rose anew when the unlikely duo of Georgia Democratic Senator Raphael Warnock and Texas Republican Senator Ted Cruz shepherded an amendment to the $1 trillion Infrastructure Investment and Jobs Act of 2021 that authorized a proposed I-14 route from Odessa, Texas, to Augusta, though allocation of funds to realize its completion remains uncertain.[6]

The lack of a true freeway along the sandhills reflected and reinforced decades of spinning in the eddies alongside the main currents of Sunbelt prosperity. Augusta, Macon, and Columbus remain satellites of Atlanta, whose state agencies, financial and corporate firms, transportation networks, and consumer markets continue to aggregate, amplify, and control the flows of capital. In the past forty years, the sandhill cities have had to abandon hopes that their rivers might restore once-thriving inland ports and that their interstate highways and regional airports could attract enough diversified industries to replace textiles. They have even had to learn not to take for granted the permanence of their well-established military bases. Decisions in the State Capitol, the Pentagon, federal offices in Washington, and Atlanta corporate and health-system boardrooms brighten or dim their hopes.

Even the surprising replication of Columbus's city-county consolidation in Augusta (in 1996) and Macon (in 2014) did little to help the cities attract a more diversified economic base to reduce overreliance on military installations and declining industries. For most of the last century, textile mills and clothing factories comprised a large part of the fall-line cities' economies, but overseas competition gradually brought American manufacturers to their knees. By the early 2000s, this sector had virtually vanished.[7] To be sure, there were some bright spots. Aerospace industries drawn by the cities' military presence included Pratt & Whitney in Columbus and Triumph Aerostructures–Vought Aircraft Division in Macon. However, even the vaunted Sunbelt was not immune to deindustrialization. The most crushing loss was the 2006 closing of Brown & Williamson Tobacco's sprawling cigarette plant in Macon following a merger with R. J. Reynolds Tobacco of Winston-Salem, North Carolina. At its peak, the plant in Ocmulgee East Industrial Park employed more than three thousand workers. After its departure, manufacturing was largely absent from Bibb County. Most of the metro area's remaining manufacturers, including a Perdue Farms poultry plant, Frito-Lay potato chip plant, and Blue Bird school bus plant, were now in Houston and Peach counties.[8]

Mirroring another national trend, the Georgia sandhill cities saw employment increases in insurance and healthcare. Macon's GEICO and Aetna regional offices and Columbus's Aflac headquarters bolstered those cities' economies, as did Augusta's Medical College of Georgia and Augusta University Health (AU Health). Increasingly, decisions made outside the cities fueled these economic engines. Maryland-based GEICO has continually expanded in Macon and now employs some 7,500 workers, but its deep economic imprint as Macon's single-largest private employer makes the Middle Georgia city highly dependent on future decisions that lie beyond its control. Nor did the boom in white-collar jobs guarantee downtown vitality as boosters had assumed in the 1970s and '80s. In 1991, Aetna's regional office left downtown Macon after only a few years for a suburban office park in North Macon, part of a broader office exodus that left nearly half of downtown's storefronts boarded up by 2008, before a tourism-led recovery in the next decade.[9] Although Macon-based Mercer School of Medicine (founded in 1982) carved out an important niche of supplying physicians across underserved rural Georgia and even added campuses in Savannah and Columbus in the past two decades, in most respects, local control over the healthcare sector diminished in the fall-line cities.[10] Atlanta-based Piedmont Health and Emory University took over Columbus's two major hospitals in 2017 and 2020, respectively. Charlotte-based Atrium Health absorbed Macon's Medical Center of Central Georgia (Georgia's second-largest hospital) in 2019, and in 2023, the University System of Georgia Board of Regents inked a merger deal between Atlanta's Wellstar Health Systems and AU Health. Although presented as opportunities to expand healthcare services, these mergers also reflect how smaller cities' hospitals are increasingly financially vulnerable and, to survive, must forfeit a degree of control over their futures to large health systems in larger cities.[11]

Even more, federal government and military employment dominate the fall-line cities while making them reliant on outside decisions. In 1933, Co-lumbus Mayor H. C. Smith had made the tongue-in-cheek comment that his city might become a suburb of Fort Benning, but his quip proved pre-scient. It did so because for the next three decades, southern politicians like Georgia's Dick Russell and Carl Vinson used their powerful congressional committee posts to keep robust federal investment flowing to what historian Bruce J. Schulman dubbed "fortress Dixie." The cumulative investment con-tinued to pay dividends.[12] In Macon's case, once-rural neighboring Houston County surpassed Bibb County in population in the 2010s, a direct result of the military-driven economy in Warner Robins. Fort Benning, Robins Air Force Base, and Fort Gordon continued to be, by far, the largest single employers in their respective metropolitan areas, as they had for many de-cades. Benning accounted for about 45,000 jobs, while Robins and Gordon employed 23,000 and 29,000, respectively. Although the U.S. Department of Energy's Savannah River Site (formerly the Savannah River Plant) has lost more than half of its early 1990s workforce since its shift to cleaning up the nuclear wastes remaining from its Cold War production, it still accounts for 11,000 jobs in metro Augusta. With its cleanup timeline now estimated to take until at least 2065, the SRS's own half-life, as it were, has turned out to make it the most predictable employment source among the fall-line cities' federal facilities.[13]

The presence of so many consumers connected to these federal instal-lations, including military families and retirees, swells every sector of the Georgia fall-line cities' economies from retail trade to financial services to healthcare. Even tourism relies to a considerable degree on the military presence. A study in 2017 credited Fort Gordon for many of the 51 percent of Augusta's tourists who went there to visit friends or family, and indeed the descriptions of many Airbnb-listed Columbus home rentals touted their proximity to Fort Benning.[14] Subject to the vagaries of foreign policy and domestic politics, however, the sandhill cities have faced recurring threats of base closures or downsizings by the Pentagon since the end of the Viet-nam War. Alarmed by the prospect of further cuts in 2002, Augusta leaders hired a retired U.S. Army colonel as a consultant to help save Fort Gordon. He helped them argue for the post's capacity to support high-tech military innovations in cybersecurity, eventually leading to the relocation of the U.S. Army Cyber Command headquarters to the base in 2013.[15] Albeit good news, the need for continual repositioning to protect the cities' outsize federal foot-prints suggests the precarity of even their biggest assets. Just as cotton and textiles enriched these cities at the cost of dependency on forces over which their boosters had limited control, so do their persisting roles as military metropolises.

The concentration of military and defense-related research and develop-ment has often played a role in eroding some of the rough edges of racism, either by exposing communities to people from other regions or by intro-ducing large numbers of highly educated, upwardly mobile scientific and technological workers. Yet, as historians have pointed out, even in locations around Boston's Route 128, Raleigh–Durham's Research Triangle Park, and the Augusta–Aiken area's Savannah River Plant, the purported progressiv-ism that came with becoming more "cosmopolitan" had limits.[16] Notwith-standing one journalist's claim that "Benning had a leavening effect on race relations in Columbus and the Chattahoochee Valley," the strong military influence was not enough to prevent all three cities from following broader patterns of white resistance to and retreat from racial integration.[17]

Indeed, as in other southern cities, Augusta, Macon, and Columbus saw a gradual breakdown of their checkerboard patterns of racial residence. The fall line hardened as a racial boundary, with most whites living to its north and most Blacks to its south. Augusta's longstanding pattern of more affluent whites living on "The Hill" remained little altered, and even the adjacent domestic-service enclave of Sand Hills, home to most of Augusta National's caddies until the Masters began allowing competitors to bring their own from out of town in 1983, gradually lost much of its African American com-munity.[18] Most of Macon's African Americans lived east and west of down-town, while North Macon remained a white redoubt. Likewise, Columbus's Wynnton Road remained an unmistakable racial boundary dividing the fashionable island suburbs to the north from what had once been known as the Bottoms. The stark divisions were especially visible in the spreading blight that reversed the progress of earlier years. Macon, for example, had more than 3,700 unoccupied homes by 2019.[19]

While consolidation prevented more lopsided economic and racial dis-parities between the sandhill cities and their respective counties, even the triumph embodied in these unifying acts could not eliminate socioeconomic disunity. As in many cities, the racial divide is magnified in their public schools. Despite having countywide districts, all three consolidated cities' schools are substantially less integrated than their overall populations, mirroring similar demographic disparities in Atlanta and Charlotte schools.[20] In 48 percent Black Columbus, the schools are 57 percent Black; 59 percent Black Augusta's schools are 75 percent Black; and in 57 percent Black Macon, they are 78 percent Black. The Black student enrollment at Macon's Central High School rose from 58.5 percent to 92.6 percent in the two decades after 1996, while the district's Academy for Classical Education near the Monroe County border in North Macon enrolls one-quarter of its white students. Macon schools' resegregation is, of course, a story that echoes across metropolitan America.[21]

The promise of consolidation to forge metropolitan unity also rings hollow. Although these cities and their hinterlands once had sizable Black populations, these eroded in the mid-twentieth century, and consolidation only temporarily curbed the inexorable divergence between the cities and their suburbs. Between 1990 and 2020, Macon's population grew only 5 percent, while Monroe County climbed 63 percent. Augusta expanded 9 percent, while suburban Columbia County soared 136 percent. Although Columbus enjoyed a somewhat more robust decade of 15 percent growth, neighboring Harris County saw a 94 percent increase. White flight has not only stunted the growth of the three cities, but it has also whitened counties that once had substantial rural Black populations. In the thirty years after 1990, Monroe County's African American population sagged from 32 to 22 percent while Harris County's dropped from 26 to 16 percent.[22]

While the fall-line cities' consolidation successes could not prevent civic fragmentation, their boosters' reframed metropolitan ambitions have begun to address the inequities of their urban cores and their promotional images. These changes reflect persistent social activism, growing diversity in civic leadership, and shifting economic conditions. Into the late twentieth century, those in positions of power and influence in the three cities held similar views to their counterparts elsewhere. They favored downtown development that would attract white-collar workers, suburban shoppers, tourists, and conventioneers. They supported the construction of new office buildings and the adaptive reuse of historic ones, as well as the beautification of streetscapes. They also worked to entice affluent, mostly white people to repopulate downtown-adjacent neighborhoods and apartments above downtown storefronts. Macon's longtime emphasis on cultivating a balance of the traditional and modern—"Where Old South Charm Meets New South Progress"—exemplified how the sandhill cities emulated both Atlanta and Savannah.

The transformations of the three cities' rivers suggest how economic, social, and cultural changes have extended and reshaped patterns of development and promotion. In the 1970s, the promise of navigation on the Chattahoochee and Savannah Rivers faded amid the mutually reinforcing problems of federal resistance to channel maintenance and disappointing levels of shipping activity. Hopes of reinstating navigation up to Macon floundered as environmentalists opposed harming cypress and gum swamps lining the Ocmulgee River. Columbus's port closed unceremoniously in 1971, as did Augusta's eight years later. Moreover, neither city's remaining textile mills had relied on direct waterpower in decades. Planning consultants, versed in emerging riverfront redevelopment trends elsewhere, did not wait for local boosters to abandon hopes of using the rivers for shipping and industrial development. Instead, planners began to prescribe public use of the three cities' rivers. In 1968, Atlanta planners Paul Muldawer and Harry Adley recommended parks, marinas, and apartment towers along the Augusta and Macon riverfronts, respectively. Columbus boosters took the lead when they began planning the city's Chattahoochee Promenade as its U.S. Bicentennial project. On July 4, 1976, they dedicated this outdoor linear museum on the grassy river bluff just south of downtown.[23]

Although Columbus's early start would later support more substantial riverfront investments immediately north of the Chattahoochee Promenade, Augusta was the first of the cities to mimic Savannah by pouring significant investment into reinventing its downtown riverfront. In 1982, the newly formed booster group Augusta Tomorrow was captivated by a revision of Muldawer's idea by the American City Corporation (ACC), a subsidiary of the Rouse Company that was lauded for its role in the recent transformation of Baltimore's Inner Harbor. Thanks to Clarks Hill Dam, Augusta no longer needed the two-mile river levee that had guarded against the repetition of earlier disastrous floods, which meant that the levee could be breached to reconnect the riverfront to downtown's Broad Street spine via perpendicular streets. As a result, Augusta Tomorrow and the City of Augusta embraced the ACC's recommended Bay Street Promenade, which opened in 1988 as the Augusta Riverwalk. With its elaborate network of brick-paved upper and lower paths, observation decks, an amphitheater, and attractive landscaping, the $3.4 million Riverwalk reinvigorated Augusta's longtime "Garden City of the South" image and won national attention for the city.[24]

Augusta not only repurposed its riverbanks for leisure and recreation but also reimagined usage of the river itself. Originally built to facilitate navigation, the New Savannah Bluff Lock and Dam thirteen miles downriver now served a different role: providing a controlled pool that could support recreational and competitive boating events. As a result, Augusta leaders augmented the city's golf-dominated sporting fame by opening the Augusta Riverfront Marina, which staged the first Augusta International Rowing Regatta in 1984, River Race Augusta in 1985, and Augusta Southern Nationals boat drag race in 1986, all of which became annual events.[25]

Determination to redevelop the Chattahoochee riverfront in downtown Columbus emerged soon after Augusta's Riverwalk opened. In 1989, the *Columbus Ledger-Enquirer* highlighted other cities' waterfront revitalization efforts, including the one in Augusta. In the next few years, Columbus leaders worked to remove obstacles to riverfront redevelopment, which included a natural gas service center, an electric substation, a textile warehouse, and railroad tracks.[26] The greatest spur to action came with a Georgia Environmental Protection Division (EPD) order to replace Columbus's antiquated sewer system, which dumped raw sewage into the Chattahoochee during heavy rains. This imperative led the city to cover its collection pipe along the river and, in turn, expand the five-block Chattahoochee Promenade into a fifteen-mile Riverwalk, which opened in 1993.[27]

Augusta learned, as many other midsized cities had, that it was not easy to maintain momentum after an initial investment. The Riverwalk proved unable to fill the long string of largely empty city blocks between the river and Broad Street. While some developments such as the Marriott convention hotel and Morris Museum of Art proved durable, others such as the Georgia Golf Hall of Fame did not.[28] Moreover, in 2017, Augusta lost its annual boat drag races after thirty-one years, and the potential that the city's abandonment of navigation created for river sports came into question in 2019 as the Corps of Engineers anticipated removing the obsolete New Savannah Bluff Lock and Dam, which would reintroduce variability in river levels at Augusta.[29] Nevertheless, the Augusta riverfront stimulated continuing efforts to unify the metropolitan area around the river that had inspired its CSRA nickname. South of downtown, Phinizy Swamp managed to survive Augusta's era of seeking intensive chemical plant development, although not without considerable environmental degradation. In 1993, in response to its own EPD order for sewerage upgrades, Augusta officials decided to create an artificial wetland near the city's airport for tertiary water treatment, which led to the establishment of Phinizy Swamp Nature Park as a form of wetlands mitigation required under the Clean Water Act. That same year, the state-chartered Augusta Canal Authority set out to remake the historic waterway, resulting in the federal designation of the Augusta Canal National Heritage Area three years later. Outcomes eventually included boat tours, kayaking, a canal museum, and a seven-mile trail along the canal towpath that connects with the Riverwalk.[30]

As these waterway improvements unfolded, planners and promoters incorporated them into systematic efforts to improve Augusta's quality of life and image. In 2009, Augusta Tomorrow adopted a new master plan dubbed *The Westobou Vision*, appropriating a Native American name for the Savannah River. The plan called for embracing the older "Garden City" identity crafted in Augusta's winter resort era. It recommended remedying the area's "disjointed open space" problem by creating greenbelts on both sides of the river.[31] Similarly, the Augusta CVB responded to the expanding leisure and recreation uses of local waterways with a new promotional campaign in 2015. Its branding of the metropolitan area as "Augusta's River Region," with the tagline "Together We Have a Lot More to Offer," reprised the regional appeal of the longstanding CSRA moniker.[32]

If Columbus lagged Augusta in using its riverfront to support downtown revitalization, it progressed steadily toward creating seamless connections between the river and Broadway. Unlike Augusta's emptiness along the Savannah, Columbus's Chattahoochee River was lined by historic mills that developers transformed into apartments.[33] Similar conversions of old mills occurred along the Augusta Canal, but they were too far from downtown to reactivate the city's core. And unlike Augusta's reliance on locks and dams to maintain a placid, lake-like river, Columbus restored a more natural, sustainable waterway. In 2013, the city demolished the obsolete City Mills Dam and the old Eagle & Phenix Dam, reverting two and a half miles of the river to a state not seen since the city's founding in 1828 and creating the world's longest urban whitewater rafting course. In 2014, the rafting operator added a new zipline spanning the river, symbolically unifying Columbus and Phenix City as a tourist destination a century after Georgia and Alabama leaders had stood on Goat Rock Dam with a shared vision of electrified mill development.[34] Although Columbus had failed decades earlier to use the Chattahoochee's passive role as a border to attract football rivalries, these newer developments made the river an active destination for outdoor recreation.

While the collapse of Augusta's and Columbus's textile industries and the failure of their inland ports had encouraged their leaders to eye national models of waterfront redevelopment in cities such as San Antonio and San Francisco, the Ocmulgee River continued to be comparatively out of sight and out of mind for Maconites. In contrast to downtown Columbus and Augusta, whose main streets paralleled their respective rivers two blocks away, Macon's Cherry Street was much farther from the nearest access point on its river. Local action in the 1960s compounded Macon's estrangement from the Ocmulgee. Macon leaders' success in securing a junction of I-75 and I-16 just over a mile from downtown "severed, physically and psychologically, the heart of Macon from its body."[35]

In July 1994, Tropical Storm Alberto dumped prodigious rainfall that caused the Ocmulgee to overtop its levees. After Alberto's floodwaters reintroduced the city to its river, civic leaders mounted their first sustained effort to make the Ocmulgee more integral to the city.[36] Three years later, Macon leaders began planning what they hoped would eventually be a thirty-five-mile riverfront park. In 1999, construction began on the initial seven-mile Ocmulgee Heritage Trail linking the mounds to Central City Park and the future Amerson River Park farther north. As the twenty-first century unfolded, the cancellation of the Eisenhower Parkway extension across the river also inspired a commitment to enlarge Ocmulgee National Monument and connect it both to long-marginalized neighborhoods like Pleasant Hill and downriver wildlife refuges and wildlife management areas, including Bond Swamp.[37] In contrast to Macon boosters' appropriation of Okmulgee (Creek) culture to drum up tourism in the 1970s, the current initiative reflects a stronger common purpose. In 2019, the National Park Service redesignated the expanded park as Ocmulgee Mounds National Historical Park, and local officials have since continued their effort to see the unit upgraded to full National Park status, which would greatly increase visitation.[38] Macon boosters continue to imagine the mounds and river corridor as one of the city's most promising pathways to becoming a tourist destination rather than merely a stopover on the way to Florida.

The same spirit that underlay boosters' efforts to repurpose rivers in Augusta, Columbus, and Macon also guided their recasting of the cities' images. Until the last decade of the twentieth century, the Old South and the Civil War dominated boosters' depictions of Georgia's sandhill cities. White-columned mansions figured prominently in tourist guides to the cities, and marble monuments to the Lost Cause dotted their expansive streets. Columbus boosters clung to the myth of being the site of the Civil War's last battle, while Macon's Cannonball House provided a fitting spot to narrate a heroic tale about thwarting Sherman's would-be destruction. As in other southern cities following the civil rights movement, African Americans gradually began to assert their roles as historical actors. They challenged the whitewashed imagery erected by Confederate descendants and crafted by white civic boosters, seeding the gradual remediation of starkly divided and exclusionary cities.

Beginning with Historic Augusta Inc.'s grant-funded documentation and historic designation of the Black vernacular architecture of the Laney–Walker neighborhood between the late 1970s and mid-1980s, the three cities' historic preservation organizations began to expand their interest to include Black neighborhoods. But the three cities took no decisive action to address the ubiquity of their Confederate symbols until the racially motivated killings of Ahmaud Arbery in Brunswick, Georgia; Breonna Taylor in Louisville, Kentucky; and George Floyd in Minneapolis in 2020 generated new momentum.[39] Task forces made recommendations for how to loosen the Confederacy's grip on civic space in the three cities. Macon made the first breakthrough, overcoming opposition from the Sons of Confederate Veterans (SCV) and United Daughters of the Confederacy (UDC) to the relocation of two downtown monuments. In 2022, the city moved monuments from Cotton Avenue and Poplar Street to a triangular plot just outside Rose Hill Cemetery, the final resting place of several hundred Confederate veterans.[40]

While the Department of Defense rechristened Fort Benning and Fort Gordon, each with Confederate general namesakes, as Fort Moore and Fort Eisenhower, respectively, in 2023, Columbus and Augusta lagged in stripping the commemorative power of white supremacy, but not for lack of effort.[41] In

2020, an Augusta task force urged moving the soaring Confederate monument on Broad Street and a smaller one on Greene Street to either Magnolia or Westover cemeteries and renaming the city's Jefferson Davis Memorial Bridge, Gordon Highway, and James C. Calhoun Expressway. In fulfilling the *Westobou Vision* recommendation to convert the one-time highway bridge into a pedestrian bridge to foster more inclusive and equitable access to parks on both sides of the Savannah River, the city hoped to rename the span Freedom Bridge, but an SCV lawsuit in 2022 thwarted the task force's recommended actions. In Columbus, a similar task force has weighed the removal of the Confederate obelisk on the Broadway parkway but leaned toward adding four monuments to African Americans who played prominent roles in the city's nineteenth-century history.[42]

Meanwhile, tourism promoters in the sandhill cities increasingly foregrounded Black history and culture as they recast their marketing, but doing so depended on a long, difficult process of overcoming their cities' long histories of politically marginalizing African Americans and neglecting or erasing Black contributions and landmarks. The shift reflects a national trend that emerged after the civil rights movement, first confined mainly to grassroots attractions and tours but eventually expanding to experiences embraced by civic boosters, a trend especially visible in New Orleans, Jackson, Montgomery, and Selma.[43] The three Georgia cities saw community-based efforts in the 1970s and 1980s to showcase Black history and culture in ways that could reshape local identity. In 1971, months after civil unrest rocked downtown Augusta, local civil rights activist Harold Suber presented a petition asking that Gwinnett Street (named for a Georgia Declaration of Independence signer and slaveholder) be renamed James Brown Boulevard to honor the Godfather of Soul, a suggestion the city council declined. Four years later, following a request from the Augusta Black Heritage Commission, the city renamed the street Laney–Walker Boulevard to honor Augusta's pioneering African American educator Lucy Craft Laney and Black pastor Rev. Charles T. Walker, whose famed Tabernacle Baptist sermons attracted regular visits by President Taft and John D. Rockefeller.[44] In 1993, African American businessman James Riles brought a new petition to the Augusta city council calling for renaming Ninth Street as James Brown Boulevard. Although one councilman groused that there was no way he would support naming a street for an ex-convict, the city approved the change.[45]

Over time, Brown's legacy became more visible in civic space. The city dedicated a statue in his honor in the center of Broad Street in 2005 just a block up the street from the Confederate monument. Just months before Brown's death the following year, the Augusta–Richmond County Coliseum Authority changed the name of the 1974 I. M. Pei–designed Civic Center to James Brown Arena. Along with the Augusta Museum of History's addition of a "James Brown, Godfather of Soul" exhibition in 2015, Visit Augusta worked closely with Brown family members and friends to bring the star's legacy literally into the city's streets in the form of "The James Brown Journey," a self-guided tour featuring twelve artistically designed vinyl record markers embedded in sidewalks in front of sites that collectively narrate Brown's life. By pairing the physical markers with QR codes that point to audio narratives by those who knew the singer, the tour provides an inclusive mode of storytelling, reconnects Laney–Walker to downtown, and helps balance the city's commemorative landscape.[46]

The effort to open African American history museums in the Georgia fall-line cities was also slow to materialize because they lacked broad support beyond local Black communities. However, a gradual change of attitude on the part of municipal leaders and boosters emerged, reflecting their growing realization that antebellum and Civil War history were no longer unchallenged objects of veneration but rather a shaky foundation for metropolitan ambitions. In 1975, the Augusta Black Heritage Commission rented a Gwinnett Street building with the intent to start a Black museum, but the effort did not outlast the Bicentennial year. A second attempt in the late 1970s and early 1980s also faded, but a third effort by the Delta Sigma Theta Sorority that began in 1987 resulted in the acquisition of Lucy Craft Laney's home on Phillips Street two years later. Amid a long, difficult fundraising effort, the Augusta CVB began providing some support in 1999. Two years later, after the Augusta Museum of History received a large sum from hotel room tax revenues, the city agreed to redirect UDAG funds to the Lucy Craft Laney Museum of Black History, a controversial move that nonetheless helped the museum toward financial stability over the next decade.[47]

Macon's Tubman African American Museum also endured its own hardships. In 1982, St. Peter Claver Catholic Church priest Fr. Richard Keil bought a Walnut Street building to serve as a temporary museum. In the 1990s, at a time when Macon leaders were working hard to remake lower

Cherry Street across from Terminal Station as a civic plaza flanked by the Georgia Music Hall of Fame, Georgia Sports Hall of Fame, and renovated Douglass Theater, the Tubman Museum's leaders also aspired to be part of this cultural center. Through repeated municipal earmarks that helped leverage foundation support, the Tubman Museum finally reopened on Cherry Street in 2015.[48] Similarly, Columbus's Gertrude "Ma" Rainey House and Blues Museum reflects a two-decade effort to highlight "The Mother of the Blues" in her hometown that began in 1984. In that year, Carver High School's Golden Owlettes alumnae organization worked to get Rainey's dilapidated Fifth Avenue house listed on the National Register, and retired Carver band director William J. Monroe raised funds to place a state historical marker in front of the house two years later. In 1991, the Columbus Council rejected funding its renovation as a museum before a tourism-minded Mayor Frank Martin broke a deadlocked vote a month later to stabilize the house. His action drew white hostility, with one detractor complaining that the city was wasting money on "a broken-down shack" while neglecting to support the Confederate Naval Museum. Ultimately, as in Augusta and Macon, the pendulum swung toward making Black heritage an integral part of Columbus's tourism offerings. In 2004, the Columbus Council matched a $150,000 Save America's Treasures federal grant secured through the efforts of Congressman Sanford Bishop and worked with the Friends of Ma Rainey Blues Museum to complete and open the shrine three years later.[49]

As the Georgia sandhill cities inscribed Black contributions in civic space, saved threatened Black landmarks, and supported Black museums, they were laying the foundation for recasting their civic image. As this book has argued, image has been inseparable from metropolitan ambitions because outsiders' impressions of a city are important in decisions to invest, whether as a business or a tourist. For too long, boosters had crafted images that reflected metropolitan ambitions that did not equitably serve their cities' people. *Macon Telegraph* publisher W. T. Anderson may have been incensed that a prospective advertiser from outside the city did not consider Macon's large Black community worthy of being counted in the local market in the 1910s, but long thereafter, boosters acted with similar disregard as they tried variously to appeal to midwestern white practitioners of diversified agriculture, northern white winter tourists, southern white college football teams, mostly white GIs, and their own growing populations of white suburbanites.

African Americans either carved out their own separate livelihoods on the other side of the color line or accepted the meanest jobs in spaces that privileged whites. Reimagined image campaigns, of course, will not in themselves reverse the legacies of long-ingrained discrimination and disinvestment that consigned Black sections of the sandhill cities to suffer blight, poverty, pollution, exclusion, and marginalization. But as statements of aspiration, these steps are not inconsequential.

It remains to be seen whether these reframed metropolitan ambitions may lift the fall-line cities' needles from the well-worn grooves of their history as places that struggled to overcome the diminution of their originally valued "natural advantages." The fall line and the rivers that traverse it once carried steamboats and barges, turned textile mill and hydroelectric turbines, provided topographic conditions conducive to resorts and military installations, and inspired a wide range of other promotional efforts. But ultimately none of these pursuits prevented Georgia's sandhill cities from losing ground to Atlanta or enabled them to match other fall-line cities that were seats of state government or flagship universities. Located on the margins of the megaregions that now dominate the modern South's economy, transformative change seems unlikely. Faced with these constraints, the Georgia sandhill cities will likely continue to showcase their distinctive intangible assets as they do now. Columbus proclaims, "We do amazing!" Augusta sells itself as "Funky. Soulful. Historic." And Macon declares itself the city "Where Soul Lives." Perhaps, in the end, modern Macon boosters' enticement of Atlantans to experience its "Soul" by sampling its museums, recording studios, auditoriums, dive bars, and music stores is not so different from their forebears' conception of "The Heart of Georgia" as a fitting place to supplant Atlanta as the state's capital. In an age where the consumption of experiences has superseded the production of goods, the Georgia fall-line cities have finally reached that point where metropolitan ambitions revolve more around *being* than *becoming*.

NOTES

ABBREVIATIONS

ACS	Alva C. Smith Collection
ACVB	Augusta Convention & Visitors Bureau, Augusta, GA
AMH	Augusta Museum of History, Augusta, GA
ARCPL	Augusta–Richmond County Public Library, Augusta, GA
BFM	Bucker F. Melton Papers
CAHA	USDA Census of Agriculture Historical Archive
CHBL	Chattanooga–Hamilton Bicentennial Library, Chattanooga, TN
CSRA	Central Savannah River Area
CSUA	Columbus State University Archives, Schwob Library, Columbus State University, Columbus, GA
CUL	Cornell University Library Division of Rare and Manuscript Collections, Ithaca, NY
DHABC	Dixie Highway Auxiliary, Bibb Co. Chapter
DHAMB	Dixie Highway Association Minutes Book
GMCC	Greater Macon Chamber of Commerce Records
GVF	Georgiana Vertical File
HAI	Historic Augusta, Inc., Augusta, GA
HOLC	Home Owners' Loan Corporation
HRBML	Hargrett Rare Book and Manuscript Library, University of Georgia, Athens, GA
JJM	John J. McKay Jr. Papers
LSM	Lester S. Moody Collection
MCCS	Macon Chamber of Commerce Scrapbook
MCW	Mary Carter Winter Collection

MGA	Middle Georgia Archives, Washington Memorial Library, Macon, GA
PZC	Macon–Bibb County Planning & Zoning Commission Records
RLSC	Reese Library Special Collections, Augusta University, Augusta, GA
SRP	Savannah River Plant
WTA	W. T. Anderson Papers

INTRODUCTION

1. Perry, "Population Distribution and Change: 2010 to 2020."

2. Blaine A. Brownell coined the term "commercial-civic elite" in the 1970s, describing the southern variant of what John R. Logan and Harvey L. Molotch later called the "growth machine," or "growth coalition" as other scholars have termed it. See Blaine A. Brownell, "Commercial Civic Elite," in Rushing, ed., *The New Encyclopedia of Southern Culture*, Vol. 15: *Urbanization*, 34–38; Logan and Molotch, *Urban Fortunes*, chap. 3.

3. Bureau of the Census, *Geographic Areas Reference Manual*, chap. 13, https://www2.census.gov/geo/pdfs/reference/GARM/Ch13GARM.pdf.

4. Goldfield, *Cotton Fields and Skyscrapers*, 87–89; Doyle, *New Men, New Cities, New South*.

5. On Sunbelt cities, see especially Watkins and Perry, eds., *The Rise of the Sunbelt Cities*; Abbott, *The New Urban America*; Bernard and Rice, eds., *Sunbelt Cities*; Sawers and Tabb, eds., *Sunbelt/Snowbelt*; Mohl, ed., *Searching for the Sunbelt*.

6. Harris, "A Portrait of North American Urban Historians." On Atlanta, see Russell, *Atlanta, 1847–1890*; Bayor, *Race and the Shaping of Twentieth-Century Atlanta*; Hunter, *To Joy My Freedom*; Newman, *Southern Hospitality*; Hickey, *Hope and Danger in the New South City*; Kruse, *White Flight*; Lands, *The Culture of Property*; Link, *Atlanta, Cradle of the New South*; Lands, *Poor Atlanta*. On New Orleans, see for example, Hirsch and Logsdon, eds., *Creole New Orleans*; Kelman, *A River and Its City*; Long, *The Great Southern Babylon*; Souther, *New Orleans on Parade*; Nystrom, *New Orleans After the Civil War*; Germany, *New Orleans After the Promises*; Horowitz, *Katrina*. On Houston, see especially Pruitt, *The Other Great Migration*. On Charlotte, see especially Hanchett, *Sorting Out the New South City*. Most Miami scholarship has yet to situate the South Florida city within a southern framework; a notable exception is Connolly, *A World More Concrete*.

7. See, for example, Moore, *Columbia and Richland County*; Huff, *Greenville*; Thomason, ed., *Mobile*; Fraser, *Savannah in the New South*; Causey, *Red Clay, White Water and Blues*; Wilson, *Charleston and Savannah*.

8. See, for example, Bolin, *Bossism and Reform in a Southern City*; Newton, *Montgomery in the Good War*; Yuhl, *A Golden Haze of Memory*; Lee, *The Tennessee-Virginia Tri-Cities*; Dotson, *Roanoke, Virginia, 1882–1912*.

9. Notable exceptions include Silver, *Twentieth-Century Richmond*; Wheeler,

Knoxville, Tennessee; Knapp, *Constructing the Dynamo of Dixie;* Lessoff, *Where Texas Meets the Sea.*

10. Doyle, *New Men, New Cities, New South,* 5. Exceptions include Silver, *Twentieth-Century Richmond;* Moore, *Columbia and Richland County;* Causey, *Red Clay, White Water, and Blues.*

11. Brownell, *The Urban Ethos in the South, 1920–1930;* Brownell and Goldfield, eds., *The City in Southern History;* Rabinowitz, *Race Relations in the Urban South, 1865–1890;* Bernard and Rice, eds., *Sunbelt Cities;* Goldfield, *Cotton Fields and Skyscrapers.* Goldfield surveys his work in relation to the early development of southern urban historiography; see Goldfield, *Region, Race, and Cities,* 4–8.

12. Lessoff, *Where Texas Meets the Sea,* 22–28. Lessoff, in turn, finds influence in Carl Abbott's work on "networked cities" in the western U.S. context; see Abbott, *The Metropolitan Frontier,* chap. 3.

13. The fall-line zone of Georgia has long trailed behind the growth rates of metropolitan Atlanta and northern Georgia; see Perry, "Population Distribution and Change." The difficulty that secondary cities face ascending in rank within a network of cities seems no less applicable to secondary cities within a state and region than within a global urban system; for context, see Hodos, *Second Cities,* 2, 5–6.

14. My understanding of early trade territories owes a particular debt to William Cronon's discussion of how Mississippi Valley grain farmers related to potential markets for their commodity; see Cronon, *Nature's Metropolis,* chap. 3.

15. Georgia Railroad, Stone Mountain Route, *Eastern Middle Georgia, the Cream of the Southland;* Russell Brown, "Georgia Railroad Bank and Trust," *New Georgia Encyclopedia,* last modified August 27, 2019, https://www.georgiaencyclopedia.org /articles/business-economy/georgia-railroad-bank-and-trust/.

16. Amee Vyas, "Georgia's County Governments," *New Georgia Encyclopedia,* last modified July 6, 2022. https://www.georgiaencyclopedia.org/articles/counties-cities -neighborhoods/georgias-county-governments/; Jasper Berry Shannon, quoted in Black and Black, *Politics and Society in the South,* 25.

17. Between 1870 and 1924, Georgia chartered twenty-seven new counties; see Newberry Library, *Atlas of Historical County Boundaries.*

18. On the concern about Black purchasing power, see Susan Myrick, "The Idealism of a Great Editor," *Publishers Service Magazine,* 15 December 1932, 14, W. T. Anderson Papers, Middle Georgia Archives (MGA), Washington Memorial Library, Macon, GA. Columbia, South Carolina, boosters similarly used their city's large rural hinterland to accentuate its apparent size and stature and deflect from the fact that many among its actual metropolitan population were African Americans "too poor to buy much of anything"; see Moore, *Columbia and Richland County,* 273.

19. Macon Chamber of Commerce Report: Economic Study of Macon, 1943, box 4, folder 47, Greater Macon Chamber of Commerce Records, MGA; John Mebane, "Mid-Georgia Council Proposed to Develop Huge Macon Area," *Atlanta Journal,* 13 February 1944, 2.

20. For context on boosters' use of "lore and myth," see Lessoff, *Where Texas Meets the Sea*, 81.

21. Douglas Appler argues similarly that understanding urban renewal requires examining smaller cities that have long been neglected by urban historians; see Appler, ed., *The Many Geographies of Urban Renewal*.

22. "Publisher Supported Educating Blacks and Battled Ku Klux Klan," *Macon Telegraph*, 5 January 1997; Causey, *Red Clay, White Water, and Blues*, 2, 62, 140, 215–16; "Robert Woodruff is Dead: Created Coca-Cola Empire," *New York Times*, March 9, 1985, B6.

23. Molotch, "The City as a Growth Machine," 315; Gaurneri, *Newsprint Metropolis*, 9.

24. Cashin, *The Story of Augusta*, 9–10, 18; Cashin, "Augusta," *New Georgia Encyclopedia*, last modified 4 May 2021, https://georgiaencyclopedia.org/articles/counties-cities-neighborhoods/augusta/.

25. Cashin, *The Story of Augusta*, 30–31, 39–40; Cashin, "Augusta"; Edwin Jackson, "Georgia's Historic Capitals," *New Georgia Encyclopedia*, last modified 14 August 2020, https://georgiaencyclopedia.org/articles/counties-cities-neighborhoods/georgias-historic-capitals/.

26. Cashin, "Augusta"; Cashin, *The Story of Augusta*, 71, 73, 93–96.

27. German, "The Queen City of the Savannah," 3–5; Cashin, *The Story of Augusta*, 121, 128.

28. Cashin, *The Story of Augusta*, 149; "The Lowell of the South," *Augusta Chronicle*, 30 June 1878, 1; Carlton, *Mill and Town in South Carolina, 1880–1920*, 13–15; German, "The Queen City of the Savannah," 17–18; Advertisement, *Augusta Chronicle*, 2 February 1908, 9.

29. Butler, *Historical Record of Macon and Central Georgia*, 98–99; Souther, "'Green Spots in the Heart of Town.'" 289.

30. "Macon Once Was Thriving River Port for State Farmers," *Macon Telegraph*, 19 April 1942, 116th Anniversary Edition, 2. For context on the erosion caused by cutting timber, cultivating cotton, roadbuilding, and misguided efforts at soil conservation, see especially Fite, *Cotton Fields No More*; Sutter, *Let Us Now Praise Famous Gullies*, chaps. 6 and 7.

31. Iobst, *Civil War Macon*, 2–3, 344–55, 450. On the Cannonball House story, see Eichhorn, *The Civil War Battles of Macon*, chap. 7.

32. Manis, *Macon Black and White*, 16.

33. Nancy Anderson, "Macon," *New Georgia Encyclopedia*, last modified 30 August 2017, https://www.georgiaencyclopedia.org/articles/counties-cities-neighborhoods/macon/.

34. Young, Gholson, and Hargrove, *The History of Macon, Georgia, 1823–1949*, 329–30, 335.

35. Anderson, "Macon."

36. "Macon Speeding Annexation Tasks," *Macon Telegraph*, May 26, 1961; Nelson

et al., "Mapping Inequality," https://dsl.richmond.edu/panorama/redlining/map #loc=8/32.4171/-83.3812. The "Mapping Inequality" website provides ratios of HOLC-surveyed city areas assigned each of the four grades, A-D, but the proportions include ungraded industrial zones. Project director Robert K. Nelson provided the author a database of cities by D-graded areas as a proportion of graded areas excluding industrial zones, and these serve as the basis for these national ranks. For more context on the HOLC in the fall-line cities, see Ella Howard, "Redlining Georgia," in Cox and Gardner, eds., *Reassessing the 1930s South*, 196–98.

37. Kruse, *White Flight*, 38.

38. John Lupold, "Columbus," *New Georgia Encyclopedia*, last modified 9 September 2019, https://www.georgiaencyclopedia.org/articles/counties-cities -neighborhoods/columbus/; Causey, *Red Clay, White Water and Blues*, 3, 18–21.

39. Causey, *Red Clay, White Water and Blues*, 34–35, 46–49.

40. Lupold, "Columbus"; Causey, *Red Clay, White Water and Blues*, 58, 86.

41. Causey, *Red Clay, White Water and Blues*, 77–83, 146–47, 217.

1. THE HEART OF GEORGIA

1. "Georgia Lawmakers' Thirst," *New York Times*, 6 August 1911, 1; Joseph R. Curtis, "Georgia Legislature is Here; Macon Makes Fine Impression," *Macon News*, 5 August 1911, 1. On the capital move to Atlanta, see Edwin L. Jackson, "Georgia's Historic Capitals," *New Georgia Encyclopedia*, 14 August 2020, https://www .georgiaencyclopedia.org/articles/counties-cities-neighborhoods/georgias-historic -capitals.

2. On earlier efforts by Macon to challenge Atlanta, see Wynne, *The Continuity of Cotton*, 94–95. On the inland shift of southern economic growth, see Doyle, *New Men, New Cities, New South*.

3. On rural hinterlands as a fundamental part of early- to mid-twentieth-century "southern urban spatial identity," see Brownell, *The Urban Ethos in the South*, 80.

4. For the "Central City" nickname, see "City of Macon, Ga.," *New York Times*, 8 June 1895, 20.

5. "Capital," *Macon Daily Telegraph*, 27 November 1910, 3. The *Telegraph* compiled several Georgia newspapers' recent editorials about the capital issue, including that of the *Savannah Evening Press*.

6. Doyle, *New Men, New Cities, New South*, 155; Brownell, *The Urban Ethos in the South*, 81–83.

7. Key, *Southern Politics in State and Nation*.

8. "Move the Capital into Georgia," *Macon Daily Telegraph*, 3 December 1910, 4. For an early example of the boosterish notion of an "Atlanta spirit," see Atlanta Chamber of Commerce, *Atlanta: A Twentieth Century City*, 5.

9. "The Capital—A Question of Courtesy," *Macon Daily Telegraph*, 5 August 1910,

4; Department of Commerce and Labor, Bureau of the Census, *Thirteenth Census of the United States Taken in the Year 1910; Statistics for Georgia* (Washington, DC: Government Printing Office, 1913), 572.

10. "A. J. Long Cigar and Grocery Company," *Macon Daily Telegraph*, 15 May 1910, sec. 4, p. 10; "Mass Meeting of the Citizens of the Various City Suburbs," *Macon Daily Telegraph*, 28 February 1909, 2; "Big Mass Meeting Favors the Greater Macon Movement," *Macon Daily Telegraph*, 4 March 1909, 7. For context on annexations in southern cities, see Blaine A. Brownell, "The Urban South Comes of Age, 1900–1940," in Brownell and Goldfield, eds., *The City in Southern History*, 135–36. On another fall-line city, see Moore, *Columbia and Richland County*, 276–83.

11. "Census Man Will Now Have Big Job," *Macon Daily Telegraph*, 21 March 1910, 9.

12. "Big Mass Meeting Favors the Greater Macon Movement"; "City Engineer Wilcox Gives Macon Population of 71,558," *Macon Daily Telegraph*, 24 September 1909, 3. For a map of Augusta annexations, see Hutchinson and Brewster, *Population Mobility*, 6. For the *Waycross Herald* editorial, see "Macon Forging Ahead," *Macon Daily Telegraph*, 27 March 1910, 4. The Wiregrass region is located in southern Georgia, northern Florida, and southeastern Alabama.

13. "The Correct Population of Augusta is 41,305, 3,479 More Than Incorrect Report of Census Bureau," *Augusta Chronicle*, 21 November 1910, 1; "Macon Increases 17,000 People Since Last the Census Was Enumerated," *Macon Daily Telegraph*, 11 October 1910, 1. I am indebted to Cashin, *The Story of Augusta*, 207, for introducing me to the 1910 census controversy.

14. "Complete 'Volunteer Census' of Augusta Will Be Taken Between Sunrise and Sunset Sunday by Patriotic Citizens," *Augusta Chronicle*, 19 November 1910, 1; "The Correct Population of Augusta is 41,305."

15. "A Message to Macon on the Census Statistics and—Macon's Reply," *Augusta Chronicle*, 21 November 1910, 1. The Macon Board of Health conducted its own recount of 41,775, which was 480 more than Augusta's, but the Bureau of the Census refused to accept it; see "Board of Health's New Census Gives to Macon 41,775," *Macon Daily Telegraph*, 22 November 1910, 1.

16. "Census Bureau Allows the Augusta Citizens Recount," *Macon Daily Telegraph*, 10 December 1910, 1. The recount, while sensational, was not unique. Indeed, after Chicago had surpassed St. Louis in population in 1880, St. Louisans demanded and were granted an opportunity to conduct a recount, which in their case was insufficient to change the city's rank; see James Neal Primm, "The Economy of Nineteenth-Century St. Louis," in Sandweiss, ed., *St. Louis in the Century of Henry Shaw*, 130.

17. "With Monster Torchlight Procession, All Augusta Celebrates Real Census," *Augusta Chronicle*, 11 December 1910, 8.

18. For the *Griffin News* editorial, see "State Press is Discussing Proposition to Move Capital," *Macon Daily Telegraph*, 4 December 1910, 1. For the *Tifton Gazette* editorial, see "What the State Newspapers Are Saying About Moving the State Capital and Mercer," *Macon Daily Telegraph*, 11 December 1910, 4. For the *Dawson*

News editorial, see "What the State Newspapers Are Saying About Moving the State Capital and Mercer," *Macon Daily Telegraph*, 14 December 1910, 4. Railroad timetables underscore the burden of reaching Atlanta from the southernmost reaches of the state. As one example, in 1910, the Central of Georgia's Pullman service took nearly 9 hours from Valdosta to Atlanta compared with 5.5 hours to Macon; see Burns et al., eds., *Official Railway Guide*.

19. For the *Cochran Journal* and *Milledgeville Union-Recorder* editorials, see "What the State Newspapers Are Saying About Moving the State Capital and Mercer," *Macon Daily Telegraph*, 10 December 1910, 4. For the *Meriwether Vindicator* [Greenville, GA] editorial, see "What the State Newspapers Are Saying About Moving the State Capital and Mercer," *Macon Daily Telegraph*, 13 December 1910, 4. One South Georgia city also associated Atlanta's capital city status with the legacy of "carpetbaggers"; see the *Valdosta Times* editorial in "What the State Newspapers Are Saying About Moving the State Capital and Mercer," *Macon Daily Telegraph*, 15 December 1910, 4. For an account of Atlanta's two-decade effort to wrest the capital from Milledgeville, see Crimmins and Farrisee, *Democracy Restored*, chap. 2.

20. Jackson, "Georgia State Capitol."

21. "What the State Newspapers Are Saying About Moving the State Capital and Mercer," *Macon Daily Telegraph*, 14 December 1910, 4; "Organization Formed for Campaign to Get Capital Moved Back into Georgia Again," *Macon Daily Telegraph*, 6 December 1910, 1; "Moving the Capital is No Joke," *Macon Daily Telegraph*, 4 December 1910, 4.

22. "Send in Your Slogan and Help in Move for a Greater Macon," *Macon Daily Telegraph*, 23 May 1910, 5; "Macon's New Slogan," *Augusta Chronicle*, 10 August 1910, 9.

23. "Publicity Bureau to Aid in Macon's Capital Fight," *Macon Daily Telegraph*, 20 December 1910, 12; "Macon Buttons Received Here," *Columbus Ledger*, 15 January 1911, 8.

24. "Location of State Capitol," *Augusta Chronicle*, 27 September 1912, 6.

25. "Half Million Dollar Hotel Pledged While One Would Breathe," *Macon Daily Telegraph*, 6 December 1910, 1.

26. "Macon is Up-to-Date; Builds Hotel That Would Do Credit to New York," *Macon Daily Telegraph*, 26 December 1912, 1; "Large Electric Sign on Top Hotel Dempsey," *Macon Daily Telegraph*, 2 October 1912, 8. For "Heart of Georgia" origin, see "Outside Towns Enter Slogan Contest with Residents of Macon," *Macon Daily Telegraph*, 30 May 1910, 8. For "blaze of truculent glory," see "Send in Your Slogan and Help in Move for a Greater Macon," *Macon Daily Telegraph*, 23 May 1910, 5.

27. Minutes of meeting, Macon, GA, 7 March 1919, regarding capital removal, W. T. Anderson Papers (WTA), Middle Georgia Archives (MGA), Washington Memorial Library, Macon, GA; John W. Hammond to Hon. Ben J. Fowler, 31 March 1919, WTA.

28. "Atlanta Begins Fight to Retain the State Capital," *Macon News*, 30 June 1919, 1; Atlanta Committee ad: "Capital Removal is Dead and Macon KNOWS It," *Macon Daily Telegraph*, 13 July 1919, WTA; W. T. Anderson to St. Elmo Massengale, 14 July 1919, WTA; William Thomas Anderson: A Short Biography, n.d., WTA.

29. Susan Myrick, "The Idealism of a Great Editor," *Publishers Service Magazine*, 15 December 1932, 14, WTA; Manis, *Macon Black and White*, 100, 105. Concerns over malapportionment under Georgia's infamous county unit system led to some idle discussion in the 1920s of dividing Georgia into North and South Georgia, enabling Atlanta to exert greater political control over its own commercial and industrial interests while allowing Macon to be "capital of the southern agricultural sections; see Montès, *American Capitals*, 128.

30. Craddock Goins, "Macon, the South's Dairy Capital?" *Macon Magazine*, July 1924, 7, box 3, folder 38c, Greater Macon Chamber of Commerce Records (GMCC), MGA; Liesch, "Chinch Bug."

31. "Macon Facing Its Best Year," *The Dixie Manufacturer*, 25 January 1924, 24, Macon Chamber of Commerce Scrapbook (MCCS), box 5, folder 51, GMCC.

32. Brownell, *The Urban Ethos in the South*, 77–79.

33. Works Progress Administration, *The Macon Guide and the Ocmulgee National Monument*, 22; Okie, *The Georgia Peach*, chap. 3.

34. Okie, *The Georgia Peach*, 79–82; Finlay, "The Failure of Chemurgy in the Depression-Era South," 82–83; "Test Farms Proposed by Central of Georgia," *Macon Daily Telegraph*, 20 August 1911, 10; W. A. Winburn, "Georgia Not Dependent Upon Cotton for Agricultural Prosperity," *Middle Georgia Supplement of the Macon Magazine*, n.d. [1924], 4, box 3, folder 38c, GMCC; "Agricultural Implements," *Iron Tradesman* (February 1915), 135.

35. Young, Gholson, and Hargrove, *A History of Macon, Georgia*, 447; Wilton E. Cobb, "Agriculture Making Wonderful Progress in Bibb County, Georgia," *Agricultural Bulletin*, 2 October 1925, MCCS, box 5, folder 51, GMCC; Giesen, *Boll Weevil Blues*, 107–18, 146–50.

36. Cobb, "Agriculture Making Wonderful Progress in Bibb County, Georgia"; Manis, *Macon Black and White*, 73–75.

37. Winburn, "Georgia Not Dependent Upon Cotton for Agricultural Prosperity"; Statement of J. F. Jackson, General Agricultural Agent, Central of Georgia Railway, House of Representatives Report No. 870: Creation of organized rural communities in the South, 10 March 1930, 9, in *House Reports, 71st Congress, 2d Session*.

38. "About Macon, Georgia; Conditions Make Outlook for 1925 Very Bright," *United States Investor*, 20 December 1924, MCCS, box 5, folder 51, GMCC.

39. Macon News, *History of Macon: The First One Hundred Years, 1823–1923* (Macon, GA: Macon News, 1929), 98–99, box 6, folder 53, GMCC; "Chamber Reports Macon's Progress," *Macon Magazine*, February 1924, 4, box 3, folder 38c, GMCC.

40. Okie, *The Georgia Peach*, 82–83, 111; "Southern Development Work of 25 Years Ago Should Be an Inspiration to the Present," *Manufacturers Record*, 9 October 1913, 43; Economic Study of Macon, Georgia Institute of Technology, 1943, box 4, folder 47,

GMCC. On the fixation with white farm settlement in the early 20th century, see also Herbin-Triant, *Threatening Property*, 193–207.

41. "A Middle Georgia Development Campaign by Macon Chamber of Commerce," *Manufacturers Record*, 6 September 1923, 99; Andrew M. Soule, "A Prosperity Program for the Farmers of Middle Georgia," *Middle Georgia Supplement of the Macon Magazine*, n.d. [1924]; "Farm Survey Made of Macon's Trade Territory Comprehensive in Scope," *Macon News*, 15 March 1925, MCCS, box 5, folder 52, GMCC; Bureau of the Census, *Thirteenth Census of the United States, 1910:* Vol. 6: *Agriculture, 1909 and 1910–Alabama to Montana:* 50–51, 359–61, 364–70, and Vol. 7: *Agriculture, 1909 and 1910–Nebraska to Wyoming*, 516–17, USDA Census of Agriculture Historical Archive (CAHA); Bureau of the Census, *United States Census of Agriculture, 1925, Part 2—The Southern States* (Washington, DC: United States Government Printing Office, 1927), 376, 379, 501, 503–4, 507–14, 828–29, CAHA; "Chamber Reports Macon's Progress," 3; "Land Project is Taken Up," *Macon News*, 22 June 1923, 1. The Middle Georgia farm survey covered Bibb, Baldwin, Wilkinson, Twiggs, Monroe, Houston, and Crawford counties. I define the Columbus trade area as including Muscogee, Chattahoochee, Harris, Marion, Stewart, and Talbot counties in Georgia and Lee and Russell counties in Alabama, and the Augusta trade area as including Richmond, Burke, Columbia, Jefferson, and McDuffie counties in Georgia and Aiken and Edgefield counties in South Carolina.

42. "Farm Survey Made"; *Middle Georgia Supplement of the Macon Magazine*, cover. Here I use the same definition as for cotton acreage in note 41; see Bureau of the Census, *Thirteenth Census of the United States, 1910:* Vols. 6–7; Bureau of the Census, *United States Census of Agriculture, 1925, Part 2—The Southern States*, 376, 379, 501, 503–4, 507–14, 828–29.

43. "More Industries," *Macon Magazine*, February 1924, 6; *Middle Georgia Supplement to the Macon Magazine*, back cover; "What the Chamber of Commerce is Doing," *Macon Magazine*, June 1924, 10, box 3, folder 38d, GMCC; "Peach Men Are Expected Back," *Macon News*, 7 December 1924; Okie, *The Georgia Peach*, 129–30.

44. "Founding," *Delta Flight Museum*, https://www.deltamuseum.org/exhibits /delta-history/founding; "Airplane Dusters to Lay Trail of Peach Petals at Festival," *The Duster Dispatch* [Macon, GA] 1, no. 1 (1925), https://www.deltamuseum .org/docs/site/aircraft-pages/hdd-duster-dispatch-1925.pdf; C. W. Berl, "Crop Protection by Airplane Duster," *Manufacturers Record*, 9 July 1925, MCCS, box 5, folder 51, GMCC; "Booster Meet Stirs Interest," *Macon News*, 24 May 1925, 12.

45. "Founding."

46. Bureau of the Census, *Fifteenth Census of the United States, 1930: Agriculture, Vol. 3: Type of Farm, Part 2—The Southern States* (Washington, DC: United States Government Printing Office, 1932), 341, 345–46, CAHA.

47. Bureau of the Census, *United States Census of Agriculture, 1925, Part 2—The Southern States*, 376, 379, 501, 503–4, 507–14, 828–29; Bureau of the Census, *Fifteenth Census of the United States, 1930: Agriculture, Vol. 3: Type of Farm, Part 2—The Southern States*, 307, 310, 339–41, 344–49, 668–69.

48. Minutes, 7 June 1927, Meeting Minutes of the Bibb County Dixie Highway Auxiliary, 1924–1927, 76–77, https://dlg.usg.edu/record/gac_dix_dix205, Dixie Highway Auxiliary, Bibb Co. Chapter (DHABC), MGA; "History National Dixie Highway Auxiliary," *The Dixie Highway* 11, no. 5 (May 1925), 1, https://dlg.usg.edu /record/gac_dix_dix189, DHABC.

49. Ingram, *Dixie Highway*, 6–7, 43.

50. Dixie Highway Association Minutes Book (DHAMB), 23 April 1915, 3, Records of the Chattanooga Automobile Club/Dixie Highway Association, Chattanooga–Hamilton Bicentennial Library, Chattanooga, TN.

51. DHAMB, 25 March 1916, 31; DHAMB, 29 March 1916, 33; "History National Dixie Highway Auxiliary."

52. Whisnant, *Super-Scenic Motorway*, 17–24.

53. The situation would be reprised decades later when Columbus became the nation's largest city left off the original interstate highway system; see Causey, *Red Clay, White Water, and Blues*, 215.

54. Myrick, "The Idealism of a Great Editor"; Ingram, *Dixie Highway*, 81, 83.

55. Ingram, *Dixie Highway*, 67; DHAMB, 25 March 1916, 32.

56. "Bee-Line Highway," *Macon News*, 7 May 1925, 6; "New Highway Zone Planned," unknown newspaper, 28 May 1925, MCCS, box 5, folder 51, GMCC; "Lions Sponsor Highway Work," *Macon News*, 14 July 1925, 1.

57. "Macon Good Will Tour Comes to Cordele on September Sixteenth," *Cordele Dispatch*, 28 August 1925, MCCS, box 5, folder 51, GMCC; "Good Will Tour," *Eastman Journal*, 20 August 1925, MCCS, box 5, folder 51, GMCC. For a regional comparison, see Huff, *Greenville*, 306.

58. "Macon Citizens Will Visit South Georgia," *Ashburn Wiregrass Farmer*, 20 August 1925, MCCS, box 5, folder 51, GMCC; "Bullish Feeling in Georgia," *American Nut Journal* 20, no, 1 (January 1924): 12; "Local Trade Territory," *Columbus Ledger*, 11 August 1925, MCCS, box 5, folder 51, GMCC; "Macon Tourists Given Welcome," *Ashburn Wiregrass Farmer*, 17 September 1925, MCCS, box 5, folder 51, GMCC.

59. "New Booklet on Macon," *Macon Telegraph*, 24 March 1917, 10; *Automobile Blue Book*, Vol. 2, 456; Souther, "'Green Spots in the Heart of Town.'"

60. Notes on work completed by the Bibb County Dixie Highway Auxiliary, 1921, DHABC, https://dlg.usg.edu/record/gac_dix_dix209; Report of Work of Dixie Highway Auxiliary, 1921 January–October, DHABC, https://dlg.usg.edu/record/gac _dix_dix215; Reynolds, "A History of Fruitland Nurseries," 9; President's Report of the Bibb County Dixie Highway Auxiliary, Macon, Georgia, 1921–1923, DHABC, https://dlg.usg.edu/record/gac_dix_dix214; Minutes of meeting, 3 February 1925, DHABC, https://dlg.usg.edu/record/gac_dix_dix205.

61. Ingram, *Dixie Highway*, 188; Minutes of Convention, National Dixie Highway Auxiliary, second session, 18 May 1928, DHABC, https://dlg.usg.edu/record/gac _dix_dix226.

62. Woolf, *Sesquicentennial of the Greater Macon Chamber of Commerce*, 38–39; "WMAZ: Doing a Peach of a Job in Georgia" (booklet), n.d. [ca. 1933], box 1, folder 19, GMCC.

63. "A New Deal for Macon's Cash Registers!" (ad), *Macon Telegraph and News*, 9 April 1933, MCCS, box 6, folder 55, GMCC.

64. "A New Deal for Macon's Cash Registers!"; "Sign Erected in Griffin to Bring Tourists Here," *Macon Telegraph and News*, 13 November 1932, MCCS, box 6, folder 55, GMCC.

65. "Macon Parks to Be Worked on WPA Funds," *Macon Telegraph*, 10 August 1935, 1; "Roads Will Be Beautified with Work-Relief Money," *Macon Telegraph*, 29 June 1935, 7; George D. W. Burt, "Builders of Middle Georgia, No. 10–Glover Glendenning Toole," *Macon Telegraph*, 26 May 1935, 9; "Paving Sought for Cleveland," *Macon Telegraph*, 30 March 1938, 3.

66. "Beautification of Macon Suggested by Publisher," *Macon Telegraph*, 26 March 1936, 11; "Beautification Program Started by Kiwanis Club," *Macon Telegraph*, 2 April 1936, 1.

67. Beverly Wallace, "Beautification Stressed by Anderson at Jackson," *Macon Telegraph*, 19 August 1936, 7; "Baldwin Women Hear Anderson," *Macon Telegraph*, 29 October 1936, 9.

68. Beverly Wallace, "Rules and Prizes in State Garden Contest Announced," *Macon Telegraph*, 18 October 1936, 14; "Cochran to Aid Chamber Project," *Macon Telegraph*, 9 July 1936, 11; "More Right-of-Way for Beauty," *Macon Telegraph*, 8 November 1936, 4; "Land is Obtained to Beautify Road," *Macon Telegraph*, 10 February 1937, 9.

69. "Beautification Program Urged for State Roads," *Macon Telegraph*, 24 September 1936, 3; "Jones County is Enthusiastic Over Beautification Program," *Macon Telegraph*, 26 August 1936, 7.

70. Wallace, "Beautification Stressed by Anderson at Jackson"; "Uniting on Highway Projects," *Macon Telegraph*, 24 November 1937, 4.

71. "Beautification Plans Grow," *Macon Telegraph*, 6 November 1936, 4; Souther, "Making 'The Garden City of the South,'" 88, 90, 97.

72. Susan Myrick, "Macon Flower Show's Success is Pointing Way to New Beauty," *Macon Telegraph*, 3 May 1936, 12.

73. Myrick, "Macon Flower Show's Success is Pointing Way to New Beauty"; "Paving Sought for Cleveland"; Susan Myrick, "Riot of Color Found in Porterdale Garden; Public Gets View of Wonderful Display Here," *Macon Evening News*, 4 May 1934, 5; "Azalea Gardens Opening Sunday," *Macon Telegraph*, 29 March 1935, 2; Works Progress Administration, *The Macon Guide and the Ocmulgee National Monument*, 108, 115–16.

74. Marsh, "Ocmulgee," 84–85.

75. Marsh, "Ocmulgee," 85–86. A parallel may be seen in attempts in the 1930s by the Columbus Chamber of Commerce to interest the National Park Service in

designating Providence Canyon, a product of erosion romanticized as a "natural" wonder in Stewart County, as a national park; see Sutter, *Now Let Us Praise Famous Gullies,* 75.

76. Marsh, "Ocmulgee," 87–88; Dr. Arthur R. Kelly, "Mound Explorer Amazed at Neglected Opportunity," *Macon Telegraph,* 23 May 1935, MCCS, box 7, folder 56, GMCC; "Indian Park May Be Lost for City Due to Finances," *Macon Telegraph and News,* 21 April 1935, MCCS, box 7, folder 56, GMCC.

77. "Park Project is Endorsed by Robert J. Taylor Here," *Macon Evening News,* 16 May 1935, MCCS, box 7, folder 56, GMCC.

78. Marsh, "Ocmulgee," 88–91.

79. "Uniting on Highway Projects," *Macon Telegraph,* 24 November 1937, 4; "Developing Ocmulgee Fields," *Macon Telegraph,* 8 February 1936, 4.

80. Ed Bernd, "Macon's Indian Mounds Are Attracting Visitors from All Parts of U.S.," *Macon Telegraph,* 27 August 1936, 1; Macon Chamber of Commerce 1937 Annual Report; Works Progress Administration, *The Macon Guide and the Ocmulgee National Monument.*

81. Works Progress Administration, *The Macon Guide and the Ocmulgee National Monument,* 18.

82. This ambivalence is exemplified in comments by Macon Chamber of Commerce executive vice president Lee S. Trimble in 1940: "It is a different city; the tempo of its life has been accelerated . . . The big job of keeping the healthy balance between industry, trade, agriculture, and culture that has been Macon's finest attribute, lies ahead. 'It's the best place in the world in which to live and rear a family' has been Macon's most frequent compliment. It must be kept so, if humanly possible." See *A Story of Progress in Macon, 1940* [Macon Chamber of Commerce], box 1, folder 3, GMCC.

83. Southern boosters' persistent embrace of agrarian urbanism into the twentieth century is explored in Goldfield, *Cotton Fields and Skyscrapers,* 89–91.

2. THE WINTER CAPITAL OF AMERICA

1. "Right Royal Welcome to President-Elect Wm. H. Taft," *Augusta Chronicle,* 19 December 1908, 1; "Terrett Cottage Selected by Taft for the Winter," *Augusta Chronicle,* 25 November 1908, 1. For biographical information on Hayne, see "United States Census, 1910," GenealogyBank (https://genealogybank.com/#), L. C. Hayne, Ward 1, Augusta, Richmond County, Georgia, United States"; "What Is Thought of Mr. Hayne in Burke," *Augusta Chronicle,* 10 October 1900, 5. Edward J. Cashin's urban biography of Augusta informs this chapter. For more detail on Taft's 1908 visit, see Cashin, *The Story of Augusta,* 196. For context on Augusta as "Lowell of the South," see Manganiello, *Southern Water, Southern Power,* chap. 1.

2. "Judge Wm. H. Taft Tells Why He Chose 'Hill' and Augusta as Place of Winter

Residence," *Augusta Chronicle*, 12 February 1909, 1; "Augusta Above Sea Level and City's Highest Points," *Augusta Chronicle*, 21 May 1911, 1.

3. Souther, "Making 'The Garden City of the South.'" 87–88.

4. Cashin, *The Story of Augusta*, 59. For the quote, see Valencius, *The Health of the Country*, 86. See also Nash, *Inescapable Ecologies*, especially chap. 2.

5. Hutchinson and Brewster, *Population Mobility*, 11, 46; "Summerville; Growth and Development of Augusta's Pretty Suburb," *Augusta Chronicle*, 7 November 1909, 86. The classic work on streetcar suburbs is Warner, *Streetcar Suburbs*. Other excellent places to start are Stilgoe, *Borderland*, and McShane and Tarr, *The Horse in the City*.

6. "A Complete Freshet," *Augusta Chronicle*, 11 September 1888, 1.

7. Starnes, *Creating the Land of the Sky*, 32–33.

8. For commentary on healthfulness, see "The Health of the Hills," *Augusta Chronicle*, 13 February 1879, 1; "The Sunny South," *Augusta Chronicle*, 31 December 1882, 2. On calls for a hotel, see "The Summerville Hotel," *Augusta Chronicle*, 9 March 1881, 4; "A Hotel on the Sand Hills," *Augusta Chronicle*, 24 March 1883, 4.

9. Anne Osborne, "The Bon Air," *Augusta Magazine* (Spring 1976): 5; "The Sand Hills Hotel Project," box 4, folder 20, Mary Carter Winter Collection (MCW), Reese Library Special Collections, Augusta University (RLSC), Augusta, GA; E. B. Hook, "The Hotel Bon-Air," *Augusta Chronicle*, 1 December 1889, 11; Cashin, *The Story of Augusta*, 170, 172.

10. "Carnival," *Augusta Chronicle*, 15 January 1890, 1; "The Carnival Crowds," *Augusta Chronicle*, 24 January 1891, 8. For context on elites' use of Carnival festivities to encourage civic unity and spur tourism, see Stanonis, "Through a Purple (Green and Gold) Haze," 115–18.

11. "Hotel Problem in Augusta," *Augusta Chronicle*, 4 March 1900, 13; "The Record is Broken," *Augusta Chronicle*, 22 February 1901, 3.

12. Cashin, *The Story of Augusta*, 178; "The Magnificent Winter Resorts," *Augusta Chronicle*, 3 November 1907, 39.

13. "The Record is Broken"; "The Country Club of Augusta," *Augusta Chronicle*, 7 November 1909, 2.

14. Osborne, "The Bon Air," 6. On the rise of golf, see Jackson, *Crabgrass Frontier*, 98–99. On the emergence of golf in southern resorts, see Moss, *Golf and the American Country Club*, 91–92; Youngs, "Creating America's Winter Golfing Mecca at Pinehurst, North Carolina"; Himel, "Greening Golf."

15. "Hotel Bon Air, Augusta, Ga., Season 1908-9," 7, box 5, folder "Augusta Resource Material 1900–1973," Augusta Metro Chamber of Commerce Collection (AMCC), Augusta Museum of History, Augusta, GA; "The Real Vandals," *Augusta Chronicle*, 13 July 1902, 12. For context on birds as consumer commodities in this era, see Smalley, *The Market in Birds*.

16. See, for example, "Tourists Are Pouring in Now," *Augusta Chronicle*, 28 January 1904, 5; "Will Close Soon," *Augusta Chronicle*, 28 March 1907, 4

17. "The Contracts Signed Up," *Augusta Chronicle*, 23 March 1902, 5; "Christmas Week at Hampton Terrace," *Augusta Chronicle*, 27 December 1903, 9.

18. "Ground Broken on the New Electric Line," *Augusta Chronicle*, 26 June 1901, 1; "The New Hotel in Aiken Near Completion," *Augusta Chronicle*, 25 October 1903, 24; "Purchasers A. R. & E. Co. in the City," *Augusta Chronicle*, 12 November 1902, 5; "New Combination Street Railway Car," *Augusta Chronicle*, 3 January 1909, 15.

19. Don Metz, "The Glory That Was Rome," *Augusta Magazine*, Fall 1966, 26, RLSC; "More Tourists Here Than Ever," *Augusta Chronicle*, 14 February 1904, 15; "Augusta Needs More Hotel Room," *Augusta Chronicle*, 11 March 1904, 10; "Several More Hotels Needed," *Augusta Chronicle*, 16 April 1905, 25; "No More Room at Tourist Hotels," *Augusta Chronicle*, 9 February 1906, 7. On hotel expansions, see "Tourist Travel Outlook Good," *Augusta Chronicle*, 21 October 1904, 8; "Hotel Will Hold a Small Town," *Augusta Chronicle*, 13 October 1907, 29; "Opening of the Bon Air Tomorrow," *Augusta Chronicle*, 15 December 1909, 5.

20. "Richest Man in America Has Arrived in Augusta," *Augusta Chronicle*, 19 January 1907, 5; "Mr. Rockefeller Leaves Augusta for the Season," *Augusta Chronicle*, 22 March 1908, 11; "Jno. D. Rockefeller and Party Here," *Augusta Chronicle*, 16 January 1909, 7; "Rockefeller Again at Bon Air Hotel for the Season," *Augusta Chronicle*, 2 February 1910, 1; "J. D. Rockefeller and Party Here," *Augusta Chronicle*, 4 February 1911, 5; "Sixth Winter for Mr. Rockefeller," *Augusta Chronicle*, 11 February 1912, 10; "Some of Augusta's Winter Residents," *Augusta Chronicle*, 7 January 1913, 44.

21. "Worst Flood in History of Savannah River Valley Covers Augusta with Water for Two Days and Nights Entailing Loss of Over $750,000 in City and Suburbs," *Augusta Chronicle*, 27 August 1908, 1; Annie R. Keil, "When the Flood Waters Came Down on Augusta," *Augusta Chronicle*, 13 December 1908, 36; Sanders et al., *Flood Frequency of the Savannah River at Augusta, Georgia*, 7.

22. "Twenty Rooms to Partridge House," *Augusta Chronicle*, 13 October 1909, 10; "Partridge Inn On-the-Hill," *Augusta Chronicle*, 21 November 1909, 1; "Augusta's Greatest and Best Advertised Asset is Well Nigh Ignored at Home," *Augusta Chronicle*, 13 March 1911, 6.

23. "Augusta's Greatest and Best Advertised Asset." The *Chronicle*'s drumbeat of promotion of Augusta's tourism potential reflects what Cashin calls the opening of Augusta's "Era of Ballyhoo"; see especially Cashin, *The Story of Augusta*, 205.

24. "Augusta's Greatest and Best Advertised Asset."

25. "An Era of Growth and Enterprise," *Augusta Chronicle-Herald*, 6 March 1960, 175th Anniversary sec., p. 5; "Thomas Loyless Was First to Develop Warm Springs," *Augusta Chronicle*, 18 May 1939, 6; "Messrs. T. K. Scott and D. B. Dyer Sell Their Entire Interest in the Augusta Chronicle," *Augusta Chronicle*, 1 February 1911, 1; Souther, "Making 'The Garden City of the South,'" 91, 93.

26. "For Tourist Hotel Business Men Met To Consider Plans," *Augusta Chronicle*, 30 March 1911, 12; "Mr. O. A. Steiner President of New Inter-Urban and Tourist Hotel Development Company," *Augusta Chronicle*, 14 December 1911, 1; "'Aumond' is

the Beautiful Name of Augusta's Beautiful New Suburb," *Augusta Chronicle*, 18 February 1912, 18; "By Almost Two to One Vote," *Augusta Chronicle*, 27 October 1911, 1-A.

27. "Work Begins This Week on Augusta's Greatest Undertaking," *Augusta Chronicle*, 3 March 1912, 6; Augusta's End of the Tourist Hotel Project Be Put Through This Week by Business Men," *Augusta Chronicle*, 31 March 1912, 2; "A Golf Town," *Augusta Chronicle*, 3 July 1916, 4.

28. "Construction of Levee Will Be Completed in the Early Spring," *Augusta Chronicle*, 10 December 1916, 1; "Augusta Swept by $6,000,000 Fire Last Night; 25 Business and Residence Blocks Burned," *Augusta Chronicle*, 23 March 1916, 1; "Fire-swept Augusta Rallying Gamely to Task of Rebuilding," *Atlanta Journal*, 24 March 1916, 1; Earl L. Bell, "Augusta's Great Conflagration," *Augusta Magazine*, Spring 1968, 14.

29. Hutchinson and Brewster, *Population Mobility*, 47–49.

30. "Hampton Terrace Hotel Fire Upsets Plans of Many Persons," *Augusta Chronicle*, 1 January 1917, 1; "Bon Air Hotel is Destroyed by Fire," *Augusta Chronicle*, 4 February 1921, 1.

31. "Thomas Loyless Was First to Develop Warm Springs"; Tobin, *The Man He Became*, 201–3.

32. On resorts in the South, see especially Starnes, *Creating the Land of the Sky*; Hillyer, *Designing Dixie*; Vivian, *A New Plantation World*. On Macon's push for a resort hotel, see "Macon is Proper Place for Big Tourist Hotel," *Macon News*, 9 February 1921, 1. On Columbus's similar effort, see "Capitalist Wants to Build a Big Tourist Hotel in Columbus," *Columbus Ledger*, 17 September 1922, 1.

33. "Bon Air Hotel Be Rebuilt by Next Season—Directors and Stockholders Accept Cohen Proposition," *Augusta Chronicle*, 11 January 1922, 1; Starnes, *Creating the Land of the Sky*, 55; Committee of Fifty Launches Active Campaign for Bon Air," *Augusta Chronicle*, 25 February 1922, 5; "Bon Air–Vanderbilt Ready for Business; Formal Opening on Monday Evening," *Augusta Chronicle*, 7 January 1923, Bon-Air Tourist Section, 1.

34. "Quarter Million Dollars in Augusta Automobiles," *Augusta Chronicle*, 26 January 1908, 10. On Asheville's highway agenda, see Whisnant, *Super-Scenic Motorway*, 19–20; Starnes, *Creating the Land of the Sky*, 55–56.

35. "Wonders Wrought in Richmond County by Judge Eve During His 31 Years of Service as Road Commissioner," *Augusta Chronicle*, 15 August 1909, 20; "Hotel Bon Air, Augusta, Ga., Season 1908-9," 9; "Hotels Filled to Overflowing Point," *Augusta Chronicle*, 29 February 1912, 7. For context on road improvements in fall-line counties with large African American populations, see Lichstenstein, "Good Roads and Chain Gangs in the Progressive South," 97–99; Ingram, *Dixie Highway*, 132–35.

36. "Are Richmond's Roads Deteriorating?" *Augusta Chronicle*, 7 August 1910, 16.

37. "Richmond County's Roads," *Augusta Chronicle*, 10 February 1915, 4.

38. "Activity and Plenty of Hard Work at Headquarters of M. & M. Ass'n," *Augusta Chronicle*, 25 April 1915, 5.

39. "Augusta the Logical Terminal for Dixie Highway, Says Mr. Haden," *Augusta Chronicle*, 16 May 1915, 3.

40. Ingram, *Dixie Highway*, 85; "Effort by Board Commerce to Bring Dixie Highway to Augusta," *Augusta Chronicle*, 3 February 1918, 1; Dixie Highway Association Minutes Book, 16 May 1918, 57, Records of the Chattanooga Automobile Club/Dixie Highway Association, Chattanooga–Hamilton Bicentennial Library, Chattanooga, TN.

41. Charles F. Rossignol, the Music Man ad, *Augusta Chronicle*, 3 November 1907, 4; Charles F. Rossignol & Co. ad, *Augusta Chronicle*, 21 August 1919, 3; "Complete Road Map is Shown on Broad Street," *Augusta Chronicle*, 13 April 1919, 8; "Auto Tourist Camp at Augusta Wrightsville Road and 15th St.," *Augusta Chronicle*, 24 February 1921, 8; "Tourists Official Road Guide," *Augusta Chronicle*, 6 March 1921, 37.

42. "Rossignol Road Map Service Proves of Great Aid to Travelers and is Discussed in Prominent Magazines," *Augusta Chronicle*, 8 November 1920, 5. Rossignol's service addressed the combination of highly variable road conditions with the general lack of reliable guidance for motorists; see Ingram, *Dixie Highway*, 113.

43. "Charles F. Rossignol," *Augusta Chronicle*, 22 July 1928, 16; "Augusta and the Tourists," *Augusta Chronicle*, 15 March 1921, 6.

44. "Auto Tourist Camp at Augusta Wrightsville Road and 15th St."; "Tourists Official Road Guide."

45. "Chronicle Produces 7th Edition of Official Highways Guide and Chas. F. Rossignol Carries Thousands to Florida," *Augusta Chronicle*, 17 April 1923, 5; "What a Department of the Augusta Chronicle is Bringing to Augusta," *Augusta Chronicle*, 25 November 1923, C–4; "Highway Report Made at Annual Session of the Board of Commerce Last Night," *Augusta Chronicle*, 16 January 1924, 5.

46. "The Dixie Highway from Augusta to Asheville; Also a Few Observances by the Way," *Augusta Chronicle*, 14 August 1921, 4; "Let's Strike Fast on the 'Broken Link' of Road," *Augusta Chronicle*, 13 July 1922, 4.

47. "Let's Strike Fast on the 'Broken Link' of Road"; "Dixie Highway to Remain as It Is," *Augusta Chronicle*, 29 May 1923, 5.

48. "Praises Augusta's Cordial Greetings for the Tourists," *Augusta Chronicle*, 14 October 1924, 6. Columbia, South Carolina, boosters also pressed for similar facilities to capture their share of auto tourism; see Moore, *Columbia and Richland County*, 333. For more on municipal auto tourist camps, see Belasco, *Americans on the Road*.

49. "Motor Tourists Pay Calls"; "Auto Tourist Camp at Augusta"; "Coming By Here on Their Way Home," *Augusta Chronicle*, 12 March 1921, 7.

50. "Swarm of Tourists to Come Thru Here," *Augusta Chronicle*, 29 July 1921, 2; Charles F. Rossignol, "Auto Tourists Coming to Augusta from Every Section of Florida," *Augusta Chronicle*, 27 March 1921, 8; "Urging Augusta to Make Strong Bid as Stopping Place for Motor Tourists," *Augusta Chronicle*, 15 September 1921, 10; "Augusta's Disgraceful Tourist Camp Facilities," *Augusta Chronicle*, 5 June 1922, 4.

51. "Making a Plea for a Better Camp Site for Auto Tourists," *Augusta Chronicle*,

21 September 1922, 5; "The Tourist Camp Again, What Are We Going to Do About It?" *Augusta Chronicle*, 31 October 1922, 4.

52. "Selection of Tourists Camp Site Still Undecided by City Council," *Augusta Chronicle*, 7 November 1922, 2; "Editorial," *Augusta Chronicle*, 26 August 1923, D–4; "Praises Augusta's Cordial Greetings for the Tourists," *Augusta Chronicle*, 14 October 1924, 6.

53. "President of Local Board of Commerce Explains Why It is Good Business to Pave Roads," *Augusta Chronicle*, 8 November 1925, 5; "Facilities Increased to Take Care of Visitors; Resort Outlook Bright," *Augusta Chronicle*, 27 December 1925, Progress and Prosperity Edition, 10.

54. "Unveiling Here Yesterday of First Federal Highway Sign an Epoch in City's History," *Augusta Chronicle*, 8 April 1926, 1.

55. "Hundreds of Visitors in Brunswick for Opening of New Coastal Highway," *Augusta Chronicle*, 12 July 1928, 1; "Advertising Aids Highway Tourists," *Augusta Chronicle*, 22 August 1929, 19.

56. "Charles F. Rossignol."

57. "Augustans Going to State Meets," *Augusta Chronicle*, 2 May 1929, 10; Philip Gourevitch, "Mr. Brown: On the Road with His Bad Self," *New Yorker*, 29 July 2002, https://www.newyorker.com/magazine/2002/07/29/mr-brown; Minutes of meeting of Resort Advertising Committee, 29 September 1930, ledger 3, 161, AMCC. For insights on the Terry of James Brown's youth, see Smith, *The One*, chap. 4.

58. Patterson, *The Mosquito Wars*; Revels, *Sunshine Paradise*.

59. Bob Parks, "Champion Keeps Up Great Game to Defeat Smith," *Augusta Chronicle*, 2 April 1930, 1.

60. Bartley, *The Creation of Modern Georgia*, 213; Augusta Chamber of Commerce and Greater Augusta Advertising Committee Annual Report, 1 June 1928, box 1, folder "Annual Reports 1928–1959," GMCC. The development's namesake, Forrest Adair, headed Atlanta-based Adair Realty and Trust Company, which provided major financing; see "Magnificent Hostelry to Lend Great Prestige to City as Tourist Resort," *Augusta Chronicle*, 11 April 1926, 28.

61. *Augusta, Georgia, the Winter Resort*; Augusta Chamber of Commerce and Greater Augusta Advertising Committee Annual Report, 1 June 1928.

62. "The Chronicle Presents a New Set of Ambitions for Augusta," *Augusta Chronicle*, 10 June 1930, 14.

63. "The Augusta National Golf Club and President 'Bobby' Jones," *Augusta Chronicle*, 15 July 1931, 4; Reynolds, "A History of Fruitland Nurseries," 10.

64. Reynolds, "A History of Fruitland Nurseries," 3–5, 7–10. For more on Redmond, see Okie, *The Georgia Peach*, 28, 31; Herrington, "Agricultural and Architectural Reform in the Antebellum South."

65. Thomas, "Fruitlands/Augusta National Golf Club."

66. "Convenience of Golfers is Principal Aim of Club House Planned for Jones Course," *Augusta Chronicle*, 28 October 1931, 2; Nick Paumgarten, "Inside the Cultish Dreamworld of Augusta National," *The New Yorker*, 24 June 2019, https://

www.newyorker.com/magazine/2019/06/24/inside-the-cultish-dreamworld-of
-augusta-national.

67. Paumgarten, "Inside the Cultish Dreamworld of Augusta National"; Earl
DeLoach, "Council is Asked for $10,000 for Great Golf Event," *Augusta Chronicle*,
8 August 1933, 1; "Council Finance Committee Votes Golf Match Fund," *Augusta
Chronicle*, 10 August 1933, 3; "Handling of Golf Course Money Called Safe," *Augusta
Chronicle*, 29 September 1933, 14; "The World's Greatest Golf Event for Augusta,"
Augusta Chronicle, 9 August 1933, 4.

68. Owen, *The Making of the Masters*, 89; "The Finest Advertising for Augusta,"
Augusta Chronicle, 2 March 1934, 4; "Business License for City of Augusta for Year
1934 Announced," 24 March 1934, 10; "Housing Bureau to Provide Accommodations
to Throngs of Visitors is Set Up Here," *Augusta Chronicle*, 7 January 1934, 7; "Social
Interest Centers in Masters' Golf Tournament," *Augusta Chronicle*, 18 March 1934, 12.

69. For the Partridge quote, see "Crowds Pack Resort Hotels as Masters' Tournament Gets Under Way," *Augusta Chronicle*, 22 March 1934, 5.

70. Tom Wall, "Augusta Was Mecca of Sports World During Masters' Event,"
Augusta Chronicle, 26 March 1934, 6.

71. Paumgarten, "Inside the Cultish Dreamworld of Augusta National"; "Advertis-
ing Budget Appears Lost with Injunction Facing Golf Tourney Appropriation,"
Augusta Chronicle, 8 January 1937, 1; "Rain Holds Up Masters,' 36 Holes Slated
Sunday," *Augusta Chronicle*, 31 March 1939, 1; "Business Men Vote Support to Golf
Meet," *Augusta Chronicle*, 15 March 1939, 8.

72. "Better Tourist Season is Seen," *Augusta Chronicle*, 1 November 1939, 12.

73. Tom Wall, "MAWNIN!" *Augusta Chronicle*, 22 September 1940, 10.

74. "Bon Air Hotel Purchased by Spartanburg Operator," *Augusta Chronicle*,
21 September 1941, 1; "Tourist Season to Open Dec. 1," *Augusta Chronicle*, 27 November 1941, 7; "Auto Finance Firm Purchases Bon Air," *Augusta Chronicle*, 11 July
1943, 1; "Sheraton Corp. Buys Bon Air," *Augusta Chronicle*, 2 December 1945, 1.

75. "Roberts Shelves Augusta Masters Golf Tournament for Duration," *Augusta
Chronicle*, 2 October 1942, 16; "Oliver General Hospital is Name of New Infirmary,"
Augusta Chronicle, 14 December 1942, 3; "Feeder Calves Will Roam Links Tract,"
Augusta Chronicle, 23 November 1942, 8.

76. Taylor, *The Augusta Survey*, 116; Hutchinson and Brewster, *Population
Mobility*, 69.

77. Souther, "Making 'The Garden City of the South," 97–98; Home Owners' Loan
Corporation area description, Areas D-9, D-10, D-11, Augusta, Georgia, 26 August
1937, in Nelson et al., "Mapping Inequality," https://dsl.richmond.edu/panorama
/redlining/#loc=13/33.456/-82.04&city=augusta-ga&area=D11&adimage=3/72.182
/-143.171. For biographical information on R. A. Dent, see "B. J. Dent Built Successful
Business by Conquering Overwhelming Barriers," *Augusta Chronicle-Herald*,
27 August 1972, Dent Furniture Company Co. Section, 2.

78. Augusta Unit, Federal Writers' Project in Georgia, *Augusta (American Guide
Series)*, 45; Hutchinson and Brewster, *Population Mobility*, 29.

79. "Tourists Are a Help to Augusta's Industrial Development" (Augusta Chamber of Commerce ad), *Augusta Chronicle*, 22 April 1931, 12.

80. Hutchinson and Brewster, *Population Mobility*, 10, 70.

3. METROPOLIS OF THE CHATTAHOOCHEE VALLEY

1. Rosa C. Gordon, "Utopia in Columbus, Or, Looking Forward 30 Years; A Paper by Mrs. Fred B. Gordon, Read at the Woman's Reading Club," *Columbus Enquirer-Sun*, 28 May 1922, 11.

2. Gordon, "Utopia in Columbus"; Causey, *Red Clay, White Water, and Blues*, 78.

3. *The Electric City of the South.* The Niagara River's discharge is vastly greater than that of the Chattahoochee River, a fact ignored by Columbus's boosters.

4. Causey, *Red Clay, White Water, and Blues*, 18–20.

5. Causey, *Red Clay, White Water, and Blues*, 77; "Names of Jordan, Tharpe, Given to Vets' Buildings," *Columbus Enquirer*, 14 October 1946, 5.

6. Causey, *Red Clay, White Water, and Blues*, 78–79.

7. Hardaway Contracting Co. advertisement, *Columbus Magazine*, 30 September 1943, folder 1, W. C. Woodall Papers (WCW), SMC 116, Columbus State University Archives (CSUA), Schwob Library, Columbus State University, Columbus, GA; Causey, *Red Clay, White Water, and Blues*, 80.

8. "Chattahoochee Waters Christen Goat Rock," *Columbus Enquirer-Sun*, 20 December 1912, 1; "Columbus Power Plant Officially Opened," *Montgomery Advertiser*, 20 December 1912, 12.

9. "Hydro-Electric Power the Study Backbone of Columbus—The City of Industries Founded on Ability to Secure Cheap Power," *Columbus Enquirer-Sun*, 29 February 1916, 19.

10. "Book Will Contain 125 Columbus Pictures," *Columbus Enquirer-Sun*, 11 November 1913, 5; *Columbus, Georgia: The Place with the Power and the Push.*

11. "Three Columbus Companies Will Be Consolidated," *Columbus Ledger*, 24 April 1922, 8; "Plans Go Forward for Power Plant," *Columbus Enquirer-Sun*, 23 March 1924, 1; "Lake Harding Name of Big Body of Water at Bartlett's Ferry," *Columbus Enquirer-Sun*, 5 December 1926, 3.

12. Columbus Electric & Power Co. and South Georgia Power Co. advertisement, *Columbus Enquirer-Sun*, 23 November 1926, 5; "Columbus Centennial Edition," *Columbus Enquirer-Sun*, 21 April 1928, 95–96. For context on how electric power provision brought far-flung rural areas into the orbit of cities, see Needham, *Power Lines.*

13. "Columbus Centennial Edition," 97–99.

14. "College Course in Agriculture," *Columbus Ledger*, 26 August 1928, 4; Columbus Electric & Power Co. and South Georgia Power Co. advertisement, *Columbus Ledger*, 6 December 1928, 2; weekly ads in *Columbus Ledger*, January–May 1929.

15. Manganiello, *Southern Water, Southern Power*, 59; "Columbus Electric & Power

Company Remains on Friendly Basis," *Columbus Enquirer-Sun*, 6 August 1929, 4; W. C. Woodall, "Good Morning," *Columbus Enquirer-Sun*, 7 October 1929, 6.

16. Georgia Power Co. advertisements, *Columbus Enquirer-Sun*, 12 February 1930, 10, and 7 May 1930, 3; W. C. Woodall, "Good Morning," *Columbus Ledger-Enquirer*, 22 June 1930, 6.

17. "Prompt Action by Congress in Survey of Chattahoochee is Promised by Sen. Harris," *Atlanta Constitution*, 28 November 1929, 2; Manganiello, *Southern Water, Southern Power*, 65–67.

18. "History of Fight to Improve Chattahoochee, Lower Rivers is Interesting Detailed," *Columbus Ledger-Enquirer*, 30 July 1939, 16; "Survey Amendment in Senate Planned," *Columbus Enquirer-Sun*, 4 May 1924, 1; "Chattahoochee Valley and Gulf Association to Be Formed Soon," *Atlanta Constitution*, 1 August 1928, 2; W. C. Woodall, "Day by Day," *Columbus Enquirer-Sun*, 18 October 1916, 4.

19. Minutes of Meeting of the Chattahoochee Valley Chamber of Commerce, held at Lake Cora, 30 March 1935, series 1, subseries 1, box 1, folder 3, James Waldo Woodruff Collection (JWW), MC 96, CSUA; "Columbus Zone Has Population of Over One-Half Million," *Columbus Enquirer*, 28 June 1935; Walter P. Pike, Secretary's Annual Report, 31 December 1935, in Chamber of Commerce Minutes—1935, box 6, folder 3, Alva C. Smith Collection (ACS), MC 34, CSUA.

20. Columbus Chamber of Commerce 101st Annual Report, 1946, box 9, folder 27, ACS; Typescript from "Woodruff—A Man of Vision," *Auburn Alumnews*, January 1947, series 1, subseries 1, box 1, folder 1, JWW; "Columbus Soon to Be Port City," *Georgia Anchorage*, May 1963, 19, box 2, folder 2, Lester S. Moody Collection, Augusta Museum of History, Augusta, GA.

21. Pollak, *The Playing Grounds of College Football*, 5.

22. "Commons to Be Sold to the City," *Columbus Ledger*, 27 September 1910, 8; Causey, *Red Clay, White Water, and Blues*, 10; "'Golden Park' Sounds Good," *Columbus Ledger*, 21 November 1920, 4.

23. "Hot on Trail of Football Game," *Columbus Enquirer-Sun*, 9 November 1911, 3; "Columbus Has Landed Big Football Game," *Columbus Enquirer-Sun*, 12 November 1911, 6; "Macon Mourns Loss of Game," *Columbus Ledger*, 14 November 1911, 5; "Great Football Game, Driving Park Today," *Columbus Enquirer-Sun*, 18 November 1911, 1.

24. "Another Big Game Landed," *Columbus Enquirer-Sun*, 9 August 1912, 6; "Ga. Alumni Held Big Meeting," *Columbus Ledger*, 23 October 1912, 8.

25. "Colleges Are Wired About Big Game," *Columbus Ledger*, 16 October 1916, 10; "Georgia Plays Auburn in Columbus November 4th," *Columbus Ledger*, 19 October 1916, 1; "Auburn Authorities Pay Columbus Visit," *Columbus Ledger*, 11 October 1916, 6.

26. "Georgia Plays Auburn in Columbus November 4th"; "Georgia–Auburn Game Clinched for Columbus," *Columbus Enquirer-Sun*, 20 October 1916, 2.

27. "Getting Spirit for Big Game," *Columbus Ledger*, 27 October 1916, 5; "Big Stand is Almost Ready; Ticket Sale On," *Columbus Enquirer-Sun*, 2 November 1916, 6.

28. "Columbus is the Place," *Columbus Ledger,* 25 September 1919, 4; "Columbus Gets Annual Football Clash," *Columbus Enquirer-Sun,* 2 October 1919, 1.

29. "Oglethorpe Petrels Meet Florida Here Thanksgiving," *Columbus Enquirer-Sun,* 7 February 1920, 5.

30. "Gridiron Battle Here Turkey Day When Petrels Will Battle Florida," *Columbus Enquirer-Sun,* 3 November 1920, 3; "Biggest Sport Year Locally," *Columbus Ledger,* 13 September 1921, 7; "Great Classic for Five Years," *Columbus Ledger,* 8 November 1921, 1. The five-year commitment was to begin in 1923 because the 1922 game had been promised under a previous contract.

31. "Great Stadium Plan Launched at Rote Meet," *Columbus Enquirer-Sun,* 28 September 1922, 1; "'Golden Park' Sounds Good."

32. "Columbus the Athletic Center," *Columbus Ledger,* 3 November 1922, 4; "Bugs" Ramsey, "Columbus Making Rapid Strides in Sports," *Columbus Ledger,* 21 January 1923, 1.

33. "Steps Are Taken to Erect Stadium," *Columbus Enquirer-Sun,* 15 October 1924, 1; "City Commission Ratifies Sale of Seat Privileges for Stadium Completion," *Columbus Ledger,* 31 May 1925, 20; "Georgia Smothers Auburn," *Columbus Enquirer-Sun,* 8 November 1925, 1; "Columbus' New Memorial Stadium with a Seating Capacity of Near 15,000; Modern Concrete Structure," *Columbus Ledger,* 28 March 1926, 86. The city's desire to build Memorial Stadium arose from the same hope to build its metropolitan stature while memorializing soldiers that motivated Chicago's concurrent building of Soldier Field, but there is no evidence that Chicago's endeavor influenced Columbus's; on this phenomenon in Chicago and other cities, see Ford, *Soldier Field,* 1, 18.

34. "Georgia–Auburn Football Game Assembles Many Visitors," *Columbus Ledger,* 7 November 1926, 16.

35. "Kiwanians After 'Bama Grid Game," *Columbus Ledger,* 11 November 1926, 11; "Alabama–Auburn Relations Asked," *Columbus Ledger,* 12 November 1926, 1.

36. "Georgia–Auburn Tilt is Shifted," *Columbus Ledger,* 9 December 1928, 1; Henry Averill, "Jaycees Sponsor Georgia–Tulane Game," *Columbus Enquirer-Sun,* 20 September 1929, 3; "Find a Use for the Stadium," *Columbus Ledger,* 27 September 1929, 6.

37. Angelique Soenarie, "SO-C 25; Club Was a Beacon for Young Blacks," *Columbus Ledger-Enquirer,* 10 February 2006, D1; Washington Heights advertisement, *Columbus Enquirer-Sun,* 22 October 1926, 12; Joseph A. Clarke, "Colored Civic Clubs at Work Planning Game," *Columbus Enquirer-Sun,* 8 November 1929, 5.

38. Clarke, "Colored Civic Clubs at Work Planning Game"; Joseph A. Clarke, "Negro Football Teams Speedy," *Columbus Enquirer-Sun,* 9 November 1929, 3; Clark–Alabama State Game to Draw Crowd," *Columbus Ledger,* 9 November 1930, 12. On the renaming of Broad Street, see Souther, "'Green Spots in the Heart of Town.'" 222.

39. The only such game they attracted in the 1930s was the Auburn–South Carolina game in 1930; see "Gamecocks Battle Auburn Tigers Here on Thursday," *Columbus Ledger,* 26 November 1930, 1.

40. "Clark–Alabama State Game to Draw Crowd," *Columbus Ledger,* 9 November 1930, 12; "Florida's Rattlers Arrive for Contest with Alabama Team," *Columbus Enquirer-Sun,* 11 November 1931, 5; "Colored Grid Teams Prepare for Tilt Here," *Columbus Ledger,* 13 October 1937, 4.

41. "E. E. Farley: Civic Leader and Real Estate Developer."

42. Bob Pruitt, "Plans to Move Football Game in the Making Five Years Ago," *Columbus Enquirer,* 19 January 1959, 7.

43. "The Green Book," *The New York Public Library Digital Collections,* https:// digitalcollections.nypl.org/collections/the-green-book; Clarke, "Colored Civic Clubs at Work Planning Game."

44. Joe Livingston, "Locker Room Lingo," *Columbus Ledger-Enquirer,* 25 October 1942, 6. For context on white racism in relation to HBCU football, see Thomas Aiello, "The Black Heart of Dixie: The Turkey Day Classic and Race in Twentieth-Century Alabama," in Wiggins and Swanson, eds., *Separate Games,* 93–108.

45. Stelpflug and Hyatt, *Home of the Infantry,* 1–7; Worsley, *Columbus on the Chattahoochee,* 421–22.

46. Worsley, *Columbus on the Chattahoochee,* 421; Hon. B. S. (Brick) Miller, "Site for Fort Benning Was Suggested to Col. Eames by B. S. Miller," *Industrial Index,* 28 July 1954, CSUA.

47. "Riverside," n.d., box 1, folder 22, F. Clayson Kyle Papers, MC 86, CSUA; Stelpflug and Hyatt, *Home of the Infantry,* 19.

48. "Fort Benning: 'Home of the Infantry," n.d., 10, CSUA.

49. "Colonel Eames Tells of the Magnitude of the Infantry School of Arms," *Columbus Enquirer-Sun,* 27 October 1918, 1.

50. Stelpflug and Hyatt, *Home of the Infantry,* 22.

51. Stelpflug and Hyatt, *Home of the Infantry,* 16.

52. Advertisement, *Columbus Enquirer-Sun,* 18 December 1918, 8; "Opposition to the Best Thing Ever in Our Reach?" *Columbus Ledger,* 18 December 1918, 4; "Rhodes Browne is Strong for Fort Benning," *Columbus Enquirer-Sun,* 19 December 1918, 1.

53. "Camp Benning Endorsed by Rousing Mass Meeting," *Columbus Ledger,* 22 December 1918, 9; "Mass Meeting at Court House Last Night Was Productive Much Good," *Columbus Enquirer-Sun,* 21 December 1918, 1.

54. R. Briggs Pekor, "Ft. Benning Largest Army School in the World," *Columbus Enquirer-Sun,* 20 April 1919, 14.

55. "Petition for Charter, The Muscogee County Agricultural Association," *Columbus Ledger,* 4 December 1935, 12; "Columbus, Georgia" (brochure), n.d. [ca. 1935], box 2, folder 88, Loretto Chappell/Bradley Library Vertical Files, MC 361, CSUA.

56. *Industrial Survey of Columbus, Georgia* (Columbus, GA: Columbus Chamber of Commerce, 1935), box 9, folder 32, ACS.

57. Simons, *Comprehensive Area Plan, City of Columbus and Muscogee County, Georgia, 1948,* 16–19, CSUA.

58. Worsley, *Columbus on the Chattahoochee*, 427.

59. Stelpflug and Hyatt, *Home of the Infantry*, 26.

60. Stelpflug and Hyatt, *Home of the Infantry*, 37; "New Buss [*sic*] Line Begins Operations Saturday," *Columbus Enquirer-Sun*, 12 August 1921, 2. The Columbus–Fort Benning route was the first route in what would eventually become the METRA transit system decades later; see Carole Marle Cropper, "Bus Stop Final," *Saturday Enquirer and Ledger*, 4 March 1978, 2.

61. Columbus Chamber of Commerce advertisement and "A Ten-Million-Dollar Year at Columbus, Georgia," *Industrial Index*, 31 December 1919, CSUA; Worsley, *Columbus on the Chattahoochee*, 430.

62. "Golf Match at the Country Club Saturday," *Columbus Ledger*, 20 November 1918, 5; "C. of C. Want Military Folks," *Columbus Ledger*, 11 March 1919, 6; "Camp Activity Committee Keeps Relations Cordial," *Columbus Ledger*, 22 February 1925, 84.

63. "Columbus Advertised by Camp Benning Men," *Columbus Enquirer-Sun*, 20 January 1921, 10.

64. "Our Columbus-Benning Edition," *Columbus Ledger*, 22 February 1925, 96.

65. Stelpflug and Hyatt, *Home of the Infantry*, 51.

66. Worsley, *Columbus on the Chattahoochee*, 423; R. Briggs Pekor, "Ft. Benning Largest Army School in the World," *Columbus Enquirer-Sun*, 20 April 1919, 14.

67. Georgia Power Co. advertisement, *Industrial Index*, 30 November 1938, 14, box 2, folder 6, Industrial Index Collection (IIC), MC 304, CSUA; "Army Payroll of $1,255,000 Received Here," *Columbus Ledger*, 29 April 1940, 1; "Textile Backbone of Industry Here," *Columbus Ledger-Enquirer*, 5 September 1937, 6. The $2 million figure included payrolls of the divisions stationed at Benning.

68. "Fort Benning," n.d. [ca. 1933], box 22, folder 7, ACS.

69. "Silver Service Presented to Club by Civilian Members," *Benning Herald*, 27 July 1934, box 22, folder 5, ACS.

70. H. C. Smith, speech script, 5 September 1933, box 22, folder 14, ACS.

71. *Columbus, Georgia* (Columbus, GA: Columbus Real Estate Board, n.d. [ca. 1934]), box 9, folder 24, ACS.

72. "No Enlisted Men in Phenix City," *Columbus Enquirer-Sun*, 5 March 1924, 4; "Gen. King Lifts Ban on Phenix," *Columbus Enquirer-Sun*, 29 June 1929, 1.

73. Causey, *Red Clay, White Water, and Blues*, 130, 162; Madison interview.

4. PLANNING "THE SOUTH'S MOST PROGRESSIVE CITY"

1. On the ways that World War II reshaped southern cities, see especially Goldfield, *Cotton Fields and Skyscrapers*, 182–83; Bartley, *The New South, 1945–1980*, chap. 1; Cobb, *The South and America since World War II*, chap. 3.

2. Pearl Smith Truman, "Our Great Neighbor," *Industrial Index*, 29 December

1943, 29, box 2, folder 87, Loretto Chappell/Bradley Library Vertical Files, MC 361, Columbus State University Archives (CSUA), Schwob Library, Columbus State University, Columbus, GA.

3. Cashin, *The Story of Augusta*, 269; Causey, *Red Clay, White Water, and Blues*, 165; Robins Air Force Base Heritage Committee, *A Pictorial History of Robins Air Force Base, Georgia*, 4–7; Gould, *Otis Redding*, 40, 44–45.

4. "Military Population of Fort Benning is 476 Officers, 5,653 Enlisted Men," *Industrial Index*, 30 November 1938, 22, box 2, folder 6, Industrial Index Collection (IIC), MC 304, CSUA; Etta Blanchard Worsley, *Columbus on the Chattahoochee* (Columbus, GA: Columbus Office Supply Co., 1951), 441, CSUA; "Columbus, Georgia," *Columbus Magazine*, 31 May 1940, 5, folder 1, WCW.

5. Marion Post Wolcott photographs; "In 15 Months, $5,591,069 of New Construction at Fort Benning—Additional New Projects Total $3,091,000," 7, *Industrial Index*, 30 October 1940, box 2, folder 11, IIC; "1,528,803 Defense Housing Project Under Construction," *Industrial Index*, 30 October 1940, 10, box 2, folder 11, IIC.

6. "Soldiers, Two Million in Pockets, Swarm All Over City and Vicinity," *Columbus Ledger*, 30 April 1940, 1; Mark Dowtin, "Public Service Buildings Being Rushed in City," *Columbus Enquirer*, 16 October 1941, 17; Nelson M. Shipp, "From the Crow's Nest," *Columbus Enquirer*, 23 May 1941, 6; "Graphic Pen Picture of Columbus; Its Fast War-Time Tempo, Its Problems and Progress," *Industrial Index*, 30 June 1943, 32, CSUA.

7. Shipp, "From the Crow's Nest"; "Cooperation with Army Imperative," *Columbus Enquirer*, 20 December 1940, 6.

8. Photo caption card, Marion Post Wolcott, *Jones Trailer Camp . . .* , December 1940, FSA-OWI, https://www.loc.gov/item/2017805824/. For context on the wartime rural-to-urban migration, see Schulman, *From Cotton Belt to Sunbelt*, 102.

9. "Duty and Opportunity," *Columbus Ledger-Enquirer*, 22 December 1940, 6.

10. "It is a Law!" *Columbus Ledger*, 15 June 1942, 4; "Contract Let for 50 Homes," *Columbus Ledger-Enquirer*, 22 June 1941, 11; Earl Watson, "123-Home Development is City's 'Biggest' Project," *Columbus Ledger-Enquirer*, 30 August 1942, 13.

11. Walter A. Richards, "Must Take Place of Home-Folks for Soldiers, Says Chamber Head," *Columbus Enquirer*, 16 April 1942, United States Army Special Edition, 15.

12. Doug Wallace, "Millions Go for Goobers," *Columbus Ledger-Enquirer*, 28 May 1961, sec. 2, p. 12; Walter Richards Dies; Civic, Business Leader," *Columbus Enquirer*, 1 August 1961, 1. Richards's correspondence with Nolen in 1924–25 is found in box 24, folder 6, John Nolen Papers (JN), Cornell University Library Division of Rare and Manuscript Collections, Ithaca, NY.

13. John B. McDermott, "Secretary of War Now at Benning," *Columbus Ledger-Enquirer*, 17 November 1940, 1; "War Camp Activities Committee May Be Set Up in Columbus Soon," *Columbus Ledger*, 19 November 1940, 2; "Mayor Says City is Working Hard to Control Vice," *Columbus Ledger*, 4 March 1942, 1; "The Story of Benning," *Industrial Index*, 2 December 1942, box 3, folder 7, IIC; "Soldier Recre-

ation Drive Plans Being Formulated," *Columbus Enquirer*, 17 January 1941, 1; "Cooperation with Army Imperative."

14. "U.S. Health Officer Webber Assigned Here," *Columbus Enquirer*, 21 January 1940, 22; "Richards Will Head Hygiene Council Here," *Columbus Enquirer*, 23 January 1940, 9.

15. Walter A. Richards to John Nolen, 23 October 1924, box 24, folder 6, JN; Walter A. Richards, "Columbus Mobilizes for Defense Service," *Columbus Enquirer*, 24 February 1941, 4; "Columbus Has Failed in Morale Boosting Work for Soldiers at Fort Benning, Richards Says," *Columbus Ledger*, 8 October 1941, 9. Alison Isenberg also points to Columbus leaders' apathy toward hiring Nolen; see Isenberg, *Downtown America*, 28.

16. Jane Raymond, "Columbus Accepts Her Responsibilities," *Columbus Ledger-Enquirer*, 3 August 1941, Sunday Magazine, 13; "Trinity Episcopal Church Has an Extended Program of Service for Men in Armed Forces," *Industrial Index*, 30 June 1943, 86, CSUA; "Presbyterian Church Establishes Center for Men in Their Country's Service," *Industrial Index*, 30 June 1943, 87, CSUA.

17. Jane Raymond, "22nd Infantry is Captivated by Charge of Modern Version of Famed 'Light Brigade," *Columbus Ledger-Enquirer*, 12 October 1941, Sunday Magazine, 3; "Entertainment Gain for Troops Announced," *Columbus Enquirer*, 9 April 1942, 3; Mrs. George Burrus Jr., "Fort Benning Gives Military Maids Glorious Opportunities," *Columbus Enquirer*, 25 March 1942, 4.

18. "City, Benning Leaders Draft Recreation Plan," *Columbus Ledger*, 15 January 1941, 14.

19. "Soldier Recreation Drive Plans Being Formulated," *Columbus Enquirer*, 17 January 1941, 1; "E. E. Farley: Civic Leader and Real Estate Developer"; "Elizabeth Mae 'Lizzie Mae' Lunsford: A Quiet Force"; "Columbus Offered Army and Navy 'Y' for Negro Troops," *Columbus Enquirer*, 21 January 1941, 1; "United States Census, 1940," database, *GenealogyBank* (https://genealogybank.com/#), Lula Mae Lunsford, Columbus, Militia District 921, Muscogee County, Georgia, United States; "Will of Richard Pierce Probated," *Columbus Ledger*, 19 January 1941, 13.

20. Worsley, *Columbus on the Chattahoochee*, 483–84; W. C. Tucker, "Top o' the Morn," *Columbus Ledger-Enquirer*, 16 February 1941, 6; "Donations Asked for Negro Army Y.M.C.A. Here," *Columbus Ledger*, 18 February 1941, 8; "Colored Baptist Conference Lauds Leaders, Workers for Colored Army–Navy YMCA," *Columbus Ledger*, 31 July 1941, 2. See also Causey, *Red Clay, White Water, and Blues*, 162.

21. Causey, *Red Clay, White Water, and Blues*, 167–69; "Mayor Says City is Working Hard to Control Vice," *Columbus Ledger*, 4 March 1942, 1; Worsley, *Columbus on the Chattahoochee*, 444.

22. "Parade in Retrospect," *Columbus Ledger*, 7 April 1942, 4; "Post Will Show War-time Might During Army Day," *Columbus Enquirer*, 2 April 1942, 1.

23. "Graphic Pen Picture of Columbus: Its Fast War-Time Tempo, Its Problems and Progress," *Industrial Index*, 30 June 1943, 32, CSUA; "'Officers' Dance at Ralston Hotel on Friday Night," *Columbus Enquirer*, 31 March 1943, 8; Brig. Gen. Leven C.

Allen to O. L. Betts Jr., 26 December 1942, and Brig. Gen. William H. Hobson to Oscar L. Betts, 17 February 1945, series 1, box 1, folder 5, Betts/Taliaferro Collection, MC 149, CSUA; "Oscar Betts Will Receive AUSA Medal," *Columbus Ledger,* 27 September 1966, 30.

24. *Columbus, Georgia: Statistical Review* (Columbus, GA: Columbus Chamber of Commerce, 1943), 12, series 2, box 1, folder 6, Columbus Public Library Pamphlet Collection, MC 302, CSUA; "Columbus and Benning Featured by Hajoca Corporation in Magazine Issue," *Industrial Index,* 30 June 1943, 84, CSUA.

25. Postwar planning was an important wartime preoccupation in many cities. See as examples Teaford, *The Rough Road to Renaissance,* chap. 1; Lubove, *Twentieth-Century Pittsburgh,* chap. 1; Thomas, *Redevelopment and Race,* chap. 2.

26. John Dunn, "Old Skeletons Lurking in Planning Closets," *Columbus Enquirer,* 30 September 1969, 15. The lack of implementation of so much of the Nolen Plan by Columbus leaders may explain why the leading monograph on Nolen omits any mention of Columbus despite detailing many other Nolen city plans; see Stephenson, *John Nolen, Landscape Architect and City Planner.*

27. "New Industries Predicted for City by Col. Ashworth," *Columbus Enquirer,* 29 August 1945, 1.

28. Causey, *Red Clay, White Water, and Blues,* 49; Sellers, *Race and the Greening of Atlanta,* 24–26, 46–47; Virginia Bailey, "Will Columbus Be State's Third City by Annexation? Voters to Decide July 25," *Columbus Enquirer,* 22 June 1945, 15.

29. "Columbus, Planned City, Plans for New Era," *Industrial Index,* 28 June 1944, 28, box 3, folder 11, IIC; "163 Plan Future Growth of City," *Columbus Ledger-Enquirer,* 27 August 1944, 1.

30. "Columbus, Planned City, Plans for New Era"; "Growing . . . Columbus, Georgia, Has Busy Year," *Industrial Index,* 28 June 1944, 5, box 3, folder 11, IIC; *Columbus, Georgia* (Columbus, GA: Columbus Chamber of Commerce, 1945), box 9, folder 27, Alva C. Smith Collection, MC 34, CSUA.

31. "Annexation Wins by 1,508–396 Count," *Columbus Enquirer,* 26 July 1945, 1; "New Areas Taken into City by Annexation," *Columbus Enquirer,* 1 January 1949, 1.

32. "Columbus' Post-War Job," *Columbus Ledger,* 3 August 1944, 4.

33. "Message to Columbus," *Columbus Ledger,* 20 April 1945, 4; "Business Expansion for Columbus," *Columbus Enquirer,* 21 April 1945, 6. Local laments about the city's decadent appearance were hardly unusual. Indeed, the Augusta Citizens Union's report at the end of the war called similar attention to the fact that the so-called Garden City of the South had allowed its prized downtown parkways to devolve into an unkempt condition. See Reed and Reed, *Report to the Citizens,* 60.

34. Nelson et al., "Mapping Inequality," https://dsl.richmond.edu/panorama /redlining/map#loc=8/32.4171/-83.3812. On HOLC's area appraisals, see Glotzer, *How the Suburbs Were Segregated,* 153–56.

35. Area Description: Columbus, GA, B2 Overlook, in Nelson et al., "Mapping Inequality," https://dsl.richmond.edu/panorama/redlining/#loc=16/32.465 /-84.975&city=columbus-ga&area=B2; "$900,000 Housing Project Assured,"

Columbus Ledger, 23 August 1944, 1; "163 Plan Future Growth of City," *Columbus Ledger-Enquirer,* 27 August 1944, 1.

36. "$900,000 Housing Project Assured." On the idea of protecting white property from assumed impacts resulting from proximity to Black occupancy, see as examples Freund, *Colored Property;* Herbin-Triant, *Threatening Property.*

37. "Bridges and Richards Are Elected to Commission in Record Balloting," *Columbus Ledger,* 18 October 1945, 1; "Richards Mayor of Columbus," *Columbus Enquirer,* 7 January 1947, 6; "Engineers Ask Area Planner Be Appointed," *Columbus Enquirer,* 7 May 1946, 1; "Study of Plan for Future to Start in Early August," *Columbus Ledger,* 10 July 1946, 3; Simons, *Comprehensive Area Plan, City of Columbus and Muscogee County, Georgia, 1948,* 8, 19.

38. "Mayor to Quit Post; 'We Should Rotate,'" *Columbus Ledger,* 18 August 1949, 1; Frank Bruer, "City Employs Simons to Direct Local Zoning," *Columbus Enquirer,* 9 December 1953, 1; Bruce Harrison, "T. Glenn Hatfield Has to Step Fast to Keep Pace with Growth of City," *Columbus Ledger-Enquirer,* 23 September 1956, D–3; Marvin Wall, "Annexation Hinted in Zone Discussion," *Columbus Ledger,* 15 March 1955, 13; Richard Beckman, "Annexation Winds Handily," *Columbus Enquirer,* 13 September 1956, 1; Richard F. Beckman, "Columbus Flexes New Muscles, Stretches Toward Bigger Role," *Columbus Enquirer,* 31 December 1958, Annexation Supplement, 18.

39. "New Industries Group to Meet," *Columbus Ledger,* 24 June 1945, 27; "$100,000 Fund Ready for Use in Macon Drive," *Macon News,* 25 August 1944, 12; "To Publicize Columbus," *Columbus Enquirer,* 18 February 1945, 4.

40. Cobb, *The Selling of the South,* 54–55; "U.S. to Discover Columbus in Fancy New Booklet," *Columbus Ledger,* 18 April 1949, 1.

41. "Columbus is Given Boost Industrially," *Columbus Enquirer,* 11 July 1952, 6; "City Becomes Example," *Columbus Ledger,* 16 September 1969, 4; Numan V. Bartley, "Prosperity and Problems: The Economy during World War II and After," in Coleman, ed., *A History of Georgia,* 2nd ed., 343.

42. Rosa C. Gordon, "Utopia in Columbus, Or, Looking Forward 30 Years; A Paper by Mrs. Fred B. Gordon, Read at the Woman's Reading Club," *Columbus Enquirer-Sun,* 28 May 1922, 11. For context on Gordon's story of Columbus's future, refer to the opening of Chapter 3.

43. "Cobb Hailed for Moves to 'Cleanse' Phenix," *Columbus Ledger,* 2 April 1946, 9; "P. C. Has Survived the Clean Up," *Columbus Ledger,* 26 July 1951, 4; "Mrs. Maddox Hits Phenix Officials," *Columbus Ledger-Enquirer,* 7 September 1952, C–6; "RBA Stresses Industry Wants 'Clean' Town," *Columbus Ledger-Enquirer,* 9 August 1953, C–7; "RBA Claims PC Rackets Will Be Election Issue," *Columbus Ledger,* 10 January 1954, 8.

44. "RBA Stresses Industry Wants 'Clean' Town"; "Patterson Shot to Death in Car Alongside Office," *Columbus Enquirer,* 19 June 1954, 1. The fullest secondary account of the murder and subsequent cleanup of Phenix City is Barnes, *The Tragedy and the Triumph of Phenix City, Alabama.*

45. "Industries Urged to Take New Look at 'Divorcee' PC," *Columbus Ledger,*
15 December 1954, 1; "Phenix City is Now Open to Military," *Columbus Enquirer,*
25 January 1955, 4.

46. "Exchangites View Movie on Planning," *Columbus Enquirer,* 22 March 1957, 18;
"Planning Commission Approved for Atlanta," *Columbus Enquirer,* 28 March 1947,
21; Marlene Bennett, "Atlanta's Planning Committee Ideas Applied to Columbus by
Menhinick," *Columbus Enquirer,* 19 December 1957, 9. For context on the Atlanta
Metropolitan Planning Commission, see Basmajian, *Atlanta Unbound,* 90–91. On
Hartsfield's promotion of annexation to whiten Atlanta, see Bayor, *Race and the
Shaping of Twentieth-Century Atlanta,* 85–87; Kruse, *White Flight,* 37–38. While no
such overt calls to dilute Black political power by annexing land into Columbus
appear in the available record, local officials surely understood the racial dimensions
of their stated intent to "capture growth."

47. Robert Schoenholt, "Georgia Cities Plan for 50-Mile Radius," *Columbus
Ledger-Enquirer,* 8 December 1957, 42; Bennett, "Atlanta's Planning Committee
Ideas"; Steve Lesher, "County Okehs Plans Council, Will Ask Enabling Measure,"
Columbus Ledger, 27 December 1957, 9; Steve Lesher, "Okeh Given Plans Unit,"
Columbus Ledger, 18 June 1958, 1.

48. Steve Lesher, "CofC Oks 2-Year Analysis of Area Economic Potential," *Columbus Ledger,* 28 March 1958, 1. For context on the formation of the Industrial Development Branch, see Cebul, *Illusions of Progress,* 92–93, 95–96.

49. Whitlatch and Van Geuns, *An Evaluation of the Economic Assets and Liabilities of the Columbus Area,* 4–5, 49, 65–66, 98. For context on the problem of military
base impermanence and fluctuations in employment, see Goldfield, *Cotton Fields
and Skyscrapers,* 184. On Broadway parkway beautification, see Souther, "'Green
Spots in the Heart of Town,'" 304.

50. Lesher, "CofC Oks 2-Year Analysis of Area Economic Potential"; Steve Lesher,
"New Planning Board Raises Jurisdiction Problem," *Columbus Ledger,* 30 June
1958, 4.

51. Lesher, "Okeh Given Plans Unit"; "Boyce Heads Metropolitan Plans Group,"
Columbus Ledger, 10 July 1958, 35.

52. "Flynt to Be Director of Plans Commission," *Columbus Ledger,* 24 December
1958, 28.

53. Ben Walburn, "Downtown Mall Again Proposed in New Study," *Columbus
Ledger,* 3 December 1959, 1; Simons, *Report on Central Business District, Columbus,
Georgia,* 38–41.

54. "Planning Board Takes Rash Step," *Columbus Ledger,* 25 May 1959, 4; Ben
Walburn, "County Votes to Cut MPC Funds for 1960 if Meets Not Opened," *Columbus
Ledger,* 22 July 1959, 1; "County Criticizes MPC for Usurping Authority," *Columbus
Ledger,* 16 March 1960, 15; Remer Tyson, "Flynt Going Back to His New York Job,"
Columbus Ledger, 19 May 1960, 1.

55. Wes Owens, "MPC to Get Cash on Monthly Basis," *Columbus Ledger,* 18 April
1961, 9.

56. "CC Group Mapping Plans for More Building Space," *Columbus Ledger,* 19 March 1947, 8; Columbus Industrial Development Corporation pamphlet, n.d. [ca. 1958], series 7, box 1, folder "Pamphlet, 'Columbus Industrial Development Corporation," James Waldo Woodruff Collection, MC 96, CSUA; Jane Gullatt, "Development Group Here Offers Aid, Advice to Prospective New Industries," *Columbus Enquirer,* 21 April 1961, 23; Ben Walburn and Paul Miles, "Merchant Says Mills Fear New Industry Will Bring in Unions," *Columbus Enquirer,* 12 June 1962, 1; Jo Anne Singley, "Chamber 'Buries Skeleton' of Control by Textile Mills," *Columbus Ledger,* 27 June 1962, 3.

57. Wes Owens and Constance Johnson, "County to Establish Own Agency to Administer Zoning, Planning," *Columbus Ledger,* 20 June 1961, 11; "New City-County Zoning Law is Adopted by Commission," *Augusta Chronicle,* 25 September 1952, 1; "County Board Backs Revised Zoning Setup," *Macon Telegraph,* 11 November 1952, 1.

58. "Voice is Needed to Give Meaning to Community's Hopes, Dreams," *Columbus Ledger,* 12 October 1961, 4.

59. "Wright Quits as Director of MPC Here," *Columbus Ledger,* 15 January 1962, 1; Neal Brogdon, "Possible Merger Halts Appointments," *Columbus Ledger,* 6 February 1962, 3.

60. Causey, *Red Clay, White Water, and Blues,* 183–84, 223; Bill Levy, "Waller Charges Merger Move Unconstitutional," *Columbus Enquirer,* 5 March 1962, 1.

61. Levy, "Waller Charges Merger Move Unconstitutional"; Carroll Lisby, "County Commissioners Oppose City Move to Annex New Areas," *Columbus Ledger,* 5 April 1955, 1; Neal Brogdon, "Amos Scores Drive to Label Merger Plan 'Dictatorship.'" *Columbus Ledger,* 14 February 1962, 1. Detractors of metropolitan government elsewhere made the same linkage with communism; see Doyle, *Nashville since the 1920s,* 212.

62. Advertisements, *Columbus Enquirer,* 13 March 1962, 10, and 24 March 1962, 12.

63. Paul Miles, "Merger Defeated, 9,070 to 6,565; Proposal Rejected by County and City," *Columbus Enquirer,* 12 April 1962, 1. Lassiter, *The Silent Majority,* 13. Lassiter's "island suburb" examples include Atlanta's Buckhead and Charlotte's Myers Park. Fall-line counterparts, as suggested earlier in this book, were "The Hill" (Summerville) in Augusta and Vineville in Macon.

64. "W. S. Persons Appointed Campaign Manager for Maddox in Lt. Gov. Bid," *Columbus Ledger,* 6 June 1962, 13.

65. Bill Levy, "Advisory Team Begins Housing Survey Here," *Columbus Enquirer,* 6 February 1962, 1; Alexander von Hoffman, "The Lost History of Urban Renewal," in Tighe and Mueller, eds., *The Affordable Housing Reader,* 19; National Association of Real Estate Boards, Build America Better Committee, *Toward a New Columbus;* Bill Levy, "Inspection Team Releases Report on Survey of City," *Columbus Enquirer,* 22 May 1962, 1.

66. National Association of Real Estate Boards, Build America Better Committee, *Toward a New Columbus,* 4–6, 11, 26–28, 47. On historic preservation in Augusta's

Pinch Gut district, see Souther, "Making 'The Garden City of the South.'" 100–101, 107. On preservation in Macon's College Hill section, see Chapter 6.

67. George Mitchell, "Inside There is No Cheer, Just the Stench of Poverty," *Columbus Ledger*, 8 July 1968, 1. On racial discrimination in the textile industry, see Causey, *Red Clay, White Water, and Blues*, 207; Minchin, *Hiring the Black Worker*.

68. "Is 'Togetherness' Near?" *Columbus Enquirer*, 6 May 1963, 4; "City Commission Agrees to Joint Planning Board," *Columbus Ledger*, 25 June 1963, 1; Constance Johnson, "1st Meet Set by Plans Unit," *Columbus Ledger*, 18 October 1963, 13.

69. "Worth of Planning," *Columbus Ledger*, 2 March 1966, 4; "Joint Plans Required," *Columbus Ledger*, 26 July 1963, 9; "'Umbrella' Plan Proposed," *Columbus Ledger*, 25 June 1969, 15. For context on how new federal policies reshaped urban planning efforts and elevated regional planning, see Basmajian, *Atlanta Unbound*, 9.

70. Tom Sellers, "Time to Get Ready Had Slipped Past," *Columbus Ledger-Enquirer*, 22 July 1962, 30.

71. "George Quits City-County Planning Job," *Columbus Enquirer*, 10 December 1965, 41; Blount Ferrell, "City May Miss Renewal Funds Due to Lack of Planning Team; Must Wait for Share of Money," *Columbus Ledger*, 10 March 1966, 1; Constance Johnson, "Planning Chief Named in County," *Columbus Ledger*, 22 September 1966, 1.

72. George Mitchell, "The Savannah Plan: Private Enterprise at Its Best," *Columbus Ledger-Enquirer*, 7 July 1968, B–7; George Mitchell, "City Beginning Attack on Slums," *Columbus Ledger-Enquirer*, 14 July 1968, 1; Patton, "Mills B. Lane, Jr. and Enterprise in a New South"; Edward Hatfield, "Mills B. Lane Jr.," *New Georgia Encyclopedia*, last modified 14 April 2021, https://www.georgiaencyclopedia.org/articles/business-economy/mills-b-lane-jr-1912–1989/. On Lane's role in Savannah restoration, see Lane, *The Wonderful World of Mills B. Lane Jr.*

73. George Mitchell, "Local War on Slums Hasn't Received Great Support," *Columbus Ledger*, 17 July 1968, 1; George Mitchell "Relieving Plight of Poor Major Challenge for '70s," *Columbus Ledger-Enquirer*, 5 January 1969, 19; Constance Johnson, "Theo McGee Will Again Serve as CHA Chairman," *Columbus Ledger*, 20 August 1968, 1.

74. "'Umbrella' Plan Proposed," *Columbus Ledger*, 25 June 1969, 15; Mickey Mills, "Two Jet Airport Studies Under Way," *Columbus Ledger*, 14 October 1968, 2; Constance Johnson, "Phenix City Disagrees on Location for New Bridge," *Columbus Ledger*, 13 November 1968, 42.

75. "Planner Resigns; Controversy Hinted," *Columbus Ledger*, 1 July 1969, 1; "What is Story on Baker?" Columbus Ledger, 3 July 1969, 4 ; "Planning Unit is Faulty," *Columbus Ledger*, 6 July 1969, 14; "Baker Blasts Planners' 'Personal Gain," *Columbus Ledger*, 15 July 1969, 13.

76. Constance Johnson, "Cash to Be Asked to Speed Study," *Columbus Ledger*, 22 August 1969, 14.

77. Wanda Padgett, "Citizens Call for Membership Cut in Planning Commission," *Columbus Enquirer*, 11 September 1969, 21; Constance Johnson, "Council Names 5-Member Panel," *Columbus Ledger*, 3 December 1970, 3.

78. "Why You Should Vote 'Yes.'" *Columbus Enquirer,* 26 May 1970, 4. On consolidation in Nashville, see Doyle, *Nashville Since the 1920s,* 193–221. On consolidation in Jacksonville, see Crooks, *Jacksonville.*

79. Bob Fort, "Merger Voted In," *Columbus Enquirer,* 28 May 1970, 1; Constance Johnson, "It's Official Now: Consolidation OKd 4 to 1 by Voters," *Columbus Ledger,* 30 May 1970, 21.

80. John Dunn, "Vote on Annexation is Scheduled Today," *Columbus Enquirer,* 25 June 1969, 1; John Dunn, "Annexation Passes," *Columbus Enquirer,* 26 June 1969, 1; "Macon Speeding Annexation Tasks," *Macon Telegraph,* May 26, 1961.

81. "City/County Consolidation: Columbus, Georgia"; Causey, *Red Clay, White Water, and Blues,* 224. On Richmond, see Lassiter, *The Silent Majority,* 281–84.

82. Donna Wilson, "Government Center Typifies Progress," *Columbus Enquirer,* 29 July 1970, 11.

83. "'Look Ma—A Skyscraper.'" *Columbus Ledger,* 30 August 1971, 15.

84. "Board Oks City Transportation Study," *Columbus Ledger,* 17 December 1970, 13.

85. Constance Johnson, "Columbus on Interstate," *Columbus Ledger,* 19 September 1979, 1, quoted in Causey, *Red Clay, White Water, and Blues,* 215.

86. Constance Johnson, "Old Houses Are Facing Renovation," *Columbus Ledger-Enquirer,* 4 June 1972, 13; Jim Houston, "Urban Renewal Has New Image," *Columbus Enquirer,* 12 September 1972, 15; Sam Hopkins, "Columbus Plans for 'Inland Port' City Fails," *Atlanta Journal and Constitution,* 18 July 1971, box 104, folder 10 "Columbus—General (2)," Georgiana Vertical File (GVF), Hargrett Rare Book and Manuscript Library, University of Georgia, Athens, GA; "Historic House Begins New Life," *Columbus Ledger-Enquirer Magazine,* 4 April 1971, 19.

87. Causey, *Red Clay, White Water, and Blues,* 226–30; James T. Wooten, "Racial Tensions in Columbus, Ga., Bring City to the Brink of Schizophrenia," *New York Times,* 27 July 1971. On Augusta's 1970 uprising, see William Winn and D. L. Inman, "Augusta, Georgia," in Southern Regional Council, *Augusta, Georgia and Jackson State University: Southern Episodes in a National Tragedy* (Atlanta: Southern Regional Council, June 1970), 21–34, Augusta, Georgia, Race Riots, 1970, MSS/210, Reese Library Special Collections, Augusta University, Augusta, GA. On the Macon uprisings, see Manis, *Macon Black and White,* 259–67.

5. WHAT AUGUSTA BUILDS, BUILDS AUGUSTA

1. Advertisement, *Augusta Chronicle,* 11 June 1950, 6–B; "Contest is Launched to Select New Name for Clark Hill Area by Mayors of Towns in Section," *Augusta Chronicle,* 9 June 1950, 1–2; "Kiwanis Club Endorses Contest to Name Clark Hill Area; Interest in Integration Drive Growing Throughout Zone," *Augusta Chronicle,* 13 June 1950, 1.

2. "'Central Savannah River Area' is New Name for This Section; Wrens Resident Wins Contest," *Augusta Chronicle,* 25 June 1950, 1.

3. *Agricultural Augusta, Georgia, Where Nature Does Your Work*, n.d. [ca. 1947], Mary Carter Winter Collection (MCW), Reese Library Special Collections, Augusta University (RLSC), Augusta, GA; *Building Augusta*, May 1951, box 2, Lester S. Moody Collection (LSM), Augusta Museum of History (AMH), Augusta, GA; *A Brief on Industrial Augusta, Georgia*, Augusta–Richmond County Public Library (ARCPL), Augusta, GA.

4. Frederickson, *Cold War Dixie*, 48. *Cold War Dixie* focuses almost entirely on the SRP's impact on the South Carolina side of the river.

5. Through a clerical error, the dam and reservoir originally carried the name Clark Hill. In 1987, a South Carolina representative's bill led Congress to redesignate the lake as J. Strom Thurmond Reservoir, a name the state of Georgia refused to recognize. For clarity, I use Clarks Hill throughout.

6. Charles Seabrook, "Savannah River," *New Georgia Encyclopedia*, last modified 2 February 2021, https://www.georgiaencyclopedia.org/articles/geography-environment/savannah-river; Lynn Willoughby, "Chattahoochee River," *New Georgia Encyclopedia*, last modified 2 January 2020, https://www.georgiaencyclopedia.org/articles/geography-environment/chattahoochee-river; Keith Hulett, "Ocmulgee River," *New Georgia Encyclopedia*, last modified 15 July 2020, https://www.georgia encyclopedia.org/articles/geography-environment/ocmulgee-river.

7. Ester Young Mewihsen, ". . . Of a Man and a River . . . ," *Augusta Magazine*, Summer 1966, 15, RLSC; "A Wall of Protection," *Augusta Chronicle*, 4 February 1916, 5; Manganiello, *Southern Water, Southern Power*, 88–90.

8. Address of L. S. Moody before Joint Meeting, Directors of the Chamber of Commerce of Augusta, Georgia, and the Augusta Merchants Association, 12 September 1946, box 2, folder 4, LSM; William S. Morris, "A Secret Ambition," *Augusta Chronicle*, 23 September 1933, 1; "T. J. Hamilton Dies Suddenly at Home Here," *Augusta Chronicle*, 2 September 1937, 1; "Approval Won on Clarks Hill," *Augusta Chronicle*, 13 December 1944, 1.

9. Manganiello, *Southern Water, Southern Power*, 56; Moody address, 12 September 1946.

10. Moody address, 12 September 1946. On the role of hydroelectric power in the larger ambitions of electric companies, see especially Manganiello, *Southern Water, Southern Power*, chap. 2; Cater, *Regenerating Dixie;* Needham, *Power Lines.*

11. Moody address, 12 September 1946; "Georgia Power Co. Willing to Take Over Clarks Hill," *Augusta Chronicle*, 21 August 1946, 1.

12. "Collier Advances Power Co. Claims," *Augusta Chronicle*, 10 September 1946, 8. For context on Collier's statement, see Manganiello, *Southern Water, Southern Power*, 101.

13. Moody address, 12 September 1946.

14. Cashin, *The Story of Augusta*, 270; Thurmond, "Clark's Hill Project." For context on Thurmond, see Crespino, *Strom Thurmond's America*, esp. chap. 2.

15. L. S. Moody, "The Nine Foot Channel Project, Savannah River, Request for an Appropriation, March 1956," box 3, LSM.

16. Fite, *Richard B. Russell, Jr., Senator from Georgia*, 319; Cashin, *The Story of Augusta*, 271, 288; Moody, "Nine Foot Channel Project"; L. S. Moody, "Augusta's Destiny is Linked to the Savannah River," *Building Augusta*, August 1957, 1, ARCPL.

17. Daniel Lang, "Our Far-Flung Correspondents: Camellias and Bombs," *New Yorker*, 7 July 1951, 38, box 2, folder 5, LSM.

18. Frederickson, *Cold War Dixie*, 79, 81, 84, 95.

19. Goldfield, *Cotton Fields and Skyscrapers*, 142–43; *Economic Analysis: Augusta–Richmond County, Phase 3: Population, November 1965* (Augusta, GA: Augusta–Richmond County Planning Commission, 1965), 7, 20, box 2, LSM. For additional context on the postwar exodus of Black farmers, see Daniel, *Dispossession*, chap. 1.

20. *The Savannah River Plant of the U.S. Atomic Energy Commission*, n.d., box 2, folder 5, LSM.

21. *The Savannah River Plant of the U.S. Atomic Energy Commission*; Frederickson, *Cold War Dixie*, 23.

22. Louis C. Fink, "When the H-Bomb Fell on Carolina," *State Magazine* [Columbia, SC], 29 June 1952, 3–4, box 2, folder 5, LSM; "United States Census, 1940," database, *GenealogyBank* (https://genealogybank.com/#), Ralph V. South, Ordway, Election Precinct 3, Crowley, Colorado, United States.

23. "Richmond County Population to Almost Double Itself within Two Years," *Building Augusta*, May 1951, 3, box 2, LSM.

24. "Augusta Growing Economically and Numerically," *Building Augusta*, June 1953, 1, ARCPL.

25. Margaret Shannon, "Where the Big Bombs Grow," *Atlanta Journal*, 14 March 1952, box 2, folder 5, LSM; Lang, "Camellias and Bombs," 39; Frederickson, *Cold War Dixie*, 110–11. For context, see Hunner, *Inventing Los Alamos*; Johnson and Jackson, *City Behind a Fence*.

26. Fink, "When the H-Bomb Fell on Carolina," 5; Herbert Yahraes, "Building the H-Bomb Plant: Biggest Construction Job," *Popular Science*, June 1952, 108, box 2, folder 5, LSM; John T. Alexander, "To Make Way for a Super Bomb Plant 6,000 Persons Are Giving Up Their Homes," *Kansas City Star*, 17 February 1952, box 2, folder 5, LSM.

27. "New Atomic Bomb Plant Hits Augusta with a Bang," *Business Week*, 10 November 1951, box 2, folder 5, LSM; Morgan Fitz, "Boom on the Savannah; It Spells Death to Ellenton, Prosperous New Life to the Nearby Communities, *Times-Herald* [Newport News, VA], 28 March 1952, 23, box 2, folder 5, LSM.

28. Yahraes, "Building the H-Bomb Plant," 108; "Bomb Means Boom in Augusta," *Building Augusta*, September 1952, 1, ARCPL.

29. "Bomb Means Boom in Augusta"; Fink, "When the H-Bomb Fell on Carolina," 3; Lang, "Camellias and Bombs," 41; Reed et al., *Savannah River Site at Fifty*, 235.

30. Reed et al., *Savannah River Site at Fifty*, 231, 234–35; "Bomb Means Boom in Augusta"; Yahraes, "Building the H-Bomb Plant," 107.

31. Cashin, *The Story of Augusta*, 284; Reed et al., *Savannah River Site at Fifty*,

235. Robbins's encouragement of yard beautification paralleled that of William Levitt and Sons at Levittown on Long Island; see Sellers, *Crabgrass Crucible*, 52–53.

32. Reed et al., *Savannah River Site at Fifty*, 224–25, 227, 229; Yahraes, "Building the H-Bomb Plant," 228.

33. Yahraes, "Building the H-Bomb Plant," 228; unpaginated reprint of Ralph McGill, "They Stuck to the South—and Won," *Saturday Evening Post*, 30 April 1949, box 2, folder 4, LSM; Southern Finance Corporation advertisement, *Augusta Chronicle*, 12 February 1950, 7–D; Southern Finance Corporation advertisement, *Augusta Chronicle*, 9 March 1952, 8; Bill Knotts Realty Co. advertisement, *Augusta Chronicle*, 18 January 1953, 11.

34. Fink, "When the H-Bomb Fell on Carolina," 3; "New Atomic Bomb Plant Hits Augusta with a Bang"; Randy Jay, "County to Join City in New $7.2 Million Sewer Project," *Augusta Chronicle*, 30 November 1962, 19.

35. Augusta Unit, Federal Writers' Project in Georgia, *Augusta (American Guide Series)*, 13.

36. *For You, Sir, a Brief on Industrial Augusta, Georgia* (Augusta, GA: Industrial Development Division, Augusta Chamber of Commerce, 1952), 2, box 2, LSM.

37. Dorothy Kilgallen, "A Big Night in Augusta," *Good Housekeeping*, May 1953, 28, quoted in Cashin, *The Story of Augusta*, 284, and Reed, *Savannah River Site at Fifty*, 244.

38. "Is It True What They Say about Augusta?" *Building Augusta*, December 1951, 1, ARCPL.

39. Cashin, *The Story of Augusta*, 284; "Last Word," *Augusta Chronicle*, 5 May 1953, 4; "Mayor Requests Apology from Columnist Kilgallen," *Augusta Chronicle*, 10 May 1953, 9. On boosters' greater sensitivity to urban image than urban problems, see Cobb, "Politics in a New South City," 86–87.

40. *For You, Sir, a Brief on Industrial Augusta, Georgia* (Augusta, GA: Industrial Development Division, Augusta Chamber of Commerce, 1953), 5, box 2, folder 2, LSM.

41. Report of the Secretary to the Annual Meeting of the Chamber of Commerce, 1946, box 1, folder 6, MCW; Hutchinson and Brewster, *Population Mobility*, 10, 70; *For You, Sir, a Brief on Industrial Augusta, Georgia* (1953), 5.

42. Causey, *Red Clay, White Water, and Blues*, 127–28; "Georgia-Pacific History."

43. "Augusta Boom is Continuing," *Augusta Chronicle*, 28 October 1964, 20; *The Inside Facts on Augusta, Georgia, Heart of the Industrial Southeast* (Augusta, GA: Industrial Development Division, Augusta Chamber of Commerce, 1954), 5, box 2, folder 2, LSM.

44. Richardson, *Augusta, Ga.*; *Economic Analysis, Augusta–Richmond County, Phase 2*, 9–11; "B&W Expansion Boomed Since End of World War II," *Augusta Chronicle*, 4 August 1968; "Drainage Work Nearing Finish," *Augusta Chronicle*, 22 January 1937, 12.

45. *For You, Sir, a Brief on Industrial Augusta, Georgia* (1952), 5; *The Inside Facts on*

Augusta, Georgia, Heart of the Industrial Southeast (Augusta, GA: Industrial Development Division, Augusta Chamber of Commerce, 1955), 5, box 2, folder 2, LSM.

46. On industrial recruitment and diversification efforts, see Cobb, *The Selling of the South*, 54–63, 87–89; Wheeler, *Knoxville, Tennessee*, 2nd ed., chap. 3; Maunula, *Guten Tag, Y'all*, chaps. 1–2. On attempts to "hatch" a new economy, see Cummings, *Brain Magnet*, 9–12; Downs, *Transforming the South*, 222–23.

47. John R. Henry, "Birmingham Eyes Relief from Economic Ills with Diversification of Industry," *Columbus Ledger-Enquirer*, 8 February 1953, 22; "'Committee of 100' Will Assist in Augusta and CSRA's Growth," *Augusta Chronicle*, 19 June 1952, 1.

48. "Committee of 100 Launches Steps to Aid Development of Georgia, S. C. Counties," *Augusta Chronicle*, 23 July 1952, 1; Josef C. Patchen, "The Industrial Future of Augusta," *Building Augusta*, September 1954, 1, ARCPL; Rod Fisher, "Large-Scale Beef Breeding is 'Hobby' with Augustan," *Augusta Chronicle*, 27 October 1957, 7.

49. James Sheppard, "Committee of 100 to Regroup and Function as Separate Unit," *Augusta Chronicle*, 16 February 1956, 1–A; "Young Savannahian Begins Work of Luring New Industry to Augusta," *Augusta Chronicle*, 23 February 1956, 1; "Augusta's Potential Wealth," *Augusta Chronicle*, 20 September 1944, 6.

50. "Paper Plant Turns Down Augusta Site," *Augusta Chronicle*, 28 November 1956, 1; "Civic Restlessness," *Augusta Chronicle*, 21 April 1957, 2–D.

51. "Open House Set Today by Committee of 100," *Augusta Chronicle*, 25 April 1957, 6–D; "Optimism is Needed by Factory-Seekers," *Augusta Chronicle*, 28 May 1957, 3. On the formation of similar industrial committees in other southern cities, see especially Cobb, *The Selling of the South*, 54–63, 87–89; Wheeler, *Knoxville, Tennessee*, 100. Knoxville's Committee of 100 formed in 1954; see "Group Formed to Spur Industrial Development," *Knoxville Journal*, 23 January 1954, 2. On the role of community pride in industrial recruitment, see Cobb, *The Selling of the South*, 151–52.

52. "Industrial Firm Buys 'Possible Plant Site," *Augusta Chronicle*, 24 December 1957, 1; "900 Acres Ear-Marked for Future Industrial Use," *Augusta Chronicle*, 23 February 1958, 6–A.

53. Barbara Milz, "G.E. to Begin Operating Augusta Plant in August," *Augusta Chronicle*, 26 June 1958, 1.

54. David Playford, "Augusta Has a New Atmosphere," *Augusta Chronicle*, 26 October 1958, 1–D.

55. "Area Hails Acquisition of Mammoth Paper Plant," *Augusta Chronicle*, 18 December 1958, 1–A; Sutter, *Let Us Now Praise Famous Gullies*, 196. The reference to the "big parade" of paper companies derives from Jonathan Daniels, *The Forest Is the Future* (New York: International Paper Company, 1957), 7, quoted in Sutter.

56. Rod Harris, "$250,000 Fund Asked; Sum Would Pay for Site of Industry," *Augusta Chronicle*, 20 January 1959, 1. On southern industrial incentive packages, see Cobb, *The Selling of the South*.

57. "Put Up or Shut Up," *Augusta Chronicle,* 20 January 1959, 1; "Pledges Pouring in for Industrial Site," *Augusta Chronicle,* 21 January 1959, 1. The provision of free land as an inducement to industry mirrored a common practice dating to the interwar period in some southern cities and towns; see Goldfield, *Cotton Fields and Skyscrapers,* 189–90.

58. Rod Harris, "Rally Brings $53,285 to Plant Site Fund," *Augusta Chronicle,* 22 January 1959, 1–A; "Plant Location Fund Past Halfway Point," *Augusta Chronicle,* 28 January 1959, 1–A; "Factory Fund at $194,000; More Likely," *Augusta Chronicle,* 4 February 1959, 1.

59. "The CSRA Has Spoken," *Augusta Chronicle,* 5 February 1959, 4; "Deed for Factory Site Going to Continental," *Augusta Chronicle,* 5 February 1959, 1; "End of Month Start Due on Paper Plant," *Augusta Chronicle,* 6 February 1959, 1–A.

60. "Committee of 100 Wasted Little Time Taking Charge," *Augusta Chronicle,* 5 September 1961, 9.

61. "Togetherness is Paying Off," *Columbus Ledger,* 22 May 1964, 4.

62. Carrol Dadisman, "400-Acre Tract to Lure Industry Due for County," *Augusta Chronicle,* 8 April 1959, 1.

63. "Dwight D. Eisenhower's Influence on Augusta National Remembered," *Augusta.com,* 28 March 2019, https://www.augusta.com/masters/story/news/2019 -03-28/dwight-d-eisenhowers-influence-augusta-national-remembered; Barry Lorge, "Masters, CBS Understated Partners," *Washington Post,* 12 April 1981, https:// www.washingtonpost.com/archive/sports/1981/04/12/masters-cbs-understated -partners/9ef7502c-bdf6-4128-b1ef-fae20e334a7c/; Committee of 100 advertisement, *Augusta Chronicle,* 3 April 1960, 41.

64. *Augusta Bicentennial 1735–1935 Pageant Book,* 45, ARCPL.

65. "In Peach Land, a New Empire of Chemicals," *Augusta Chronicle,* 29 August 1965, 16–F; "Railroad Buys Land in Miracle Mile," *Building Augusta,* February 1963, 4, RLSC; *Economic Analysis, Augusta–Richmond County, Phase 2,* 13–14. Paper and chemicals were among the "new type" industries that appeared with greater frequency in the postwar South; see Bartley, *The New South 1945–1980,* 143.

66. "Beckum Warns of Complacency," *Building Augusta,* April 1964, 3, RLSC; "State's First Lady Will Break Ground," *Augusta Chronicle,* 19 June 1964, 5.

67. Margaret Twiggs, "CSRA Planning Group Aids Area Development," *Augusta Chronicle,* 21 July 1963, 4; Margaret Twiggs, "Planning Group Two Years Old," *Augusta Chronicle,* 25 August 1963, 86; "Development Group Plan is Proposed for CSRA," *Augusta Chronicle,* 21 April 1961, 3–B; "CSRA Planning Group to Meet at Swainsboro," *Augusta Chronicle,* 21 October 1961, 2. On Rome's Coosa Valley Area Planning and Development Commission, see Cebul, *Illusions of Progress,* 97–102. Macon and Columbus later opened their own area planning and development commissions like Augusta's; see "Seventh Year of Progress" (1967–68 Annual Report), Central Savannah River Area Planning and Development Commission, unpaginated insert, ARCPL.

68. "Seventh Year of Progress," 5–6, ARCPL.

69. "Seventh Year of Progress" 6; Don Fererell, "Plans of Industrial Park Finalized at $25 Million," *Augusta Chronicle*, 4 May 1968, 1; Souther, "Making 'The Garden City of the South.'" 100–101; John Alston, "Request Withdrawn for Phinizy Funds," *Augusta Chronicle*, 28 June 1969, 9.

70. Nix and Dudley, *Community Social Analysis of Augusta–Richmond County*, 4, 12, 17–18, 22.

71. The shifting priorities may be seen in the Central Savannah River Area Planning & Development Commission annual reports, 1968–77, ARCPL; Nix and Dudley, *Community Social Analysis*, 17–18.

72. *Economic Analysis, Augusta–Richmond County, Phase 2*, 21–22; 1990 U.S. Census of Population. Between 1960 and 1990, the population of Augusta's seven-county SMSA increased by more than 55 percent while the surrounding rural counties in the CSRA grew by a mere 0.6 percent.

73. Goldfield, *Cotton Fields and Skyscrapers*, 152–53; George Doss, "Merger Failed Repeatedly, but City Grew by Annexation," *Macon Telegraph*, 17 February 1983, 1–A; "From 2.3 to 26.62 Miles in 130 Years City Story," *Columbus Enquirer*, 31 December 1958, 22; Wayne Partridge, "Revenue Growing with City," *Augusta Chronicle*, 21 April 1996.

74. Neumann, "Reforging the Steel City," 586.

75. U.S. Census of Manufactures, 1958–1963, cited in *Augusta Regional Transportation Study*, 39; Clason Kyle, "ABC Stands for A Booming Columbus," *Columbus Ledger-Enquirer Magazine*, 17 January 1965, box 104, folder 21 "Columbus—Business and Industry (4)," Georgiana Vertical File (GVF), Hargrett Rare Book and Manuscript Library, University of Georgia, Athens, GA; "Airport Industrial Park Transferred to Authority," *Macon Mover*, 29 June 1964, box 2, folder 23, John J. McKay Jr. Collection, Middle Georgia Archives, Washington Memorial Library, Macon, GA.

76. "Columbus Soon to Be Port City," *Georgia Anchorage* [Georgia Ports Authority], May 1963, 19, box 2, folder 2, LSM; Sam Hopkins, "Columbus Plans for 'Inland Port' City Fails," *Atlanta Journal and Constitution*, 18 July 1971, box 104, folder 10 "Columbus—General (2)," GVF; Col. Marvin Griffin, "The Fate of the Lock and Dam in Augusta, but First a Little History," *US Army Corps of Engineers Savannah District*, 12 February 2018, https://www.sas.usace.army.mil/Media/News-Stories /Article/1438784/column-the-fate-of-the-lock-and-dam-in-augusta-but-first-a-little -history/.

77. *Economic Analysis: Augusta–Richmond County, Phase 2*, 13–14; "Beckum Warns of Complacency," *Building Augusta*, April 1964, 3, RLSC; Goldfield, *Cotton Fields and Skyscrapers*, 190.

78. Frederickson, *Cold War Dixie*, 173–75; Doug Pardue, "Deadly Legacy: Savannah River Site Near Aiken One of the Most Contaminated Places on Earth," *Post and Courier* [Charleston, SC], 21 May 2017, https://www.postandcourier.com/news /deadly-legacy-savannah-river-site-near-aiken-one-of-the-most-contaminated -places-on-earth/article_d325f494-12ff-11e7-9579-6b0721ccae53.html; Angelon-Gaetz, Richardson, and Wing, "Inequalities in the Nuclear Age."

79. Cobb, "Politics in a New South City," 169–70, 184; *Economic Analysis: Augusta-Richmond County, Phase 3*, 54.

80. Checker, *Polluted Promises*, 4–6, 88–90; Cashin, *The Story of Augusta*, 298–301.

81. The same reliance on the fall line to evacuate sewage and industrial wastes was a hallmark of other fall-line cities, including Baltimore; see Glotzer, *How the Suburbs Were Segregated*, 19. On the impact of chemical industries in Savannah, see Goldfield, *Cotton Fields and Skyscrapers*, 190.

82. John Alston, "New Waste Treatment Will Go into Operation," *Augusta Chronicle*, 5 January 1969, 12–B; John Alston, "Oates Creek Drainage Study Faults Savannah Flood Control," *Augusta Chronicle*, 30 September 1971, 1–D; Tommy Tomlinson, "Richmond, U.S. Officials to Sign Oates Creek Agreement, *Augusta Chronicle*, 10 March 1988, 1–B.

6. BUILDING THE FUTURE FROM OUR PAST

1. "Bright, Unusual Plants Create the Right Mood," *Macon News*, 29 July 1975, Macon Mall Supplement, 26; "Exciting Events Being Planned at Macon Mall" and "Mall Designed for its Customers," *Macon News*, 29 July 1975, Macon Mall Supplement, 8. Hypothetical purchases reflect items that appeared in advertisements in the Macon Mall Supplement.

2. "Mall Tenant List Has Variety," *Macon News*, 29 July 1975, Macon Mall Supplement, 6.

3. "Downtown Considers New Program," *Macon News*, 14 August 1977, 1A.

4. "Buys Saxon–Cullum Co.; Davison, Paxon Co., Macy Affiliate, Closes Augusta Deal," *New York Times*, 17 August 1944, 25; Annie Wheat Smith, "Union Dry Goods Company Bought by Davison-Paxon," *Macon Telegraph and News*, 5 November 1944, 1; Susan Long, "Another Downtown Store Closing Its Doors Soon," *Macon Telegraph and News*, 9 November 1975, 5C. Davison's also built a store on Columbus's Broadway in 1949; see Carlton Johnson, "Crowds Cheer Davison's Debut," *Columbus Ledger*, 14 February 1949, 1.

5. "Downtown Considers New Program." On downtown merchants' preference for luring white suburbanites over serving the more working-class shoppers who lived close to downtown; see Isenberg, *Downtown America*, chap. 5.

6. Susan Long, "Downtown Area Tries to Cope," *Macon Telegraph and News*, 10 August 1975, 4C; Cecil Bentley, "The Mall; Macon Learns to Live with a 'Second City,'" *Macon News*, 6 August 1980, 3B.

7. For an apt comparison, see Alan Lessoff's discussion of Corpus Christi's move from lofty metropolitan ambitions to acceptance of regional satellite status; Lessoff, *Where Texas Meets the Sea*, 22–28.

8. The sandhill cities' lag in mall development following postwar suburbanization echoed a national pattern, but the lag was longer because mall developers needed to

reach a certain market threshold before investing in a major regional center; see Cohen, *A Consumers' Republic*, 257–58.

9. "Postwar Campaign to Seek Individual Contributions," *Macon News*, 12 May 1944, 13; Gould, *Otis Redding*, 53; Bob Blair, "Competition Keen for New Industry," *Macon Telegraph*, 13 April 1958, 2.

10. "W. A. Fickling Picked Head Planning Unit," *Macon News*, 3 July 1944, 8; "Fickling to Head Industrial Unit," *Macon News*, 28 November 1962, 12; "Maconites Urged to Back Road Plan," *Macon News*, 6 November 1957, 1. For context on how aggressive local leverage helped determine precise freeway routes, see the example of Phoenix, Arizona, in Rose, *Interstate*, 2nd ed., 102–5.

11. "Industrial Park Proposed," *Macon Mover*, 14 October 1963, 1, box 4, folder 30, John J. McKay Jr. Papers (JJM), Middle Georgia Archives (MGA), Washington Memorial Library, Macon, GA; Grace T. Crawford, "Chamber Cites Importance of Interstate Highway Here," *Macon News*, 25 April 1963, 32; "Airport Industrial Park Transferred to Authority," *Macon Mover*, 29 June 1964, 2, box 4, folder 31, JJM. For broader context on interstate highways' impact on cities and metropolitan regions, see Rose and Mohl, *Interstate*, 3rd ed., chap. 8.

12. Causey, *Red Clay, White Water and Blues*, 215.

13. "Fast Growth Seen for Macon Area," *Macon News*, 10 July 1967, 1.

14. "Macon Advertised in January 'Wall Street Journal," *Macon Mover*, 5 February 1968, 1, box 5, folder 39, JJM; "Wall Street Journal Ad Promotes Macon as Area Office Center," *Macon Mover*, 26 February 1968, 1, box 5, folder 39, JJM.

15. See, for example, the reprinted advertisement in *Macon Mover*, 27 September 1971, 2, box 5, folder 46, JJM.

16. Minutes of Business Communications Committee, Greater Macon Chamber of Commerce, March 8, 1978, box 8, folder 21, Bucker F. Melton Papers (BFM), MGA; Mary Burdette and Ron Woodgeard, "Macon Seeks Help for Industrial Park," *Macon News*, 4 January 1979, 1A; Bill Cutler, "Who's In, Who's Out, and What's Up in Macon," *Brown's Guide to Georgia*, June 1982, 48, box 105, folder 33 "Macon—General," Georgiana Vertical File, Hargrett Rare Book and Manuscript Library, University of Georgia, Athens, GA.

17. Neil Skene, "Plans for Downtown Reaching Fruition," *Macon Telegraph and News*, 22 February 1970, 1B.

18. "Downtown Bloc Forming Council," *Macon News*, 14 February 1963, 1; "Downtown Council Meeting Introduces Plans, Officers," *Macon Mover*, 27 July 1964, 1, box 4, folder 32, JJM; "Council Begins Colorful Park and Shop Campaign," *Macon Mover*, 14 September 1964, 2, box 4, folder 32, JJM; "Downtown Gets Planters, Trees," *Macon Mover*, 21 December 1964, 1, box 4, folder 32, JJM; "Parade Becomes Regional Event," *Macon Mover*, 21 September 1964, 1, box 4, folder 32, JJM.

19. "C of C Plans First Shopping Tour of City," *Macon News*, 3 March 1965, 14; "Second V.I.P. Tour Scheduled," *Macon News*, 1 June 1965, 2; "Griffin Club to Visit Downtown," *Macon Mover*, 26 July 1965, 5, box 4, folder 34, JJM; "Berrien Group Here on Tour," *Macon News*, 31 August 1965, 5; "Coffee Group Due Today," *Macon*

Telegraph, 21 September 1965, 8; "V.I.P. Group from McRae Visits Today," *Macon Telegraph,* 12 October 1965, 3; R. F. (Bob) Jones, "Welcome to Downtown Macon," n.d. [1965], box 1, folder 7, JJM.

20. Souther, "Making 'The Garden City of the South,'" 101.

21. Adley Associates Inc., *Macon Central Business District Improvement Program: Plan for Physical Improvements* (Macon, GA: Macon-Bibb County Planning & Zoning Commission, 1968), box 1, folder 3c, Macon–Bibb County Planning & Zoning Commission Records (PZC), MGA.

22. "C&S Bank to Build $30 Million Complex at Terminal Station," *Macon Mover,* 29 January 1968, 1, box 5, folder 39, JJM; Edward Hatfield, "Mills B. Lane Jr.," *New Georgia Encyclopedia,* last modified 14 April 2021, https://www.georgiaencyclopedia .org/articles/business-economy/mills-b-lane-jr-1912-1989/. Macon's financial sector was controlled from outside the city so thoroughly that when Georgia Bank and Trust Company formed in 1960, it billed itself as Macon's only locally owned bank; see advertisement, *Macon Telegraph and News,* 9 October 1960, 7.

23. "Banker Sees Rich's Here by 1974," *Macon Telegraph,* 12 September 1969, 3A; Nancy Lewis, "Terminal Station Complex Given Go Ahead Here," *Macon Telegraph,* 18 June 1970, 1A; "Rich's Bolsters Plans for Commerce Square," *Macon News,* 25 May 1972, 1A.

24. Joe Kovac Jr., "Former Mayor Ronnie Thompson Dies," *Macon Telegraph,* March 29, 2020; "Mayor Planning Avenue of Flags," *Macon News,* 21 May 1969, 8.

25. Lassiter, *The Silent Majority,* 11; Manis, *Macon Black and White,* 260–62; Phil Dodson, "Shoot Anarchists 'To Kill,' Mayor Tells Macon Police," *Macon News,* 19 June 1970, 1A. Mayor William B. Hartsfield had dubbed Atlanta "The City Too Busy to Hate" in the 1950s.

26. "Tourist Project Leaders Named," *Macon News,* 21 December 1962, 16, "United States Census, 1910," database, *GenealogyBank* (https://genealogybank.com/#), John J. McKay, Ward 4, Bibb, Georgia, United States; "Mrs. J. J. McKay Dies at Home," *Macon News,* 23 October 1956, 8; George Doss, "John McKay Dies," *Macon News,* 29 March 1982, 1B; "Macon C of C Maps Tours as Part of Stay-See Plan," *Macon News,* 30 January 1963, 8.

27. "Macon, the Heart of Historic Georgia" (brochure), n.d. [ca. 1965], box 1, folder 9, JJM; "See and Enjoy Beautiful + Historic Macon: Heritage Tour" (brochure), n.d. [ca. 1966], box 1, folder 9, JJM; "Heritage Tour Signs Going Up Around Macon," *Macon News,* 24 January 1967, 11. On women's roles in using historic preservation as a mixture of historical memory and ancestral worship, see especially Dubrow, *Restoring Women's History Through Historic Preservation,* 24–30; Yuhl, *A Golden Haze of Memory,* 30–32; Stanonis, *Creating the Big Easy,* 142; Falck, *Remembering Dixie,* 170–72. As Yuhl argues, Charleston was an unusual early adopter of the notion of turning "old buildings into bridges that spanned the generations and helped the Old South adapt to the New"; see Yuhl, *A Golden Haze of Memory,* 26.

28. "Macon, the Heart of Historic Georgia"; "Enjoy Macon's Colonial Charm in the Heart of Historic Georgia" (brochure), n.d. [1960s], box 1, folder 9, JJM; "See and

Enjoy Beautiful + Historic Macon: Heritage Tour"; "Enchanting Macon, Georgia: Historical . . . Beautiful . . . Old South Charm" (brochure), n.d. [1960s], box 1, folder 9, JJM. The reconstruction of the Fort Hawkins blockhouse reflected a quarter-century effort by the Nathaniel Macon Chapter of the DAR; see Donald G. Mitchell Jr., "Full-Sized Replica of Fort Dedicated," *Macon News*, 20 March 1939, 1. On the Baconsfield Park struggle, see Manis, *Macon Black and White*, 236–39.

29. Selby McCash, "New Roads Aid Coliseum Traffic," *Macon Telegraph and News*, 13 October 1968, S–5; Digital Scholarship Lab, "Renewing Inequality," https://dsl .richmond.edu/panorama/renewal/#view=0/0/1&viz=cartogram&city=maconGA& loc=14/32.8400/-83.6281; *Macon Coliseum Dedication* (pamphlet), Historical Reference Files, MGA; "Tourist Information Center to Be Opened," *Macon News*, 26 July 1968, 12; "Stay and See Award Big Honor for Macon," *Macon News*, 12 November 1971, 4A.

30. "Greater Macon Sells Itself: Atlanta Developers Hear of Local Efforts," *Macon Mover*, 3 November 1969, 2, box 5, folder 42, JJM.

31. "Creek Indian Trading Post Opens Soon," *Macon Mover*, 30 May 1972, 1, box 5, folder 47, JJM; Mike Webb, "Creeks Wary of Invitation," *Macon Telegraph and News*, 14 August 1977, 1D; Cutler, "Who's In, Who's Out, and What's Up in Macon," 37.

32. "Indians Arrive Here for Park Celebration," *Macon News*, 2 November 1951, 1; "Parade Here Will Open Annual Indian Festival," *Macon Telegraph*, 17 September 1952, 1. The use of Native Americans to entice tourists has a long history; see especially Dilworth, *Imagining Indians in the Southwest*; Rothman, *Devil's Bargains*; West, *The Enduring Seminoles*; Shaffer, *See America First*; Beard-Moose, *Public Indians, Private Cherokees*.

33. Hyatt, *Charles H. Jones*, 148–49.

34. Phil Garner, "Some Creeks Come Home to Macon," *Atlanta Journal and Constitution Magazine*, 26 November 1972; 42; Hyatt, *Charles H. Jones*, 135–36; Webb, "Creeks Wary of Invitation."

35. Webb, "Creeks Wary of Invitation"; "Scholarships Offered by Mercer to Indians," *Macon Telegraph and News*, 6 Feb 1972, 6A; Leonard Ray Teel, "Creek Indians Are Still Close to the Land," *Atlanta Journal and Constitution*, 13 February 1972, 11–B; "Two Indians to Arrive This Week," *Macon News*, 2 May 1972, 4B.

36. Lyn Martin, "'Trail of Cheers'?; For the Creeks in Macon It Was a 'Trail of Tears," *Atlanta Journal and Constitution*, 4 January 1976, 6–A; Mike Webb, "A Creek is Not a Stream," *Macon News*, 17 August 1977, 1B.

37. Hyatt, *Charles H. Jones*, 149.

38. Garner, "Some Creeks Come Home to Macon."

39. "Macon Gets All Ready to Observe Creek Week," *Macon News*, 1 October 1972, 1A; "Creek Indian Week," *Macon Telegraph and News*, 24 September 1972, 61.

40. Garner, "Some Creeks Come Home to Macon." On the John B. Rogers Producing Company of Fostoria, Ohio, see Glassberg, *American Historical Pageantry*, 236–37.

41. Jean Bush, "Creeks Return, More Coming," *Macon Telegraph and News*, 28 May 1972, 1A; Webb, "A Creek is Not a Stream."

42. Kathleen Myler, "Macon is No 'Trail of Tears' for Creek Couple Who Stayed," *Macon Telegraph and News*, 18 January 1976, 1B; Mike Webb, "Creeks Dislike 'Museum' Image," *Macon News*, 16 August 1977, 1B; Martin, "'Trail of Cheers'?"

43. Phil Dodson, "State Delays Parkway Plan," *Macon News*, 18 September 1973, 1A; Gertrude Trawick, "Down Area Plan is Studied," *Macon News*, 6 November 1973, 1A; Gertrude Trawick, "Four Major Stores Anchor Macon Mall," *Macon News*, 15 August 1973, 1A.

44. Gertrude Trawick, "Monorail Idea Considered for Macon," *Macon News*, 2 November 1973, 1A; "The Monorail Plan: Appropriately Bold," *Macon News*, 6 November 1973, 4A; Eddie Robinette, "Officials, Banker to Visit Europe," *Macon News*, 15 November 1973, 1B; "Globetrotting Mayor an Offense to Macon," *Macon News*, 1 December 1973, 4A. On the history of pedestrian malls, see Hardwick, *Mall Maker*; Vega-Barachowitz, "Festival Modernism"; Gregg, "Placing the North American Post-war Pedestrian Mall Within the Legacy of Downtown Urban Renewal."

45. Although Macon did not face the same "urban crisis" that Rustbelt cities endured, Melton fit the mold of so-called messiah mayors in his downtown-focused interest in reframing urban image, attracting tourists, and fostering public-private partnerships. Comparisons include Mayor William Donald Schaefer in Baltimore and Mayor George V. Voinovich in Cleveland; see Cowan, *A Nice Place to Visit*, 130–34; Biles and Rose, *A Good Place to Do Business*, 127–40.

46. Cutler, "Who's In, Who's Out, and What's Up in Macon," 37; City of Macon; Bibb County, *Intown Redevelopment and Revitalization Plan*, n.d. [1977], box 4, folder 12f, PZC.

47. Robert Hodder, "Savannah's Changing Past: Historic Preservation and the Social Construction of a Historic Landscape, 1955 to 1985," in Sies and Silver, eds., *Planning the Twentieth-Century American City*, 366–72.

48. McKay, "Story of the Middle Georgia Historical Society, Inc.," 157–58; Joe Heiterer, "Preservation is Their Aim," *Augusta Chronicle*, 4 June 1973, 13; Lupold, "Historic Columbus Foundation, 1966–1978," 130, 132. For additional context, see Goldfield, *Cotton Fields and Skyscrapers*, 157–58; Weyeneth, *Historic Preservation for a Living City*, 55–60; Lyon, "From Landmarks to Community," 77–97.

49. *A Neighborhood Conservation Study: The Macon In-Town Historic District* (Macon, GA: Macon–Bibb County Planning & Zoning Commission, 1976), 38, box 3, folder 11a, PZC; George W. Simons Jr. and Associates, *A Plan to Grow By* (Macon, GA: Macon–Bibb County Planning & Zoning Commission, 1958), 57, box 1, folder 1a, PZC.

50. Joyce R. Ellison, "A Lot of Living's Left in Macon's Older Homes," *Macon Telegraph and News*, 20 July 1975, 1D.

51. *A Neighborhood Conservation Study*, 1.

52. National Association of Real Estate Boards, Build America Better Committee, *Toward a New Columbus* (Washington, DC: National Association of Real Estate Boards, 1962), 26–28, Columbus State University Archives, Schwob Library, Columbus State University, Columbus, GA; G. Baker, "Olde Towne, Old Neighborhood but New Name and Outlook," *Augusta Magazine,* Fall 1979, 21, Augusta–Richmond County Public Library, Augusta, GA; Morton McInvale and Joyce R. Ellison, "Historic District Approved," *Macon Telegraph and News,* 1 February 1975, 1A.

53. Gould, *Otis Redding,* 142–43, 148; Susan Long, "Capricorn to Restore Old Downtown Building," *Macon News,* 24 July 1975, 1A; Sherry Howard, "Capricorn Park Honors Artists, Enhances Avenue," *Macon Telegraph and News,* 6 June 1976, 1A; "Capitalizing on Charm," *Macon Telegraph and News,* 27 July 1975, 6A. The emphasis on "charm" calls to mind Baltimore's "Charm City" branding of the 1970s; see Cowan, *A Nice Place to Visit,* 132.

54. Long, "Capricorn to Restore Old Downtown Building"; Mary Swint, "How Political is Walden? He Says He Won't Run," *Macon Telegraph and News,* 10 August 1975, 1D; Cutler, "Who's In, Who's Out, and What's Up in Macon," 44; Linda Wilson, "Walden Resigns Commission Seat," *Macon Telegraph and News,* 10 July 1976, 1B.

55. Gertrude Trawick, "New Authority Proposed to Revitalize Downtown," *Macon News,* 3 January 1974, 1A; "City, County Okay Panel," *Macon News,* 29 May 1974, 1B. Special purpose districts became increasingly common in the post–World War II decades as vehicles for raising and channeling funds toward specific development outcomes in defined areas; see Foster, *The Political Economy of Special-Purpose Government,* 19–20.

56. "Team Studying Macon Offers Three Proposals," *Macon News,* 14 January 1975, 1A.

57. On the Black business district on Cotton and Poplar, see Hayden, *Where Poplar Crosses Cotton,* 7. On Bridge Row, see "Bridge Row is Doomed at Last," *Macon Telegraph,* 24 July 1900, 8; "Nope, Bridge Row Has Not Reformed," *Macon Telegraph,* 4 May 1915, 8; Souther, "'Green Spots in the Heart of Town.'" 294–95.

58. Souther, "Making 'The Garden City of the South.'" 106; Souther, "'Green Spots in the Heart of Town.'" 310.

59. Linda Wilson, "New Cherry Street Plan Unveiled," *Macon Telegraph,* 4 December 1975, 1A.

60. *Urban Design and Planning Study: Macon Central Business District* (Macon, GA: Macon–Bibb County Planning & Zoning Commission, 1976), 5, 17–20, box 3, folder 11b, PZC.

61. Jane Oppy, "Building Restorations Considered," *Macon Telegraph,* 5 December 1977, 1A; Yvonne Shinhoster, "Downtown Hopes for Facelift," *Macon Telegraph,* 30 July 1978, 1D. On Pittsburgh's pioneering facade easement program, see Stephanie Ryberg-Webster, "Combatting Decline: Preservation and Community Development in Pittsburgh and Cincinnati," in Mason and Page, eds., *Giving Preservation a History,* 2nd ed., 234.

62. Sidney Hill, "Macon-Bibb Capital Improvements in 1978 Centered on Three Areas," *Macon Telegraph*, 25 February 1979, 2F; Terry D. Aronoff, "New Downtown Starting to Take Shape," *Macon Telegraph and News*, 24 February 1980, 1G; Philip Morris, "Shaping Livable Southern Cities," *Southern Living*, January 1980, 6s; Jenny Munro, "Augusta to Spend $100,000 of Grant for Facade Work," *Augusta Chronicle*, 5 October 1979, 10B.

63. Philip A. Dodson, "Readers Heap Criticism on Downtown Promenade," *Macon Telegraph*, 17 October 1977, 1A; Tethel White, "So You Want to Be Mayor?" *Macon Telegraph*, 26 March 1978, 1F; "Some Like It . . . Most Want It Changed; Downtown Promenade," *Macon Telegraph*, 14 October 1980, 4A.

64. Nancy Anderson, "Downtown Macon Has Turned the Corner," *Macon Telegraph*, 3 September 1976, 4A.

65. Lassiter, *The Silent Majority*, 213. This sort of rupture was not novel in the 1970s. For decades, the notion of "spatial harmony" between urban center and periphery, however compelling, was not unquestioned in cities; see Fogelson, *Downtown: Its Rise and Fall, 1880–1950*, 207–8.

66. Molly Cole, "Sewer Line Delay Sought," *Macon News*, 17 July 1977, 1C.

67. Randall Savage, "Dusty Orchard Avenue; When It Rains, It's Mud," *Macon Telegraph and News*, 1 August 1976, 8A; "United States Census, 1940," database, *GenealogyBank* (https://genealogybank.com/#), Richard Penniman, Ward 3, Macon, Militia District 1085, Bibb County, Georgia, United States.

68. Linda Wilson, "Housing Effort Vowed," *Macon Telegraph and News*, 11 December 1977, 1D. For regional context on the relative absence of street improvements in Black neighborhoods, see Goldfield, *Cotton Fields and Skyscrapers*, 151–52.

69. "Charles Henry Douglass," *Macon Telegraph*, 7 February 2000, 6A; "Charles H. Douglass listings in Macon City Directories, 1888–1940," and "Charles Henry Douglass, 1870–1940," (typescripts), n.d., and "Visit the Historic Douglass Theatre," (pamphlet), n.d., Douglass Business Records (DBR), MGA. On the 1922 incident, see Manis, *Macon Black and White*, 63–65.

70. On the idea of "blight" as a color-blind but racially coded term, see N. D. B. Connolly, "Sunbelt Civil Rights: Urban Renewal and the Follies of Desegregation in Greater Miami," in Nickerson and Dochuk, eds., *Sunbelt Rising*, 181.

71. *Urban Design and Planning Study*, 22. On white leaders' consensus favoring removal of Black areas along downtown fringes, see Biles and Rose, *A Good Place to Do Business*, 7. On Knoxville, see Wheeler, *Knoxville, Tennessee*, 2nd ed., 135. On Chattanooga, see Knapp, *Constructing the Dynamo of Dixie*, 85–87.

72. The Broadway redevelopment plan was a vision with echoes from three and a half decades earlier when then-mayor Glen Toole had urged building a Third Street Bridge over the river so that tourists arriving from the east would be routed away from the unsavory Bridge Row area on Fifth Street and instead enter downtown on the beautiful, expansive Third Street; see "Stewart Urging Third Span Here; Chamber of Commerce Highway Committeeman Wants Bridge at Third Street," *Macon Telegraph*, 10 September 1933, 1.

73. Vincent J. Bellafiore to John J. Holley, 11 April 1978, box 2, folder 4, BFM; *Urban Design and Planning Study*, 25.

74. *Urban Design and Planning Study*, 25–26; Maria Saporta, "About $1 Million Would Put Theater in Top Shape," *Macon Telegraph*, 2 September 1980, 1B.

75. Peter Robbins, "No Apparent Savior for Douglass Theater," *Macon News*, 22 May 1978, 8A; Pam Keene and Randall Savage, "The Fate of Douglass Theater Rests on Dwindling Support," *Macon Telegraph*, 13 November 1980, 1A; "Maconite Wins Black Award," *Macon News*, February 6, 1978, 7B.

76. Pam Keene, "City Begins Cleanup of Douglas Theater," *Macon News*, 30 May 1980, 7D; Pam Keene, "Restoration: Something New Every Day," *Macon News*, 27 June 1980, 1C; Lupold, "Historic Columbus Foundation," 129.

77. "Douglass Bungling Can Doom Project," *Macon News*, 22 October 1980, 10A; David Beasley, "$150,000 Recommended for Douglass," *Macon News*, 27 January 1982, 1A; Historic Preservation Services Inc., "Architectural History: The New Douglass Theatre," Landmark Museum Application prepared for the City of Macon, 1994, DBR.

78. Yvonne Shinhoster, "Poplar Street Blues; Problem-Plagued Block Untouched by Downtown Renaissance," *Macon News*, 6 May 1979, 1A; Larry D. Wilder, "Poplar's 400 Closing an Era," *Macon Telegraph*, 26 January 1986, 1A; "Entertainment-Business Notes," *Macon Telegraph*, 22 March 1949, Personal and Social News for Colored People, n.p.

79. Pellerin and Pellerin, *Poplar Street 400 Block Redevelopment Plan, Executive Summary* (Macon, GA: City of Macon Community Development Department, 1980), 8–9, 12–14, box 21, Macon City Records, MGA; Maria Saporta, "Office Park Possible Cure for Ailing Poplar," *Macon Telegraph and News*, 7 December 1980, 1A; Carol Marie Cropper, "Kamensky; Rankin Square's Developer Stays on the Move," *Columbus Enquirer*, 5 June 1978, A–1; Clason Kyle, "The Past Can Be As Much a Stimulus to the Future as Anything Else," *Sunday Ledger-Enquirer Magazine*, 13 July 1969, 12; Maria Saporta, "One Developer, One Downtown Block Are Keys to Renovation of Columbus," *Macon Telegraph and News*, 11 January 1981, 1C. On Larimer Square, see Morley, *Preservation & the Imagined West*, 43–66.

80. John Gaines, "Poplar Street Grant Sought," *Macon News*, 20 October 1982, 1A; John Gaines, "Poplar Street Renovation Worries Blacks," *Macon News*, 26 October 1982, 1A; Peter Robbins, "Blacks to Join Downtown Project," *Macon News*, 13 September 1978, 10A; John Finotti, "National Notebook: Macon, Ga.; A New Blow Against Blight," *New York Times*, 5 June 1988, sec. 8, p. 1.

81. Paula Crouch, "Macon in the Pink Again; Cherry Blossom Festival a Good Reason to Visit," *Atlanta Journal and Constitution*, 17 March 1984, Weekend, 41.

82. George Doss, "Cherry Blossom Day Proclaimed," *Macon News*, 24 March 1982, 1B.

83. Steve Bills, "More Cherry Trees Coming," *Macon News*, 2 September 1982, 1B; Crouch, "Macon in the Pink Again." For a detailed history of the Cherry Blossom Festival, see Grisamore, *The Pinkest Party on Earth*.

84. Skippy Lawson, "Cherry Festival a Tribute to Fickling," *Macon Telegraph and News,* 23 January 1983, 1D; Bob Lystad, "A Three-Ton Touch of the Orient Adds to Macon's Japanese Flavor," *Macon Telegraph and News,* 12 March 1983, 1B.

85. Randall Savage, "Cherry Street Project Officially Under Way," *Macon Telegraph and News,* 31 July 1982, 1B; Terri K. Smith, "Cherry Jubilee; Ribbon-Cutting and Gala Party Will Mark Reopening of Cherry Street," *Macon Telegraph,* 28 October 1983, 1D; Harley Bowers, "Bourbon Street Rival," *Macon Telegraph,* 28 March 1984, 1D.

86. Bob Lystad, "Turn-of-the-Century Fountain Discovered with Some Sleuthing," *Macon News,* 7 March 1983, 1B; Katherine Knott, "Dempsey Opens to Residents," *Macon News,* 15 July 1983, 1A; Jane Oppy, "Dempsey Considered for Elderly Housing," *Macon News,* 4 May 1977, 1A; Steve Bills, "Festivities Welcome New Cherry Street," *Macon Telegraph,* 2 November 1983, 1A; Steve Bills, "Terminal Station Contract Awarded to Macon Firm," *Macon News,* 22 July 1983, 2B.

87. "War! Macon, Ga., Challenges D.C. for 'Cherry Blossom' Crown," *Naples Daily News* [Naples, FL], 22 March 1987, 1E.

88. "Fly Macon: A Joint Program of the City of Macon and the Greater Macon Chamber of Commerce," May 1978, box 3, folder 11, BFM; Melton to Clint Sweazea, 15 August 1978, box 3, folder 11, BFM; Clint Sweazea to Melton, 21 August 1978, box 3, folder 11, BFM; Melton, Answer of City of Macon to Application of Eastern Air Lines, Inc., 10 July 1978, box 3, folder 12, BFM. For context on deregulation, see Bednarek, *Airports, Cities, and the Jet Age,* 18–30.

89. William Lee Robinson, unidentified speech, n.d. [1991], series 2, box 11, folder 14, William Lee Robinson Papers, Hargrett Rare Book and Manuscript Library, University of Georgia, Athens, GA.

90. Andrea Varga, "Auditorium Means Boost for Economy," *Macon News,* 5 April 1979, City Auditorium Tabloid, 7; "Officers Elected for Visitors Bureau," *Macon News,* 25 May 1976, 8A; "Macon's Convention Growth Phenomenal," *Macon Telegraph and News,* 29 July 1979, CVB Tabloid, 2; "Macon, Georgia: A Mid-Size City Still Intact," *Southern Living,* April 1986, 110; Susan Long, "Recycling a City," *Macon Magazine,* Winter 1986, 19, MGA.

91. Sherry Howard, "Downtown; City Skyline Emerging but Local Architects Hope for Bigger Effort," *Macon Telegraph and News,* 6 June 1976, 1C; "White Collar Job Push a Good Idea," *Macon Telegraph and News,* 31 January 1981, 4A.

92. "Discover Historic Macon." For an astute explication of Macon leaders' gradual tilt toward embracing the city's access to Atlanta's airport, amenities, and investors, see Cutler, "Who's In, Who's Out, and What's Up in Macon," 47.

EPILOGUE

1. "Where Soul Lives" (Visit Macon advertisement), 2023, received by the author via email from Visit Macon; *Trails—Tour Macon.* On the historical basis for Macon's music city image, see Wynne, *Something in the Water.*

2. Linda S. Morris, "New Logo Revealed for Macon-Bibb County," *Macon Telegraph*, 22 January 2016, A5; "Convention and Visitors Bureau Introduces New Black Heritage Brochure and Tour," Macon–Bibb County Convention and Visitors Bureau press release, February 14, 1991, folder "Black History—Tours and Tourism," and *Black Heritage, Macon, Georgia* (brochure), n.d. [1991], Historical Reference Files, Middle Georgia Archives (MGA), Washington Memorial Library, Macon, GA.

3. Anna Clark and Stacy Lam, "Marketing Downtown Macon," *Macon Telegraph*, 8 November 1998, 1A.

4. Wynne, *Something in the Water*, 276–77; "Branding Process | Macon's Official Branding Site," *Macon, Where Soul Lives* (Visit Macon), https://www.maconga.org /official-branding-site-/branding-process/.

5. "All Roads Lead to Macon" (Visit Macon advertisement), 2023, received by the author via email from Visit Macon.

6. "Georgia Authorizes $29 Million for Fall Line Freeway in Baldwin, Washington, Wilkinson, Twiggs Counties," *Macon Telegraph*, 22 October 2011, 1A; Caleb Slinkard and Jenna Eason, "Proposed Interstate Could Help Economy," *Macon Telegraph*, 8 August 2021, 1A; Mella McEwen, "Baby Steps Will Eventually Result in New Interstate 14," *Midland Reporter-Telegram*, 3 February 2023, https://www.mrt.com /news/local/article/baby-steps-eventually-result-new-interstate-14-17762714.php; Falon Brown, "Proposed Interstate 14 Would Run Through Central Louisiana, Connect Texas with Georgia," *WBRZ* [Baton Rouge, LA], 18 October 2023, https:// www.wbrz.com/news/proposed-interstate-14-would-run-through-central-louisiana -connect-texas-with-georgia/.

7. Arden Williams, "Textile Industry," *New Georgia Encyclopedia*, last modified 28 October 2021, https://www.georgiaencyclopedia.org/articles/business-economy /textile-industry/.

8. Cindy Sams, "Facts, Figures Reveal Macon's Economic Identity," *Macon Telegraph*, 7 January 2001, 5C; Linda S. Morris, "'A Critical Juncture'" *Macon Telegraph*, 19 January 2005, 1A; Linda S. Morris, "Largest Employers," *Macon Telegraph*, 3 October 2014, 5H.

9. Becky Purser, "Geico Will Hire 500 or More 'as Soon as Possible' at Macon Office," *Macon Telegraph*, 30 April 2021, 2A; Skip Krueger, "Downtown Sector Faces 2nd Decline," *Macon Telegraph*, 17 March 1991, 1D; Laura Corley, "Retail Shift Has Wound Through Macon for Over Half a Century," *Macon Telegraph*, 30 June 2019, 1A.

10. Tony Adams, "Mercer University to Set Up Medical School in Columbus," *Columbus Ledger-Enquirer*, 11 February 2012, A1.

11. Chuck Williams, "Company Exploring Possibility of Affiliation or Partnership," *Columbus Ledger-Enquirer*, 6 May 2016, 1A; Chuck Williams, "Hospital Pursues Merger with Atlanta-Based Provider," *Columbus Ledger-Enquirer*, 10 May 2017, 1A; Chuck Williams, "Piedmont to Assume Columbus Regional Debt," *Columbus Ledger-Enquirer*, 21 January 2018, 1A; "Joint Ownership, New Brand for St. Francis Hospital," *Columbus Ledger-Enquirer*, 15 February 2020, 3A; Andy Miller, "Navicent Deal with Atrium, Based in N.C., Shakes Up Georgia's Hospital Landscape," *Macon*

Telegraph, 2 January 2019, A1; Abraham Kenemore, "AU Health, Wellstar Agreement Brings Mixed Responses," *Augusta Chronicle*, 13 April 2023, 1A.

12. Schulman, *From Cotton Belt to Sunbelt*, 142.

13. "Major Employers," *Choose Columbus*, https://www.choosecolumbusga.com /site-selectors/major-employers; Tamari Perrineau, "Robins AFB Prepares for Mission Changes, Starting This Fall," *Macon Telegraph*, 6 June 2021, 2A; "Largest Employers," *Augusta Economic Development Authority*, https://augustaeda.org /business-industry/largest-employers/; Jeffrey Collins, "SC Senators Debate How to Spend $525 Million," *Florence Morning News*, 30 September 2021, A1; Matthew Schofield, "S.C. Wants to Know Where Waste Will Go," *The State*, 5 March 2017, C12.

14. Alexa Lightle, "Augusta Tourism Study Shows Significant Increase in Visitors," *WRDW*, 12 July 2017, https://www.wrdw.com/content/news/Augusta-Tourism-Study -Shows-Significant-Increase-in-Visitors-434143633.html; *Tourism Report and 2018 Marketing Plan*, 5.

15. Causey, *Red Clay, White Water, and Blues*, 256; Damon Cline, "City Seeks Protector for Post," *Augusta Chronicle*, 30 January 2002, 5D; Associated Press, "Security Role Might Save Fort Gordon," *Columbus Ledger-Enquirer*, 11 May 2005, 5C; Dan Chapman, "Army's Cyberwarriors Coming to Georgia Base," *Atlanta Journal-Constitution*, 20 December 2013, A1.

16. Geismer, *Don't Blame Us*, esp. chaps. 2–3; Cummings, *Brain Magnet*, 89–98; Frederickson, *Cold War Dixie*, 97–105, 167–69.

17. Billy Winn, "African American Soldiers at Fort Benning," n.d., series 1, box 2, folder 14, Virginia Causey Research Collection, MC 413, Columbus State University Archives, Schwob Library, Columbus State University, Columbus, GA. Neither Virginia Causey nor Andrew Manis identifies nearby military bases as having had a "leavening effect" on Columbus's or Macon's racial climate; see Causey, *Red Clay, White Water, and Blues*, and Manis, *Macon Black and White*.

18. Jack Bantock, "For Nearly 50 Years, Only Black Men Caddied The Masters. One Day, They All but Vanished," *CNN*, 5 April 2023, https://www.cnn.com/2023/04/05 /golf/black-caddies-masters-augusta-national-spt-spc-intl/index.html.

19. Samantha Max, "No Shortage of Ideas on How to Fix Bibb's Blight," *Macon Telegraph*, 26 May 2019, 1C.

20. Kruse, *White Flight*, 239–40; Lassiter, *The Silent Majority*, 327.

21. *U.S. Census Bureau QuickFacts: Muscogee County, Georgia*, https://www .census.gov/quickfacts/muscogeecountygeorgia; "Muscogee County Public Schools," *U.S. News & World Report*, https://www.usnews.com/education/k12/georgia /districts/muscogee-county-100651; *U.S. Census Bureau QuickFacts: Richmond County, Georgia*, https://www.census.gov/quickfacts/richmondcountygeorgia; "Richmond County Public Schools," *U.S. News & World Report*, https://www.usnews .com/education/k12/georgia/districts/richmond-county-103214; *U.S. Census Bureau QuickFacts: Bibb County, Georgia*, https://www.census.gov/quickfacts/bibbcounty georgia; "Bibb County Public Schools," *U.S. News & World Report*, https://www

.usnews.com/education/k12/georgia/districts/bibb-county-103595; Debbie Blanken-ship and Adam Ragusea, "Racial Concentration on Rise in Bibb Schools," *Macon Telegraph*, 15 January 2017, 1A. On resegregation of public schools following the collapse of busing, see Erickson, *Making the Unequal Metropolis;* Lassiter, *The Silent Majority.*

22. U.S. Census Bureau, *1990 Census of Population, General Population Character-istics: Georgia,* https://www2.census.gov/library/publications/decennial/1990/cp-1/cp-1–12.pdf; *U.S. Census Bureau QuickFacts: Monroe County, Georgia,* https://www.census.gov/quickfacts/fact/table/monroecountygeorgia; *U.S. Census Bureau QuickFacts: Harris County, Georgia,* https://www.census.gov/quickfacts/harriscountygeorgia.

23. Augusta Commercial Areas Study Committee, *Downtown Augusta: A Plan for Expansion and Revitalization of the Central Area of Augusta, Georgia* (Augusta, GA: Commercial Areas Study Committee of Augusta, 1968), Augusta–Richmond County Public Library, Augusta, GA; Adley Associates, Inc., *Macon Central Business District Improvement Program* (Macon, GA: Macon-Bibb County Planning & Zoning Commission, 1968), box 1, folder 3c, Macon–Bibb County Planning & Zoning Commission Records, MGA; Causey, *Red Clay, White Water, and Blues,* 236; Constance Johnson, "City Readies Real Work Downtown," *Sunday Ledger-Enquirer,* 12 May 1974, B–3; Constance Johnson, "Valley, Nation Celebrate," *Columbus Ledger-Enquirer,* 4 July 1976, A–1.

24. Souther, "Making 'The Garden City of the South.'" 108–9; Ernie Rogers, "Festival to Mark Opening of Downtown's Riverwalk," *Augusta Chronicle,* 23 March 1988, 1B.

25. James Palmer, "Taking a Chance on the River," *Macon Telegraph and News,* 18 July 1989, 3–B.

26. Bill Winn, "Augusta's Riverfront Has Cultural Flair," *Columbus Ledger-Enquirer,* 24 July 1989, A–1; Bill Winn, "Columbus Searching for Right Riverfront Plan," *Columbus Ledger-Enquirer,* 26 July 1989, A–1.

27. Causey, *Red Clay, White Water, and Blues,* 240.

28. Bill Winn, "Waterfront Rainbow's End for Some Cities," *Columbus Ledger-Enquirer,* 23 July 1989, A–1; Souther, "Making 'The Garden City of the South," 109; "Georgia Golf Hall of Fame Officially Closed," *Augusta Tomorrow | Our History.*

29. Damon Cline, "Savannah River Crucial to Augusta Sports Tourism, Recre-ation," *Augusta Chronicle,* 20 May 2019. As of this writing, Augusta leaders' lobbying had succeeded in securing federal approval to preserve the lock and dam; see Joe Hotchkiss, "'Could Not Be Prouder': President Signs Bill Saving New Savannah Bluff Lock and Dam," *Augusta Chronicle,* 7 January 2025, https://www.augustachronicle.com/story/news/local/2025/01/07/lock-and-dam-near-augusta-saved-after-biden-signs-new-water-bill-congress-army-corps-engineers/77490285007/.

30. "Our History," *Phinizy Center for Water Sciences,* https://phinizycenter.org/our-history/; *Augusta Canal National Heritage Area,* https://augustacanal.com;

Kennedi Harris, "New Augusta Canal Trail Extension Connects the CSRA Together," *WRDW*, 28 September 2020, https://www.wrdw.com/2020/09/28/new-augusta -canal-trail-extension-connects-the-csra-together/.

31. ICON Architecture, Inc., *The Westobou Vision Urban Area Master Plan: Part 1*, 9–10.

32. *Tourism Report and 2016 Marketing Plan*, 19, ACVB; *Tourism Report and 2017 Marketing Plan*, 22–23, ACVB.

33. Causey, *Red Clay, White Water, and Blues*, 248–49, 257, 263.

34. Causey, *Red Clay, White Water, and Blues*, 265. Columbus was not the first southern city to promote whitewater rafting. On the development of a similar course in downtown Richmond in the 1990s, see Hambrick, *Transforming the James River in Richmond*, chap. 6.

35. "Community Coalition Calls for Changes to Interchange Plans," *Macon Telegraph*, 30 August 2008, 4A.

36. Charles Richardson, "The Little River That Can," *Macon Telegraph*, 28 September 1999, 10.

37. Ed Grisamore, "Bringing Our River to Life," *Macon Telegraph*, 28 February 1997, 16; Ocmulgee Heritage Greenway advertisement, *Macon Telegraph*, 26 September 1999, 9; S. Heather Duncan, "Ocmulgee Mounds Expansion Proposal Almost Done," *Macon Telegraph*, 22 December 2012, 1A; Liz Fabian, "Converging Paths," *Macon Telegraph*, 20 July 2003, 1B.

38. Lisa Mayfield Spence, "Preserving Our Past, Protecting Our Present, Planning for Our Future: The Muscogee Nation Speaks Out," *Macon Magazine*, December/ January 2021, https://maconmagazine.com/preserving-our-past-protecting-our -present-planning-for-our-future-the-muscogee-nation-speaks-out/; Lisa Mayfield Spence, "Preserving Our Past, Protecting Our Present, Planning for Our Future: The Ocmulgee National Park and Preserve Initiative," *Macon Magazine*, August/ September 2021, https://maconmagazine.com/preserving-our-past-protecting-our -present-planning-for-our-future-the-ocmulgee-national-park-and-preserve -initiative/.

39. On the trend toward more racially inclusive historic preservation in southern cities, see Weyeneth, *Historic Preservation for a Living City*, 163–70. On Historic Augusta Inc.'s work in Laney–Walker, see "Black Historic Sites Identified," *Historic Augusta* 10, no. 3 (Fall 1979), 5, Historic Augusta Inc. (HAI), Augusta, GA; "NEH Grant Work Completed," *Historic Augusta* 12, no. 1 (Winter 1981), 2, HAI; "Planning for Laney–Walker Rehabilitation Program," *Historic Augusta* 12, no. 1 (Winter 1981), 5, HAI; Brooks, "Laney–Walker North Historic District." On opposition to the ongoing presence of Confederate monuments in civic space, see Cox, *No Common Ground;* Giguere, "The (Im)Movable Monument"; Goldfield, *Still Fighting the Civil War,* updated ed.; Marie Tyler-McGraw, "Southern Comfort Levels: Race, Heritage Tourism, and the Civil War in Richmond," in Horton and Horton, eds., *Slavery and Public History*, 151–68.

40. Micah Johnston and Caleb Slinkard, "2 Confederate Monuments in Macon Moving to New Site," *Macon Telegraph*, 23 June 2022, 1A.

41. Arin Yoon, "How a Military Base's New Name Honors a Military Spouse and Mother," *New York Times*, https://www.nytimes.com/2023/05/14/us/politics/fort -benning-renamed-fort-moore.html; Abraham Kenmore, "A Celebration of Legacy: Fort Gordon Officially Becomes Fort Eisenhower at Renaming Ceremony," *Augusta Chronicle*, October 27, 2023, https://www.augustachronicle.com/story/news /military/2023/10/27/officially-fort-eisenhower-fort-gordon-renaming-complete /71334586007/.

42. Miguel Legoas, "Augusta Approves Renaming 5th Street Bridge, Moving Confederate Plaques to Museum," *Augusta Chronicle*, 15 November 2022, https:// www.augustachronicle.com/story/news/politics/2022/11/15/augusta-georgia-oks -renaming-fifth-street-bridge-removing-confederate-ties/10703513002/; Miguel Legoas, "Augusta Sued Over Removing Confederate Ties from 5th Street Bridge," *Augusta Chronicle*, 6 December 2022, https://www.augustachronicle.com/story /news/local/2022/12/06/augusta-ga-lawsuit-removing-confederate-ties-from-5th -street-jefferson-davis-bridge/69705531007/; Abraham Kenmore, "As Fort Eisen- hower Becomes Official, Augusta Confederate Names Stay in Place," *Augusta Chronicle*, 24 October 2023, https://www.augustachronicle.com/story/news /military/2023/10/24/augusta-confederate-monuments-names-remain-as-fort -gordon-changed/71245304007/; Nick Wooten, "Panel Has Two Final Options for Confederate Monument in Columbus," *Columbus Ledger-Enquirer*, 27 August 2021, 1A.

43. On Black heritage tourism since the Civil Rights era, see Thomas, *Desire and Disaster in New Orleans*, esp. chap. 1; King and Gatchet, *Terror and Truth*; Glenn T. Eskew, "Selling the Civil Rights Movement: Montgomery, Alabama, since the 1960s," in Stanonis, ed., *Dixie Emporium*, 175–201; Glenn T. Eskew, "Selling the Civil Rights Movement Through Black Political Empowerment in Selma, Alabama," in Cox, ed., *Destination Dixie*, 160–83.

44. "James Brown Blvd. Petition is Received," *Augusta Chronicle*, 2 November 1971, 11; Laurie Dooley, "Black Assails Loitering Law Enforcement," *Augusta Chronicle*, 16 November 1971, 15; Laurie Gregory, "Black Group Requests Street Name Change," *Augusta Chronicle*, 10 October 1975, 2B; "Merited Honor," *Augusta Chronicle*, 17 December 1975, 4A. Macon's city council renamed the Fifth Street Bridge near downtown the Otis Redding Memorial Bridge in 1974 without fanfare; see "Redding's Memorial," *Macon Telegraph*, 21 June 1974, 4A.

45. Charles T. Gay, "Augusta Follows Lead of Colorado Town," *Augusta Chronicle*, 19 October 1993, 1A; Charles T. Gay, "Signs to Direct Soul Singer's Bandwagon," *Augusta Chronicle*, 4 November 1993, 1B.

46. Jozsef Papp, "James Brown Tour Unveiled in Downtown Augusta," *Augusta Chronicle*, 12 August 2020, https://www.augustachronicle.com/story/news/2020 /08/12/james-brown-tour-unveiled-in-downtown-augusta/43073071/.

47. "Displays to Depict the Role of Blacks in Augusta's Growth," *Augusta Chronicle-Herald*, 9 May 1976, 14A; Sharon H. Polansky, "Center for Black Cultural Arts in Works," *Augusta Chronicle*, 22 December 1978, 6B; Toni Baker, "$3 Million Plan Announced for Afro-American Museum," *Augusta Chronicle*, 9 May 1980, 2B; Hal Hewell, "Laney House Renovation Gets $60,000 State Grant," *Augusta Chronicle*, 1 September 1989, 1B; Heidi Coryell, "Museum Closes in on Funds," *Augusta Chronicle*, 12 June 2001, 5C; "What About Next Year?" *Augusta Chronicle*, 18 June 2001, 4A.

48. Constance Prater, "Priest Working to Put Black History on View," *Macon Telegraph*, 2 December 1982, 1B; Jim Gaines, "New, Larger Tubman Will Open in May," *Macon Telegraph*, 3 April 2015, 1A; Wayne Crenshaw, "New Tubman Museum Has a Joyful Opening," *Macon Telegraph*, 17 May 2015, 1A.

49. Causey, *Red Clay, White Water, and Blues*, 137; Charles Nix, "Fund Near Goal to Honor 'The Mother of the Blues," *Columbus Ledger*, 14 May 1984, B2; "Markers Honoring 'Ma' Rainey, Fletcher Henderson to Be Unveiled," *Columbus Enquirer*, 26 September 1986, B2; Kimball Perry, "Council Votes $90,000 for Rainey House," *Columbus Ledger-Enquirer*, 27 November 1991, 1A; "Readers Protest Renovating 'Ma' Rainey House," *Columbus Ledger-Enquirer*, 9 December 1991, A13; "Readers Upset Over Museum Neglect," *Columbus Ledger-Enquirer*, 6 November 1992, A11; Billy Winn, "Bird in the Hand is Worth . . . ," *Columbus Ledger-Enquirer*, 20 August 1992, A10; Kelli Esters, "Investing in a Legacy," *Columbus Ledger-Enquirer*, 18 February 2004, A1; "Celebrate the Ma Rainey House."

BIBLIOGRAPHY

ARCHIVAL COLLECTIONS

Anderson, W. T., Papers. MGA.

Augusta Metro Chamber of Commerce Collection. AMH.

Augusta, Georgia, Race Riots, 1970, MSS/210. RLSC.

Betts/Taliaferro Collection, MC 149. CSUA.

Causey, Virginia, Research Collection, MC 413. CSUA.

Chappell, Loretto/Bradley Library Vertical Files, MC 361. CSUA.

Columbus Public Library Pamphlet Collection, MC 302. CSUA.

Dixie Highway Auxiliary, Bibb Co. Chapter Records. MGA.

Douglass Business Records. MGA.

Georgiana Vertical File. HRBML.

Greater Macon Chamber of Commerce Records. MGA.

Historical Reference Files. MGA.

Industrial Index Collection, MC 304. CSUA.

Kyle, F. Clayson, Papers, MC 86. CSUA.

Macon City Records. MGA.

Macon–Bibb County Planning & Zoning Commission Records. MGA.

McKay, John J., Jr., Collection. MGA.

Melton, Bucker F., Papers. MGA.

Moody, Lester S., Collection. AMH.

Nolen, John, Papers. CUL.

Records of the Chattanooga Automobile Club/Dixie Highway Association. CHBL.

Robinson, William Lee, Papers. HRBML.

Smith, Alva C., Collection, MC 34. CSUA.

USDA Census of Agriculture Historical Archive. CUL.

Winter, Mary Carter, Collection. RLSC.

Woodall, W. C., Papers, SMC 116. CSUA.

Woodruff, James Waldo, Collection, MC 96. CSUA.

LOCAL NEWSPAPERS, NEWS SITES, AND PERIODICALS

Augusta Chronicle

Augusta Chronicle-Herald

Augusta Magazine

Columbus Enquirer

Columbus Enquirer-Sun

Columbus Ledger

Columbus Ledger-Enquirer

Industrial Index (Columbus, GA)

Macon Daily Telegraph

Macon Magazine

Macon News

Macon Telegraph

Macon Telegraph and News

WRDW (Augusta, GA)

OTHER NEWSPAPERS, NEWS SITES, AND PERIODICALS

American Nut Journal (Rochester, NY)

Atlanta Constitution

Atlanta Journal

Atlanta Journal and Constitution

CNN

Florence Morning News (Florence, SC)

The Iron Tradesman (Atlanta, GA)

Knoxville Journal

Midland (TX) Reporter-Telegram

Naples (FL) Daily News

New York Times

The New Yorker

Post and Courier (Charleston, SC)

Southern Living

The State (Columbia, SC)

U.S. News & World Report

Washington Post

WBRZ (Baton Rouge, LA)

OTHER PRIMARY SOURCES

Atlanta Chamber of Commerce. *Atlanta: A Twentieth Century City*. Atlanta: Atlanta Chamber of Commerce, 1904.

Augusta, Georgia, the Winter Resort. Augusta, GA: Augusta Chamber of Commerce, 1927. RLSC.

Augusta Regional Transportation Study: Trends in Land Development and Transportation. Augusta, GA: Augusta–Richmond County Planning Commission, 1968. ARCPL.

Augusta Unit, Federal Writers' Project in Georgia. *Augusta (American Guide Series)*. Augusta, GA: Tidwell Printing Supply for City Council of Augusta, 1938.

Automobile Blue Book, Vol. 2. Chicago: Automobile Blue Books, 1922.

A Brief on Industrial Augusta, Georgia. Augusta, GA: Industrial Development Division, Augusta Chamber of Commerce, 1947. ARCPL.

Bureau of the Census. *Geographic Areas Reference Manual*. Washington, DC: U.S. Department of Commerce, Economics and Statistics Administration, Bureau of the Census, 1994. https://www2.census.gov/geo/pdfs/reference /GARM/Ch13GARM.pdf.

Burns, Andrew J., et al., eds. *Official Railway Guide; North American Passenger Travel Edition*. New York: National Railway Publication Co., 1910. https://catalog.hathitrust.org/Record/000046063.

"Celebrate the Ma Rainey House." *Historic Columbus*. 1 May 2020. https:// www.historiccolumbus.com/post/ma-rainey-house.

Central Savannah River Area Planning & Development Commission annual reports, 1968–77. ARCPL.

Columbus, Georgia: The Place with the Power and the Push. Columbus, GA: Board of Trade, 1914. Chattahoochee Valley Regional Library System Collection. https://dlg.usg.edu/record/chat_scp_cv137.

Department of Commerce and Labor, Bureau of the Census. *Thirteenth Census of the United States Taken in the Year 1910; Statistics for Georgia*. Washington, DC: Government Printing Office, 1913.

Digital Scholarship Lab. "Renewing Inequality." Robert K. Nelson and Edward L. Ayers, eds. *American Panorama*. https://dsl.richmond.edu /panorama/renewal.

"Discover Historic Macon" (brochure). n.d. [ca. 1984]. Author's collection.

Economic Analysis, Augusta–Richmond County, Phase 2: Economic Highlights of the Augusta Region, October 1965. Augusta, GA: Augusta–Richmond County Planning Commission, 1965. ARCPL.

The Electric City of the South: Columbus, Georgia. Columbus, GA: Columbus Board of Trade, 1906. CSUA.

Georgia Railroad, Stone Mountain Route. *Eastern Middle Georgia, the Cream of the Southland*. Augusta, GA: Georgia Railroad, 1895. Library of Congress.

House Reports, 71st Congress, 2d Session (December 2, 1929–July 3, 1930), vol. 2. Washington, DC: U.S. Government Printing Office, 1930.

ICON Architecture, Inc. *The Westobou Vision Urban Area Master Plan*. Boston: ICON Architecture, Inc., 2009.

"Largest Employers," *Augusta Economic Development Authority*, https:// augustaeda.org/business-industry/largest-employers/.

Madison, Robert. Interview by Dee Perry. 2 February 2017. Cleveland Regional Oral History Collection. Interview 501034. https://engagedscholarship.csuohio.edu/crohc000/1188/.

National Association of Real Estate Boards, Build America Better Committee. *Toward a New Columbus: An Advisory Team Report.* Washington, DC: National Association of Real Estate Boards, 1962. CSUA.

Nelson, Robert K., et al. "Mapping Inequality." Robert K. Nelson and Edward L. Ayers, eds. *American Panorama.* https://dsl.richmond.edu/panorama/redlining.

Nix, Harold L., and Charles J. Dudley. *Community Social Analysis of Augusta-Richmond County, February 1966, Community Social Analysis Series no. 3.* Athens, GA: Georgia Department of Public Health, 1966. ARCPL.

Reed, Thomas H., and Doris D. Reed. *Report to the Citizens: A Survey of the Government of the City of Augusta, Georgia, May 1945.* Augusta, GA: Augusta Citizens Union, 1945. ARCPL.

Richardson, George W. *Augusta, Ga.* Augusta, GA: Commercial Printing Co., 1926. RLSC.

Simons, George W., Jr. *Comprehensive Area Plan, City of Columbus and Muscogee County, Georgia, 1948.* Jacksonville, FL: George W. Simons Jr., 1948. CSUA.

——. *Report on Central Business District, Columbus, Georgia.* Jacksonville, FL: George W. Simons Jr., 1958. George W. Simons Jr. Planning Collection. University of North Florida, Thomas G. Carpenter Library Special Collections and Archives. https://digitalcommons.unf.edu/simons_ga/1/.

Taylor, Carter. *The Augusta Survey: A Community Improvement Study of Augusta and Richmond County.* Augusta, GA: The Augusta Kiwanis Club, 1924. ARCPL.

Tourism Report and 2016 Marketing Plan. Augusta, GA: Augusta Convention & Visitors Bureau, 2016. ACVB.

Tourism Report and 2017 Marketing Plan. Augusta, GA: Augusta Convention & Visitors Bureau, 2017. ACVB.

Tourism Report and 2018 Marketing Plan. Augusta, GA: Augusta Convention & Visitors Bureau, 2018. ACVB.

Thurmond, Strom. "Clark's Hill Project." 1947. Strom Thurmond Collection. Clemson University Libraries, Clemson, SC. https://tigerprints.clemson.edu/strom/154.

Trails—Tour Macon, https://tourmacon.stqry.app.

United States Census (database). *GenealogyBank* (https://genealogybank.com/#).

US Census Bureau QuickFacts. https://www.census.gov/quickfacts/.

Whitlatch, George I., and Robert E. Van Geuns. *An Evaluation of the Economic Assets and Liabilities of the Columbus Area*. Atlanta: Engineering Experiment Station, Georgia Institute of Technology, 1959. CSUA.

Wolcott, Marion Post, photographs. 1940. Farm Security Administration–Office of War Information Photograph Collection. Library of Congress Prints and Photographs Division. Washington, DC.

Works Progress Administration. *The Macon Guide and the Ocmulgee National Monument*. Macon, GA: J. W. Burke Co., 1939.

SECONDARY SOURCES

Abbott, Carl. *The Metropolitan Frontier: Cities in the Modern American West*. Tucson: University of Arizona Press, 1993.

———. *The New Urban America: Growth and Politics in Sunbelt Cities*. Chapel Hill: University of North Carolina Press, 1981.

Angelon-Gaetz, Kim A., David B. Richardson, and Steve Wing. "Inequalities in the Nuclear Age: Impact of Race and Gender on Radiation Exposure at the Savannah River Site (1951–1999)." *New Solutions: A Journal of Environmental and Occupational Health Policy* 20, no. 2 (July 2010): 195–210.

Appler, Douglas R., ed. *The Many Geographies of Urban Renewal: New Perspectives on the Housing Act of 1949*. Philadelphia: Temple University Press, 2023.

Augusta Tomorrow | Our History. https://www.augustatomorrow.com/our -history/.

Barnes, Margaret Anne. *The Tragedy and the Triumph of Phenix City, Alabama*. Macon, GA: Mercer University Press, 1998.

Bartley, Numan V. *The Creation of Modern Georgia*. Athens: University of Georgia Press, 1983.

———. *The New South, 1945–1980: The Story of the South's Transformation*. Baton Rouge: Louisiana State University Press, 1995.

Basmajian, Carlton Wade. *Atlanta Unbound: Enabling Sprawl through Policy and Planning*. Philadelphia: Temple University Press, 2013.

Bayor, Ronald H. *Race and the Shaping of Twentieth-Century Atlanta*. Chapel Hill: University of North Carolina Press, 1996.

Beard-Moose, Christina Taylor. *Public Indians, Private Cherokees: Tourism and Tradition on Tribal Ground*. Tuscaloosa: University of Alabama Press, 2009.

Bednarek, Janet R. *Airports, Cities, and the Jet Age: US Airports Since 1945*. New York: Palgrave Macmillan, 2016.

Belasco, Warren. *Americans on the Road: From Autocamp to Motel, 1910–1945*. Cambridge, MA: MIT Press, 1979.

Bernard, Richard M., and Bradley Robert Rice, eds. *Sunbelt Cities: Politics and Growth Since World War II*. Austin: University of Texas Press, 1983

Biles, Roger, and Mark Rose. *A Good Place to Do Business: The Politics of Downtown Renewal Since 1945*. Philadelphia: Temple University Press, 2022.

Black, Earl, and Merle Black. *Politics and Society in the South*. Cambridge: Harvard University Press, 1987.

Bolin, James Duane. *Bossism and Reform in a Southern City: Lexington, Kentucky, 1880–1940*. Lexington: University Press of Kentucky, 2000.

Brooks, Carolyn. "Laney–Walker North Historic District." National Register of Historic Places nomination form. 20 June 1985. National Register of Historic Places Inventory. https://npgallery.nps.gov/AssetDetail/NRIS /85001976.

Brownell, Blaine A. *The Urban Ethos in the South, 1920–1930*. Baton Rouge: Louisiana State University Press, 1975.

Brownell, Blaine A., and David R. Goldfield, eds. *The City in Southern History: The Growth of Urban Civilization in the South*. Port Washington, NY: Kennikat Press, 1977.

Butler, John C. *Historical Record of Macon and Central Georgia*. Macon, GA: J. W. Burke & Co., 1879.

Carlton, David L. *Mill and Town in South Carolina, 1880–1920*. Baton Rouge: Louisiana State University Press, 1982.

Cashin, Edward J. *The Story of Augusta*. Augusta, GA: Richmond County Board of Education, 1980.

Cater, Casey P. *Regenerating Dixie: Electric Energy and the Modern South*. Pittsburgh: University of Pittsburgh Press, 2019.

Causey, Virginia E. *Red Clay, White Water, and Blues: A History of Columbus, Georgia*. Athens: University of Georgia Press, 2019.

Cebul, Brent. *Illusions of Progress: Business, Poverty, and Liberalism in the American Century*. Philadelphia: University of Pennsylvania Press, 2023.

Checker, Melissa. *Polluted Promises: Environmental Racism and the Search for Justice in a Southern Town*. New York: New York University Press, 2005.

"City/County Consolidation: Columbus, Georgia." *Columbus Consolidated Government*. https://www.columbusga.gov/history/consolidation.htm.

Cobb, James C. "Politics in a New South City: Augusta, Georgia, 1946–1971." PhD dissertation, University of Georgia, 1975.

———. *The Selling of the South: The Southern Crusade for Industrial Development, 1936–1990*. Baton Rouge: Louisiana State University Press, 1982.

———. *The South and America Since World War II*. New York: Oxford University Press, 2012.

Cohen, Lizabeth. *A Consumers' Republic: The Politics of Mass Consumption in Postwar America*. New York: Alfred A. Knopf, 2003.

Coleman, Kenneth, ed. *A History of Georgia*. 2nd ed. Athens: University of Georgia Press, 1991.

Connolly, N. D. B. *A World More Concrete: Real Estate and the Remaking of Jim Crow South Florida*. Chicago: University of Chicago Press, 2014.

Cox, Karen L., ed. *Destination Dixie: Tourism & Southern History*. Gainesville: University Press of Florida, 2012.

———. *No Common Ground: Confederate Monuments and the Ongoing Fight for Racial Justice*. Chapel Hill: University of North Carolina Press, 2021.

Cox, Karen L., and Sarah E. Gardner, eds. *Reassessing the 1930s South*. Baton Rouge: Louisiana State University Press, 2018.

Cowan, Aaron. *A Nice Place to Visit: Tourism and Urban Revitalization in the Postwar Rustbelt*. Philadelphia: Temple University Press, 2016.

Crespino, Joseph. *Strom Thurmond's America*. New York: Hill and Wang, 2012.

Crimmins, Timothy J., and Anne H. Farrisee. *Democracy Restored: A History of the Georgia State Capitol*. Athens: University of Georgia Press, 2007.

Cronon, William. *Nature's Metropolis: Chicago and the Great West*. New York: W. W. Norton, 1991.

Crooks, James B. *Jacksonville: The Consolidation Story, from Civil Rights to the Jaguars*. Gainesville: University Press of Florida, 2019.

Cummings, Alex Sayf. *Brain Magnet: Research Triangle Park and the Idea of the Idea Economy*. New York: Columbia University Press, 2020.

Daniel, Pete. *Dispossession: Discrimination Against African American Farmers in the Age of Civil Rights*. Chapel Hill: University of North Carolina Press, 2013.

Dilworth, Leah. *Imagining Indians in the Southwest: Persistent Visions of a Primitive Past*. Washington, DC: Smithsonian Institution Press, 1996.

Dotson, Rand. *Roanoke, Virginia, 1882–1912: Magic City of the New South*. Knoxville: University of Tennessee Press, 2007.

Downs, Matthew L. *Transforming the South: Federal Development in the Tennessee Valley, 1915–1960*. Baton Rouge: Louisiana State University Press, 2014.

Doyle, Don H. *Nashville since the 1920s*. Knoxville: University of Tennessee Press, 1985.

———. *New Men, New Cities, New South: Atlanta, Nashville, Charleston, Mobile, 1860–1910*. Chapel Hill: University of North Carolina Press, 1990.

Dubrow, Gail Lee. *Restoring Women's History Through Historic Preservation.* Baltimore: Johns Hopkins University Press, 2003.

"E. E. Farley: Civic Leader and Real Estate Developer." *Historic Columbus.* 18 February 2021. https://www.historiccolumbus.com/post/e-e-farley-civic -leader-and-real-estate-developer.

Eichhorn, Niels. *The Civil War Battles of Macon.* Charleston, SC: The History Press, 2021.

"Elizabeth Mae 'Lizzie Mae' Lunsford: A Quiet Force." *Historic Columbus.* 18 March 2021. https://www.historiccolumbus.com/post/elizabeth-mae -lizzie-mae-lunsford-a-quiet-force.

Erickson, Ansley T. *Making the Unequal Metropolis: School Desegregation and Its Limits.* Chicago: University of Chicago Press, 2016.

Falck, Susan T. *Remembering Dixie: The Battle to Control Historical Memory in Natchez, Mississippi, 1865–1941.* Jackson: University Press of Mississippi, 2019.

Finlay, Mark R. "The Failure of Chemurgy in the Depression-Era South: The Case of Jesse F. Jackson and the Central of Georgia Railroad." *Georgia Historical Quarterly* 81, no. 1 (Spring 1997): 78–102.

Fite, Gilbert C. *Cotton Fields No More: Southern Agriculture, 1865–1980.* Lexington: University Press of Kentucky, 1984.

———. *Richard B. Russell, Jr., Senator from Georgia.* Chapel Hill: University of North Carolina Press, 1991.

Fogelson, Robert M. *Downtown: Its Rise and Fall, 1880–1950.* New Haven: Yale University Press, 2001.

Ford, Liam T. A. *Soldier Field: A Stadium and Its City.* Chicago: University of Chicago Press, 2009.

Foster, Kathryn A. *The Political Economy of Special-Purpose Government.* Washington, DC: Georgetown University Press, 1997.

Fraser, Walter J. *Savannah in the New South: From the Civil War to the Twenty-First Century.* Columbia: University of South Carolina Press, 2018.

Frederickson, Kari. *Cold War Dixie: Militarization and Modernization in the American South.* Athens: University of Georgia Press, 2013.

Freund, David M. P. *Colored Property: State Policy and White Racial Politics in Suburban America.* Chicago: University of Chicago Press, 2007.

Geismer, Lily. *Don't Blame Us: Suburban Liberals and the Transformation of the Democratic Party.* Princeton: Princeton University Press, 2015.

"Georgia-Pacific History." *Georgia-Pacific.* https://www.gp.com/about-us /history.

German, Richard. "The Queen City of the Savannah: Augusta, Georgia, During the Urban Progressive Era, 1890–1917." PhD dissertation, University of Florida, 1971.

Germany, Kent B. *New Orleans After the Promises: Poverty, Citizenship, and the Search for the Great Society*. Athens: University of Georgia Press, 2007.

Giesen, James C. *Boll Weevil Blues: Cotton, Myth, and Power in the American South*. Chicago: University of Chicago Press, 2011.

Giguere, Joy M. "The (Im)Movable Monument: Identity, Space, and The Louisville Confederate Monument." *The Public Historian* 41, no. 4 (November 2019): 56–82.

Glassberg, David. *American Historical Pageantry: The Uses of Tradition in the Early Twentieth Century*. Chapel Hill: University of North Carolina Press, 1990.

Glotzer, Paige. *How the Suburbs Were Segregated: Developers and the Business of Exclusionary Housing, 1890–1960*. New York: Columbia University Press, 2020.

Goldfield, David R. *Cotton Fields and Skyscrapers: Southern City and Region, 1607–1980*. Baton Rouge: Louisiana State University Press, 1982.

———. *Region, Race, and Cities: Interpreting the Urban South*. Baton Rouge: Louisiana State University Press, 1997.

———. *Still Fighting the Civil War: The American South and Southern History*. Updated ed. Baton Rouge: Louisiana State University Press, 2013.

Gould, Jonathan. *Otis Redding: An Unfinished Life*. New York: Crown Archetype, 2017.

Gregg, Kelly. "Placing the North American Post-war Pedestrian Mall within the Legacy of Downtown Urban Renewal." *Journal of Urban History* 23, no. 3 (August 2024): 167–96.

Grisamore, Ed. *The Pinkest Party on Earth: Macon, Georgia's International Cherry Blossom Festival*. Macon, GA: Mercer University Press, 2014.

Guarneri, Julia. *Newsprint Metropolis: City Papers and the Making of Modern Americans*. Chicago: University of Chicago Press, 2017.

Hambrick, Ralph. *Transforming the James River in Richmond*. Charleston, SC: History Press, 2020.

Hanchett, Thomas W. *Sorting Out the New South City: Race, Class, and Urban Development in Charlotte, 1875–1975*. Chapel Hill: University of North Carolina Press, 1998.

Hardwick, M. Jeffrey. *Mall Maker: Victor Gruen, Architect of an American Dream*. Philadelphia: University of Pennsylvania Press, 2015.

Harris, Richard. "A Portrait of North American Urban Historians." *Journal of Urban History* 45, no. 6 (November 2019): 1237–45.

Hayden, Dolores. *Where Poplar Crosses Cotton: Interpreting the Urban Land-scape in Macon, Georgia.* College Park: School of Architecture Planning and Preservation, University of Maryland, 2007.

Herbin-Triant, Elizabeth A. *Threatening Property: Race, Class, and Campaigns to Legislate Jim Crow Neighborhoods.* New York: Columbia University Press, 2019.

Herrington, Philip Mills. "Agricultural and Architectural Reform in the Antebellum South: Fruitland at Augusta, Georgia." *Journal of Southern History* 78, no. 4 (November 2012): 855–86.

Hickey, Georgina. *Hope and Danger in the New South City: Working-Class Women and Urban Development in Atlanta, 1890–1940.* Athens: University of Georgia Press, 2003.

Hillyer, Reiko. *Designing Dixie: Tourism, Memory, and Urban Space in the New South.* Charlottesville: University of Virginia Press, 2014

Himel, Matthew Taylor. "Greening Golf: Grass, Agriculture, and Pinehurst in the Sandhills." PhD dissertation, Mississippi State University, 2020.

Hirsch, Arnold R., and Joseph Logsdon, eds. *Creole New Orleans: Race and Americanization.* Baton Rouge: Louisiana State University Press, 1992.

Hodos, Jerome I. *Second Cities: Globalization and Local Politics in Manchester and Philadelphia.* Philadelphia: Temple University Press, 2013.

Horowitz, Andy. *Katrina: A History, 1915–2015.* Cambridge: Harvard University Press, 2020.

Horton, James Oliver, and Lois E. Horton, eds. *Slavery and Public History: The Tough Stuff of American Memory.* New York: The New Press, 2006.

Huff, Archie Vernon, Jr. *Greenville: The History of the City and County in the South Carolina Piedmont.* Columbia: University of South Carolina Press, 1995.

Hunner, Jon. *Inventing Los Alamos: The Growth of an Atomic Community.* Norman: University of Oklahoma Press, 2004.

Hunter, Tera W. *To 'Joy My Freedom: Southern Black Women's Lives and Labors After the Civil War.* Cambridge: Harvard University Press, 1997.

Hutchinson, Glenn, and Maurice R. Brewster. *Population Mobility: A Study of Family Movements Affecting Augusta, Georgia, 1899–1939.* Augusta, GA: Federal Works Agency; Work Projects Administration of Georgia, 1942. https://catalog.hathitrust.org/Record/102193339.

Hyatt, Richard. *Charles H. Jones: A Biography.* Macon, GA: Mercer University Press, 2003.

Ingram, Tammy. *Dixie Highway: Road Building and the Making of the Modern South, 1900–1930.* Chapel Hill: University of North Carolina Press, 2014.

Iobst, Richard W. *Civil War Macon: The History of a Confederate City.* Macon, GA: Mercer University Press, 1999.

Isenberg, Alison. *Downtown America: A History of the Place and the People Who Made It.* Chicago: University of Chicago Press, 2004.

Jackson, Kenneth T. *Crabgrass Frontier: The Suburbanization of the United States.* New York: Oxford University Press, 1985.

Johnson, Charles W., and Charles O. Jackson. *City Behind a Fence: Oak Ridge, Tennessee, 1942–1946.* Knoxville: University of Tennessee Press, 1981.

Kelman, Ari. *A River and Its City: The Nature of Landscape in New Orleans.* Berkeley: University of California Press, 2003.

Key, V. O. Jr., *Southern Politics in State and Nation.* New York: Alfred D. Knopf, 1949.

King, Stephen A., and Roger Davis Gatchet. *Terror and Truth: Civil Rights Tourism and the Mississippi Movement.* Jackson: University Press of Mississippi, 2023.

Knapp, Courtney Elizabeth. *Constructing the Dynamo of Dixie: Race, Urban Planning, and Cosmopolitanism in Chattanooga, Tennessee.* Chapel Hill: University of North Carolina Press, 2018.

Kruse, Kevin M. *White Flight: Atlanta and the Making of Modern Conservatism.* Princeton: Princeton University Press, 2005.

Lands, LeeAnn. *The Culture of Property: Race, Class, and Housing Landscapes in Atlanta, 1880–1950.* Athens: University of Georgia Press, 2009.

———. *Poor Atlanta: Poverty, Race, and the Limits of Sunbelt Development.* Athens: University of Georgia Press, 2023.

Lane, Mills. *The Wonderful World of Mills B. Lane Jr.* Savannah, GA: the author, 1990.

Lassiter, Matthew D. *The Silent Majority: Suburban Politics in the Sunbelt South.* Princeton: Princeton University Press, 2006.

Lee, Tom. *The Tennessee-Virginia Tri-Cities: Urbanization in Appalachia, 1900–1950.* Knoxville: University of Tennessee Press, 2005.

Lessoff, Alan. *Where Texas Meets the Sea: Corpus Christi & Its History.* Austin: University of Texas Press, 2015.

Lichstenstein, Alex. "Good Roads and Chain Gangs in the Progressive South: 'The Negro Convict is a Slave.'" *Journal of Southern History* 59, no. 1 (February 1993): 85–110.

Liesch, P. J. "Chinch Bug: How a Tiny Insect Helped Wisconsin Become the Dairy State." *UW Madison Department of Entomology Insect Diagnostic Lab.* 14 June 2018. https://insectlab.russell.wisc.edu/2018/06/14/chinch -bug-wisconsin-dairy/.

Link, William A. *Atlanta, Cradle of the New South: Race and Remembering in the Civil War's Aftermath*. Chapel Hill: University of North Carolina Press, 2013.

Logan, John R., and Harvey L. Molotch. *Urban Fortunes: The Political Economy of Place*. Berkeley: University of California Press, 1987.

Long, Alecia P. *The Great Southern Babylon: Sex, Race, and Respectability in New Orleans, 1865–1920*. Baton Rouge: Louisiana State University Press, 2005.

Lubove, Roy. *Twentieth-Century Pittsburgh: Government, Business, and Environmental Change*. Pittsburgh: University of Pittsburgh Press, 1995.

Lupold, John S. "Historic Columbus Foundation, 1966–1978." *Georgia Historical Quarterly* 63, no. 1 (Spring 1979): 129–37.

Lyon, Elizabeth A. "From Landmarks to Community: The History of Georgia's Historic Preservation Movement." *Georgia Historical Quarterly* 83, no. 1 (Spring 1999): 77–97.

Manganiello, Christopher J. *Southern Water, Southern Power: How the Politics of Cheap Energy and Water Scarcity Shaped a Region*. Chapel Hill: University of North Carolina Press, 2015.

Manis, Andrew M. *Macon Black and White: An Unutterable Separation in the American Century*. Macon, GA: Mercer University Press, 2004.

Marsh, Alan. "Ocmulgee: The Making of a Monument." *Proceedings and Papers of the Georgia Association of Historians* 7 (1986): 81–98. https://www.columbusstate.edu/archives/gah/toc1986.php.

Mason, Randall, and Max Page, eds. *Giving Preservation a History: Histories of Historic Preservation in the United States*, 2nd ed. New York: Routledge, 2020.

Maunula, Marko. *Guten Tag, Y'all: Globalization and the South Carolina Piedmont, 1950–2000*. Athens: University of Georgia Press, 2009.

McKay, John J., Jr. "Story of the Middle Georgia Historical Society, Inc." *Georgia Historical Quarterly* 63, no. 1 (Spring 1979): 156–60.

McShane, Clay, and Joel Tarr. *The Horse in the City: Living Machines in the Nineteenth Century*. Baltimore: Johns Hopkins University Press, 2007.

Minchin, Timothy J. *Hiring the Black Worker: The Racial Integration of the Southern Textile Industry, 1960–1980*. Chapel Hill: University of North Carolina Press, 1999.

Mitman, Gregg. *Breathing Space: How Allergies Shape Our Lives and Landscapes*. New Haven: Yale University Press, 2007.

Mohl, Raymond A., ed. *Searching for the Sunbelt: Historical Perspectives on a Region*. Knoxville: University of Tennessee Press, 1990.

Molotch, Harvey. "The City as a Growth Machine: Toward a Political Economy of Place." *American Journal of Sociology* 82, no. 2 (September 1976): 309–32.

Montès, Christian. *American Capitals: A Historical Geography.* Chicago: University of Chicago Press, 2014.

Moore, John Hammond. *Columbia and Richland County: A South Carolina Community, 1740–1990.* Columbia: University of South Carolina Press, 1993.

Morley, Judy Mattivi. *Preservation & the Imagined West: Albuquerque, Denver, & Seattle.* Lawrence: University Press of Kansas, 2006.

Moss, Richard J. *Golf and the American Country Club.* Urbana: University of Illinois Press, 2001.

Nash, Linda. *Inescapable Ecologies: A History of Environment, Disease, and Knowledge.* Berkeley: University of California Press, 2006.

Needham, Andrew. *Power Lines: Phoenix and the Making of the Modern Southwest.* Princeton: Princeton University Press, 2014.

Neumann, Tracy. "Reforging the Steel City: Symbolism and Space in Postindustrial Pittsburgh." *Journal of Urban History* 44, no. 4 (July 2018): 582–602.

New Georgia Encyclopedia, https://www.georgiaencyclopedia.org.

Newberry Library. *Atlas of Historical County Boundaries.* https://digital .newberry.org/ahcb/pages/Georgia.html.

Newman, Harvey K. *Southern Hospitality: Tourism and the Growth of Atlanta.* Tuscaloosa: University of Alabama Press, 1999.

Newton, Wesley Phillips. *Montgomery in the Good War: Portrait of a Southern City, 1939–1946.* Tuscaloosa: University of Alabama Press, 2000.

Nickerson, Michelle, and Darren Dochuk, eds. *Sunbelt Rising: The Politics of Space, Place, and Region.* Philadelphia: University of Pennsylvania Press, 2014.

Nystrom, Justin A. *New Orleans After the Civil War: Race, Politics, and a New Birth of Freedom.* Baltimore: Johns Hopkins University Press, 2010.

Okie, William Thomas. *The Georgia Peach: Culture, Agriculture, and Environment in the American South.* New York: Cambridge University Press, 2016.

Owen, David. *The Making of the Masters: Clifford Roberts, Augusta National, and Golf's Most Prestigious Tournament.* New York: Simon & Schuster, 1999.

Patterson, Gordon M. *The Mosquito Wars: A History of Mosquito Control in Florida.* Gainesville: University Press of Florida, 2004.

Patton, Randall L. "Mills B. Lane, Jr. and Enterprise in a New South." *Essays in Economic & Business History* 27 (2009): 93–106.

Perry, Marc. "Population Distribution and Change: 2010 to 2020." *U.S. Census Bureau.* https://www.census.gov/content/dam/Census/newsroom/press -kits/2021/redistricting/20210812-presentation-redistricting-perry.pdf.

Pollak, Mark. *The Playing Grounds of College Football: A Comprehensive Directory, 1869 to Today.* Jefferson, NC: McFarland, 2018.

Pruitt, Bernadette. *The Other Great Migration: The Movement of Rural African Americans to Houston, 1900–1941.* College Station: Texas A&M University Press, 2013.

Rabinowitz, Howard N. *Race Relations in the Urban South, 1865–1890.* New York: Oxford University Press, 1978.

Reed, Mary Beth, et al., *Savannah River Site at Fifty.* Washington, DC: U.S. Department of Energy, 2002.

Revels, Tracy J. *Sunshine Paradise: A History of Florida Tourism.* Gainesville: University Press of Florida, 2011.

Reynolds, Michael. "A History of Fruitland Nurseries, Augusta, Georgia and the Berckmans Family in America." *Magnolia; Bulletin of the Southern Garden History Society* 18, no. 1 (Winter 2002–3): 1–10.

Robins Air Force Base Heritage Committee. *A Pictorial History of Robins Air Force Base, Georgia.* Macon, GA: Air Force Logistics Command, 1982.

Rose, Mark H. *Interstate: Highway Politics and Policy, 1939–1989,* 2nd ed. Knoxville: University of Tennessee Press, 1990.

Rose, Mark H., and Raymond A. Mohl. *Interstate: Highway Politics and Policy Since 1939,* 3rd ed. Knoxville: University of Tennessee Press, 2012.

Rothman, Hal. *Devil's Bargains: Tourism in the Twentieth-Century American West.* Lawrence: University Press of Kansas, 1998.

Rushing, Wanda, ed. *The New Encyclopedia of Southern Culture,* Vol. 15: *Urbanization.* Chapel Hill: University of North Carolina Press, 2010.

Russell, James M. *Atlanta, 1847–1890: City Building in the Old South and the New.* Baton Rouge: Louisiana State University Press, 1988.

Sanders, Curtis L., Jr., et al. *Flood Frequency of the Savannah River at Augusta, Georgia,* Water-Resources Investigations Report 90–4024. Columbia, SC: U.S. Geological Survey and U.S. Army Corps of Engineers, 1990. https://doi.org/10.3133/wri904024.

Sandweiss, Eric, ed. *St. Louis in the Century of Henry Shaw: A View Beyond the Garden Wall.* Columbia: University of Missouri Press, 2003.

Sawers, Larry, and William K. Tabb, eds. *Sunbelt/Snowbelt: Urban Development and Restructuring.* New York: Oxford University Press, 1984.

Schulman, Bruce J. *From Cotton Belt to Sunbelt: Federal Policy, Economic Development, and the Transformation of the South, 1938–1980.* Durham, NC: Duke University Press, 1994.

Sellers, Christopher C. *Crabgrass Crucible: Suburban Nature and the Rise of Environmentalism in Twentieth-Century America.* Chapel Hill: University of North Carolina Press, 2012.

————. *Race and the Greening of Atlanta: Inequality, Democracy, and Environmental Politics in an Ascendant Metropolis.* Athens: University of Georgia Press, 2023.

Shaffer, Marguerite S. *See America First: Tourism and National Identity, 1880–1940.* Washington, DC: Smithsonian Institution Press, 2001.

Sies, Mary Corbin, and Christopher Silver, eds. *Planning the Twentieth-Century American City.* Baltimore: Johns Hopkins University Press, 1996.

Silver, Christopher. *Twentieth-Century Richmond: Planning, Politics, and Race.* Knoxville: University of Tennessee Press, 1984.

Smalley, Andrea L., with Henry M. Reeves. *The Market in Birds: Commercial Hunting, Conservation, and the Origins of Wildlife Consumerism, 1850–1920.* Baltimore: Johns Hopkins University Press, 2022.

Smith, R. J. *The One: The Life and Music of James Brown.* New York: Avery, 2012.

Souther, J. Mark. "'Green Spots in the Heart of Town': Planning and Contesting the Nation's Widest Streets in Georgia's Fall Line Cities." *Georgia Historical Quarterly* 104, no. 4 (Winter 2020): 282–322.

————. "Making 'The Garden City of the South': Beautification, Preservation, and Downtown Planning in Augusta, Georgia." *Journal of Planning History* 20, no. 2 (May 2021): 87–116.

————. *New Orleans on Parade: Tourism and the Transformation of the Crescent City.* Baton Rouge: Louisiana State University Press, 2006.

Stanonis, Anthony J. *Creating the Big Easy: New Orleans and the Emergence of Modern Tourism, 1918–1945.* Athens: University of Georgia Press, 2006.

————, ed. *Dixie Emporium: Tourism, Foodways, and Consumer Culture in the American South.* Athens: University of Georgia Press, 2008.

————. "Through a Purple (Green and Gold) Haze: New Orleans Mardi Gras in the American Imagination." *Southern Cultures* 14, no. 2 (Summer 2008): 109–31.

Starnes, Richard D. *Creating the Land of the Sky: Tourism and Society in Western North Carolina.* Tuscaloosa: University of Alabama Press, 2005.

Stelpflug, Peggy A., and Richard Hyatt. *Home of the Infantry: The History of Fort Benning.* Macon, GA: Mercer University Press, 2007.

Stephenson, R. Bruce. *John Nolen, Landscape Architect and City Planner.* Amherst: University of Massachusetts Press, 2015.

Stilgoe, John R. *Borderland: Origins of the American Suburb, 1820–1939.* New Haven: Yale University Press, 1988.

Sutter, Paul S. *Let Us Now Praise Famous Gullies: Providence Canyon and the Soils of the South.* Athens: University of Georgia Press, 2015.

Teaford, Jon C. *The Rough Road to Renaissance: Urban Revitalization in America, 1940–1985.* Baltimore: Johns Hopkins University Press, 1990.

Thomas, June Manning. *Redevelopment and Race: Planning a Finer City in Postwar Detroit.* Baltimore: Johns Hopkins University Press, 1997.

Thomas, Kenneth H., Jr. "Fruitlands/Augusta National Golf Club." National Register of Historic Places nomination form, 12 April 1979. https://npgallery.nps.gov/AssetDetail/ef870057-e6de-4096-9cae-d30b8a5b289a.

Thomas, Lynnell L. *Desire and Disaster in New Orleans: Tourism, Race, and Historical Memory.* Durham, NC: Duke University Press, 2014.

Thomason, Michael, ed. *Mobile: The New History of Alabama's First City.* Tuscaloosa: University of Alabama Press, 2001.

Tighe, J. Rosie, and Elizabeth J. Mueller, eds. *The Affordable Housing Reader.* New York: Routledge, 2013.

Tobin, James. *The Man He Became: How FDR Defied Polio to Win the Presidency.* New York: Simon & Schuster, 2013.

Valencius, Conevery Bolton. *The Health of the Country: How American Settlers Understood Themselves and Their Land.* New York: Basic Books, 2002.

Vega-Barachowitz, David Eli. "Festival Modernism: Downtown Plans & Pedestrian Malls, 1956–1974." Master's thesis, Massachusetts Institute of Technology, 2016.

Vivian, Daniel J. *A New Plantation World: Sporting Estates in the South Carolina Lowcountry, 1900–1940.* New York: Cambridge University Press, 2018.

Warner, Sam Bass, Jr. *Streetcar Suburbs: The Process of Growth in Boston, 1870–1900.* Cambridge: Harvard University Press, 1962.

Watkins, Alfred J., and David C. Perry, eds. *The Rise of the Sunbelt Cities.* Beverly Hills, CA: Sage Publications, 1977.

West, Patsy. *The Enduring Seminoles: From Alligator Wrestling to Ecotourism.* Gainesville: University Press of Florida, 1998.

Weyeneth, Robert R. *Historic Preservation for a Living City: Historic Charleston Foundation, 1947–1997.* Columbia: University of South Carolina Press, 2000.

Wheeler, William Bruce. *Knoxville, Tennessee: A Mountain City in the New South,* 2nd ed. Knoxville: University of Tennessee Press, 2005.

Whisnant, Anne Mitchell. *Super-Scenic Motorway: A Blue Ridge Parkway History.* Chapel Hill: University of North Carolina Press, 2006.

Wiggins, David K., and Ryan Swanson, eds. *Separate Games: African American Sport Behind the Walls of Segregation.* Fayetteville: University of Arkansas Press, 2016.

Wilson, Thomas D. *Charleston and Savannah: The Rise, Fall, and Reinvention of Two Rival Cities.* Athens: University of Georgia Press, 2023.

Woolf, Joni. *Sesquicentennial of the Greater Macon Chamber of Commerce:*

Celebrating the Chamber's Contributions to the Cultural, Political, Social and Economic Life of Macon, Georgia. Macon, GA: Greater Macon Chamber of Commerce, 2011.

Worsley, Etta Blanchard. *Columbus on the Chattahoochee.* Columbus, GA: Columbus Office Supply Co., 1951.

Wynne, Ben. *Something in the Water: A History of Music in Macon, Georgia, 1823–1980.* Macon, GA: Mercer University Press, 2021.

Wynne, Lewis Nicholas. *The Continuity of Cotton: Planter Politics in Georgia, 1865–1892.* Macon, GA: Mercer University Press, 1986.

Young, Ida, Julius Gholson, and Clara Nell Hargrove. *A History of Macon, Georgia, 1823–1949.* Macon, GA: Lyon, Marshall & Brooks, 1950.

Youngs, Larry R. "Creating America's Winter Golfing Mecca at Pinehurst, North Carolina: National Marketing and Local Control." *Journal of Sport History* 30, no. 1 (Spring 2003): 25–45.

Yuhl, Stephanie E. *A Golden Haze of Memory: The Making of Historic Charleston.* Chapel Hill: University of North Carolina Press, 2005.

INDEX

advertising, 34, 89, 132, 288n1; and news, 75–76; reach of, 32, 36, 188; and sports, 60, 64, 67, 81; and tourism, 57–58, 150, 174
aerospace industry, 176
Aetna, 172, 177
Aflac, 1, 111, 177
African Americans, 2; in city government, 116; civic leadership of, 82–85, 185, 186; discrimination against, 118, 166, 188–89; exodus of, 26, 179–80; and housing, 104, 157; labor of, 88, 112–13, 127–28; perspectives of, 7, 164, 173; policing of, 55, 153; and segregation, 66–67; soldiers, 92, 101. *See also* Black neighborhoods; Black populations of fall-line cities
agriculture: dependence on, 3–7, 37, 68; diversification of, 17, 25–27, 30, 58, 87–88; employment in, 127; and hydropower, 76–77, 121; industrialization of, 31, 34; and urban economies, 13, 16, 19, 25, 33. *See also* cotton; peaches
Aiken–Augusta Electric Railway, 51
Aiken County, SC, 125, 129, 179, 199n41; industry in, 127, 134; population of, 128, 130–32
airports, 96, 115, 143, 171

Alabama, 5, 70, 79–80, 196n12; and Columbus, 73, 78, 106–7, 115, 184, 199n41. *See also* Phenix City, AL
Alabama Polytechnic Institute (Auburn), 80
Alabama State Teachers College, 84
Allen, J. R., 116
Allman Brothers Band, 161
American Can Company, 28
American City Corporation, 181
American Family Life Assurance Company. *See* Aflac
Amos, John B., 111
Anderson, Peyton T., 34
Anderson, W. T., 7, 23, 25, 169; and the Black population of Macon, 26, 188; and civic beautification, 38–40, 42; and the Dixie Highway, 31–32
annexations, 13, 14, 36, 142; by Columbus, 103, 105, 108; by Macon, 19–21, 25; opposition to, 111. *See also* city-county consolidation
Arbery, Ahmaud, 185
Arkwright, Preston S., 77–78, 124
Asheville, NC, 49, 55
Ashworth, Maynard R., 101, 105, 110–11
Atlanta, GA, 4; Black neighborhoods of, 103; centrality of, 6, 17–18, 114, 169,

Atlanta, GA (*continued*)
175–76; economic dominance of, 134,
152–53, 156, 172; expansion of, 108; as
Georgia's capital, 21–25, 197n19,
198n29; population of, 1, 3, 12, 36,
193n13; postwar development of, 106;
rivalries with, 19–20, 43–44, 148, 189;
trade territory of, 75; travel to, 196n18
Auburn University, 80–83
Augusta, GA, 1, 6–7, 9–11, 14, 15; beautification of, 40; Black heritage of, 174, 187;
Confederate monuments of, 10, 185–86;
consolidation of, 176; downtown of, 148,
162, 164; economic development of,
45–48, 120–22, 127–28, 134–39, 143;
environment of, 144–46; geography of,
48–49, 122–23; and golf, 62–65; and
highway construction, 55–60, 175;
hinterland of, 27–28; and historic
preservation, 159–61; metropolitan
ambitions of, 66–68; military presence
in, 95–96, 178; planning commission of,
152; population of, 12, 36, 129–33, 142,
196n15, 227n72; racial division of,
179–80; red-shading of, 13; and river
development, 124–27, 181–83; social
development of, 142; trade territory of,
4–5, 8, 30, 140–41, 199n41; as a winter
resort, 32, 49–54, 60–61, 204n23. *See
also* Central Savannah River Area
(CSRA)
Augusta and Summerville Railroad, 48
Augusta Beautification Commission, 66
Augusta Black Heritage Commission, 186,
187
Augusta Canal, 10–11, 134, 183
Augusta Carnival, 49–50, 62
Augusta Chamber of Commerce, 21, 54,
60–62; and industrial development,
121, 135–37, 142; roads committee of,
56, 58
Augusta Chronicle, 53, 57–58, 204n23
Augusta Committee, 100, 136–41
Augusta Country Club, 45, 50, 60
Augusta Motor Club, 56
Augusta National Golf Club, 63–65, 66, 139

Augusta Tomorrow, 181, 183
Augusta Woman's Club, 59
automobiles, 31, 34; guides for, 206n42;
and tourism, 37, 53, 55–60, 206n48. *See
also* Dixie Highway; interstate highway
system

Baconsfield Park, 38, 41, 154–55. *See also*
city parks
Baker, Ed, 114–15
Baker Village, 97, 104
Bamberg County, SC, 129
Barnwell County, SC, 60, 125, 128, 129,
130–31
Barrett, Thomas, Jr., 54, 62
Battle of Columbus (1865), 14
beautification, 180; of cities, 37–41, 66–67;
of highways, 30–31, 34–35. *See also*
blight; city parks; gardens; historic
preservation
Berckmans, Louis E., 62–63
Berckmans, Prosper J. A., 62–63
Berckmans, Robert C., 35
Bibb County, GA, 20, 91; development of,
164; economy of, 30, 147, 149, 172, 177;
highways of, 30–31, 34–35, 169, 176;
population of, 27, 36, 151, 178. *See also*
Macon, GA
Bibb County Dixie Highway Auxiliary, 31,
35–36, 37–38, 169
Bibb Manufacturing Company, 41, 42, 72
Birmingham, AL, 82, 86, 135–36, 138
Black, Eugene R., 24
Black Belt, 27, 55, 97
Black neighborhoods, 2–3; housing in,
103–4, 144; neglect of, 47, 58, 66–67,
122, 165, 234n72; preservation of, 185;
rebranding of, 160–61; redevelopment
of, 168; removal of, 149, 152, 162, 166,
179. *See also* African Americans; Black
populations of fall-line cities; Laney-
Walker (Augusta); "Negro Territory"
(Terry, Augusta); Pleasant Hill (Macon)
Black populations of fall-line cities, 5, 7,
10–12, 14, 16; of Augusta, 21, 52, 144–45;
of Columbus, 82–84, 85, 88, 92, 112–13;

discrimination against, 118, 154–55; heritage of, 173, 186–88; inclusion of, 188–89; institutions of, 165–67; labor of, 26–27, 122; of Macon, 22, 32, 39, 147–48, 159; and the military, 101; opportunities for, 97; political power of, 2, 108, 111, 116, 218n46; purchasing power of, 193n18; removal of, 128–29, 156, 180. *See also* African Americans; demographics; Jim Crow; race; racism; segregation; white populations of fall-line cities

Bleckley County, GA, 39

blight, 104–5, 112, 114, 160, 167; racial connotations of, 166, 168, 179, 189. *See also* beautification; downtown revitalization; urban renewal

Bon Air Hotel, 45–46, 49–52, 54

Bon Air–Vanderbilt Hotel, 54–55, 60–61, 65

Bradley, W. C., 96–97, 114

brickyards, 11, 12, 41, 126, 134–35; and housing, 131; work in, 67, 122

Broadway Arts Alliance (BAA, Macon), 166–67

Brown, James, 2, 165, 186–87

Brown and Williamson Tobacco, 151, 176

Burke County, GA, 56, 66, 136, 199n41

Camp/Fort Benning, 1, 14, 15, 36; and Columbus, 69–70, 72, 90–93, 94–95, 108; employment provided by, 178; expansion of, 97–98, 100, 102, 119; founding of, 86–89; obstacle of, 105; renaming of, 185; segregation of, 101; social impact of, 179

Camp/Fort Gordon, 96, 126, 132–33, 145, 178; renaming of, 185. *See also* military

Cannonball House (Macon), 12, 170, 185

Capricorn Records, 161, 173

Cargill, J. Ralston, 74, 78, 79

Census Bureau, 21, 103, 142, 196n15. *See also* demographics

Central Capital Association (Macon), 17, 22–23

Central of Georgia Railway, 19, 81, 138–39, 196n18; and agriculture, 26, 28

Central Savannah River Area (CSRA), 5, 120–21, 126–27, 140–41, 145; pollution of, 144, 227n72; population of, 129, 142; revitalization of, 182

Central Savannah River Area Planning and Development Commission (CSRAPDC), 140–41

chain gangs, 55–56, 81

Chappell, Lucius H., 73

Charleston, SC, 3, 7; and historic preservation, 13, 160, 230n27; and tourism, 38, 39–40

Charlotte, NC, 3, 111, 180, 219n63

Chattahoochee County, GA, 87–88

Chattahoochee River, 13, 15; and hydropower, 72–77, 145; redevelopment of, 181, 182, 183–84; trade corridor of, 70–71, 78–79

Chattahoochee Valley, 5; agriculture in, 27, 88; development of, 78–79; metropolis of, 70, 79, 92, 106–7

Chattahoochee Valley Chamber of Commerce (CVCC), 78–79

Chattahoochee Valley Council of Local Governments, 115

Chattahoochee Valley & Gulf Association (CVGA), 78

Checotah, Ben, 158

chemical industry, 15, 122, 126, 135, 139–40, 226n65; employment in, 143–44; pollution from, 145, 183. *See also* Du Pont

Cherry Blossom Festival. *See* International Cherry Blossom Festival

Cherry Street Promenade (Macon), 159, 162, 164, 166, 170. *See also* pedestrian malls

churches, 22, 99–100, 186, 187

Citizens and Southern (C&S) National Bank, 114, 152–53, 158

Citizen's Annexation Association (Macon), 20

city-county consolidation, 14, 25, 179–80; and Augusta, 142; and Columbus, 69, 105, 110–12, 113, 116, 118–19. *See also* annexation

city parks: in Augusta, 58–59, 66; in
  Columbus, 69, 80–81, 102; and
  downtown revitalization, 162–64, 170,
  181; and the environment, 183, 201n75;
  in Macon, 37–38, 41, 161; and public
  space, 186; segregation of, 154–55; and
  tourism, 184. *See also* National Park
  Service; Ocmulgee Mounds National
  Historical Park
civic boosterism, 2, 4–9, 16, 192n2; of
  Augusta, 11, 46, 55, 60, 66–68, 121; and
  city reputation, 133, 172, 185, 188; of
  Columbus, 14, 70–72, 74, 82, 87–88;
  and county annexation, 108–9, 142–43;
  and industrial diversification, 135–38,
  149; of Macon, 15, 18, 19, 23, 29, 44, 175;
  and race, 82–85, 91–92, 104, 119, 144,
  173–74; and rural areas, 140, 193n18;
  and tourism, 37–40, 148–49, 153–54,
  156. *See also* metropolitan ambitions
civil rights movement, 144, 155, 185, 186
Civil War, 3, 6; and fall-line cities, 10–11, 12,
  14; monuments of, 185–87
Civil Works Administration (CWA), 41
Clarks Hill Lake, 121, 125, 222n5. *See also*
  dams
Clark University, 84
class, 84, 119, 144, 160–61
Clemson Agricultural College, 80
climate, 15, 68; and agriculture, 44; and
  tourism, 37, 49, 51–53, 61, 65–66. *See*
  also environment
Coca-Cola Company, 7, 24, 134
Cold War, 92, 128–29
College Hill (Macon), 112, 154, 160, 175
Columbia, SC, 6, 86, 193n18, 206n48
Columbia Nitrogen, 139–40
Columbus, GA, 1, 6–7, 13–14, 15; as an
  athletics center, 80–82, 85–86; Black
  heritage of, 188; confederate monuments of, 186; consolidation of, 111, 116,
  117–18, 176, 218n46; downtown of, 162,
  168, 228n4; highway system of, 175,
  200n53, 226n67; hinterland of, 5, 28,
  88, 102; and historic preservation,
  160–61, 167; industrial development of,

72–79, 106, 143; metropolitan
  ambitions of, 69–71, 79, 94–95, 113,
  211n33; as a military metropolis, 89–93,
  97–102; musical heritage of, 174;
  planning of, 13, 96, 102–5, 108–10,
  113–15, 216n26; population of, 12, 36,
  86; racial division of, 118–19, 179–80;
  riverfront of, 181, 182, 183–84, 240n34;
  suburbs of, 46, 54, 84; trade territory of,
  8, 30, 35, 145, 199n41. *See also* Camp/
  Fort Benning; Chattahoochee Valley
Columbus Board of Trade, 74
Columbus Chamber of Commerce, 78,
  80–81, 86–87, 201n75; camp activities
  committee of, 89–90; Jaycees of, 82, 84;
  weakness of, 105–6, 109–10
Columbus Defense Service Committee
  (CDSC), 99–101, 105
Columbus Electric Company, 73
Columbus Electric & Power Company
  (CE&P), 75–77, 84
Columbus Enquirer-Sun, 54, 75
Columbus Industrial Development
  Committee (CIDC), 110
Columbus Ledger, 75–76, 82
Columbus Ledger-Enquirer, 85, 111
Columbus Manufacturing Company, 70
Columbus–Muscogee County Planning
  Commission (CMPC), 113–15, 168
Columbus Planning Association (CPA),
  103–5, 109
Columbus Power Company, 72–73
Committee of the Plain People (Columbus),
  111
communism, 111, 219n61
Community Development Block Grants
  (CDBG), 164
Confederacy, 10, 12, 14, 41, 154; monuments
  to, 185–87, 188; and tourism, 44
Continental Can Company, 137–38
cotton, 5, 10–14; dependence on, 25–27, 30,
  47, 58, 68; diversification from, 39, 76,
  127–28; environmental impact of, 40.
  See also agriculture
Cox, Claude A., 157
Crayton, Carolyn, 169

Creek Nation, 9, 11, 41, 156–58; expulsion
of, 13; in tourism promotion, 44,
154–58, 184. *See also* Native Americans;
Ocmulgee Mounds National Historical
Park
crop-dusting, 28
Cruz, Ted, 176

dams: on the Apalachicola River, 79; on the
Chattahoochee River, 72–75; removal
of, 183, 239n29; repurposing of, 181–82;
on the Savannah River, 121, 123–26,
128, 143, 145, 222n5, 239n29. *See also*
hydropower
Daughters of the American Revolution
(DAR), 154, 230n28
Delta Air Lines, 29, 134, 171
Democratic Party, 2, 6, 45, 106
demographics, 1–3, 5, 10–13; and the
African American population, 27, 32,
82; of Augusta, 128–29, 133, 142, 150;
and the census, 20–21, 196n15, 196n16;
of Columbus, 94, 97, 103, 119; of Macon,
116, 151; of rural counties, 36, 88, 91,
178, 193n18, 227n72; and schools, 180;
of suburbs, 48; and urban planning, 113.
See also Black populations of fall-line
cities; Metropolitan Statistical Areas
(MSAs); midsized cities; white
populations of fall-line cities
Dempsey Hotel, 23, 38, 42, 170
Dent, R. A., 66
Dimon, Homer, 90
Dixie Highway, 14–15, 59, 175; and Augusta,
55–58; and Macon, 30–36, 37, 44, 68,
149. *See also* highways
Dixie Highway Association (DHA), 31–32,
35, 56
Douglas, Allen H., 136–37
Douglass, Charles Henry, 165
Douglass Theatre, 165–67, 188
Dow Chemical, 143
downtown revitalization, 180, 216n33,
233n55, 234n65; of Augusta, 141–42; of
Columbus, 104, 112, 119; and employ-
ment, 177; and historically Black

neighborhoods, 166–69; of Macon,
147–49, 151–52, 158–65. *See also*
beautification; blight; historic
preservation; urban renewal
D-rated residential areas (redlining), 13,
104, 194n36. *See also* housing
Du Pont, 122, 127–28, 139, 143. *See also*
Savannah River Plant/Site (SRP/S)
Dyer, Daniel B., 50, 51, 53

Eagle & Phenix mill, 14, 96
Eames, Henry E. (Col.), 86–87
Economic Development Administration
(EDA), 141
Eisenhower, Dwight D., 126, 139
electricity. *See* hydropower
Ellenton, SC, 127, 128, 129
Empire Mills, 7
environment, 15, 176, 194n30; and
beautification, 40, 42; erosion of,
201n75; and health, 48, 143–46;
pollution of, 3, 183, 228n81; protection
of, 181; and tourism, 50–53, 65, 68; and
urban development, 48–49. *See also*
climate; flooding
Eve, William F., 55

fall line, 2, 175–76; cities of, 3–5, 189,
193n13; as a color line, 179; environment of, 228n81; and hydropower
generation, 74
Fall Line Freeway, 175–76
Farley, E. E., 85, 101
Feiss, Carl, 160
Fickling, William A., Sr., 149, 164, 169
fire, 47, 53–54
flooding, 48–49, 52, 53–54, 122–23, 184;
and public health, 145
Florida, 6, 7, 51; competition of, 15, 47, 61,
63, 64; and Georgia, 69–70; tourism
routes to, 32, 43, 56, 59–60, 68
Florida Agricultural and Mechanical
College, 84
Floyd, George, 185
Flynt, Roy A., Jr., 109
football, 15, 69, 79–85, 184, 211n30

Forrest Hills–Ricker Hotel, 60–61, 65, 207n60
Fort Benning. *See* Camp/Fort Benning
Fort Eisenhower. *See* Camp/Fort Gordon
Fort Gordon. *See* Camp/Fort Gordon
Fort Moore. *See* Camp/Fort Benning
Forward Four Counties Development Company, 141
Fruitland Nurseries, 35, 62–64

gardens, 38, 39–41, 42, 66, 67, 133. *See also* beautification; city parks
General Assembly of Georgia, 5, 17, 79
geography, 2, 4, 16; resources of, 6, 11, 15, 52, 70, 134; and tourism, 66; and urban development, 46, 48–49. *See also* environment; fall line
Georgia (state), 6; capital city of, 17–18, 19, 21–25, 195n5, 197n19; counties of, 193n17, 198n29, 199n41; demographics of, 20, 193n13; highway construction in, 59, 113; industrialization of, 122; military presence in, 95–96; and tourism, 153
Georgia Association, 29
Georgia–Auburn Football Association, 82
Georgia Baptist Convention, 19
Georgia-Pacific, 134
Georgia Peach Carnival, 26
Georgia Peach Growers' Exchange (GPGE), 27–28
Georgia Power Company, 77–78, 124, 170
Georgia Railroad, 4, 21
Georgia State College of Agriculture, 28, 76
golf, 11, 46, 48; in Augusta, 60–65, 68; development of, 50–52
Good Roads Movement, 31
Gordon, Frederick B., 70, 72
Gordon, Rosa C., 69, 106
Government Employees Insurance Company (GEICO), 151, 172, 177
Great Depression, 32; in Augusta, 48, 62, 63, 68; in Columbus, 72, 91; in Macon, 42; public works during, 36, 40
"Greater Macon" movement, 19–20, 23, 25
Griffin, Marvin, 127
Gulf of Mexico, 2, 15, 69, 78

Haden, Charles J., 56
Hamilton, Hugh L., 133
Hamilton, Thomas J., 123–24
Hampton Terrace Hotel, 51–52, 54
Hardaway, B. H., 73, 91
Harjo, Gerald, 157
Harris, Walter A., 41
Harris, William J., 78, 86
Harris County, GA, 73, 180, 199n41
Hayne, Lynwood C., 45
healthcare industry, 1, 6, 142, 177, 178
highways, 31, 34; beautification of, 39–40; construction of, 59–60; maintenance of, 55; and tourism, 37–38, 44, 48, 54. *See also* Dixie Highway; interstate highway system
hinterlands, 4, 5, 34, 193n18; Black populations of, 180; dependency on, 20, 25, 88, 102, 125; mapping of, 56. *See also* trade territories
historically Black colleges and universities (HBCUs), 82, 83, 84–85, 101
Historic Augusta Inc., 159, 185
Historic Columbus Foundation (HCF), 115, 160
historic preservation, 7, 16, 230n27; and Black neighborhoods, 185; and Columbus, 112, 114–15, 118; of Macon, 148, 159–63, 167. *See also* downtown revitalization; tourism
Holloway, Murphy, 137
Home Owners' Loan Corporation (HOLC), 104, 194n36
Horne, Lena, 165
housing: for Black residents, 103–4, 144, 157; need for, 64, 97, 99, 129–32; preservation of, 160; stock of, 114, 118. *See also* Black neighborhoods; blight; D-rated residential areas (redlining); suburbs
Houston, TX, 3, 6
Houston County, GA, 30, 150, 151, 177, 178, 199n41
Howard, Charles, Jr., 87–88
Howard Bus Lines, 89, 92, 97, 100, 213n60
Howell, Clark, 31–32, 56
Huff Daland, 28–29, 30

Hyde and Aragon Park Improvement Committee (HAPIC), 144
hydropower, 14, 15, 69–75, 121, 124–25; demise of, 181. *See also* dams

Indian removal, 154, 156. *See also* Native Americans
industrialization, 5, 10–16, 226n57; after World War II, 108–10; in Augusta, 67–68, 139; diversification of, 119, 134–36, 143, 176; and hydropower, 74–77, 121; in Macon, 149–50, 159; and transport, 31
industrial parks, 141, 143; in Augusta, 138–39, 144; and downtowns, 159; in Macon, 148, 149, 151, 176, 177
insurance industry, 6, 7, 87, 172, 177. *See also* Aflac; Government Employees Insurance Company (GEICO)
International Cherry Blossom Festival, 1, 169–70
interstate highway system, 14, 95, 175–76, 200n53; and Columbus, 113–14, 118, 119; and Macon, 149–50
In-Town Macon Neighborhood Association (IMNA), 160. *See also* College Hill (Macon)
Intracoastal Waterway, 78
Israel, George, 167, 169

Jackson, James U., 51
Jackson, J. F., 26, 28
Jacksonville, FL, 32, 111, 116
Jefferson, Thomas, 11, 154
Jennings, W. D., 120
Jim Crow, 101, 104, 144, 155, 165. *See also* segregation
John P. King Manufacturing Company, 45
Johnson, Lyndon B., 141
Jones, Bobby, 48, 60, 62–64
Jones, Charles H., 156–57
Jordan, G. Gunby, 72, 77, 86, 88
Junior League, 160

Kimberly-Clark, 122, 139
Kiwanis Club, 38–39, 82
Knox Brothers, 132, 140, 161

Korean War, 132
Ku Klux Klan, 25, 165

labor: of Black workers, 26, 88, 127; costs of, 18, 128; housing of, 129; market for, 134, 143–44; unionized, 110. *See also* chain gangs
Lane, Mills B., Jr., 114, 152
Laney, Lucy Craft, 186, 187
Laney-Walker (Augusta), 47, 186–87. *See also* "Negro Territory" (Terry, Augusta)
Little Richard, 2, 165, 173–74
Loyless, Thomas W., 53, 54
Lunsford, Lizzie, 101

Macon, GA, 1–2, 6–7, 11–13, 15–16, 230n22; beautification of, 35, 38–39, 41–42, 169–71; Black heritage of, 187–88, 241n44; Civil War monuments of, 185; consolidation of, 176, 226n67; downtown development of, 152–53, 158–69, 172, 232n45; efforts to become Georgia's capital of, 4, 21–25; and heritage planning, 153–55; hinterland of, 20; industrial development of, 149–51, 177; metropolitan ambitions of, 17–19, 36–37, 42–44, 68, 202n82; military presence in, 96–97; musical heritage of, 173–75, 189; population of, 36, 196n15; racial division of, 179–80; rivalry with Augusta of, 19–21; riverfront of, 181, 184; suburbs of, 46; and tourism, 58, 156–58; trade territory of, 5, 8, 26–30, 75, 199n41; and transportation, 31–34. *See also* Middle Georgia
Macon–Bibb County Industrial Authority, 149
Macon–Bibb County Urban Development Authority (UDA), 162–64
Macon Chamber of Commerce, 5, 202n82; and agriculture, 25, 27–30, 37; Area Development Committee of, 105, 149–51; and highway construction, 34, 39; and historic preservation, 148, 153–58, 162; and industry, 149; Jaycees of, 36, 41–42; and military installations, 97

Macon Coliseum, 155–56, 157
Macon Daily Telegraph, 7, 32, 34
Macon Heritage Foundation (MHF),
  160–61
Macon Historic District, 161, 163, 169
Macon Lions Club, 34
Macon Mall, 147–49, 158–59, 161–62,
  228n1
Maddox, Lester, 111
manufacturing, 5, 16, 74; decline of, 122,
  126, 142, 176–77; development of, 27,
  49, 72, 106, 136; jobs in, 68, 103, 108,
  113, 134–35, 143. *See also* industrializa-
  tion
Marshall, Janice, 173–74
Martin, Frank, 188
Massey, Alma Anderson, 31, 35
Masters Golf Tournament, The, 15, 63–66,
  139
McCoy, S L., 66
McKay, John J., Jr., 153–54
Medical College of Georgia, 1, 6
megaregions, 4, 16, 189
Melton, Buckner F., 159, 165, 232n45
Memorial Stadium (Columbus), 81–85,
  211n33
Mercer University, 19, 80
metropolitan ambitions, 2, 7, 11, 16; and
  city image, 188–89; and development,
  45, 71, 90, 103–4, 127; fragility of, 53, 77,
  94–95, 113, 175, 187; and hinterlands, 5,
  37, 75; and historic preservation, 148,
  156, 159; and inclusivity, 180; and
  regional reinvention, 40, 79, 92, 120;
  and social equity, 119. *See also* annexation; *and specific cities*
metropolitanism, 2, 16
metropolitan planning: ambitions of, 119;
  and county annexation, 108; of
  downtowns, 152; for postwar growth,
  102–3, 113–14, 216n25; and vested
  interests, 115; and World War II, 94–95,
  96, 100. *See also* annexation; city-
  county consolidation; demographics;
  zoning
Metropolitan Planning Commission (MPC,
  Columbus), 108–10

Metropolitan Statistical Areas (MSAs), 2,
  8, 142, 227n72
Miami, FL, 32, 56, 59, 64, 192n6
Middle Georgia, 5, 15, 21–22, 145, 199n41;
  agricultural diversification of, 25–28,
  30; economy of, 12, 171; environment of,
  40; Macon as hub of, 18, 25, 36–37,
  43–44; military presence in, 96–97; and
  transportation, 31, 34–35, 39
Middle Georgia Development Campaign
  (MGDC), 25, 27
Middle Georgia Historical Society
  (MGHS), 159–60
midsized cities, 3, 7, 16, 193n13; metropolitan areas of, 148; renewal of, 172,
  194n21; and transportation, 171
military, 6, 11–16; buildup of, 95–96, 97–98;
  economic impact of, 69, 70, 86–88, 143,
  176, 177–79; social impact of, 72, 89,
  179, 238n17. *See also* Camp/Fort
  Benning; Camp/Fort Gordon;
  Columbus, GA
military-industrial complex, 92
"Military Maids," 100
Milledgeville, GA, 10, 22, 32, 37, 39
Mobile, AL, 38, 41, 119
Monroe County, GA, 22, 30, 35, 165, 180,
  199n41
Monsanto, 122, 139
Montgomery, AL, 3, 6, 71, 80–81, 84; Black
  history of, 186; and the military, 86
Moody, Lester S., 121, 123–27
Morehouse College, 85
Morris Brown College, 84
Murrah, Edward, 99
Muscogee. *See* Creek Nation
Muscogee County, GA, 14, 81; consolidation
  with Columbus of, 105, 108–11, 116–17;
  population of, 36, 91, 93. *See also*
  Columbus–Muscogee County Planning
  Commission (CMPC)
museums, 157, 173, 181–83, 187–89. *See also*
  historic preservation

Nashville, TN, 6, 19, 111, 116, 172
National Association of Real Estate Boards
  (NAREB), 112, 115

National Defense Housing Program, 99
National Dixie Highway Auxiliary
    (NDHA), 31, 35–36, 38
National Historic Preservation Act, 160
National Park Service, 157, 184, 201n75. *See
    also* Ocmulgee Mounds National
    Historical Park
National Pecan Growers Association, 35
Native Americans, 6, 9, 11, 13, 183;
    settlement sites of, 41; in settler
    imagination, 42, 44, 154–58. *See also*
    Creek Nation; Ocmulgee Mounds
    National Historical Park
"Negro Territory" (Terry, Augusta), 47, 58,
    66–67, 103. *See also* Laney–Walker
    (Augusta)
New Deal, 37–38, 42
New Orleans, LA, 3, 5, 78, 101; and
    tourism, 7, 186
New South, 3, 9, 27, 114; economy of, 4, 154;
    Macon in, 42–44, 153–54, 173, 181. *See
    also* Sun Belt
Nolen, John, 71, 96, 99–100, 102, 216n26
North Augusta, SC, 51, 113, 132
nuclear weapons, 128

Ocmulgee Mounds National Historical
    Park, 1, 41–43, 44, 153–55, 157;
    enlargement of, 184–85
Ocmulgee River, 11, 38, 40, 152; redevelop-
    ment of, 181, 184
Oglethorpe University, 81
Olson, Robert, 162, 164–65
organized crime, 95, 106–7
Owens, Hubert B., 40, 66

paper mills, 15, 122, 126, 137–38, 139,
    226n65; employment in, 143
Partridge Inn, 52, 54
Patchen, Josef C., 136–37
Patterson, Albert L., 106–7
Peach County, GA, 29–30, 177
peaches, 5, 18–19, 25–30, 62, 76; frozen, 99
pedestrian malls, 109, 151–53; in Macon,
    159, 162, 164, 166, 169, 170. *See also*
    downtown revitalization
Persons, Gordon, 107

Persons, W. S., 111
Phenix City, AL, 15, 73, 92; and Columbus,
    106–8, 113–14, 133, 145, 184; crime in,
    95, 100; public health in, 101
Phinizy Swamp, 134, 141; pollution of, 122,
    132, 145; restoration of, 183
Piedmont Plateau, 2, 6, 73, 122
Pinch Gut (Augusta), 53, 54, 112, 161
Pittsburgh Plate Glass (PPG), 139, 143
plantation agriculture, 3–4, 10–12, 26,
    62–63, 87
Pleasant Hill (Macon), 12, 149, 165, 184
police, 118, 153, 165
pollution. *See* environment
press. *See* specific newspapers
Procter & Gamble, 122, 139
public education, 144, 179–80
public health, 100–101, 142, 144
public-private partnerships, 170, 232n45

race, 119, 144; and the military, 179–80,
    238n17; and politics, 218n46; and
    tourism, 173–74. *See also* Black
    populations of fall-line cities; white
    populations of fall-line cities
racism, 85, 92, 128, 153
railroads, 3, 4, 10–14, 175; and agricultural
    development, 28; construction of, 41;
    and tourism, 51, 54; travel by, 196n18
Rainey, Gertrude "Ma," 2, 165, 188
real estate industry, 7, 91, 109, 165, 194n36;
    conflicts of interest in, 115; and
    segregation, 13. *See also* D-rated
    residential areas (redlining); housing
Reconstruction, 3, 11, 22
Redding, Otis, 2, 97, 161, 165, 173, 241n44
redlining/red-shading. *See* D-rated residen-
    tial areas (redlining)
Redmond, Dennis, 62–63
Republican Party, 22, 176
Richards, Walter A., 99–101, 102–3, 105
Richmond County, GA, 55, 59, 91, 121, 129,
    132; consolidation with Augusta of, 142,
    176; industry in, 134–35, 140; pollution
    of, 145
Rich's department store, 152–53
Roberts, Clifford, 62–63, 65

Robins Air Force Base, 97, 150, 178
Rockefeller, John D., 52, 55, 186
Roosevelt, Franklin D., 36–37, 54, 97, 123
Rossignol, Charles F., 56–59, 206n42
Rotary Club, 80–81
Royal Crown Cola, 1, 114
Russell, H. J., 169
Russell, Richard B. (Dick), 123, 126, 178
Russell County, AL, 99, 106, 115, 199n41
Rust Belt, 1, 3, 232n45

sandhills, 2, 24, 66–68, 93, 134; development of, 17, 176; resorts of, 11, 15, 49–52; suburbs on, 46, 48; and tourism, 55, 60. *See also* climate; environment; fall line; geography
Savannah, GA, 3, 9, 17–18, 148; beautification of, 40, 66; and historic preservation, 159–60
Savannah River, 9, 47; flooding of, 48, 52, 53–54; industrialization of, 15, 68, 120–21, 122–28; pollution of, 145; redevelopment of, 181–83, 186; rehabilitation plan for, 114
Savannah River Electric Company, 124
Savannah River Plant/Site (SRP/S), 121, 126, 127–32, 143–44, 145; employment at, 135, 178; social impact of, 179
segregation, 13, 16, 84, 92, 97; end of, 110, 118, 141–42, 144; in the military, 101; persistence of, 154–55, 165, 179; politics of, 111, 125; of public schools, 179–80. *See also* Black populations of fall-line cities; Jim Crow; racism; white populations of fall-line cities
sexually transmitted diseases, 101
Sherman's March to the Sea, 6, 11
shopping malls, 147–49, 161–62, 228n8. *See also* downtown revitalization; suburbs
Simons, George W., Jr., 96, 105, 109, 160
slavery, 10, 39, 164
slogans: of Augusta, 11, 15, 45–47, 49, 121, 182; of Columbus, 14, 74, 77, 85, 96; of Macon, 2, 16, 19, 23, 34–36, 149, 154, 173–75; regional, 4–5, 31
Smith, H. C., 91, 178
Smithsonian Institution, 41

Social and Civic Club 25 (So-C-25), 84
socialism, 111, 125
social welfare, 143–46. *See also* public health
Sons of Confederate Veterans (SCV), 185–86
South Carolina, 113, 120–21, 123–26, 127–31, 222n5; trade territories in, 133, 139, 145, 199n41. *See also* Central Savannah River Area (CSRA)
Southern Railway, 45, 68, 81
South Georgia, 19, 21–22, 24, 198n29
South Georgia Power Company, 75–76
Southwest Georgia, 75–78
Soviet Union, 128
sports, 79, 92; African American, 82–85; and riverfront redevelopment, 182, 184, 240n34. *See also* football; golf
States' Rights Party (Dixiecrats), 125
Stimson, Henry L., 100
Stone and Webster, 72–73
Suber, Harold, 186
suburbs, 6, 219n63, 234n65; annexation of, 11, 13, 36, 49, 53, 103; of Augusta, 45, 50–51, 142; of Columbus, 70, 91, 104, 111, 179; competition of, 159–60, 166; expansion of, 93, 95, 132; flight to, 46, 119, 148–49; and highways, 38, 175; of Macon, 20, 25, 35, 151; sprawl of, 16, 170; and transportation, 48, 118; white, 179, 180. *See also* shopping malls; white flight
Summerville (Augusta), 45–46, 48–52, 53
Sun Belt, 1, 176; city growth in, 92, 122, 133, 150; scholarship on, 3

Taft, William Howard, 21, 45–46, 48, 52, 53, 186
Taylor, Breonna, 185
Terry, K. H., 84
textile industry, 10–14; in Augusta, 134–35; collapse of, 93, 176; in Columbus, 69–70, 72, 82, 95–97, 102; employment in, 127; and hydropower, 72–73; reliance on, 108, 110, 119
Thomas, Landon A., 45
Thompson, Ronnie, 153, 158–59, 165

Thurmond, Strom, 125, 222n5
Toole, G. Glen, 37–38, 234n72
tourism, 6–7, 12–14, 15–16; and African
    Americans, 186–88; and Augusta,
    47–48, 49–54, 65, 68, 204n23; by
    automobile, 55–58; and beautification,
    35, 38, 41–42; and Columbus, 79, 82;
    competition for, 23, 232n45; and
    heritage, 118, 143, 148, 153–56, 159–60,
    171; and industry, 67, 139; and Macon,
    17–18, 30–32, 35, 36, 43–44, 167; and
    the military, 178; and Native Ameri-
    cans, 156–58, 184–85; and race, 173–74
trade territories, 4–6, 193n14; and city
    stature, 36, 75, 133, 145; of Columbus,
    70, 73, 79, 88; cross-border, 120–21;
    and transportation, 34. See also
    hinterlands; and specific cities
trailer parks, 98, 129–32
Trail of Tears, 156–58
transportation, 17, 142, 175–76; planning
    for, 113–14, 115, 117–18; and tourism, 171.
    See also airports; automobiles;
    highways; interstate highway system;
    railroads
Truman, Harry S., 128
Tulane University, 82
Turner, E. J., 84
Tuskegee Institute, 85

United Daughters of the Confederacy
    (UDC), 12, 154, 185
United Service Organizations (USO),
    100–102
United States federal government:
    Congress of, 6, 78–79; funding from,
    37–38, 95, 113–15, 141, 143; and
    highways, 35, 39, 118; and historic
    preservation, 160, 162–64; and housing,
    104, 112; military spending of, 92,
    177–79; support for hydro dams from,
    123–27
University of Alabama, 80, 82
University of Florida, 81
University of Georgia, 6, 80–83
Urban Development Action Grant
    (UDAG), 168, 170, 187

urban planning. See metropolitan planning
urban renewal, 112, 194n21; and Black
    neighborhoods, 156; of Columbus, 118;
    grants for, 113–14, 155. See also
    beautification; blight; downtown
    revitalization; historic preservation
U.S. Atomic Energy Commission (AEC),
    121, 127–29
U.S. Department of Agriculture (USDA),
    28–29
U.S. Supreme Court, 154

Vineville (Macon), 35, 46, 219n63
Vinson, Carl, 97, 178
Voting Rights Act, 116

Walden, Phil, 161, 174
Walker, Charles T., 186
Wallace, Fielding H., 62, 64
Waller, Roy M., 109, 111
Warnock, Raphael, 176
War on Poverty, 141
Waynesboro, GA, 40, 45, 56
white flight, 11, 54, 111, 148, 180. See also
    blight; suburbs
white populations of fall-line cities, 2,
    10–11, 26–27, 39; boosterism of, 82,
    84–85, 91–92, 188–89; and downtown
    planning, 152, 166; and heritage
    planning, 154–55; and housing, 104;
    political power of, 108, 111; and
    Reconstruction, 22; and segregation,
    179; violence of, 165. See also demo-
    graphics; Jim Crow; segregation; white
    flight
white supremacy, 153, 185
Wimberly, James H., 166
Wiregrass region, 20, 22, 35, 56, 75, 196n12
WMAZ, 36
Woman's Reading Club (Columbus), 69
women: and boosterism, 31, 34–35; and
    civic beautification, 38–39, 109, 154;
    and downtown revitalization, 151–52;
    and historic preservation, 154, 160;
    hospitality of, 100
Woodruff, George C. "Kid," 80–82
Woodruff, George W., 7

Woodruff, James W., Jr., 79, 110, 118
Woodruff, James W., Sr. (Jim), 7, 78–81, 121
Works Progress Administration (WPA),
     37–38, 40, 42, 66–67, 154
World War II, 65, 92, 94–95, 97–99
Wynnton (Columbus), 46, 104, 111, 179

YKK, 151
YMCA, 100–101, 105

zoning, 95, 105–6, 115, 152; industrial, 149,
     194n36; and urban renewal, 114, 161. *See
     also* metropolitan planning